Modern Sports around the World

Modern Sports around the World

History, Geography, and Sociology

David Asa Schwartz

BLOOMSBURY ACADEMIC
NEW YORK • LONDON • OXFORD • NEW DELHI • SYDNEY

BLOOMSBURY ACADEMIC
Bloomsbury Publishing Inc
1385 Broadway, New York, NY 10018, USA
50 Bedford Square, London, WC1B 3DP, UK
29 Earlsfort Terrace, Dublin 2, Ireland

BLOOMSBURY, BLOOMSBURY ACADEMIC and the Diana logo are trademarks of
Bloomsbury Publishing Plc

First published in the United States of America by ABC-CLIO 2021
Paperback edition published by Bloomsbury Academic 2025

Copyright © Bloomsbury Publishing Inc, 2025

For legal purposes the Acknowledgments on p. xvii constitute an extension of this copyright page.

COVER PHOTOS: (Yuri_Acurs/iStockphoto); (OSTILL/iStockphoto);
(isitsharp/iStockphoto); (simonkr/iStockphoto).

All rights reserved. No part of this publication may be reproduced or transmitted
in any form or by any means, electronic or mechanical, including photocopying,
recording, or any information storage or retrieval
system, without prior permission in writing from the publishers.

Bloomsbury Publishing Inc does not have any control over, or responsibility for,
any third-party websites referred to or in this book. All internet addresses given
in this book were correct at the time of going to press. The author and publisher
regret any inconvenience caused if addresses have changed or sites have
ceased to exist, but can accept no responsibility for any such changes.

Library of Congress Cataloging-in-Publication Data
Names: Schwartz, David Asa, author.
Title: Modern sports around the world : history, geography, and sociology / David Asa Schwartz.
Description: Santa Barbara, California : ABC-CLIO, 2021. | Includes bibliographical references and index.
Identifiers: LCCN 2021005920 (print) | LCCN 2021005921 (ebook) | ISBN 9781440868795 (hardcover) |
ISBN 9781440868801 (ebook)
Subjects: LCSH: Sports—History. | Sports—Social aspects. |
Sports in popular culture.
Classification: LCC GV571 .S35 2021 (print) | LCC GV571 (ebook) |
DDC 796.09—dc23
LC record available at https://lccn.loc.gov/2021005920
LC ebook record available at https://lccn.loc.gov/2021005921

ISBN: HB: 978-1-4408-6879-5
PB: 979-8-7651-4014-7
ePDF: 978-1-4408-6880-1
eBook: 979-8-2161-1880-0

To find out more about our authors and books visit www.bloomsbury.com
and sign up for our newsletters.

To my coauthors: Annie, Josie, and PJ

Contents

Preface xi

Acknowledgments xvii

Introduction xix

The Entries

Action Sports 1

Archery 8

Australian Rules Football 14

Auto Racing 21

Badminton 29

Baseball 35

Basketball 43

Bodybuilding 51

Bowling 58

Boxing 64

Bullfighting 71

Cricket 79

Cross-Country Skiing 85

Curling 92

Cycling 98

Diving 106

E-Sports 113

Field Hockey   120

Figure Skating   126

Football   133

Golf   142

Gymnastics   149

Handball   157

Horse Racing   163

Ice Hockey   171

Jai Alai   179

Kabaddi   186

Kickboxing   192

Lacrosse   200

Marathon   207

Mixed Martial Arts   214

Olympics   222

Ping-Pong   231

Rodeo   237

Rowing/Crew   243

Rugby   250

Sailing and Yachting   257

Soccer   263

Softball   270

Speed Skating   276

Squash   284

Sumo   290

Surfing   297

Swimming   303

Tennis   312

Track and Field   319

Volleyball   327

Water Polo   334

Weightlifting and Powerlifting 340

Wrestling 347

Bibliography 355

Bibliography by Sport 361

Index 371

Preface

Over the last century, humanity has transformed sport from a recreational, regionally based distraction into a globalized network of commerce, spectacle, and national pronouncement. To understand sports is to understand the path of history. China's rise to international prominence, the United States' racist legacy, and Western Europe's specter of imperialism play out in real time in our stadiums and arenas. *Modern Sports around the World* provides us a model of the world we live in within the games we watch and play.

Structuring this book for college and high school students gives them the academic starting point they need to walk through the front door of numerous disciplines, including foreign policy, gender studies, geography, history, international relations, media and celebrity culture, politics, pop culture, psychology, sociology, and technology. From here they will see how sport ties their world together. This book also identifies common threads of human behavior, themes that are as prevalent in sports today as they were millennia ago. Humanity is unified by its curiosity, by its determination and competitiveness, to identify the best individuals, the best groups, the best cultures.

This book examines the history and geography of 50 of the world's most popular, influential sports. The list of sports is not exhaustive; hundreds of sports exist worldwide, each with potentially dozens of regionally driven variations. *Modern Sports around the World* selected an inclusive range of sports that recognizes their diverse global impact. It focuses heavily on identifying a dynamic range of sports that represent all parts of the world, people and places of varying economic prosperity, gender representation, and regional characteristics.

Our attention often turned to the regions of eastern and southern Asia, northern Africa, Oceania, the United States and Canada, and Western Europe for two crucial reasons. First, modern sport revolves heavily around money, and these regions represent pillars of the 20th- and 21st-century economies. Second, each of these regions has paid special attention to documenting and protecting its history and making it available to researchers. They all have given us open access to their sporting legacies.

Modern Sports around the World respects ancient cultures and their influence on today's games. Without first understanding contributions made by ancient civilizations in China, Eastern Europe, Mongolia, North Africa, North America, Polynesia, and others, we cannot understand today's sports landscape. Therefore, each of the 50 sport entries traces a sport back to its origins, whether 3,000, 300, or 30 years ago. Research was conducted in American university libraries, public libraries, and electronically via digital archives maintained throughout the world. From the beginning, this book set forth to gather its research from a worldwide pool of perspectives.

It is crucial to acknowledge British imperialism in the creation of the modern sporting world, but it is equally important to recognize that sports history neither begins nor ends with the United Kingdom. This book took great care to recognize that sports history is a global collaboration that spans millennia. The ancient Polynesians, Mongolians, Chinese, Egyptians, Greeks, Romans, Scandinavians, Indigenous Americans, and North, central, and southern Africans contributed to the origins of sport. Today, sports are a cultural phenomenon: part spectacle, part escape, part commercial enterprise. Yet it is vital we remember that sports began as a curiosity, to test our bodily limits. Who is the fastest? The strongest? The most coordinated? The most fit? The best hunter? The swiftest rower? The mightiest warrior?

This book is defined by the similarities and differences of the 50 sports it examines. Sports that at first appear quite different have much in common. The ancient sport of rowing, for example, and the world's newest sport, eSports, both grew out of a human desire to connect with those not near us in proximity. Conversely, two sports that seem similar, tennis and squash, both of which were modernized in 19th-century Great Britain and are contested with rackets, have opposite origins. Tennis enjoyed a royal birth and became a game of upper-class leisure; squash was born in a prison.

Patterns emerge throughout this book. As readers turn the pages, they will increasingly discover that even before we became a digitally connected world, sports found a way to globalize. To help make these connections, the 50 sport entries in this volume are organized into 10 distinct sections, most of which—but not all—appear in each entry.

1. HISTORICAL CONTEXT

We lay the foundation of a sport by examining the skills involved, where the sport began, and the time period in which it began. We can learn much about a sport by contextualizing it. Consider three examples: diving, which began hundreds of years ago as a royal test of loyalty and manliness; basketball, invented in the late 19th century as a safer alternative to the violence of American football; and auto racing, which because of technology has evolved so rapidly that in the 21st century the sport's officials have tried to make cars *slower*. This section sets the stage for the chapter, giving us the starting point to understand more specific details.

2. GLOBALIZATION

To understand how a sport spread to other parts of the world is to understand the path of history itself. This section attempts to draw lines from the ancient world to the modern world. Readers of this book will find emergent patterns. One country invades another and brings along its sports; the colonized country learns the skills and adapts them to its own customs and traditions. Or one country invades another, discovers in its conquests a new sport, and brings it back to the homeland. Canada's First Nation people taught European immigrants the sport of lacrosse. In time, those immigrants forcibly colonized the First Nation people, rewrote the rules of lacrosse, and then attempted to ban First Nation people from playing it. The tribes resisted, but they did accept the new rules. By the 20th century, Curt Styres became the first First Nations person to own a professional sports team, when he entered professional lacrosse.

3. WHERE IT'S PLAYED TODAY

Here we reach the modern era. Following a discussion about a sport's origins and then about its spread across the world, we consider both recreational and competitive participation as it exists today. This space is careful to distinguish a sport's popularity within a given region, such as Australian rules football's inability to find a sustainable audience outside of Australia, North America's monopoly on rodeo, or soccer's worldwide influence. The Olympics, both summer and winter, play a big role in this section because they help us understand how much a sport has penetrated a region. It is instructional when a sport such as water polo boasts clubs across the world, yet only European teams win Olympic medals, while another sport, such as track and field, regularly includes top athletes from every continent. When available, participation numbers are provided.

4. ECONOMICS AND MEDIA

Professional soccer, American football, cricket, basketball, rugby, track and field—professional sports have become billion-dollar industries. Understanding modern sports means understanding organized labor, player salaries, equipment sales, stadium construction, corporate–government partnerships, and media contracts. In 1984 Sut Jhally coined the term "sports/media complex," which identified the unbreakable bond between organized sports, sports media, and their financial relationship. To watch sports today is to watch mediated sport. Jhally, born in Kenya, educated in Europe, and employed in the United States, gave us the language we need to understand how sports, media, and money overlap. This section helps us understand the degree of a sport's impact as measured through these factors.

5. DIMENSIONS OF THE SPORT

This nuts-and-bolts section gets into the details of each sport. It is a straightforward section that discusses a sport's terminology, rules, equipment, and other necessary details.

6. IMPORTANT FIGURES

This section recognizes individual people who have made an outsized impact on their sport. Some, such as volleyball's William G. Morgan, are recognized as a sport's inventor. Others have made differences along the periphery, like Judy Glenney, a female weightlifter who could only compete against men because the world's governing bodies refused to sanction women's weightlifting. Eventually she became a coach, referee, and administrator who helped women's weightlifting receive international recognition. This section also pays special attention to the athletes, especially those whose records and achievements have set the standard for a sport. Russian wrestler Aleksandr Karelin, for example, cut through the tensions of the Cold War by going undefeated for 13 consecutive years. Even American wrestling fans waited with anticipation for Karelin's matches and were shocked in 2000 when he lost at the Olympics while attempting to win a fourth consecutive gold medal.

7. POP CULTURE

Sports make great subjects for films, books, and other forms of art. Movies, especially, love tales of underdog athletes. They often reflect a culture's values as much as a sport itself does. This section celebrates the high, low, and obscure pop-cultural references of sport. This might include a movie with an entire premise built around a sport, such as *Cool Runnings*, a film about the Jamaican bobsled team. It might reference a specific scene in an obscure movie, like *Knockaround Guys*, a forgettable film that includes two Hollywood legends squaring off in a game of handball. It also might focus on an athlete who transcended sports, such as the early 20th-century Austro-Hungarian Johnny Weissmuller, the winner of multiple gold medals for swimming who became a worldwide movie star for his portrayal of the fictional character Tarzan. This section exists to help us understand how sports extend beyond the playing fields and into our broader culture.

8. SCANDALS

From the illegal to the profane to the unbelievable, sports can be at their most dramatic when they challenge our moral codes. Three primary themes emerge in this section: gambling, drugs, and money. However, this is also the section that gives us examples of the absurd, such as badminton teams trying to lose on purpose, as well as the horrific, including a gymnastics doctor who attacked his clients for decades. Sports scandals transcend time. They live forever as cautionary tales and examples of our fragile ethical foundations. Scandals can alter the trajectory of a sport. This section documents and contextualizes those moments.

9. POLITICS

Although traditional definitions of politics are included in this section, we built this section upon a broader understanding of the term *political*. As such, this section examines political moments and struggles faced within sports. Examples include battles for gender equity, the perils of using public funding for privately owned sports franchises, and the struggles of transgendered people to find their place in a sporting world desperate to split everything into one or the other of just two categories: men and women. This section also includes moments of international intrigue, such as when half of the Hungarian water polo team, at that time living under communist rule, won an Olympic gold medal and defected before they could return home. Sports hold the ability to carry deep political meanings, and it is crucial to understand how sports are used to achieve goals beyond winning and losing.

10. PATRIOTISM AND NATIONAL PRIDE

The Olympics, military conflicts, and historical traditions have transformed sport into a canvas for patriotic—and sometimes nationalistic—moments. This section gives this book the opportunity to investigate events such as Mongolia's "Great Naadam Festival," which celebrates its three great sporting traditions: archery, horse racing, and wrestling. This section also runs the chapter's anchor leg because of how it brings together so many other elements of the chapters; historical context, globalization, economics, key figures, and politics build the bedrock of the pride that different nations, regions, and individuals feel in watching their athletes—as extensions of themselves, as their representatives—succeed.

These 10 sections embody the elements that help us understand sports' historical impact and provide a road map into how our cultures might continue to develop. Additionally, each of the 50 entries includes reading recommendations. Books and articles were selected to paint an accurate, diverse picture of each sport, from how-to books, to wild tales of heroic individuals, to historiographies that capture important moments in time.

Acknowledgments

Two books in particular made themselves invaluable to the production of *Modern Sports around the World*: Gary Osmond and Murray G. Phillips's *Sports History in the Digital Era* and Andrea Bundon's *Digital Qualitative Research in Sport and Physical Activity*. I am grateful to my editor, Julie Dunbar, whose steady hand and bottomless well of patience guided me through this process. My family, especially my wife, Sam, gave me endless support and encouragement. Lastly, *Modern Sports around the World* is indebted to—and likely would not exist—were it not for the efforts of passionate people across the world who tend to the history of the sports they love. Their devotion to maintenance and archiving do not go unnoticed, and we hope the creation of this book, which preserves their knowledge so that generations of students and future scholars may learn from them, helps them feel their hard work was not done in vain.

Introduction

There is no way William Webb Ellis could have known what he set in motion in 1823 when, playing a sport that looked something like football, he ran with the ball. Ellis attended Rugby School, a boarding school in Warwickshire, England. For centuries school children had played versions of the game, which had evolved over time and been adjusted to compensate for regional flavors. The version Ellis and his classmates played forbid running with the ball; they could catch it, punt it and move to another position, but not run with it.

Although the tale is likely exaggerated or apocryphal, the idea gained traction. Within 10 years some versions of the game had come to allow players to run with the ball, and by 1845 rules had been written down, which led to standardization, which allowed for teams and clubs to play one another with a uniform understanding of what the game should be. Yet that was only the beginning. Ellis's run unwittingly planted the seed for what would become the global, social, and economic future of organized sports across the world.

By the mid-1800s, a philosophical split had ruptured the United Kingdom's football community. Some preferred the game when it did not allow players to use their hands, while others preferred being able to run while holding the ball. Arguments between the two parties became heated and, in time, irreconcilable. Finally, in 1863 the two sides officially split into rugby football and association football (or "soccer" for short, possibly an abbreviation that stems from the third through fifth letters of "association," although debate remains among historians). Rugby football allowed its players to use their hands. Soccer, within a few years of its official formation, would outlaw the use of hands completely except by goalkeepers.

The wheels of history began to turn faster. Great Britain's imperialist ambition forced its games upon subjects in such regions as South Africa and South Asia, while its commercial interests and political allegiances introduced it to other parts of the world. Much of the world picked sides—rugby or soccer—just as local athletes had done in England. Many added their own local ideas. Australia favored rugby but tweaked a few of the rules to create a game that today is known as Australian rules football. Of all the world's football-centric sports, Aussie football most resembles the game played by Ellis, which is not as violent as other forms of football but still calls for physical ambition.

The United States also adopted rugby rules, but within a few decades the game had evolved to include new features, such as forward passes and set plays that, when completed, led to a short break to set up another attempted play. American football, unlike Australian rules football, embraced violence. Players regularly shattered their noses, arms, and legs. In the late 19th century, so many players died that the U.S. government threatened to ban American football unless officials created rules to make the game safer, which they did.

Still, for many the violence remained too much. American physical education teacher James Naismith, searching for a safer alternative to keep his students fit, invented basketball. That game, too, proved popular. Then one of Naismith's students, William G. Morgan, saw what his teacher had done and created yet another new game, one that required even less physical exertion than basketball so that workers could enjoy the game over their lunch break without returning to work full of sweat: volleyball.

Meanwhile, Europe, South America, and parts of western Asia and northern and central Africa gravitated toward soccer. The speed and gracefulness of the game transformed its players from athletes into artists. Injuries occurred in soccer, as they did in any sport, but not like they did in rugby. Soccer's restriction of hand use forced players to improvise with their feet. They were ballet dancers with the ball, and the world quickly became transfixed.

In 1904 soccer associations from eight nations—Belgium, Denmark, France, Germany, the Netherlands, Spain, Sweden, and Switzerland—collaborated on the formation of the Fédération Internationale de Football Association, or FIFA, a governing body to administer and organize international competition. In 1930 FIFA held its first World Cup. It was held not in Europe but rather in the South American nation of Uruguay. As if the world needed any more proof that soccer had already gone global, Uruguay defeated Argentina to win the championship, the United States took third, and Yugoslavia took fourth to mark the highest finish by any squad from Europe, the continent where soccer and FIFA were born.

Over the last century, soccer's accumulative financial impact on the world has exceeded a trillion dollars. The women's and men's FIFA World Cups have become the most lucrative single-sport events in the world. Only the Olympics, which combine 40 sports and 200 countries, are worth more. American broadcasting company Fox Sports paid $400 million to broadcast the World Cup, a three-week event, in the United States, and FIFA receives broadcast fees from companies in every country that wants to broadcast the World Cup, which is nearly all of them.

Soccer is the world's most popular sport and its most valuable. The one country soccer officials have been unable to penetrate, despite countless attempts, is the United States. Although the United States includes loyal soccer fans, its most popular sport has become American football. Its most successful professional organization, the National Football League (NFL), has, behind FIFA, grown into the world's second most valuable sports property outside of the Olympics. As of 2020 the 32 NFL franchises have an average individual value of $2.5 billion. By the mid-1960s the NFL became the most-watched sport on American television, an honor it won 55 consecutive years.

Just as soccer has failed to find a consistently large U.S. audience, American football has been unable to expand beyond the United States. Sports fans outside the United States have called it too slow or too violent. However, a different U.S.

sport, basketball, has successfully penetrated the global market. Participation numbers show that basketball has become the second most popular sport in the world. Argentina, Brazil, Cameroon, Canada, China, Lithuania, Serbia, and Spain have produced some of the world's best players. American basketball player Stephon Marbury became so popular in China that a statue was erected in his honor; Lithuanian player Arvydas Sabonis is in both the American and European basketball halls of fame.

William Webb Ellis changed the world when he broke the rules, picked up the ball, and ran. What first must have appeared as an unorthodox moment instead created a rift in the historic game of football. Unable to reconcile their differences, soccer and rugby fans split their sport into two separate sports. Soccer conquered the world. The Brits introduced it to South America, and before long South America taught the world how to do it better. Rugby, meanwhile, led to the creation of new sports in Australia and North America, most notably American football. And when that proved too violent, entrepreneurial teachers invented two new games—basketball and volleyball—that continue to excite the world. Ellis's whimsical decision set the world on new athletic and financial courses with effects that today influence the everyday life of billions of people across every continent.

Action Sports

Action sports, or extreme sports, have soared in popularity since the back half of the 20th century. "Action sports" is the collective name for several sports, including skateboarding, snowboarding, motocross, and BMX (bike motocross). Motocross, or off-road motorcycle racing, first drew interest around the same time as other motorsports such as auto racing, in the early 20th century. The rest, however, were born in U.S. counterculture, mostly in California, Michigan, and Vermont. Action sports are more than just athletes competing in a sport they find interesting: they are a lifestyle, spawning fashion trends, clothing lines, and their own traveling series of exhibition and professional events. Automotive and soda companies build ad campaigns around attracting the action sports market, even though the market by definition often rejects mainstream materialism. What once was on the outskirts of culture, however, inevitably becomes mainstream itself, which is how action sports went from niche to billion-dollar industry in the blink of an eye.

HISTORICAL CONTEXT

With the exception of motocross, which debuted in the first decade of the 20th century as the world became interested in motorsports, action sports grew mostly out of 1960s California counterculture, starting with skateboarding. Skateboards do not resemble miniature surfboards by accident. Many early skateboarders referred to the sport as street surfing. Prior to the first patented skateboard in 1963, youth and other enthusiasts pried the wheels off of roller skates and mounted them to the bottom of planks of wood. It became a niche hobby with a devoted, even rabid, fan base.

The 1970s completed action sports' base. The BMX movement took off in the early 1970s following the release of the documentary *On Any Sunday*. What riders thought could only previously be done on motocross bikes could also be done on specially designed or modified bicycles. That gave access to a whole new market of riders, kids who challenged themselves and each other to off-road races and to attempt new tricks with their bikes. Around the same time, a "snurfer" named Jake Carpenter manufactured the first snowboard. Snurfing—attaching two skis together and riding them down a snowy hill or mountain—started in Michigan, the idea of an engineer. Snowboards, a single plank the approximate width of two skis, were the logical next step.

One other key moment in action sports took place in the 1970s. Japanese motorcycle manufacturers took an interest in motocross. Their engineers revolutionized, among other things, how bikes were cooled while being ridden, which opened the door to other advancements. Action sports, although still well off the mainstream's international radar, now had all the ingredients they needed to become a global force in the coming decades.

The final step to mainstream acceptance took place in the mid-1990s, when ESPN, the American-based cable network and most valuable media property in the world, saw in action sports an opportunity to simultaneously expand its audience and locate new content to fill its growing stable of channels. In 1995 ESPN produced, hosted, and broadcasted the first "X Games," a multiday, Olympic-like celebration of action sports. Less than two years earlier, ESPN launched ESPN2, a second all-sports channel that originally was supposed to cater to younger audiences. A year later the Vans shoe brand began to sponsor a national skateboarding tour, and in 1997 ESPN started the winter X Games, which included snowboarding. Both the X Games and the Vans tour continue to this day.

Skateboards were invented in the mid-20th century. By the turn of the millennium, competitors such as Tony Hawk (pictured) captured the imagination of millions of kids around the world with their athleticism and willingness to risk their own bodies. (Carlos Carvalho/Dreamstime.com)

GLOBALIZATION

European nations dominated motocross for its first 70 years. Motocross des Nations began in 1947, about 40 years after the first motocross race in the United Kingdom. The Netherlands hosted the first Motocross des Nations, which has been held annually since the first event, and countries throughout Europe rotated hosting until 1981, when the United States hosted its first of 13 consecutive Motocross des Nations before the event returned to Belgium in 1995. Great Britain hosted the 1994 event.

Two factors led to motocross's expansion in the late 1960s. First, some of the sport's top racers toured the United States to compete against—and defeat—the best American riders. Undeterred by their defeat, the Americans were instead inspired by the European competitors to improve. Second, Japanese motorcycle builders began to challenge European makers for motocross supremacy. Within just a few years, motocross went from mostly a European sport to one with heavy fan interest on three continents.

WHERE THEY'RE PLAYED TODAY

This is a difficult question to succinctly answer since four primary sports fall under action sport's umbrella: BMX, motocross, skateboarding, and snowboarding. Snowboarding takes place across the world wherever there are snow-covered hills and mountains. It is just as common in some parts of the world, including Europe and the United States, for young athletes to be pulled toward a snowboard as to a pair of skis. BMX and skateboarding, meanwhile, are more universal; wherever there is a dirt road or rough terrain, one can find casual athletes messing around with BMX, and wherever there is pavement, one can find skateboarders.

Motocross, as ever, requires more funding and, occasionally, a pit crew for support, so it mostly is limited to places where there is access to dirt roads or tracks conducive to the sport.

Hawk Held Out for More

Some say a sport is only as good as its most popular, charismatic stars. That would help explain the first meteoric rise of action sports. The cultural arrival of skateboarder Tony Hawk could not have come at a better time for action sports. He was daring—not just completing difficult moves but inventing them as well. He was successful, winning competitions just as mainstream media began to pay attention to skateboarding. He oozed charisma, indulging kids, adults, and every camera pointed in his direction. He also knew how to market himself, appearing in dozens of television shows and films. Starting in the late 1990s, wherever there were action sports, there was Hawk.

Perhaps most importantly, Hawk had an entrepreneurial spirit. His video game series, especially *Tony Hawk's Pro Skater*, may have done as much to elevate the sport as anything anyone ever accomplished on the halfpipe. Between 1999 and 2020, Hawk, in a video game series published by Activision, released video games that have sold tens of millions of units around the world, with a total revenue reaching $1.5 billion. His very first game, *Tony Hawk's Pro Skater*, sold 1.3 million units. That game alone spawned four sequels, including *Pro Skater 4*, considered by gaming magazines the best skating video game ever made, plus four spinoff games and five rereleases, including the first two *Pro Skaters* together in one package in 2020.

Hawk has a mind for business. When Activision first approached him about video games in the late 1990s, they offered him $500,000 to put his name on the box in exchange for them holding all future rights. He declined, instead seeking a long-term deal. The hard-line approach paid off. Hawk got the deal he wanted, and the franchise is one of the most popular in video game history. Hawk's reward is a fortune worth nearly $150 million.

ECONOMICS AND MEDIA

The skateboarding industry alone is worth as much as $5 billion annually, according to some estimates. This includes decks and other parts, apparel, media, and other properties. Professional skateboarders, on average, earn $3,000 to $5,000 a month through sponsorships and supplement their incomes through competition awards and product endorsements. The top professionals can earn anywhere from several hundred thousand dollars per year to the low millions. The most publicly influential skateboarder in the sport's short history, Tony Hawk, possesses a net worth of more than $100 million.

BMX riders and snowboarders build their livings similar to skateboarders, although the money is slightly less than skateboarding because of skateboarding's wider interest base. Motocross is significantly more, with the top 3 or 4 riders earning as much as $10 million annually and another 15 earning as much as $1 million per year. Motocross racing teams are better financed because of maintenance upkeep and transportation costs. The sport is also able to negotiate broadcast rights and other media contracts across the world, including Australia, where interest in motocross continues to grow. Typically, motocross league officials seek to negotiate multiyear deals with broadcast companies.

DIMENSIONS OF THE SPORT

The common denominator among action sports is safety gear: helmets, knee and elbow pads, and other sport-specific equipment. Violent, often terrifying injuries are part of action sports. Some participants even celebrate their injuries, compiling them into YouTube videos for others to consume. It is common to find action sport athletes boasting and laughing about their injuries on internet message boards.

Motocross typically takes place on dirt tracks. Racers compete using varying models of motorcycles, at various distances, and under different sorts of track conditions. BMX competes under similar conditions—minus the engines. Professional skateboarders compete in skate parks on equipment known as half-pipes or quarter-pipes, vertical ramps, full pipes, and banked ramps. Snowboarders compete in three Olympic events, including half-pipe, snowboard cross, and parallel giant slalom, but as one snowboarder innocently told an American newspaper, "Who knew that someday snowboarders would have their own video games?" (Jenkins 2005, D1).

IMPORTANT FIGURES

John F. Humphrey's 2012 obituary read like something out of a movie. It was almost too perfect. Had he been a movie character, critics could have complained that no one could have accomplished as much in one life as Humphrey did: received the Distinguished Flying Cross for his World War II fighter-pilot heroics; helped build his family's home from the ground up; and moved his family across the country after buying a small business, which, naturally, he transformed into a successful venture with ties to Fortune 500 companies. Always a tinkerer, in 1963 he engineered and produced the first patented skateboard. For his contributions to the sport, he was inducted into the Skateboarding Hall of Fame.

Before the coronavirus pandemic postponed the 2020 Summer Olympics, Sky Brown had her sights on becoming the youngest Olympic athlete in British history. Only 11 years old, Brown was set to compete in skateboarding. She had already won bronze at the World Championships and gained further notoriety by winning an American reality television show centered on dancing, not action sports.

Even for those who do not skateboard, Vans shoe company, which has become synonymous with the action sports lifestyle, has played a significant role in youth culture. The unofficial official shoe of skateboarding, Vans first appeared in 1966 in Southern California. Two brothers and their business partner started the company, which they sold in the late 1980s. In 1996 Vans became the primary sponsor of the largest skateboard tour in the United States, a partnership it continues. The company also sponsors BMX, motocross, and snowboarding teams. But those who do not participate—or even watch—any of those sports needn't worry: Vans are sold in malls and online stores across America.

POP CULTURE

Cupid struck at the 2001 X Games when motocross racer Carey Hart met pop singer Alecia Moore, better known as P!nk. The two hit it off instantly. The celebrity couple injected action sports with a dose of mainstream publicity. P!nk proposed in 2005 while Hart was in the middle of a race. Assisting his pit crew, P!nk wrote on a sign "Will you marry me? I'm serious!" (Lester 2013, electronic edition), which Hart saw during the race. He immediately pulled over to accept, they embraced, and Hart jumped back on his motorcycle to finish the race. Hart, the first motocross racer ever to successfully complete a backflip on a 250cc motorcycle in competition, and P!nk, a three-time Grammy winner, have two children.

In 1985 actor Michael J. Fox starred in the film *Back to the Future*, which became a worldwide sensation that spawned two sequels and multiple video games. In the film, Fox's character travels back in time from 1985 to 1955, where he finds himself in precarious positions. In one scene high school bullies chase Fox. To get away, he steals a kid's scooter, breaks off the basket and handle, and turns it into a skateboard—something he excels at riding in 1985. In 1955 onlookers are confused but curious about this new form of transportation. One character asks what Fox is riding. The line received praise from the real-world skateboarding community for its accuracy: skateboards were invented in 1962, seven years after the movie takes place.

Although skateboarding was a small part of *Back to the Future*, movies centered on action sports traditionally have done poorly with moviegoers. Action sports participants dislike the films for their lack of realism, while casual movie fans simply do not find the movies entertaining. In 1989 actor Christian Slater's star was on the rise. Starting that year and over the next five, he appeared in some of the era's iconic teen films. He also starred in *Gleaming the Cube*, about a skateboarder who stumbles into a government conspiracy. Urban Dictionary defined something that is "gleaming the cube" as a failure so spectacular that there is beauty in the failure. The film created a cult following, and it also marked one of the first on-screen appearances of a then 20-year-old Tony Hawk. One exception to action sports' lack of success in film: the XXX movie franchise about a secret agent who uses action sports to fight crime.

SCANDALS

In 2011 American news anchor Anderson Cooper became the host of a daytime talk show. Producers decided to make a show on the teenage mind. A teen skateboarder, approached by one of Cooper's producers, was asked to film himself doing some of his typical skateboard tricks so the show could air the footage. The teen fell and suffered a major head injury. The show never aired. It is not known whether the show accepted any responsibility for the accident, but Cooper was said to be distraught, according to media sources. The incident led to scrutiny of whether the producers of Cooper's program should be held liable for encouraging dangerous behavior. Replied a guest on another network that was discussing the accident: "The principle of 'do no harm' applies not just to physicians but to TV and producers too" (Wemple 2011).

PATRIOTISM AND NATIONAL PRIDE

American snowboarder Shaun White said he had a vision of appearing on the cover of *Rolling Stone* magazine. Not just appearing on it, but appearing on it while wearing a pair of pants designed like the American flag. White had seen the rock singer Axl Rose wear a pair of American flag shorts and thought it would be fun if he wore a similar pair of pants on the magazine cover.

First, White had to win the 2010 Olympic gold medal in snowboarding. He won in 2006, but in the four years since, competition had grown more difficult. Still, White won his second gold. *Rolling Stone* asked him to be on the cover, and on the March 18, 2010 edition, White appeared shirtless in American flag pants celebrating over a burning snowboard, an homage to rock legend Jimi Hendrix, who famously burned his guitar on stage in 1967.

Timeline

1906 – First off-road motorcycle race is held in the United Kingdom.

1921 – Although scooters date as far back as the 19th century, this was when someone applied for the first patent. Skateboards come from the base (foot part) of the scooter.

1930s – The "scooter skate" is invented, a three-wheeled contraption that comes with a removable scooter handle.

1947 – The first Motocross des Nations is held in the Netherlands and won by Great Britain.

1950s – Kids across the United States, especially the West Coast, hastily remove wheels from roller skates and attach them to wood boards, essentially inventing the modern skateboard.

1962 – California surf shop Val Surf manufactures and sells its own skateboards, the first retail skateboard shop in the world.

1963 – World War II navy veteran John Humphrey makes and patents the first mass-produced skateboard.

1965 – Engineer Sherman Poppen inadvertently invents the snowboard when he ties two skis together to help his daughters learn control on ski slopes. At first the event is called "snurfing."

1966 – Motocross makes its North American debut.

1971 – The documentary film about racing, *On Any Sunday*, inspires legions of kids to begin racing their bikes on dirt tracks. BMX (bike motocross) is born.

1977 – Snurfer Jake Carpenter manufactures the first snowboards.

1977 – The American Bicycle Association, which oversees BMX events, is founded in Arizona.

1982 – First USA Nationals snowboard competition is held.

1983 – First World Championships in international snowboarding are held.

1985 – The hit movie *Back to the Future* is released, in which the lead character in the year 1955 teaches a small town about skateboards when he tears the handle off a kid's scooter.

1995 – American cable television network ESPN produces and broadcasts the first X Games, an annual action sports event that includes skateboarding, motocross, and BMX.

1997 – Winter X Games debuts.

1998 – Snowboarding debuts as an Olympic sport.

1999 – Skateboarder Tony Hawk lands the first "900," an aerial trick that calls for the skater to complete 2.5 midair revolutions in one jump.

2008 – BMX debuts as an Olympic sport.

2020 – Skateboarding is supposed to debut as an Olympic sport, but the Olympics are postponed because of the coronavirus pandemic.

See also: Cross-Country Skiing; Cycling; Surfing.

Further Reading

Bulltjens, J. and Sweeney, C. (2018). *Ride: BMX Glory, Against All the Odds*. Pitch Publishing: Sussex, United Kingdom.

Crist, S. (2012). *Locals Only: California Skateboarding 1975–1978*. AMMO Books: Los Angeles.

Hawk, T. (2010). *How Did I Get Here? The Ascent of an Unlikely CEO.* Wiley: Hoboken, New Jersey.

Jenkins, L. (2005). "The Flying Tomato McTwists His Way to the Top." *New York Times*, Dec. 6, 2005, D1.

Lester, P. (2013). *Split Personality: The Story of Pink.* Omnibus Press: London.

Louison, C. (2011). *Impossible: Rodney Mullen, Ryan Sheckler, and the Fantastic History of Skateboarding.* Lyons Press: Lanham, Maryland.

Lucas, G. and Robinson, S. (2012). *Rad Bikes: The Best BMX Bikes of All Time.* Laurence King Publishing: London.

Mullen, R. and Mortimer, S. (2005). *The Mutt: How to Skateboard and Not Kill Yourself.* It Books: New York.

Prescott, S. (2020). *Shredders: Girls Who Skate.* Ten Speed Press: Berkeley, California.

Santella, C. (2013). *Fifty Places to Ski and Snowboard before You Die: Downhill Experts Share the World's Greatest Destinations.* Harry N. Abrams: New York.

Wemple, E. (2011). "Anderson Cooper Skateboarder Scandal Draws Tsk from Today Show." *Washington Post*, Oct. 3, 2011. https://www.washingtonpost.com/blogs/erik-wemple/post/anderson-cooper-skateboarder-scandal-draws-tsk-from-today-show/2011/10/03/gIQA5ntLIL_blog.html.

Archery

Pick up a bow. Pick up an arrow. Aim it. Shoot it. Archery sounds so simple, but it is not. This contest of skill, rooted in ancient human civilization, has frustrated people for millennia. Their target might have been a large animal that their tribe needed for food, or a charging enemy threatening their family, or a stationary, fabricated target with a bull's-eye in the middle, its only reward a gold medal or cash prize. Archery is the art of using a bow and arrow with precision. Archers practice their craft around the world today as they have for thousands of years, albeit with modern equipment. Humanity celebrates archery, commemorating it through sport, books, and—perhaps more than any sport—a legacy of art and popular culture dating back centuries. Guns and bombs have replaced archery as the most lethal forms of killing, but neither of these reflect the historical appreciation or romanticism attached to the bow and arrow.

HISTORICAL CONTEXT

Along with wrestling, archery is one of the most ancient sports on earth, and like wrestling, archery was an activity born not out of leisure but necessity. Archery exists because people needed food. They needed to hunt animals far larger than themselves. Firing a piercing, fatal arrow into a large beast provided an efficient, safe way to take down animals such as buffalo.

Historians date the earliest arrows to about 20,000 years ago, while some traces of what might be arrows were found at a southern African site possibly as old as 70,000 years. Evidence of arrows dating to 15,000 BCE was found in Germany. It took about another 15,000 years for humans to realize that not only could they kill animals with arrows but they could also more easily kill people. Around 3000 BCE the ancient Egyptians began to standardize archery as a tool for warfare and hunting. Many ancient skills and games, such as kabaddi, were seeded through military training exercises. The Chinese, for example, employed archers in chariots for military use around 1600 BCE.

Archery did not become an organized sport until the late 16th century in England, with the first documented competition taking place around 1580, in Finsbury. The date is notable because the most famous literary archery contest, the one won by British character Robin Hood, is imagined to have taken place during the 14th or 15th century. It makes sense, then, that some of the earlier, apocryphal tales of Robin Hood begin to appear during the early 16th or late 15th centuries.

The modern Olympic Games began in 1896. Men's archery made its Games debut in 1900 and women's in 1904, and the sport appeared sporadically until 1920, at which point it disappeared from the Games until reappearing permanently in 1972.

GLOBALIZATION

Given that bows and arrows are tens of thousands of years old, with centuries and even millennia of history across multiple continents, pinpointing the skill's global migration is nearly impossible. Did different cultures independently create some form of a bow, given its importance to hunting? Or did the craftsmanship of the bow and arrow begin in one culture and then spread to others?

Modern Olympic archery medal counts show how decentralized the sport is. Cold, northern European countries tend to dominate many cold-weather sports; Americans dominate popular global sports that began in the United States. Archery is different. South Korea has won 23 golds, more than any other country. The United States sits second with 14. Belgium comes in third, with 11, meaning the top three gold-medal-winning countries in archery come from three different continents. Australian archers have also won gold.

WHERE IT'S PLAYED TODAY

The World Archery Foundation, formed in 1931 in Poland, includes 159 countries and oversees administration of the sport, including the World Championships. It administers events for outdoor and indoor events, youth, para-athletes, and college and university students. Archery takes place all over the world, with recent championship events taking place in Turkey, Sweden, Indonesia, Mexico, South Korea, China, Croatia, and the United States.

The sport's rich, ancient history contributes to its global participation numbers. Recent Olympic medal winners in archery have come from Mexico, South Korea, Germany, China, Indonesia, Russia, Great Britain, France, Italy, Australia, and Japan, among other nations. Archery skills also continue to attract young recreational participants. Nerf, for example, the Hasbro-owned toy company that is the most valuable maker of children's toy weapons in the world, makes a full line of archery toys.

ECONOMICS AND MEDIA

In most parts of the world, archery receives almost no local, regional, or international media coverage except during the Olympics. Even then, it is rare to see a full event as one might get to see for gymnastics, ice skating, or basketball; instead, it is relegated to highlights or a less popular television time slot during the middle of the night.

The big money in archery comes through pop culture, not the sport itself (see "Pop Culture"). A small handful of professional archers supplement their income through endorsement deals or equipment manufacturing. Harry Drake rose to archery fame in the mid-20th century by firing arrows record distances using bows he designed himself. He expanded his business by expanding his notoriety.

DIMENSIONS OF THE SPORT

Although there are different forms of archery, the most commonly recognized is loading an arrow into a bow to fire at a target. To do so, archers should line up their body perpendicular to what they are shooting at, feet even with the shoulders. Use the three middle fingers to hold the arrow on the string of the bow. Point the bow toward the target and aim the arrowhead toward the bull's-eye, pull back the string until the tension is tight, and release. Hopefully, the arrow finds its target.

A standard target includes 10 rings, with 1 color for every 2 rings for a total of 5 colors. Working from the outside-in, a standard target goes white for the outside 2 rings, then black, then blue, then red, and finally yellow for the inner 2 rings, which includes the bull's-eye, or what is considered dead center (not the actual eye of a bull). Distances from the archer to the target vary by age, gender, and skill level. Standard outdoor range for Olympic archery is 70 meters.

IMPORTANT FIGURES

The most important, influential, and sustaining figure in the sport's history was a fictional character, or rather, a fictionalized version of someone who was most likely—at some point—real: Robin Hood.

Robin Hood. Robin of Sherwood. Robin of Loxley. Robert Huntingdon. Poets began telling stories in the late 14th century of a British noble turned outlaw who fought on behalf of the commoners. He employed several weapons over the centuries but no weapon more than his bow and arrow. An expert marksman, Robin Hood has appeared in sonnets, books, plays, and movies. The universality of his story has helped it survive more than 600 years, and it appears as popular today around the world as it was hundreds of years ago across Great Britain.

In one of the more popular versions of the story, Robin's nemesis, the Sheriff of Nottingham, challenges Robin to an archery contest. Robin appears in disguise, not wanting to get caught. He wins, eventually reveals his identity, and a battle between the Sheriff's men and Robin's supporters follows. In film, the modern role of Robin Hood was most famously ushered in by Australian actor Errol Flynn, who appeared in 1938's *The Adventures of Robin Hood*. More recent actors to portray the character include Russell Crowe, Kevin Costner, Cary Elwes, Taron Egerton, and Sean Connery. Walt Disney Company gave the character the animated treatment in 1973's *Robin Hood*. It received favorable reviews, with several movie critics calling it Disney's best animated movie since the company founder's death in 1966.

As for nonliterary heroes, a motorbike accident could have ended Neroli Fairhall's life. Instead, it opened a pathway to a new one. Fairhall, a New Zealander, in 1984 became the first paraplegic to compete in the Olympics when she represented her country in archery at the Los Angeles Games. Fairhall finished 35th. She also won numerous Paralympic medals, coached archery, and earned the honor Member of the Order of the British Empire for services to the disabled. She died in 2006 at age 61 from complications related to the motorbike accident from years earlier, but the mark she left on her sport lives on.

POP CULTURE

The two most profitable comic-book companies of the 20th and 21st centuries, Marvel Comics and DC Comics, created archers as superheroes. In 1941 DC debuted Green Arrow. Wealthy playboy Oliver Queen wore an outfit that updated the classic Robin Hood look, which did not violate international copyright law since the Robin Hood story went back about 500 years and was legally considered fair use.

Using his wits, financial resources, and his trusty bow and arrow, Queen, either alone or alongside such mainstream heroes as Batman, fought to bring justice to the DC universe. The Green Arrow character endured. In addition to occasionally getting fashion makeovers, in 2012 the character got its own American television show, called *Arrow*. It ran for eight years, leaving fans in tears when the production company announced the series would come to an end.

Marvel Comics wanted its own archer superhero but sought to separate itself from DC's Green Arrow. In 1964, the company created Hawkeye, who wore purple and came from a low socioeconomic background. Clint Barton, Hawkeye's alter ego, was orphaned after his parents died. He joined a circus where he learned acrobatics, physical conditioning, and archery. The character proved so popular that Marvel's writers made him a member of the Avengers, their most popular team of heroes.

When Marvel got into the moviemaking business, the character of Hawkeye followed. Played by Jeremy Renner, a multiple-time Academy Award acting nominee, Hawkeye stood out as one of the few heroes without special powers. Like DC's Green Arrow, Hawkeye had only his bow, arrows, and intellect. The character became so popular that when it failed to appear in the 2018 Marvel movie *Avengers: Infinity War*, fans numbering in the thousands contacted the studio to voice their displeasure. The first scene in the sequel, *Avengers: Endgame*, focused on Hawkeye and his family, appeasing fans and kick-starting the movie. The message from fans, however, was loud and clear: Don't mess with our archers.

In 2008 author Suzanne Collins published a dystopian novel about a girl forced to fight to the death for the entertainment of the ruling class. The character, Katniss Everdeen, could bring just one weapon with her into the arena. She chose a bow and arrow, the weapon she had mastered to hunt animals to help feed her family. *The Hunger Games* proved a global smash. It inspired two follow-up novels and a prequel as well as four movies, elevating Collins from successful, surviving author into a global icon.

Everdeen became a hero for the ages. Using her bow, she shot bull's-eyes during training sessions and brought down enemies whether they were on foot or flying in an aircraft. The trilogy of books about Everdeen has sold 70 million copies to date and been translated into dozens of languages, while the movies collectively earned about $1.5 billion. The series concludes with Everdeen taking down not one, but two, government presidents, including one, naturally, with a bow and arrow.

SCANDALS

In 2017 members of Great Britain's para-archery team came forward with complaints of mistreatment, a toxic environment, and most alarming, sexual assault by a coach against an athlete. Not wanting the bad publicity, a team staff member told the assault victim that the coach's job and her position on the team could be damaged if she reported the attack—a common tactic used against assault victims to scare them into not coming forward.

She ultimately decided to report, opening the door for others to speak out about mistreatment within the team. "Some of us have nothing but archery in our lives," a teammate told the British Broadcasting Corporation (BBC). "If we lose this, we lose everything. They know that and they take huge advantage of that by bullying, intimidating, and discriminating against us" (Rumsby 2017).

Archery Great Britain, the organizational administrator for national-level archery in the country, suspended the coach and opened an investigation into the program. AGB's para-archers won three gold medals at the 2016 Paralympic Games held in Rio de Janeiro, Brazil, the most among any nation competing in archery.

PATRIOTISM AND NATIONAL PRIDE

The Secret History of the Mongols, dating to the late 1200s and one of the oldest books in the Mongol language, details what has become the three official sports of Mongolia's annual Great Naadam Festival: horse racing, wrestling, and archery. The festival, which attracts spectators from across the world, includes archery

Archery

contests for adults and children. The target is a traditional bull hide stretched across a wood frame.

Archery, which Mongols once used for battles, sport, and hunting, is now mostly relegated exclusively to sport, including at festivals. At the festival, coed teams of 10 archers compete at varying distances. There also are individual competitions. The winners earn the title National Markswoman or National Marksman.

Timeline

68,000 BCE – Scientists have found evidence of arrowheads in South Africa that they believe date back this far.

3000 BCE – The ancient Greeks use bows and arrows to hunt and wage war.

1600 BCE – The ancient Chinese employ archers in their military chariots.

Late 13th century CE – Poets begin to describe the character who would become Robin Hood.

1580 – The first documented archery contest takes place in Finsbury, England.

17th century – Chinese writer Gao Ying puts Chinese archery techniques into writing, paving the way for the country's *The Way of Archery* manuals, which will be studied for centuries.

1781 – British businessperson Ashton Lever founds the Royal Toxophilite Society, the oldest archery club in the United Kingdom, which exists to this day.

1900 – Archery makes its Olympic debut.

1938 – The film *The Adventures of Robin Hood*, starring Errol Flynn, debuts and is an indisputable success, ushering the character into the modern era. Over the next 80 years, more than two dozen Robin Hood films are made—and those are just the ones made in English.

1941 – Dressed in "Robin Hood green" DC Comics introduces superhero Green Arrow, whose only power is his superhuman ability to accurately use a bow and arrow.

1964 – American Harry Drake, using a bow he designed himself, fires an arrow 1,077 yards.

1971 – Using a footbow—a bow controlled by the feet and legs—Drake sends an arrow 2,028 yards, or 1.15 miles.

1972 – Archery returns to the Olympics following a 52-year absence.

1999 – Two years after learning how to use a bow, Academy Award–winning actor Geena Davis qualifies to try out for the U.S. Olympic team. She makes it to the semifinal round, ultimately finishing 24th, not good enough to qualify but more than enough to earn the sport some much-deserved mainstream attention.

2012 – Arrow, based on the DC Comics hero Green Arrow, debuts on American television. It lasts eight seasons and 170 episodes.

2012 – South Korea wins gold in women's archery for the fourth consecutive Olympic Games.

See also: Horse Racing; Olympics; Wrestling.

Further Reading

Collins, S. (2008). *The Hunger Games*. Scholastic Press: New York.

Ferguson, B. and Helgeland, G. (1994). *Become the Arrow*. Target Communication Corporation: Milwaukee, Wisconsin.

Fraction, M., Aja, D., and Pulido, J. (2013). *Hawkeye, Vol. 1: My Life as a Weapon*. Marvel Comics: New York.

Herrigel, E. (1999). *Zen in the Art of Archery*. Vintage: New York.

Hill, J. (2018). *Howard Hill's Method of Shooting a Bow and Arrow*. Self-published.

Lee, K. and Benner, T. (2019). *Total Archery–Inside the Archer*. Astra Archery: Chula Vista, California.

Pyle, H. (2017). *The Merry Adventures of Robin Hood*. Digireads.com: Overland Park, Kansas.

Ritson, J. (1795). *Robin Hood: A Collection of All the Ancient Poems, Songs, and Ballads Now Extant, Relative to that Celebrated Outlaw*. Cambridge University Press: Cambridge, England.

Rumsby, B. (2017). "Archery the Latest Olympic and Paralympic Sport Hit by Sexual Abuse Allegations." *The Telegraph*, June 30, 2017. https://www.telegraph.co.uk/archery/2017/06/30/archery-latest-olympic-paralympic-sport-hit-sexual-abuse-allegations.

Sorrells, B. (2004). *Beginner's Guide to Traditional Archery*. Stackpole Books: Mechanicsburg, Pennsylvania.

Various authors and illustrators. (2016). *Green Arrow: A Celebration of 75 Years*. DC Comics: New York.

Australian Rules Football

It is rare when a country's most popular sport is a mere afterthought in the rest of the world. Yet in Australia there exists a sport that drums up the passions of rabid fan bases and casual observers alike, while barely making a dent in the international conversation. Australian rules football, a hybrid of rugby, soccer, and Australian ingenuity, provokes fanaticism and emotional peaks and valleys. Like kabaddi in South Asia and NASCAR in the United States, Australian rules football generates excitement for millions within the host region yet very little outside of it. Its best players become national celebrities. Statues are built, T-shirts printed and sold, Halls of Fame erected in their honor. However, as popular as it is within Australia, it just never caught on extensively outside of it. Which is fine, because Aussies love Aussie football. The rest of the world does not know what it is missing.

HISTORICAL CONTEXT

In the 1850s Australia was still under British rule. Around 1858 Tom Wills, an Aussie educated in Great Britain, and three others adapted rugby to create a new sport designed to keep athletes fit during winter months. The Melbourne Football Club was formed, and a match took place between Scotch and Melbourne Grammar Schools that incorporated more rugby rules than football. During this period within the sport, soccer and rugby were splitting the skills into

Australian rules football is a sport unique to the region. It resembles rugby, but called "footy," as it is known locally, and although hugely popular in Australia, has not experienced much global spread. (Max421/Dreamstime.com)

separate sports. That match between Scotch and Melbourne Grammar on July 31, 1858, although crude by today's measures, is considered the first contest in what would become Australian rules football.

Scotch and Melbourne Grammar played the first match under a new set of rules, adopted that day. They first were called Melbourne rules. By the late 1870s Australian rules football saw the birth of "intercolonial matches," a term for matches played between different Australian states and territories. The sport found early popularity in the states of Victoria, which includes Melbourne, and South Australia, and eventually spread to other parts of the country, although it remains most popular in Victoria. Rule changes reflected the will of the players and coaches beginning as early as the 1860s. A club that had an idea would pitch it to one of the early governing bodies, such as the South Australian National Football League. Sometimes new rules became permanent, and sometimes they did not, until eventually the game took on its current form.

Many of those rules were introduced to slightly reduce the risk of injury, a trait that came to distinguish Australian rules football from other games under the football family tree, most notably rugby. The game remains rough and, at times, violent, but it can be tame compared with rugby and American football. One of the first rugby components removed from Australian football was "hacking," the act of tripping or kicking opposing players. Players who caught balls in the air were awarded free kicks without the fear of being hit while performing the kick. It was also during this period that game officials began to require ball carriers to bounce the ball at least once every 33 feet in exchange for protection while carrying the ball.

On January 1, 1901, Australia became an independent nation. The Victorian Football League (VFL), formed three years earlier, emerged as the new nation's dominant governing body for Aussie football, outmaneuvering rivals through innovations such as postseason playoffs and championships. It hosted its first championship, known as the Grand Final, in 1898. It also devised the beginnings of a modern scoring system, including six points for a goal. The VFL further cemented its spot atop the sport by attracting and/or poaching teams from other leagues, including the rival Victorian Football Association. By the end of the 20th century's first decade, the VFL boasted 10 teams. A few years after the conclusion of World War I, it was up to 12. Today the VFL, which changed its name to the Australian Football League (AFL) in 1990, includes 18 teams, although Victoria remains the sport's hub.

Melbourne alone is home to 9 of the AFL's 18 teams, and 10 teams in total reside in Victoria. The other 8 teams are spread across the states of New South Wales, Queensland, South Australia, and Western Australia. Today Australian rules football is the country's most popular domestic sport, while rugby remains a popular international sport. In Victoria, Aussie football rules the television ratings among all sports broadcasts. The AFL has tried to boost interest beyond Victoria, and specifically Melbourne, but Victoria remains by far the most rabid state for Aussie football.

GLOBALIZATION

Australian rules football as a participatory sport has not experienced much globalization. There are clubs throughout the world on most continents, but their following is small compared to many other sports. In 2017 the AFL played an in-season match in China for the first time. It drew 10,000 fans, a paltry number compared to the size of crowds for imported soccer matches and basketball games.

As the 19th century ended and the 20th century began, a series of exhibition matches took place between Australian and British clubs, but the game never took off in the United Kingdom. The United Kingdom at that time cultivated two other strands of football: soccer and rugby. Both were proving extremely popular, and perhaps there simply was not room for a third, especially one that sought to minimize the violence of rugby while lacking the pure speed and precision of soccer. The United States during that period was growing its own strand of football—what today is known as American football, with set plays, no bouncing of the ball, and so much violence that ex-players have described it as getting into a car crash on every play.

Where Aussie football did gain some global traction was as an early attraction on cable television. In 1980, less than a year after its debut, American cable television network ESPN paid $100,000 for the rights to show AFL games in the United States. It was not allowed to show the games live. The sport gained a cult following in the United States that continued well after ESPN let the contract expire in 1986. Now an established media entity, ESPN's wallet had grown large enough to attract more American sports partnerships, such as college sports, and in 1987 it struck gold when it made its first deal with the National Football League, the most popular pro sports league in the United States. Once that happened, ESPN no longer needed Aussie football.

WHERE IT'S PLAYED TODAY

Australian rules football is played almost exclusively in Australia, even more exclusively in the state of Victoria and, to be even more specific, in the city of Melbourne inside Victoria. The AFL in 2002 started the Australian Football International Cup, an event held once every three years. Amateurs representing nations from across the world compete for the Cup, which is always held in Australia.

Australians are not allowed to compete in the men's division because they would almost certainly win. No other nation comes close to competing in the sport at the level of Australia, so the event is held as a gesture of ambassadorship and goodwill. Papua New Guinea has either won the event or finished second in all six of the International Cups. They have won three times. Ireland has won twice, and New Zealand earned one championship. In all, teams from 26 nations have competed in the men's and women's events. They are Australia (women's only), Canada, China, Croatia, Denmark, Fiji, Finland, France, Germany, Great Britain, India, Indonesia, Ireland, Israel-Palestine (united team), Japan, Nauru, New Zealand, Pakistan, Papua New Guinea, Samoa, South Africa, Spain, Sri Lanka, Sweden, Timor-Leste, Tonga, and the United States.

ECONOMICS AND MEDIA

Between 2014 and 2019, the AFL Grand Final, or championship game, was the highest-rated television program for the year in Australia. The only exception occurred in 2015 with the finals of the Cricket World Cup, which Australia hosted. The Grand Final generally pulls between 2.5 million and 3.2 million viewers, or just more than 10 percent of the country's population.

DIMENSIONS OF THE SPORT

Although some rules vary based on age and skill level, the most standard version of Aussie football includes a game split into four 20-minute quarters. Each quarter includes stoppage time, similar to injury time in soccer, and each game includes a halftime. Where Aussie football sometimes confuses casual observers is in trying to keep track of the positions. There are 18 players playing 18 different positions at any one time: 3 ruck-rovers, 3 full forwards, 3 half forwards, 3 centers, 3 halfbacks, and 3 fullbacks. Players come and go throughout a match, similar to line changes in ice hockey.

Goals occur when an attacking team boots the ball through the goal posts, either on the fly or by first bouncing it off the ground. Own-goals, the act in soccer of scoring for the other team by accidentally kicking it into your own goal, do not exist in Australian rules football. "Behinds" are worth one point and can be scored different ways, including on a goal attempt in which the kicked ball sails between a goal post and one of the two outside—or behind—posts; when the ball hits one of the taller posts; or when the ball is handballed or carried by a player across the goal line.

Unlike rugby, soccer, and American football—Aussie's football's closest relatives—an Aussie football field can be oval-shaped, and there are no uniform dimensions. The ideal field is between 110 and 155 meters in width and between 135 and 185 meters long.

IMPORTANT FIGURES

There was only one legitimate choice when it came time to vote on the top AFL player of the 20th century: Leigh Matthews. Matthews, a four-time Premiership winner (most valuable player) and four-time Premiership coach, helped redefine the game through his influence as player and teacher. He won the most-valuable-player award so many times that the AFL renamed it in his honor. The top player now receives the Leigh Matthews Trophy.

Matthews played professionally from 1969 to 1985 and then coached for another 20 years following his retirement as a player. He mostly played midfield, finishing his career with 915 goals in 332 games, the most ever by a nonforward. He began his career at the age of 16, and although people could not have suspected they were looking at the future greatest player in league history, it was apparent from his start that he was destined for greatness.

The Melbourne Football Club in 1953 so badly wanted Ron Barassi Jr. that it went to the VFL and had the league create a new rule in order to get him. Barassi's father, Ron Sr., had played for the Demons. He was an excellent player whose career ended when he went to fight for Australia in World War II, during which he was killed in action. The new rule, aptly called the "father-son rule," gave teams leeway when recruiting a player whose father played for that club. Certain rules exist to keep the recruiting process fair among all AFL squads, but it might be an embarrassment to a team or an emotional blow to a player to not be able to play in the same uniform as his father. The league agreed and created the rule, which exists to this day.

Barassi Jr. did not disappoint. He not only lived up to his father's reputation as a footballer but also he exceeded it. He was one of the first three players inducted into the AFL Hall of Fame with "legend status," an honor reserved for the game's elites. The other elite players were Matthews and Ted Whitten. Just as Matthews's name became attached to the most-valuable-player award, Barassi is the namesake of the equivalent award for youth players. Although his presence led to the father-son rule, Barassi did not spend his entire career with Melbourne. He spent the final five seasons of his career with Carlton, ending his career with 330 goals in 254 games.

POP CULTURE

In 1977 Australian playwright David Williamson debuted *The Club*, his take on the exploits of an Australian rules football club. It became a huge success, shattering box-office records. Then it found new life in secondary schools. Drama and theater clubs regularly pick *The Club* as one of their school-year performances.

In 1980 *The Club*, on the heels of its success as a play, became a feature film, and that, too, proved successful. In 2013 *The Guardian* newspaper wrote "The Club surely deserves its status among the best of all sports films made in Australia" (Jackson 2013).

SCANDALS

In 2013 Australian and international sports agencies began an investigation into the Essendon Football Club, an AFL franchise. The investigation ended with a coach and general manager suspended along with 32 players receiving two-year suspensions for their involvement with performance-enhancing drugs. Some of the involved players appealed their case to the Federal Supreme Court of Switzerland, but they could not get their suspensions overturned.

PATRIOTISM AND NATIONAL PRIDE

When World War II took Peter Chitty away from Australia and his precious Australian rules football, Chitty helped bring Aussie football to World War II. Chitty was a prisoner of war being kept by the Japanese in Singapore's Changi Prison. To occupy themselves, Chitty and some of his fellow countrymen organized a four-team prison Aussie rules football league. One team was made up mostly of Victorians, the Australian state most passionate about the sport. The other three teams were made up mostly of everyone else.

Chitty had not played professionally in the VFL since 1936, his career cut short by injuries. Within Changi's walls in 1942 and 1943, Chitty's playing career was revitalized. He captained the Victorian team in a match that reportedly drew 10,000 fans—Changi contained 15,000 Australian prisoners of war. Chitty played spectacularly and earned the Brownlow, awarded annually to the VFL's top player. The Changi Brownlow, as it came to be known, is alleged to have been made from the metal of a downed World War II fighter jet. It was the only Changi Brownlow ever awarded. Perhaps most coincidentally, Wilfred Smallhorn, a VFL Brownlow winner in 1933, was also being held in Changi. He presented the Changi Brownlow to Chitty.

The matches and the stories from inside Changi were captured in Perry Roland's 2010 book, *The Changi Brownlow*. Chitty survived Changi and eventually made it home to Australia, where he lived with his wife and family until his death in 1996.

An Australian newspaper reported in 2004 that Lillian Chitty, Peter Chitty's widow, gave the Changi Brownlow to an Australian war museum after her husband's death.

Timeline

1858 – The sport is born in Melbourne when the first match—between Melbourne Grammar and Scotch schools—is played.

1868 – The Adelaide Football Club forms to become the first football organization in South Australia.

1877 – The Victorian Football Association (VFA) is formed. Infighting eventually leads some clubs to break away.

1888 – An English team of Australian rules players tours Australia for a series of exhibition games.

1897 – Eight clubs, including some from the VFA, form the Victorian Football League (VFL), which later becomes the Australian Football League.

1930 – Collingwood wins its fourth consecutive premiership (championship). No team since has won four in a row.

1941 – Footballer Ron Barassi Sr. is killed during World War II.

1957 – VFL matches are televised for the first time.

1960 – The VFL suspends television coverage when fan game attendance begins to drop. It returns a year later, but matches for another several years are shown on replay only, not live.

1965 – Ron Barassi Jr. retires as one of the most important figures in Australian football history. He continues his success as a coach.

1969 – Leigh Matthews begins his professional career, which lasts until 1985 and ends with him considered by many the greatest player of the 20th century.

1980 – Upstart American cable network ESPN pays the VFL $100,000 for the right to show games on delay.

1986 – The first VFL national draft is held.

1986 – ESPN broadcasts its final Australian rules game. The next year it begins broadcasting American football.

1987 – The Brisbane Bears and West Coast Eagles pay entry fees into the VFL, effectively dooming the financial well-being of some other teams and leagues that had tried to compete against the VFL.

1990 – After nearly 90 years as the VFL, it rebrands as the Australian Football League (AFL).

1995 – Two Australian rules clubs are founded in Germany: in Frankfurt and Munich.

2013 – The first in-season AFL game is held outside of Australia, in New Zealand.

2017 – The National Women's League begins play.

2017 – The first in-season AFL game in China takes place.

See also: Football; Rugby; Soccer.

Further Readings

Flanagan, M. (2018). *A Wink from the Universe: The Inside Story of the AFL's Greatest Fairytale, the Bulldogs' 2016 Premiership.* Viking Australia: Camberwell, Victoria, Australia.

Jackson, R. (2013). "The Joy of Six: Australian Sports Movies." *The Guardian*, Sept. 9, 2013. https://www.theguardian.com/sport/blog/2013/sep/10/joy-of-six-australian-sport-movies.

Krien, A. (2013). *Night Games: Sex, Power and Sport.* Read How You Want: Sydney, Australia.

Marshall, K. (2019). *Stronger and Bolder: Inside the 2019 AFL Finals Series with Richmond.* Hardie Grant Books: Richmond, Victoria, Australia.

Matthews, L. (2014). *Accept the Challenge: The Autobiography.* Penguin Random House Australia: Melbourne, Australia.

Murphy, B. (2019). *Leather Soul: A Half-Back Flanker's Rhythm and Blues.* Nero: Carlton, Victoria, Australia.

Riewoldt, N. and Hanlon, P. (2017). *The Things That Make Us: Life, Loss and Football.* Allen and Unwin: Crows Nest, Australia.

Roland, P. (2010). *The Changi Brownlow.* Hachette Australia: Sydney, Australia.

Soraghan, K. (2017). *The Mighty West: The Bulldogs' Journey from Daydream Believers to Premiership Heroes.* Nero: Carlton, Victoria, Australia.

Wilson, T. (2020). *1989: The Great Grand Final.* Hardie Grant Books: Richmond, Victoria, Australia.

Auto Racing

First humans became obsessed with who could run the fastest. Then they domesticated horses, and they became obsessed with who could ride the fastest. It was only natural, then, that when during the Industrial Revolution humans invented automobiles, it became only a matter of time before they obsessed over who could drive the fastest. Over the last century auto racing has become one of the world's most popular and lucrative sports. During that span, cars have developed from social novelties, rickety and slow, into finely tuned machines capable of going so fast that racing leagues sometimes have to force them to slow down. Races may cover 500 miles in as little as just a few hours. The Indianapolis Motor Speedway in the United States draws 235,000 fans to a single race. Other fans wake up in the middle of the night to watch races live on television that take place in another hemisphere. Auto racing stands as a monument to human ingenuity and bravery. Daring and dangerous, breathtaking and dizzying, few sports marry the physical and intellectual quite like automobile racing.

HISTORICAL CONTEXT

It took just two years from when Karl Benz invented the first car in 1885 for someone to create the first automobile race. In 1887 a Parisian magazine publisher sponsored a race that featured a combustion engine for the first time. Georges Bouton won, but since he was the only driver who showed up, there wasn't much

Formula One racing, shown here in Monaco, is the most expensive racing league in the world. The top three teams spend close to a billion dollars annually combined to compete. (Alexander Sandvoss/Dreamstime.com)

competition. Another seven years passed before drivers drove against other drivers. Again, a Paris magazine sponsored a race, this time from Paris to Rouen, with 25 cars entering in 1894. With a top speed of 19 kilometers per hour, Jules-Albert de Dion earned the victory.

City-to-city racing dominated the landscape, whether in Western Europe or the U.S. Midwest, such as in Chicago. Races took place on roads. By 1906 racetracks were built exclusively for auto racing, with the first going up in Australia. Racing took place on racetracks prior to 1906, including in Knoxville, Iowa, and Milwaukee, Wisconsin, in the United States, but neither of those tracks was built for auto racing. In fact, as of 2020 the Knoxville track, still in use, still runs races on a dirt track. One of the first asphalt tracks in the United States opened in Indianapolis, Indiana, 1909, three years after Australia had built its first. Indiana's track, the Indianapolis Motor Speedway, today hosts the famous Indy 500, which is run annually in May. Its seating capacity—just less than 250,000—makes it the largest venue for sports fans in the world.

By the 1930s race-car manufacturing had become its own industry, whereas earlier in the 20th century races were run in cars available for purchase by the general public. This led to the establishment of racing leagues based on the type of car, such as sprint-car racing (1948), stock-car racing (1948), Formula One racing (1950), and drag racing (1951). Mainstream automobile companies like Ferrari out of Italy, Renault out of France, and Ford out of the United States fielded competitive racing teams, regularly spending hundreds of thousands of dollars per year in the early days to earn victories, which they believed looked good in the eyes of fans. Auto companies thought wins could boost sales, but it also boosted their egos.

Formula One racing, a form of open-wheel racing, captured the imagination of fans in Europe and South America as well as South Africa. Its precision engineering separated race cars from mainstream cars built for consumers, with rpms (revolutions per minute) of F1 cars reaching 20,000 by 2006. F1's governing body, the Fédération Internationale de l'Automobile (FIA) actually put in new rules to bring down the quality of F1 cars, because engineering had become so precise—close to flawless—that all the cars were the same, and whichever driver managed to sneak into the lead on the first or second lap would often stay in the lead as other cars played follow the leader for the rest of the race. In the United States, meanwhile, stock-car racing grew in popularity. Stock cars closely resembled cars driven by fans but with much more under the hood.

An American form of open-wheel racing, IndyCar, also gained popularity. The cars were less relatable than stock cars, but the racing was faster. In 1996 American Paul Tracy's IndyCar hit 411 kilometers per hour—nearly 400 kilometers per hour faster than the top speed in the first car race 99 years earlier.

GLOBALIZATION

Auto racing went international in 1900 with the inaugural Gordon Bennett Cup, a race challenge between representatives of countries, not automakers. The races, sponsored by New York newspaper publisher James Gordon Bennett, featured mostly European nations. The Gordon Bennett Cup lasted for six years, from 1900 to 1905. France won four cups and Germany and Great Britain each won one.

The same year as the final Bennett Cup, 1905, India hosted its first auto race. It, too, was a city-to-city race, about 800 miles from Mumbai to Delhi. At the same time, automobile racing continued to grow in Australia, the United States, and parts of South America. The birth of automobile manufacturing occurred during two historical sweet spots, the tail ends of the Industrial Revolution and European imperialism. This allowed nations across the world to combine interests in new technologies with some, but not all, resources to pursue them. Plus, auto racing was just cool. They were fancy new machines that went fast, and if a country had the economic and structural capacity to tinker with automobiles, they would. Because of this, interest and participation in automobile racing required material resources, not a mere casual interest like, say, soccer, which can be played with a cheap ball on any dirt field or open lot.

WHERE IT'S PLAYED TODAY

Automobile races take place all over the world on international and local scales. Formula One's 2019 schedule included events in the following countries and regions, listed alphabetically: Abu Dhabi, Australia, Austria, Azerbaijan,

Bahrain, Belgium, Brazil, Canada, China, France, Germany, Great Britain, Hungary, Italy, Japan, Mexico, Monaco, Russia, Singapore, and the United States.

As a marker of auto racing's regional influence, consider the following South American countries that host local events: Argentina, Bolivia, Brazil, Chile, Colombia, Ecuador, Guyana, Paraguay, Uruguay, and Venezuela. Additionally, all 50 states in the United States feature some sort of auto racing, as do most countries on six continents. In other words, auto racing is everywhere.

ECONOMICS AND MEDIA

Drivers and crews of teams at the top levels of automobile racing make large incomes, but entry into the sport also requires enormous sums of money and resources. Its closest, most accurate comparison might be horse racing. According to the financial publication *Forbes*, the top three Formula One teams over a several-year period—Mercedes, Red Bull, and Brawn—sunk an average of $285 million annually into their respective racing teams. That was by a wide margin the most expensive of any racing league in the world. NASCAR racing in the United States costs teams about $400,000 per week, or $20 million annually in expenses. Expenses include car maintenance, salaries, and transportation to events across the country. Racing teams recoup costs in two ways: prize money and corporate sponsorships.

Television networks throughout the world jockey for the rights to broadcast auto racing. For example, Sky Sports and the British Broadcasting Corporation hold

---

More than a Trailblazer, a Champion

In 1965 Shirley Muldowney became the first female driver to earn her National Hot Rod Association professional license. History commemorates trailblazers, people who accomplish something never done before, even when their accomplishment does not go beyond merely being the first to do something. But Muldowney's accomplishments extend far beyond breaking a gender barrier.

By 1973 Muldowney had graduated to Top Fuel drag racing, driving the fastest accelerating race car in the world and drag racing's crown jewel. Top Fuel racers have been known to accelerate from 0 to 100 miles per hour in just less than 1 second. In 1977 Muldowney won the NHRA's Top Fuel championship, the first woman to do so. In 1980 she won a second championship, which made her the first Top Fuel driver to win multiple championships. In 1982 she won her third.

In 1983 the film company 20th Century Fox released *Heart like a Wheel*, a biopic based on Muldowney's life. She did not like the film, nor did she think it was particularly accurate, but she said she appreciated what it did for the sport of drag racing. A year after the movie's release, Muldowney suffered major injuries in a significant crash that crushed her hands and legs. She required months of therapy and rehabilitation and did not race again for nearly five years. She did, however, return, first to the International Hot Rod Association and then eventually to the NHRA. She continued to race until retiring on her own terms in 2003. Muldowney spends her retirement tending to various business interests, has written a book, and makes public appearances at racing conventions and other events, where she remains one of the most popular draws.

Formula One rights in parts of Europe, Globo broadcasts the series in Brazil, and China Central Television, a state-owned network, broadcasts throughout China. Sky Sports pays Formula One about $150 million annually in broadcast rights.

DIMENSIONS OF THE SPORT

There are different types of auto racing depending on the make of the car, size of the engines, race distances, track composition, and other variables. Four of the more common types of cars include drag racers, open-wheel racers, sprint cars, and stock cars. Their differences are as follows:

Drag cars: Usually compete two at a time, head to head over short distances, straight ahead, and with no turns. Distances can include a quarter-mile, eighth of a mile, or 1,000 feet. Drag racing is most commonly found in Australia and New Zealand, parts of Europe, and the United States and the Caribbean.

Open-wheel: Most popular in Formula One and IndyCar. These cars traditionally have just one seat, and the wheels sit outside the car's chassis (body). Open-wheel races are run on oval and road tracks and can run up to several hundred miles.

Sprint cars: Notable for running on dirt (and sometimes paved) tracks, sprint cars have no starter motor and must be pushed onto the track by another vehicle. They are among the lightest cars, with drivers encased in a tube frame within an 84-inch wheelbase. The driver must straddle the driveshaft. Most notable are the wings on top of the car, designed to increase downforce, protect drivers, and carry advertising.

Stock cars: Popular in the United States, stock cars are amplified versions of everyday automobiles. They are slower than open-wheel cars, generate fewer rpms, and carry far more advertising.

IMPORTANT FIGURES

Mario Andretti never met a car he could not drive. The most successful race-car driver in history, Andretti won the Formula One series championship (European open-wheel), the Indianapolis 500 (American open-wheel), and the Daytona 500 (American stock car)—the only driver to win all three. He also was part of a team that finished second at 24 Hours of Le Mans. Born in what is now Croatia and raised in Italy and the United States, Andretti earned U.S. Driver of the Year in three different decades: 1967, 1978, and 1984.

In 2009 the Sports Car Club of America inducted late actor Paul Newman into its Hall of Fame. Newman fell in love with racing while training for a movie in 1969 and ended up racing competitively for the rest of his life. He was good, too, winning his class at the 1995 24 Hours of Daytona. His last starring role came in the 2006 animated film *Cars*, in which he voiced Doc Hudson, a car made by the real-life Hudson Motor Car Company during the first half of the 20th century.

POP CULTURE

Pop culture loves auto racing, whether it is a fascination with celebrities, such as the driver Dario Franchitti's former marriage to actress Ashley Judd, or through art, most notably its representation in mainstream films throughout the last century. The art-consuming public loves auto racing, too, making hits of such movies as 1929's *Speedway*, which focused on romance and the Indianapolis 500, and the 2006 film *Talladega Nights*, a comedy about NASCAR that became a huge hit. Many films and film franchises about the sport have found vast commercial success, regardless of the era in which they came out.

Between 2001 and 2019, the *Fast & Furious* street-racing franchise produced nine films that earned a combined $5.9 billion worldwide. Pixar's *Cars* franchise, three animated movies about talking race cars, earned a combined $1.4 billion internationally. In 2019 *Ford vs. Ferrari*, the true story of the racing teams' 1960s rivalry at 24 Hours of Le Mans, earned more than $200 million worldwide and received an Academy Award nomination for best motion picture. From the early 1900s through 2020, the American movie industry produced more than 150 movies about automobile racing. Even auto racing movies that are not critically well received, such as the animated 2013 film *Turbo* about a racing snail, can find success: it made nearly $280 million.

SCANDALS

Cheating happens often in auto racing, especially in NASCAR. Crew members get suspended. Teams get fined. Cars get disqualified. As former driver and broadcaster Darrell Waltrip said, "If you don't cheat, you look like an idiot. If you do it and you don't get caught, you look like a hero. If you do it and get caught, you look like a dope" (Krmpotich 2011).

PATRIOTISM AND NATIONAL PRIDE

NASCAR team owners and fans behaved shamefully in 2004 when Toyota became the first non-American car company to enter the stock-car racing industry. At that point NASCAR racing teams drove Ford, Chevrolet, and Dodge—all American companies. Toyota drivers were met with boos. Drivers from other teams invoked Pearl Harbor and other World War 2 references. Many fans said they would never consider buying a Toyota.

Attitudes, however, change. Within a decade, Toyota cars had won hundreds of stock-car races, and many fans cared less what car a driver competed in. Dodge/Chrysler, one of the big three American automakers, even dropped out of NASCAR in 2012, leaving Ford, Chevrolet, and Toyota to run the sport.

Timeline

1885 – Karl Benz builds what is considered the first automobile.

1887 – The first automobile race with an internal combustion engine takes place in Paris.

1900 – Automobile racers achieve speeds of 80 kilometers per hour.

1901 – Knoxville Raceway in Knoxville, Iowa, hosts its first racing event. It is the oldest automobile racing facility in the United States.

1906 – French auto manufacturers, upset by limitations placed upon them by the Bennett Trophy Race, establish the French Grand Prix Race at Le Mans.

1906 – The first venue built specifically for auto racing (Knoxville was built for horse racing) opens in Aspendale Park, Victoria, Australia.

1908 – Six teams from four countries—France, Germany, Italy, and the United States—compete in a six-month, 22,000-mile race in Europe. Three teams complete the race.

1927 – The first Mille Miglia road race is run in Italy. Benito Mussolini bans the race in 1938 after spectators are killed. It returns in 1947 but is ended for good in 1957, when 13 people—11 spectators and 2 drivers—are killed.

1939 – Enzo Ferrari founds an automobile company and names it after himself. Ferrari goes on to become the most successful automobile in the history of European auto racing.

1948 – The National Association for Stock Car Auto Racing, or NASCAR, is founded.

1949 – Sara Christian becomes the first woman to drive NASCAR.

1950 – Formula One racing is founded in Europe as the World Drivers' Championship. It becomes the world's foremost driving series.

1990 – The company Hubbard Downing Inc. is founded, producing what later becomes known as the HANS (head and neck support) device, which a decade later revolutionizes driver safety.

1996 – Paul Tracy's Indy car reaches 256.948 miles per hour (411.9 km/hour) at Michigan International Speedway.

2001 – NASCAR driver Dale Earnhardt dies in a crash at Daytona International Speedway.

2006 – Jimmie Johnson wins the first of five consecutive NASCAR championships.

2008 – American Danica Patrick becomes the first woman to win an IndyCar Series race.

2008 – Following years of competition that watered down the quality of both leagues, the Indy Racing League and Champ World Car Series merge, returning IndyCar racing to a level unseen for more than a decade.

2009 – Formula One introduces new rules to make its sport more competitive after fans complained that master levels of engineering removed the skill of actual driving from the series.

See also: Horse Racing; Soccer; Track and Field.

Further Reading
Baime, A. J. (2010). *Go Like Hell: Ford, Ferrari, and Their Battle for Speed and Glory at Le Mans.* Mariner Books: Boston.

Donovan, B. (2008). *Hard Driving: The Wendell Scott Story.* Steerforth Press: Hanover, New Hampshire.

Earnhardt, D. and McGee, R. (2018). *Racing to the Finish: My Story.* Thomas Nelson Publishing Company: Nashville, Tennessee.

Folley, M. (2010). *Senna versus Prost: The Story of the Most Deadly Rivalry in Formula One.* Random House: London.

Krmpotich, L. (2011). "The 30 Best Quotes in NASCAR History." *Bleacher Report*, July 3, 2011. https://bleacherreport.com/articles/691527-the-30-best-quotes-in-nascar-history.

Macy, S. and Patrick, D. (2017). *Motor Girls: How Women Took the Wheel and Drove Boldly into the 20th Century.* National Geographic: Washington, DC.

Matchett, S. (1999). *The Mechanic's Tale: Life in the Pit-Lanes of Formula One.* Weidenfeld & Nicholson: London.

Muldowney, S. with B. Stephens. (2005). *Tales from a Top Fuel Dragster: A Collection of the Greatest Drag Racing Stories Ever Told.* Sports Publishing: New York.

Stewart, J. (2007). *Jackie Stewart: Winning Is Not Enough.* Headline Publishing Group: London.

Thompson, N. (2007). *Driving with the Devil: Southern Moonshine, Detroit Wheels, and the Birth of NASCAR.* Broadway Books: New York.

B

Badminton

To some, badminton represents a game of leisure, something to install in the backyard for a few hours of fun on a lazy summer afternoon. To others, it requires some of the quickest reaction times of any of the world's racket sports: matkot, pickleball, racquetball, squash, table tennis, and tennis, among others. Badminton is game of waiting and reaction. Its unorthodox shuttlecock—not a ball, not a glider—with its weighted base has to be struck just right by the racket to give a player a chance to win. There is nothing in sport quite like the shuttlecock. Science teachers use them in teaching experiments about weight, mass, and proportion. Physical education teachers include badminton because the flight pattern of the shuttlecock allows less athletic students a chance to compete. At the highest levels of the sport, however, badminton players learn how to strike the shuttlecock with such ferocity that an opponent has just a small fraction of a second to respond, to strike the shuttlecock back over the net before it hits the ground.

HISTORICAL CONTEXT

Before there was badminton, there was the shuttlecock, a cone-shaped object with a weight at the bottom used to volley between rackets. Some historians believe the shuttlecock came into existence nearly 2,000 years before the game of badminton had been invented. Shuttlecocks, or shuttlecock-like objects, were used in games in Asia and Europe toward the start of the first modern millennium. After the shuttlecocks came the specialized rackets. During the 1600s upper-class Brits used rackets to volley a shuttlecock in a skill designed to see how long they could keep it going without the shuttlecock hitting the ground. It was a joint contest of skill—called battledore, or simply shuttlecock—not a one-on-one competition. There was no net.

The net entered the game during the mid- to late 19th century. A member of the British military stationed in India, mostly likely an officer, added the net to battledore. The game caught on among his troops and local citizens. They called the game "Poona," named so only because it first became popular in the town of the same name. Poona made its way back to the United Kingdom when military officers returned home. The game was played at the estate of the Duke of Beaufort in Gloucestershire. The name of the estate: Badminton. Brits abandoned the name Poona in favor of the more Anglophile term.

Badminton proved so popular that by the end of the 19th century, only 20 years after the game's invention, Brits were taking part in national badminton championships. Although lawn tennis was also popular at the time, badminton could be played in a smaller area, and upkeep of playing areas was far easier than that of a tennis court. That might have been one reason for the game's rapid growth. Another reason was badminton from an early stage adopted mixed doubles competition—women and men playing together. It became a leisure activity that could be enjoyed by couples.

Badminton underwent a few rule changes along the way. A number of "official" badminton organizations formed, merged, and dissolved. The Badminton Association of England (BAE) was founded in 1893 and grew to become the national leader of the sport. In addition to mixed doubles, badminton made way for men's doubles and women's doubles. Single badminton did not debut until very early in the 20th century. Once again, the sport was designed to bring people together. There were many competitive players, but there were even more who used badminton for social purposes. Sociologist Thorstein Veblen observed in his groundbreaking 1899 book, *The Theory of the Leisure Class*, that certain activities appealed to the upper class's desire for recreation, social interaction, and segregation from those with less status and wealth. "The lawn, or the close-cropped yard or park," he wrote, appealed to "the taste of the well-to-do classes" (Veblen 1899, 89).

The second modern Olympic Games, 1900 in Paris, took place just as badminton began to reach a cultural peak. The Paris Games also marked the first time the Olympics included team sports, yet badminton was not seriously considered, nor did any influential party lobby hard for it with any level of effectiveness. This reinforced the idea that badminton was, first, more recreational activity than competitive sport and, second, an activity the upper classes wished to keep to themselves. As the 20th century began, the best English badminton players had competed against players from only one other country—Ireland, also a member of the United Kingdom.

GLOBALIZATION

Badminton became more competitive. Nine nations in 1934 formed the Badminton World Federation (BWF): Canada, Denmark, England, France, Ireland, the Netherlands, New Zealand, Scotland, and Wales. They allowed India—the country of badminton's birth—into the BWF two years later; still, bigotry prevented India from being a full member. Instead, it received "affiliate" status. The Danish did not have badminton until the 1920s, but they soon became Europe's most dominant nation. Historians wrote that badminton came to Denmark when the owner of a sporting-goods store traveled abroad and brought back four rackets. At first he played just with friends when he introduced the sport to a club in Copenhagen.

Denmark remains a world badminton power, but overall the sport's balance of power tilts heavily toward East and Southeast Asia, including China, Indonesia, Japan, Malaysia, and South Korea. During the early to mid-20th century, visitors to and from the regions came to enjoy badminton, so much so that by 1958, badminton had become a demonstration sport at the Asian Games. Four years later, in

1962, badminton became an official part of the Asian Games. Competitors in the Asian Games have emerged as the world's best players. In the half century after badminton's Asian Games debut, only Denmark consistently remained competitive on the world scene alongside China, South Korea, and other East and Southeast Asian nations.

By 1992 the International Olympic Committee (IOC) had to give up its Western biases and could no longer ignore badminton's popularity in—and dominance by—East Asian nations. It became an official Olympic sport during the Games in Barcelona, Spain. Of the 102 total Olympic medals in badminton awarded since 1992, for men's and women's singles, men's and women's doubles, and mixed doubles, China has earned 39, by far the most of any nation. Indonesia and South Korea each have won 19. Countries with gold medal winners in addition to China include Denmark, Indonesia, Japan, South Korea, and Spain. The only other nations to win at least one medal are Great Britain, India, Malaysia, the Netherlands, and Russia.

WHERE IT'S PLAYED TODAY

Recreationally, badminton is played throughout the world. Sporting-goods companies mass-produce cheap sets that people use to play in parks, backyards, and other green or open areas. In 2019 retailers earned about $500 million worldwide from the sale of badminton rackets. Competitively, the most successful badminton programs reside in China, Denmark, Indonesia, Japan, and South Korea, but other nations, mostly in Asia and Europe but also Canada (North America), regularly produce competitive players.

More than 50 nations from across 6 continents qualified teams for the 2016 Olympics in Rio de Janeiro. In the United States, organizations that help set physical education curricula regularly encourage the inclusion of badminton. In addition to recommending the sport, advocates provide lesson plans and other tips. One nonprofit organization pushes for badminton inclusion because it fills kids with "the confidence and skill needed to be active whenever a badminton opportunity develops" (Knapp and Hart 2018).

ECONOMICS AND MEDIA

There is money to be made in professional badminton, most of which takes place throughout Asia. Earnings from the biggest, most reputable tournaments can reach up to $50,000 for the winner. Numerous players have earned millions playing professional badminton. The average annual earnings are less. Some regional tournaments offer just a few hundred dollars in prize money. Still, as badminton remains popular throughout the world, including emerging markets in countries such as Vietnam, the best players can count themselves among other high earners in sport.

The Premier Badminton League debuted in India in 2013. To distribute players fairly, each team was required to enter the league with hundreds of thousands of dollars in resources in order to pay the players. The league has had as many as seven or eight teams in the league at any given time.

DIMENSIONS OF THE SPORT

The full size of an official badminton court is 44 feet long by 20 feet wide; it is then split in two by the net for each competing side. Doubles matches use the full 20-foot width, which is reduced to 17 feet for singles matches. Matches are played best of three, which means the first player or team to win two games wins the match. Each game goes to 21 points, and points can be scored by either the serving or receiving team. Older versions of the game used to award points only to the serving team.

Play begins when one player serves the shuttlecock over the net, which in a standard match stands 5 feet, 1 inch at its peak. Unlike the ball in lawn tennis, the shuttlecock may not touch the ground. Once it hits the ground, the point is over. The players or teams engage in what is called a "rally," or the act of hitting the shuttlecock back and forth with a racket. It is common for hard-hit shuttlecocks to travel as much as 190 miles per hour. A handful have been clocked at 200. After the serving player or team loses a point, it becomes the other team's turn to serve.

IMPORTANT FIGURES

There is a reason Lin Dan is nicknamed "Super Dan." Few dispute that Dan is the most successful professional badminton player in history. He is the only player to win all nine of badminton's major championships, including the Olympics, while representing China; World Championships; Asian Games; and Super Series Masters Finals. Dan owns two Olympic gold medals, having won twice, in 2008 and 2012, and five World Championships, all in men's singles. He won all by the age of 28 and has amassed a net worth of more than $40 million.

POP CULTURE

Badminton has not received a lot of mainstream-entertainment attention, but there is some, often in animation. The 1970s and 1980s were considered a less successful period for Walt Disney Company's famous animation studio as it tried to find its way after its founder's death, but one film that resonated well with fans was 1973's *Robin Hood*. In one scene, iconic literary character Maid Marian, a fox, and her lady-in-waiting, Lady Kluck, play badminton. In another animated movie, *Hotel Transylvania 2* (2015), Dracula runs a hotel for monsters who are looking for rest and relaxation. One of the activities he provides is the traditional recreational activity of badminton.

The mid-20th-century American *Tom and Jerry* animated cartoon, about a cat and mouse locked in constant combat, included the 1962 short "High Steaks," which centers on a man trying to have a cookout for his family while Tom and Jerry do battle. In one moment, Jerry places a shuttlecock over his body to provide cover, but Tom finds him, serves him in the air, and strikes him into a net using a badminton racket. The shuttlecock ricochets off the net and into the mouth of the man, who takes out his anger by breaking the strings of the racket over Tom's head.

SCANDALS

The IOC authorized the disqualification of eight women's doubles players—or four teams—during the 2012 London Games because the teams all tried to lose on purpose. The teams recognized that losing one match would give them an easier draw in the tournament, which means they could play a worse team later on and have an easier chance of advancing toward a gold medal. In basketball this is known as "tanking," doing poorly on purpose to advance a long-term goal. In basketball, however, no team ever loses on purpose. Instead, coaches play less-talented players, who try their hardest but end up losing to the more talented teams.

In 2012 the eight women's badminton players deliberately served the shuttlecock out of bounds or hit it into the net, giving a point to the other team. On some points, a player tried to serve out of bounds, but the opposing player raced to get it just so she could return it into her own net. The teams were in a contest to see who could be better at losing. Olympic spectators had never seen anything like it. It was inconceivable; imagine a sprinter jogging the 100 meters or a diver belly flopping on purpose.

The crowd broke into boos to express their displeasure. The Badminton World Federation took action, convening an emergency hearing to determine what to do. All eight players, from China, Indonesia, and South Korea, were immediately disqualified from the Olympics. The decision also led to a historic result in women's doubles badminton, as a nation from neither East nor Southeast Asia won a medal for the first time since it became an official Olympic sport at the 1992 Barcelona Games. Russia earned the bronze.

POLITICS

The moment passed with barely a whisper. In 1996 South Korea's Kim Dong-moon and Gil Young-ah won gold in mixed doubles at the Summer Olympics in Atlanta. Although few marked the occasion, it was the first time in 72 years that women and men competed against each other at the Olympics. The previous time it happened was at the Paris Games in 1924, when Hazel Wightman and Norris Williams won gold for the United States in mixed doubles tennis.

The IOC removed mixed doubles tennis following the 1924 Games. It returned at the 2012 London Games, which meant badminton's mixed doubles inclusion in 1996 paved the way for a return to intergender Olympic competition. Mixed doubles badminton has proved popular and been included in every Summer Olympics since 1996, with China winning gold three times, South Korea twice, and

Indonesia once, when Liliyana Natsir and Tontowi Ahmad defeated Malaysia's Goh Liu Ying and Chan Peng Soon in the 2016 gold medal match.

PATRIOTISM AND NATIONAL PRIDE

In 2014 India's Saina Nehwai became even more of a national hero after she declared how proud she was to represent her country in international competition even if it meant risking earning potential on the professional circuit. Nehwai, who won bronze in women's singles at the 2012 London Games, spoke up after some men's players said they would not represent India because international competition might jeopardize their ability to earn a living professionally. In most sports around the world, professional income far outweighs income from playing for one's country. "I don't think anyone would not want to play for their country," Nehwai told Indian media. "Everyone would want to play for the country. Sometimes you can't ignore that there is injury or a player goes through some difficult situation" (Press Trust of India 2014).

Timeline

c. 20 CE – Ancient civilizations in Europe and Asia play a game called battledore, or shuttlecock, that resembled badminton in some aspects.

1600s – Battledore (shuttlecock) becomes popular in Europe, mostly among the upper classes.

Mid–1800s – British soldiers in India add a net to battledore and call the game Poona.

1873 – Poona is now known as badminton after the Duke of Beaufort's estate, Badminton.

1877 – The newly formed Bath Badminton Club writes the first set of rules.

1893 – The Badminton Federation of England is created.

1899 – The first All England Championships for men are organized.

1900 – The first badminton tournament for women is organized.

1902–1903 – England's first international match is played against Ireland.

1934 – The International Badminton Federation (IBF) is formed. The original nine members are England, Wales, Ireland, France, Scotland, Denmark, Holland, Canada, and New Zealand.

1936 – India joins the IBF as an affiliate.

1939 – The Thomas Cup is conceptualized.

1948 – The first major IBF tournament, the Thomas Cup—or world men's team championships—is held.

1951 – The first badminton match is televised.

1957 – The first world championships for women's badminton, the Uber Cup, are held in Lancashire, England.

1972 – Badminton becomes a demonstration sport at the Munich Olympics.

1977 – The first World Championships are held for individual events.

1984 – China joins the Uber Cup and wins the championship, the first of its record 14 titles.

1989 – The first Sudirman Cup is held for mixed-gender teams.

1992 – Badminton becomes an official Olympic sport.

1992 – The first World Junior Championships are held.

1996 – Mixed doubles play is introduced to the Summer Olympics in Atlanta. Badminton at the time is the only sport with mixed doubles in the Olympics.

2001 – The final World Grand Prix of Badminton, a tournament between the world's eight top-ranked players, is held.

2006 – The IBF changes its name to the Badminton World Federation (BWF).

2006 – The BWF switches to "rally scoring," a system that allows either team to score at any time, as opposed to points only being awarded to the serving side.

See also: Jai Alai; Squash; Tennis.

Further Reading

Brahms, B. (2014). *Badminton Handbook*. Meyer & Meyer Sport: Germany.

Chen, G. and Chen, C. (2009). *Coaching Badminton 101*. Coaches Choice: Monterey, California.

Chong, W. L. (2012). *Dare to Be a Champion*. Bukuganda Digital & Publication: Butterworth, Malaysia.

Edwards, J. (1997). *Badminton: Techniques, Tactics, Training*. Crowood Press: Marlborough, England.

Grice, T. (2007). *Badminton: Steps to Success*. Human Kinetics: Champaign, Illinois.

Knapp, J. and Hart, A. (2018). "Tools for Learning Badminton." Open Physical Education Network. https://openphysed.org/curriculum_resources/hs-badminton.

Paup, D. (2017). *Skills, Drills & Strategies for Badminton*. Routledge: Abingdon, England.

Plitt, S. (2017). *Badminton for Beginners: Techniques, Tactics, Skills, and Drills for Shuttlecock Success*. CreateSpace Independent Publishing Platform: Scotts Valley, California.

Press Trust of India (2014). "For Saina Nehwal, It Is Always about Playing for India." *News 18*, Oct. 30, 2014. https://www.news18.com/news/india/for-saina-nehwal-it-is-always-about-playing-for-india-723258.html.

Uribe, D. (2017). *The Badminton Psychology Workbook: How to Use Advanced Sports Psychology to Succeed on the Badminton Court*. CreateSpace Independent Publishing Platform: Scotts Valley, California.

Veblen, T. (1899). *The Theory of the Leisure Class*. MacMillan Company: London.

Baseball

Baseball is a sport played by two teams with nine players on each side. It is the only major professional team sport in North America that does not have a clock. Instead, the game is broken into nine innings (seven for younger children) in

Baseball player Robert Clemente died in a plane crash while trying to get relief supplies from his native Puerto Rico to the nation of Nicaragua following an earthquake. This statue was built in his honor in Pittsburgh, Pennsylvania, where he played professionally. (Mike D. Tankosich/Dreamstime.com)

which the fielders, led by their pitcher, try to force the hitters into committing three outs, at which point the two teams swap places.

A pitcher throws a baseball toward a hitter, who tries to hit the ball with a wood or aluminum bat in order to advance around the bases. Advancing all the way around the four bases results in a run being scored. The team that has scored more runs at the end of nine innings is declared the winner.

Baseball's longevity and popularity in the United States has earned it the title of "national pastime," even though football long ago surpassed baseball as the country's most popular spectator sport. Children in the United States begin playing the sport as early as age 4, and some people play the sport recreationally into their 70s and 80s. Its signature event, the World Series, has been held almost every fall since 1903.

HISTORICAL CONTEXT

Baseball's history is steeped in mythology and misconceptions. Sporting-goods magnate Al Spalding heavily promoted Abner Doubleday as the game's founder. Spalding tried—and succeeded—to sell Doubleday, a decorated U.S. military officer alleged to have fired the first shot of the American Civil War, as the person who invented baseball. Doubleday, whose brilliant mind helped bring cable cars to San Francisco, in fact never made any mention of the game. Stories of his involvement in baseball didn't surface until the early 20th century, more than a decade after his death, and most credible sports historians long ago concluded that Doubleday's involvement was little more than a successful marketing ploy.

Most likely, baseball is an amalgamation of cricket, the British game rounders, and a game called town ball, plus a healthy dose of originality, with early participants in the United States and Canada making up their own rules in the modern game's earliest days during the mid-19th century. Baseball historian David Block found documented evidence of baseball dating to the mid-18th century, which has led some to think that rounders and baseball grew up around the same time and fed off each other, with baseball eventually winning out as the more popular game in North America.

Members of the Knickerbocker Base Ball Club in New York formally adopted a set of rules in 1845. Again, however, historians question the validity of this part of the game's history. Some argue that the rules already existed before the Knickerbocker Club came into being and that all the club did was write them down, although the club does get credit for determining that each team gets to make three outs per inning.

The National Association of Base Ball Players formed in 1867, making it the game's first governing body. It eventually gave way to the more professionally run, better organized National League in 1876, which exists to this day (along with the American League, formed in 1901) as part of Major League Baseball.

Initially there were no rules banning African American players from taking part in professional baseball. Moses Fleetwood Walker debuted in the major leagues for the Toledo, Ohio, team in 1884 and was later joined that season by his brother, Weldy Wilberforce Walker. A few years before that, African American William Edward White played one game. However, in 1887, as Moses Walker's team was set to play the Chicago White Stockings, White Stockings player and manager Cap Anson, who had begrudgingly played against Walker a few years earlier, insisted Walker be removed from the game because of his race. Walker was kicked out, and white professional baseball agreed from that moment to no longer sign African American players. That rule held for 60 years, until the Brooklyn Dodgers signed Jackie Robinson in 1947. Robinson won the National League's Rookie of the Year award and went on to earn induction into the Baseball Hall of Fame in 1962. (Anson had been inducted in 1939.) In the 60 years between Walker and Robinson, professional leagues for African Americans, dubbed Negro Leagues, flourished throughout the United States.

GLOBALIZATION

American baseball ambassadors worked to spread the game in the late 19th century, starting with Cuba in 1878. The game quickly caught on in Cuba and spread to other Caribbean countries and territories, most notably Puerto Rico and the Dominican Republic.

American professor Horace Wilson, hired by the Japanese government in the 1870s to help modernize Japan's education system, thought Japanese students needed more exercise. He brought balls and bats to Japan, where the game became a hit and soon spread to Taiwan and Korea. The game first appeared in the South Pacific and Oceania in the late 1880s. And in February 1889 Al Spalding—he of Abner Doubleday fame—introduce Italy to baseball. By the end of World War II, professional baseball leagues existed in Australia, Japan, the Netherlands, Puerto Rico, Mexico, Italy, and Venezuela.

WHERE IT'S PLAYED TODAY

Although the game has some following in Europe, it is most popular in North America, East Asia, the Caribbean, Central America, and parts of South America, most notably Venezuela. The World Baseball Classic, which started in 2006, included the Dominican Republic, United States, Japan, Venezuela, Mexico, Cuba, Netherlands, Chinese Taipei, Canada, Colombia, Italy, Australia, and Israel, among others.

The Little League World Series, an event started in 1947 for boys ages 10 to 12, has been won by Taiwan more than any other team. The Taiwanese have won 17 championships, followed by Japan's 11. California has been the United States' most successful representative, winning 7 Little League World Series championships.

ECONOMICS AND MEDIA

Baseball's first professional team opened play in Cincinnati in 1869. The two most dominant organizations—the National League (founded in 1876) and American League (1901)—formed an alliance in 1903 that became Major League Baseball. From its origins through the 1970s, team owners notoriously tried to drive down player salaries using something called the "reserve clause," which essentially bound a player to a team for that player's entire career, which meant the team owners could pay well below market value because the player was unable to leave. St. Louis Cardinals outfielder Curt Flood challenged the reserve clause and lost, which cost him his career, but several years after his retirement, the players' union took up Flood's cause and worked to have the reserve clause removed from professional contracts.

Within a decade, player salaries began to soar, and most team owners still managed to turn a significant profit. The average major-league salary in 1967 was $19,000. By 2010 it was just more than $3 million annually.

Baseball revenue comes from local, regional, and national broadcasting rights as well as ticket and paraphernalia sales. Revenue rose every season from 2003 to 2018, reaching $10 billion in annual revenue for the first time in 2017.

Before the age of television and climbing salaries, sportswriters unofficially worked with baseball players to help raise their profiles, which made sportswriters especially powerful. They traveled with the players on trains and often dined with them. The reserve clause stripped the players of nearly all bargaining power, so they aligned themselves with sportswriters, who could make a hero out of a player that the fans loved, therefore incentivizing owners to pay them more money because more fans would pay to come the stadium to watch them play.

DIMENSIONS OF THE SPORT

All baseball fields hold the same measurements on the infield. The distance from the pitcher's mound to home plate is 60 feet, 6 inches. Until the late 19th century, the distance was 45 feet, but such a close distance gave pitchers too much of an advantage, so the National League decided to move it back to 60 feet, 0 inches. However, someone misread the 0 inches as 6 inches, and as a result, 60 feet, 6 inches became the norm. The distance between each of the four bases—home plate, first, second, and third base—is 90 feet, which is why a baseball field is sometimes referred to as "the diamond."

Unlike infields, the baseball outfield is not standardized. Some outfield walls—sometimes called home run walls, are 360 feet from home plate, others are 375 feet away, still others are 400 feet, and so forth.

IMPORTANT FIGURES

In most sports one can argue about who is the greatest player, but in American baseball there is no valid alternative to George Herman "Babe" Ruth. Ruth, who played from 1914 to 1935, mostly for the New York Yankees, spent his first five seasons as one of the game's best pitchers, but he soon switched to full-time hitting and became the game's greatest hitter. In 1920 he hit more home runs by himself than 15 other Major League teams. In the near-century since he last played, a few players have surpassed Ruth's accomplishments as a hitter, but none also pitched as Ruth did.

When an Earthquake Shook the World Series

The 1989 World Series had Northern California buzzing. Never before had its two teams, the San Francisco Giants and the Oakland Athletics, two cities just across Bay Bridge from each other, squared off for the Major League Baseball championship.

But California is known for many things, including earthquakes. Just 30 minutes before Game 3 of the World Series was scheduled to begin, and with players warming up on the field and fans entering the stadium, a magnitude 6.9 earthquake struck Northern California. It caused major damage throughout the region. Sixty-three people died in what came to be known as the Loma Prieta Earthquake.

Inside Candlestick Park, then home to the Giants, confusion and fear spread, but police and other safety and security officials kept most fans and players from serious harm. Adding to the drama was the fact that television viewers across the United States could watch the events unfolding live. American television network ABC was broadcasting from inside the stadium when the earthquake struck, and because the World Series draws national interest, millions were watching.

Initially, the broadcasters appeared as confused and startled as anyone else. The television feed sputtered, and audio, usually clear, became less audible. They soon regained their composure and transitioned from sports broadcasters to news reporters, relaying whatever information they had on the earthquake to listeners at home. No one stood out quite like Al Michaels, the iconic American sports broadcaster most known for his call of the U.S. Men's Hockey team's upset of the Soviet Union at the 1980 Winter Olympics. Michaels's cool demeanor and reporter's instincts that night guided Americans through a scary moment.

As for the World Series, it was delayed five days. Oakland swept San Francisco, four games to none.

Roberto Clemente died New Year's Eve 1972 while trying to fly a humanitarian-relief mission to his native Puerto Rico, which had suffered an earthquake. Clemente had a reputation among his teammates and around the sport for his charity work and friendly demeanor, but he was also one of baseball's best players, totaling exactly 3,000 hits. In 1973 Major League Baseball renamed the Commissioner's Award, given annually to the player who most exemplified community and sportsmanship, in Clemente's honor.

Following Babe Ruth's path of pitcher to hitter, Sadaharu Oh led Japanese baseball in home runs 15 times. He played from 1959 to 1980. His 868 career home runs rank as the most by any professional baseball player ever in any league around the world. Oh, raised in Taiwan and originally named Wang-Chen-chih, also spent nearly 20 seasons as a manager.

POP CULTURE

Vassar College fielded a women's baseball team in the mid-19th century, but women's baseball experienced a boom period from 1943 to 1954, during the existence of the All-American Girls Professional Baseball League (AAGPBL). The American film *A League of Their Own*, which starred Geena Davis, Lori Petty, and Tom Hanks, was a massive success upon its debut in 1992, earning more than $100 million despite a budget of just $40 million. The film told the story of a league that formed to provide entertainment to a nation immersed in World War II, and to generate an alternative revenue stream for Major League Baseball owners, whose businesses suffered as some of their best players left to fight oversees.

American film has a full catalog of baseball-themed movies. No actor has contributed more to that catalog than Kevin Costner, who to date has starred in three baseball films: 1988's *Bull Durham*, which won numerous writing awards; 1989's *Field of Dreams*, which was nominated for an Academy Award for Best Picture; and 1999's *For the Love of the Game*.

SCANDALS

Baseball has endured its share of scandals. Its first significant one occurred in 1919, when eight members of the Chicago White Sox conspired with gamblers to intentionally lose the World Series. Frustration with the team's cheap owner, Charles Comiskey, and greed motivated the players. White Sox pitcher Eddie Cicotte, for example, was due to earn a $10,000 bonus, equivalent to $150,000 in 2019 dollars, if he won 30 games. He sat at 29 wins on the last day of the season and his team held the lead while he pitched, but his manager, allegedly on orders from Comiskey, pulled Cicotte from the game in the second inning, which meant he was ineligible to earn his 30th win.

Baseball attendance dropped, and public trust in the game plummeted when word leaked of the White Sox's intentional loss. As a result, Major League Baseball owners appointed Judge Kenesaw Mountain Landis as baseball's first commissioner. He permanently banned eight White Sox players from the game for life, including, most famously, "Shoeless" Joe Jackson.

Baseball faced another scandal in the early 2000s after retired player Jose Canseco published his book *Juiced*, which revealed widespread use of performance-enhancing drugs—mostly steroids—by present-day players. Players and baseball officials initially tried to discredit Canseco, but it soon became clear that Canseco had written the truth after some of the game's best players began to fail drug tests, federal law enforcement officials opened investigations that implicated players, and players who once sported the bodies of Greek gods rapidly lost muscle weight and returned to a more normal size.

Many of baseball's most hallowed records fell during what came to be known as the "steroid era," and many of the era's most dominant players, including all-time home run leader Barry Bonds and seven-time Cy Young Award winner Roger Clemens, have failed to gain admission into the Baseball Hall of Fame, even though neither ever officially tested positive for steroid use. The implications of playing during the steroid era were enough to tarnish their legacies.

POLITICS

Baseball's historical ties to the United States have led it to occasionally cross over into political arenas. In 1922 the U.S. Supreme Court ruled in *Federal Baseball Club v. National League* that baseball was an "amusement," not a corporation, and therefore exempt from the Sherman Antitrust Act of 1890 that aimed to prevent companies from colluding to fix prices or salaries. This allowed baseball's reserve clause to exist well into the 1970s, when the Major League Baseball's players' union grew in power and forced owners to allow players to enter free agency at the end of their contracts.

Congress threatened Major League Baseball's antitrust exemption during the 1994–1995 labor work stoppage that included the canceling of the 1994 World Series. Baseball owners also lost a decision by the National Labor Relations Board after they tried to impose a salary cap. Additionally, Congress held hearings in the early 21st century to question baseball owners and players about the use of illegal performance-enhancing drugs.

PATRIOTISM AND NATIONAL PRIDE

Baseball became popular so quickly in the United States in the mid-19th century that in just a few years writers and journalists began to call it America's national pastime. From 1974 to 1976, the American car company General Motors ran a commercial with the line, "Baseball, hot dogs, apple pie and Chevrolet—they go together in the good ol' USA" (Elliott 2006). W. P. Kinsella's 1982 novel *Shoeless Joe* includes the line, "America has been erased like a blackboard, only to be rebuilt and then erased again. But baseball has marked the time while America has rolled by like a procession of steamrollers."

The United States' national anthem, "The Star-Spangled Banner," first played at a baseball game in 1862 in Brooklyn, New York. It became customary to play the anthem before the start of every game during World War II. Following the September 11, 2001, terrorist attacks, it became customary at some ballparks to also play "America the Beautiful" during the seventh-inning stretch, the brief period between the top and the bottom of the seventh inning typically reserved for the 1908 song, "Take Me Out to the Ball Game."

Timeline

1749 – A British newspaper carries a short item about royalty playing a game of "Bass-Ball."

1845 – Members of the Knickerbocker Base Ball Club of New York write down rules, helping to standardize the game.

1859 – The first game between two African American teams takes place in New York.

1873 – The first formal baseball game in Japan takes place.

1876 – The National League is formed.

1887 – Moses Fleetwood Walker, a baseball player of African American heritage, is removed from his team because opposing player/manager Cap Anson does not want to play against people of color. Major League Baseball remains segregated for the next 60 years.

1901 – The American League is formed.

1903 – The first World Series is held between the National and American Leagues.

1908 – The Chicago Cubs win the World Series. They won't win another until 2016, a span of 108 years.

1910 – The Japanese Pacific Coast Baseball League is formed in the United States in response to the sport's huge popularity among Japanese American people.

1914 – Babe Ruth debuts for the Boston Red Sox.

1943 – The All-American Girls Professional Baseball League forms. It survives until 1954, peaking with more than 900,000 total spectators in 1948.

1947 – Jackie Robinson joins the Brooklyn Dodgers, integrating Major League Baseball.

1952 – African American baseball leagues reach their end because of low ticket sales after more than 150 African American players sign with Major League Baseball.

1959 – Sadaharu Oh debuts in Japan. He retires with 868 career home runs, the most by any professional player in baseball history.

1964 – Masanori Murakami becomes the first Japanese-born player to play Major League Baseball.

1966 – The Major League Baseball Players Association is formed, forever altering labor dynamics between players and team owners.

1980 – At age 54, Cuban-born Minnie Minoso, who debuted in 1949, plays two games for the Chicago White Sox, making him the first and only (as of 2020) Major League Baseball player to play in five separate decades.

1986 – Casey Candaele debuts for the Montreal Expos. He becomes the only Major League player whose mother (Helen Callaghan St. Aubin) played professionally in the All-American Girls Professional Baseball League. His aunt, Marge Callaghan, also played.

1994 – Major League Baseball cancels the World Series for the first time since 1904, this time because of a work stoppage caused by a labor disagreement between players and owners.

1998 – Players Mark McGwire and Sammy Sosa both break Roger Maris's single-season home run record of 61. Neither player, both of whom played during baseball's "steroid era," makes the Baseball Hall of Fame.

2006 – The St. Louis Cardinals win their 10th World Series, joining the New York Yankees as the only two organizations in Major League Baseball history to win at least 10 championships.

2014 – Mo'ne Davis, 14, becomes the first girl to pitch a shutout in the Little League World Series, and she is the first African American girl to play in the Series.

2017 – Major League Baseball single-season revenues reach $10 billion for the first time.

See also: Cricket; Football; Softball.

Further Reading
Bouton, J. (1970). *Ball Four.* Dell Publishing Company: New York.
Davis, M. (2016). *Mo'ne Davis: Remember My Name: My Story from First Pitch to Game Changer.* HarperCollins: New York.
Elliott, S. (2006). "Baseball, Hot Dogs and Chevy, Redux." *New York Times*, June 30, 2006. https://www.nytimes.com/2006/06/30/business/media/30adco.html.
Helyar, J. (1995). *Lords of the Realm: The Real History of Baseball.* Ballantine Books: New York.
Johnson, S. E. (1994). *When Women Played Hardball.* Seal Press: Seattle, Washington.
Klein, A. (2014). *Dominican Baseball: New Pride, Old Prejudice.* Temple University Press: Philadelphia.
Levy, J. (2018). *The Big Fella: Babe Ruth and the World He Created.* HarperCollins: New York.
Mochizuki, K. (1993). *Baseball Saved Us.* Lee & Low Books: New York.
Pessah, J. (2015). *The Game: Inside the Secret World of Major League Baseball's Power Brokers.* Little, Brown and Company: Boston.
Ribowsky, M. (1995). *A Complete History of the Negro Leagues: 1844–1955.* Birch Lane Press: New York.
Whiting, R. (2009). *You Gotta Have Wa.* Vintage Books: New York.

Basketball

Unlike some sports, which may hold centuries of vague history, the origin of basketball (originally "basket ball") can be traced directly to Springfield, Massachusetts, in 1891. At the time, American football's popularity was beginning to grow,

After soccer, basketball has become the world's second most played sport. It includes top professional leagues on nearly every continent, including the Women's National Basketball Association (pictured) in the United States. (Danny Raustadt/Dreamstime.com)

but it had earned a reputation as a dangerous game. Its players were not just spraining their ankles and breaking their noses—they were dying. American physical education instructor James Naismith recognized the importance of young people's need to survive sports, so he found a ball and attached a peach basket to opposite sides of a gymnasium. Basketball was born. The ultimate goal, Naismith wrote in his original 13 rules for the game, was the same then as it is today: shoot the ball into the basket.

HISTORICAL CONTEXT

Winter temperatures in the American Northeast hover around freezing, making outside play difficult. Naismith developed basketball specifically as a safe athletic outlet to be played during America's coldest months. He set up the rules to strictly forbid any rough physical contact while maximizing other athletic skills such as hand-eye coordination, teamwork, and cardiovascular conditioning.

In the early 20th century, basketball spread throughout the Northeast for three reasons. First, it was fun. Second, it was affordable to play and easy to find space. Unlike some sports, which required a playing area tailored to a game's dimensions—baseball, football, boxing—all basketball needed was a gymnasium, which many communities had. Surely someone had a basket—not necessarily a peach basket—and as long as one person had a ball, a group of players could have their game.

Third, during a time of great immigration on the American East Coast, which led to cultural pockets of young men, women, and children, basketball offered a healthy outlet for teamwork and camaraderie. Leagues sprang up in European American communities of varying ethnicities, African American communities, Jewish communities, and rural communities, among others. Jewish people in particular took to the game, helped usher its adoption by colleges, and contributed to its early popularization. In 1934, for example, demand for tickets to a game between City College of New York and New York University, in which 9 of the 10 starters were Jewish, was so great that the game had to be moved to Madison Square Garden. White Americans discriminated against African American players during this period, banning African Americans from most organized leagues and refusing to let them play alongside or against white players in most colleges. Although the National Basketball Association (NBA) opened its league to three African American players in 1950, some teams in the league for another two decades made a point to have at least one white player in the starting lineup because they believed that having no white players would alienate white audiences while others worried that hiring African American coaches or general managers would push white players out of the game.

Basketball's rules were adapted for women in 1892—just one year after Naismith invented the game—by Senda Berenson, an instructor at Smith College. She read about the rules in a YMCA publication and brought the game to her physical education students, who appeared bored with traditional calisthenics and gymnastics.

The American Association for Health, Physical Education and Recreation first organized intercollegiate sports for women during the 1940s, with basketball falling under the jurisdiction of its Division for Girls' and Women's Sport. Participation number in women's basketball climbed in the 1970s and 1980s because of the passing by the U.S. federal government of Title IX, a law that required, among other things, equal access to college resources for women. The Women's National Basketball Association (WNBA) began play in 1997 with teams in 8 cities and 28 regular-season games. As of 2018, the league played a 34-game season with teams in 12 cities.

Various men's professional leagues sprang up and vanished during the first half of the 20th century. The Basketball Association of America (BAA) opened play in 1946 and was consolidated a few years later with 11 teams in what today is known as the NBA. In 1954 the NBA introduced a shot clock, which discouraged stalling by giving teams 24 seconds to either shoot the ball or give it up to the other team. This creation stemmed largely from the presence of the Minneapolis Lakers' George Mikan, a center so dominant that opposing teams played keep-away from him the whole game in hopes of winning a low-scoring contest. The league realized it had a problem when the Fort Wayne Pistons defeated Mikan's Lakers, 19 to 18. "If that's basketball," said Lakers coach John Kundla, "I don't want any part of it" (Pincus 2010).

GLOBALIZATION

Behind soccer, basketball ranks as the second most popular sport in the world. Competitive national and professional teams exist across the world, from Argentina in South America, to China in Asia, to Nigeria in Africa, to Spain in Europe, to Australia's national team, and, of course, to the United States in North America. The 2014 NBA Draft provides a picture of how wide the sport has spread: The first overall selection was Canadian player Andrew Wiggins, American Jabari

Parker went second, Cameroon's Joel Embiid went third, American Aaron Gordon was selected fourth, and Australian Dante Exum was picked fifth.

The first five picks included players from four different countries on three different continents. Later in the draft, teams selected players from Croatia, Bosnia and Herzegovina, Brazil, Switzerland, French Guiana, Cape Verde, Greece, Italy, France, and Serbia. The 60 total players selected represented 5 continents and 13 different countries.

WHERE IT'S PLAYED TODAY

Basketball is played regularly in arenas on every continent except Antarctica. Leagues exist for children and adults, women and men, private profit and national pride. It became an Olympic event for men in 1936 and for women in 1976. The former commissioner of the NBA, David Stern, receives credit for growing basketball. Stern, who died in 2020, drove basketball's globalization partially because of his love for the game but mostly because of profit potential. "We're determined to make the NBA a global marketing vehicle for global marketers," Stern said in 1995 (Madkour 2014).

In February 2019 FIBA and the NBA launched a joint venture, the Basketball Africa League, which aimed to capitalize on earlier professional basketball initiatives on the continent. The league, which suffered some delays in opening because of the worldwide COVID-19 pandemic, included teams in Angola, Egypt, Kenya, Nigeria, South Africa, and other African nations, as well as ready-made sponsorships from some of the world's biggest companies.

ECONOMICS AND MEDIA

Modern basketball earns revenue from two primary sources: consumers and media rights. Consumers (fans) pay money for the right to watch a game. This could be as little as $2 to watch a high school basketball game or as much as $100 for the face-value cost of an NBA ticket. In 2017 a fan paid $133,000 for two courtside tickets to an NBA Finals game. In addition to tickets, consumers buy team merchandise, such as shirts adorned with a team's logo, concessions during the game, parking spots for their cars outside a team's arena, and media streams such as access to television channels to watch their teams when they cannot go to the games.

The governing body of American college basketball, the National Collegiate Athletic Association (NCAA), signed two contracts between 2010 and 2016—for a combined worth of nearly $20 billion—to give American broadcasting network CBS and cable property Turner Broadcasting exclusive rights to broadcast its end-of-season tournament to crown a champion. The NCAA earns additional media revenue from selling the rights to its regular-season games and conference tournaments to networks such as ESPN and Fox Sports. NBA player salaries, meanwhile, are determined largely by the value of the league's media contracts. Despite annual revenues of at least $1 billion, which comes to nearly $250,000 generated per college basketball player per year, the NCAA does not pay college players, many of whom instead receive base-level college scholarships to cover the cost of their tuition and room and board.

DIMENSIONS OF THE SPORT

Although basketball courts are similar in size throughout the world, there are variations. The court of Fédération International de Basketball (FIBA, or International Basketball Federation) measures 91.9 feet by 49.2 feet (20 by 15 meters). The NBA and WNBA courts are slightly bigger: 94 feet by 50 feet (28.6 by 15.2 meters).

Each team plays five athletes to a side at one time. Typically, although not always, the five players include one center, usually the tallest player, who plays closest to the basket; two guards, who usually are the smallest players, play farthest from the basket, and control the ball most of the time; and two forwards, who float between playing close to and away from the basket.

Players can score three types of goals. A field goal is a basket scored during the normal course of the game. A two-point field goal is scored from inside the three-point line. A three-point field goal is scored from beyond the three-point line, a concept popularized by the short-lived American Basketball Association (1967–1976) that rewards players who shoot well from long distances. Different leagues put the line at varying distances. A free throw counts as one point and takes place when the game clock has stopped because a foul has been committed.

IMPORTANT FIGURES

Naismith invented basketball, but he was far from alone in playing a role in its development. Naismith started the basketball program at the University of Kansas. One of his players was Phog Allen, a pivotal figure in the development of college basketball. Allen coached the University of Kansas from 1919 to 1956 and mentored future head college coaches such as Dean Smith, who coached North Carolina for 36 years, and Adolph Rupp, who coached Kentucky for 41 seasons. Over the course of a century, the Kansas, North Carolina, and Kentucky programs, all with Naismith and Allen roots, became college basketball's most storied and among the most consistently successful programs.

Key early professional players include, but are by no means limited to, Mikan, who in addition to inspiring the shot clock helped the Minneapolis Lakers become the NBA's first dynasty; Dolph Schayes, who started his career in the BAA in 1948 and remained a member of the NBA until 1964; and Bill Russell, one of the league's all-time greatest players and first African American stars. Russell played 13 NBA seasons, won 11 championships, and was lauded by ex-players and journalists as a superb teammate. Russell's chief rival was Wilt Chamberlain, a 7-foot-1 center who had been recruited to Kansas by Phog Allen. As a professional, Chamberlain remains the only NBA player to score more than 100 points in a game (as of 2020).

The modern era of professional basketball was ushered in by players such as Julius "Dr. J" Erving, Earvin "Magic" Johnson, and Larry Bird. However, the player most responsible for the game as it is today was their younger peer, Michael Jordan. Jordan, who played professionally from 1984 to 2003, found success on the court by winning six NBA championships and five NBA most-valuable-player awards. His greatest influence may have been off the court, where he became a global icon through product endorsements. He served as spokesperson most famously for Nike shoes but also for many other products, amassing a fortune that allowed him to later purchase his own NBA team and inspire future generations of basketball players who dreamed not only of winning games but of becoming their own "brands," such as LeBron James.

In 1931 Babe Didrikson, the most successful female athlete of the first half of the 20th century, led her team to the American Athletic Union (AAU) women's basketball national championship. Nancy Lieberman starred at Old Dominion University in the 1970s, setting numerous college records before embarking on a professional career that ended at age 50. Other notable figures included Cheryl Miller, whose career at the University of Southern California in the 1980s was so successful that the school never let another men's or women's basketball player wear her jersey number; Lisa Leslie, who won four Olympic gold medals as a member of the U.S. Women's National Team; and Becky Hammon, who after a successful WNBA career became the first woman to serve as a head coach for an NBA team.

Stars emerged across the globe as basketball's popularity grew. Among the more influential players during the game's growth period was Brazil's Oscar Schmidt, whose career spanned 30 years. Lithuania's Arvydas Sabonis six times won the Euroscar, the award given to Europe's best player. His career spanned 25 seasons. Late in his career he spent 7 seasons in the NBA, but despite his age and mounting injuries, he played so well that he earned induction into the Naismith Memorial Basketball Hall of Fame.

POP CULTURE

Basketball has been the subject of numerous sports-themed movies. The Michael Jordan vehicle *Space Jam*, released in 1996, grossed more than $250 million worldwide and—more than two decades later—remains popular with kids and nostalgic fans. *Air Bud*, a 1997 film about a basketball-playing dog, grossed more than eight times its production budget.

SCANDALS

During the 1950–1951 American college basketball season, seven schools implicated themselves in a point-shaving scandal. Point shaving can occur when gambling is involved and players accept bribes from gamblers. The practice calls for players to deliberately miss shots to affect wagers made against a point spread.

> ### Michael Jordan, Magic Johnson, and Larry Bird Take Over the World
>
> The gold medal for men's basketball at the 1992 Olympics was not in doubt after world basketball officials ruled that the United States could send its professional players to the games. Players from the National Basketball Association (NBA), including Michael Jordan, Magic Johnson, and Charles Barkley, came together to form the "Dream Team," or as *Sporting News* magazine called them, "the greatest collection of talent" the basketball world had ever seen (Bender 2017). The United States won gold after winning every game by an average of 44 points.
>
> The Dream Team accomplished another goal: it accelerated global interest in basketball. The team was the undisputed main attraction of the Barcelona games. Jordan could not go anywhere without an entourage of security guards. While he, Johnson, and Larry Bird came in as the top-billed names, Barkley became the breakout star. He posed for pictures with any opposing player or fan who asked, attended live events and mingled with others throughout the games, and he was merciless on the court, famously declaring, "I don't know anything about Angola, but I know they're in trouble" (Thamel 2010, B10). The Dream Team beat Angola, 116–48.
>
> Basketball's global footprint spread. During the 1991–1992 NBA season, the league had just 23 international players from 18 countries. At the start of the 2018–2019 season, it had 108 international players from 42 countries. Basketball has become the second most profitable sport in the world, behind soccer. The United States won basketball gold again in 1996 and 2000, but in the surest sign that basketball had taken a global turn, Argentina won Olympic gold in 2004 by beating Italy in the gold-medal game. The United States and its roster of NBA players settled for the bronze.

The school at the center of the scandal was City College of New York (CCNY) and also involved the University of Kentucky, Long Island University (LIU), Bradley University, and others. CCNY, which had won the National Invitational Tournament (NIT) the year before, ended up leaving the NCAA's top division and never returned.

POLITICS

By the mid-1960s, although most NBA teams still practiced racial discrimination, the Boston Celtics' entire starting lineup was African American. In 1966 Texas Western University won college basketball's championship with an all African American starting lineup by defeating the University of Kentucky, a program made up entirely of white players coached by Adolph Rupp, notable for his unwillingness to recruit Black players. Gradually, the American professional and college games came to be dominated, with some exceptions, by African American players—especially the NBA. As of 2016, out of 420 NBA players, 43 (10.2 percent) were white Americans, 74.3 percent were African American, and the rest were international players.

Professional basketball also blazed trails within organized labor. In 1966 Major League Baseball players unionized, yet they were shown the way by NBA players. In 1964 the NBA's best players refused to take the court before the All-Star Game until the owners recognized their union. The players won the day, and later in the decade and into the early 1970s, players such as Kareem Abdul-Jabbar and Bill Walton were symbols of the NBA's social activism. In 2012, when Trayvon Martin, an unarmed, 17-year-old African American boy, was shot and killed by a security guard, several NBA players drew awareness to the killing by publicly discussing Martin and similar victims. In summer 2018 the NBA and WNBA operated a float in the New York City LGBTQ Pride March.

PATRIOTISM AND NATIONAL PRIDE

European basketball follows a model similar to soccer. EuroLeague is considered the most competitive professional league in the world after the NBA. However, while the NBA dominates the weekly schedule during its season, EuroLeague takes weekends off to let players return home to play in separate leagues within their home countries. In addition to the Olympics, international competitions include the FIBA World Cup, AmeriCup, and other events worldwide.

Timeline

1891 – Physical educator James Naismith invents basketball.

1892 – Senda Berenson adapts basketball for women.

1894 – Naismith asks A. G. Spalding & Bros to create the first basketball.

1896 – The first intercollegiate women's game—California-Berkeley vs. Stanford—is played.

1897 – Players from Yale University introduce the tactic of "dribbling" the basketball.

1902 – Harry Lew becomes the first African American to play professional basketball.

1904 – The first recognized "basketball sneaker" is invented.

1917 – Converse Rubber Company enters the basketball-shoe business. Its business grows behind salesperson Charles Taylor, who is so successful that 15 years later the company puts his name, "Chuck Taylor," on each shoe.

1929 – The first women's Amateur Athletic Union (AAU) All-American team is named.

1940 – Basketball appears for the first time on television.

1953 – The first women's World Championships, won by the United States, is held.

1954 – A shot clock is introduced to encourage scoring and prevent deliberate stalling.

1967 – The American Basketball Association forms as a rival to the NBA. Although it lasts only until 1976, it drives much of the NBA's later innovation and is home to stars such as Julius "Dr. J" Erving.

1976 – Women's basketball becomes an Olympic event.

1979 – Indiana State's Larry Bird and Michigan State's Earvin "Magic" Johnson compete head-to-head for the college basketball championship. That fall they enter the NBA and reinvigorate a league besieged by low television ratings, uncreative leadership, and a perceived drug problem among the players.

1984 – Georgeann Wells becomes the first woman to slam dunk during a college basketball game.

1984 – The NBA's Chicago Bulls draft Michael Jordan, whose talent, charisma, and nose for marketing catapult the league into an era of massive economic growth.

1997 – The Women's National Basketball Association opens play. The official game ball, as it was in 1894, is developed by Spalding.

2003 – LeBron James enters the NBA. In addition to career playing and endorsement earnings that are expected to surpass $1 billion, James helps reclaim the league's spirit of social activism lost during the 1980s and '90s.

See also: Baseball; Football; Olympics.

Further Reading

Bender, B. (2017). "June 28, 1992: That Time the Dream Team Crushed Cuba by 79 Points in Emphatic Debut." *Sporting News*, June 28, 2017. https://www.sportingnews.com/ca/other-sports/news/dream-team-1992-olympics-roster-highlights-michael-jordan-magic-johnson-larry-bird/10hu69jme1wnezyaow3wvem7m.

Blais, M. (1995). *In the Girls, Hope Is a Muscle: A True Story of Hoop Dreams and One Very Special Team*. Grove Atlantic: Boston.

Cornelius, M. (2016). *The Final Season: The Perseverance of Pat Summitt*. University of Tennessee Press: Knoxville.

Grundy, P. and Shackelford, S. (2007). *Shattering the Glass: The Remarkable History of Women's Basketball*. University of North Carolina Press: Chapel Hill.

Iguodala, A. (2019). *The Sixth Man: A Memoir*. Penguin Books: London.

LaFerber, W. (2002). *Michael Jordan and the New Global Capitalism*. W. W. Norton & Company: New York.

Madkour, A. D. (2014). "Stern's Vision, Passion Propelled NBA Forward." *Sports Business Journal*, Jan. 20, 2014. https://www.sportsbusinessdaily.com/Journal/Issues/2014/01/20/Opinion/From-the-Executive-Editor.aspx.

Nelson, M. R. (2005). *Bill Russell: A Biography*. Greenwood: Santa Barbara, California.

Pincus, D. (2010). "Today in Sports History: November 22." SB Nation, Nov. 22, 2010. https://www.sbnation.com/2010/11/22/1026510/today-in-sports-history-november-22nd.

Pluto, T. (1990). *Loose Balls: The Short, Wild Life of the American Basketball Association*. Simon & Schuster: New York.

Rosen, C. (2017). *The Chosen Game: A Jewish Basketball History*. University of Nebraska Press: Lincoln.

Thamel, P. (2010). "Aggressive from the Start, the U.S. Leaves No Doubt." *New York Times*, Sept. 6, 2010, B10.

Bodybuilding

Beyond training their bodies, bodybuilders do not have to do anything athletic. They do not jump, run, or wield their strength against an opponent. They do not display flexibility, tumble across a mat, or strategize to offset a competitor's offensive maneuver. Judges, not a head-to-head result, determine champions, and their culture is so intertwined with performance-enhancing substances—most legal and some not—that it is impossible to discuss the sport's history without approaching the subject. Despite these perceived drawbacks, many consider bodybuilders to represent the peak of athletic performance. Their goal, to maximize the aesthetic potential of every muscle in the body, has pushed the limits of what a human being, regardless of gender, can look like. What previously existed only in comic books, cartoonish muscle mass and definition, has become reality in the world of bodybuilding, a stage of Greek gods come-to-life who risk their health to create one perception of physical human perfection.

HISTORICAL CONTEXT

Strength, not physical appearance, was the original benchmark for athletic manliness, an antiquated concept that has survived in various forms through thousands of years. Different cultures came up with unique feats of strength, including moving logs, rocks, and other natural objects. A new branch of manliness began in the late 19th century, when German Eugen Sandow, hired to perform feats of strength at World's Fairs and other variety shows, instead attracted audiences because of his powerful and unique physical appearance.

Sandow was not only strong. Lots of people were strong, but they were also stout, or even obese. Sandow's muscles looked sculpted, like something created by a Renaissance artist, a statue come to life. Soon those who hired Sandow worried less about what he performed and more about just getting him into the show. Considered the first contemporary bodybuilder, Sandow also served as an ambassador for the sport, especially in the United Kingdom and United States. By the early 1900s, Sandow sold fitness products and helped judge the first bodybuilding competitions. The winner was presented with a trophy in the likeness of Sandow. Replicas of that trophy continue to be awarded today to winners of Mr. Olympia, bodybuilding's most prestigious annual event for male competitors.

Bodybuilding was a popular but niche sport until the 1950s, when Joe Weider (see "Important Figures") helped drive it into the mainstream through his magazines and other promotions. Hollywood beach films sometimes featured a bodybuilder walking along the sand. He might not have any lines of dialogue, but he stood out enough to spark curiosity. Two bodybuilders in particular helped build a bridge between the sport and the popular entertainment that would become a bodybuilding staple. Steve Reeves won both the Mr. America and Mr. Universe competitions before going on to star in two Hollywood films about the Greek god Hercules, in which he played the title character. Reeves's peer, Jack LaLanne, took up Sandow's mission, promoting fitness and strength and new ideas about what people could look like. He emphasized diet and cardiovascular conditioning in addition to weight training, arguing that strength alone did not make one impressive. LaLanne personified his fitness style, living as a picture of health until his death at age 96 in 2011.

By the 1960s the Weider family had established the Mr. Olympia competition, cultivated media coverage, and learned how to promote its stars. Bodybuilding had become a recognized sport with highly visible, marketable athletes.

GLOBALIZATION

For as long as bodybuilding has been a sport, people from across the world have competed or become fans. As the sport grew, broadcast networks carried events that were seen internationally. Joe Weider's magazines boasted subscribers from across the world. It also helped greatly that its greatest ambassador, Arnold Schwarzenegger, who was born in Austria and maintains deep ties in Europe despite becoming an American citizen, benefited from the U.S. mass-media machine; before he even made his first movie he had a following on multiple continents, and therefore, so did the sport.

WHERE IT'S PLAYED TODAY

Bodybuilding takes place mostly everywhere. Mr. and Ms. Olympia champions have been born in Austria, Cuba, Finland, Italy, Jamaica, Lebanon, the Netherlands, the United Kingdom, the United States, and Venezuela, while events have been hosted across Australia, in Europe, in South Africa, and in the United States.

There are even bodybuilding competitions for children, although they have come under scrutiny by physiologists and other fitness experts who point out that children's bodies, which have not finished growing, might not be ready for such intense physical training. The National Center for Biotechnology Information in the United States recommends that children focus more on strength training than bodybuilding and that they be educated about how to properly exercise to improve health while reducing the risk of injury.

ECONOMICS AND MEDIA

Prize money for 2013's Olympia Fitness & Performance Weekend, a celebration of the sport that includes competitions in eight categories, reached a milestone for the annual event: $1 million total. The organization shared the good news with anyone who would listen, but they were tone deaf in their perception about how winnings would be distributed. The winner of Mr. Olympia, the event's showcase for male performers, was to receive $675,000, the most in the event's half century of existence.

And what about Ms. Olympia?

$60,000.

That women earn cents on the dollar around the world for doing the same jobs as men is hardly a secret, but this was a new low that revealed bodybuilding's chauvinism in giant, flashing neon lights. Ms. Olympia's prize money was just 9 percent of Mr. Olympia's prize money. Even the winner of the 212 Showdown, an event for smaller, lighter men's bodybuilders, was awarded a larger cash prize.

As for media, Mr. and Mrs. Olympia and other events, such as Mr. Universe, draw millions of television viewers across the world. Cable networks such as Fox Sports, ESPN, Sky News, and others have at one time or another broadcast bodybuilding championships. Arnold Schwarzenegger's international success is one reason why, and he has paid back bodybuilding by working as an advocate for the sport despite retiring decades ago. While he served two terms as governor of California, Schwarzenegger mostly put aside his acting and competitive pasts to focus on running the most economically powerful American state. After leaving office, he returned to his roots. Those who followed him on social media often were treated to behind-the-scenes looks at bodybuilding competitions, courtesy of Schwarzenegger's feeds, which helped humanize the competitors who gushed over the chance to meet one of their idols.

DIMENSIONS OF THE SPORT

As bodybuilding is a sport with champions determined exclusively by judges, similar to gymnastics and diving, its athletes are required to showcase certain skills, poses, and abilities. For example, the rules require judges to look for competitors' symmetry, which means how well proportioned their entire bodies are. An athlete with massive biceps and quad muscles but underdefined calves gets marked down for not having a "complete" body. The two sides of an athlete's upper torso should narrow like a V shape as it draws down to the athlete's waist.

Poses help judges and the crowd determine the superior competitors. In some competitions bodybuilders, who compete in skimpy swimwear, are required to demonstrate as many as 11 different poses. Some of these include the "hands on hips most muscular," front double biceps, rear lat spread while simultaneously flexing the calf muscles, and the "crab" or "hulk" pose, in which they bend their arms at the elbows and bring them down in front of their waist while flexing every muscle in the top half of their body. Depending on the event, there will be either one or two rounds of poses and judging to determine the winner.

IMPORTANT FIGURES

Schwarzenegger is synonymous with bodybuilding. Not only is he the most notable face in the sport's history but he also is one of the most popular celebrities in modern history—a global icon. Yet even Schwarzenegger recognizes that bodybuilding's most important figure, Joe Weider, almost singlehandedly carried the sport to where it is today. Weider, along with his brother Ben, took bodybuilding from a carnival sideshow and transformed it into a global endeavor.

Himself a bodybuilder in his youth, Joe Weider organized bodybuilding, helping to form the International Federation of Bodybuilders; led the effort to create its two foundational competitions, Ms. and Mr. Olympia; devised and oversaw media to cover the sport and communicate information about it across the world; pushed dietary supplements that both benefited (and potentially damaged) competitors; and saw so much potential in one of the sport's stars, Schwarzenegger, that he lied to movie producers, claiming Schwarzenegger was a German-trained Shakespearean actor, which led to Schwarzenegger being cast in his first starring movie role. Weider's longevity—he was born in 1919—and health bolstered his influence. His family founded a nutrition company in the 1930s, Weider started his first magazine in the 1940s, and he remained active in the bodybuilding community until his death in 2013.

POP CULTURE

The most famous bodybuilder in history, Schwarzenegger, also happens to be one of the most famous pop-culture celebrities in history. Few might have guessed that Schwarzenegger would achieve such fame as he was winning Mr. Olympia after Mr. Olympia, each one from 1970 through 1975 and then again in 1980. He had a great look, standing six-foot-two with the most iconic bodybuilding physique in the world. He also had a strong Austrian accent, hardly ideal for Hollywood, and by his own admission was not much of an actor. The 1977 documentary film about bodybuilding, *Pumping Iron*, showed that Schwarzenegger possessed charisma. He was funny too. That would be enough to make up for his lack of thespian training. Brushing off some of his earlier film attempts, including the unintentional hilarity and low production value of 1970's *Hercules in New York*, Schwarzenegger in the 1980s and 1990s became the biggest movie star in the world. Some of his iconic films include the *Terminator* franchise, *Total Recall*, *Kindergarten Cop*, and *True Lies*. In 2003 he stepped away from acting when he was elected governor of California. A naturalized American citizen, Schwarzenegger served two terms in office.

Schwarzenegger was not the only bodybuilder whose career was launched after *Pumping Iron*. Lou Ferrigno, occasionally the butt of Schwarzenegger's jokes in the documentary, was cast as Marvel Comics superhero the Incredible Hulk in a television show that ran for five seasons. Bill Bixby starred as mild-mannered scientist David Banner, but when he got angry, he turned into the giant green monster with muscles, played by Ferrigno.

It is safe to say neither Schwarzenegger nor Ferrigno—and perhaps not even the sport of bodybuilding—could have reached great heights were it not for Charles Atlas. Sandow was the first celebrity bodybuilder, but Atlas was the first celebrity bodybuilder who came of age during the 20th century and also understood marketing and branding. Atlas, born Angelo Siciliano, achieved his greatest fame selling his personal fitness routine through comic books and magazines. In the ads, a puny boy would get bullied on the beach, turn to Atlas's fitness regimen, and return to the beach to beat the bully and win the girl. The ads ran for more than a half century, turning Atlas into a household name long after his bodybuilding days were behind him.

SCANDALS

Bodybuilders most likely would not look anywhere near as large and defined as they do had it not been for the development of anabolic steroids in the 1950s. Anabolic steroids were the first mainstream performance-enhancing drug used by athletes, and a version of them is still used today. In bodybuilding, football, soccer, kabaddi, baseball, and virtually every other competitive sport at some point over the last half century, at least one athlete has been caught using anabolic steroids.

In bodybuilding some have traced anabolic steroids to the huge growth of the athletes dating back, not surprisingly, to the 1950s. Although modern nutrition and training techniques have played a large role, observers of the sport, including Schwarzenegger himself, have discussed steroids' role. Schwarzenegger, one of the tallest Mr. Olympias of all time, never grew heavier than 240 pounds. He stands about 6-feet-2. Today, athletes who stand 5-feet-10 and 5-feet-11 regularly surpass 275 pounds and even flirt with 300. Anabolic steroids remain illegal, but as the old cliché in sports goes, "It's only illegal if you get caught." The problem with sports like bodybuilding and cycling, where so many athletes have a history of doping, is that sometimes it is hard to distinguish between who is clean and who has turned to performance-enhancing drugs.

POLITICS

If it feels like Schwarzenegger dominates the conversation around bodybuilding, even 40 years after he last competed, it is because of how diverse, ambitious, and successful his postcompetition career has been. In addition to his success as an entertainer, Schwarzenegger has been a climate-change activist and politician, serving two terms as governor of California.

Even his personal life became political in 1986 when he married journalist Maria Shriver. Shriver, an Emmy and Peabody Award winner for the American broadcasting company NBC, one of the largest and most reputable newsgathering organizations in the world, is also a member of the famous Kennedy family of American politics. Her mother, Eunice Kennedy Shriver, was sister to former U.S. president John F. Kennedy and senators Robert and Ted Kennedy. Maria Shriver has numerous cousins in political service and has herself become active in various nonprofit organizations. She filed for divorce from Schwarzenegger after 25 years of marriage and his revelation that he had had extramarital affairs.

PATRIOTISM AND NATIONAL PRIDE

The Austrians are not exactly known for their ethnic and cultural diversity. In World War II their soldiers seamlessly blended with Germany's Nazi regime. A poll conducted in 2018 by one of the most trusted news agencies in the world, the British Broadcasting Corporation (BBC), revealed that immigrants found Austrians among the most inhospitable people in Europe. Of European countries with the highest rates of violence against people of color and immigrants, Austrian ranked the second worst. The country maintains a rule to this day that if one of its citizens accepts citizenship from another country, the Austrian government will divest the person of Austrian citizenship—unless, of course, the person's name is Arnold Schwarzenegger. He received the rarest of honors in the early 2000s when Austria let him retain citizenship despite becoming a naturalized American citizen nearly 20 years earlier. "We would have been idiots if we had denied Schwarzenegger's express wish . . . to be allowed to keep his Austrian citizenship," an Austrian politician said. "After all, today Arnold is the best-known Austrian in the world" (Geiger 2003). Excommunicating Schwarzenegger would have been a public-relations disaster for Austria, a country for which the retired bodybuilder has always professed his love, even as he built his new life in the United States.

Timeline

1892 – Angelo Siciliano, who later changes his name to Charles Atlas, is born in Acri, Italy.

1893 – At the World's Fair in Chicago, Eugen Sandow, originally brought in to demonstrate feats of strength, instead draws crowds interested in the size and shape of his muscles.

1901 – The world's first recognized bodybuilding competition is held in London. One of the judges is Sir Arthur Conan Doyle, author of the Sherlock Holmes stories.

1922 – Atlas, now a successful bodybuilder, begins a health and fitness company that exists to this day: Charles Atlas Ltd.

1925 – Sandow, now known as the "Father of Modern Bodybuilding," dies in London.

1946 – The International Federation of Bodybuilders is founded by brothers Joe and Ben Weider.

1965 – The first Mr. Olympia bodybuilding competition, organized by Joe Weider, is held in New York. It will become the most prestigious bodybuilding competition in the world.

1971 – Paris hosts the first Mr. Olympia competition held outside of the United States.

1977 – The documentary film *Pumping Iron* debuts and turns Austrian bodybuilder Arnold Schwarzenegger into an international celebrity.

1980 – The first Ms. Olympia competition, organized by Joe Weider, is held in Philadelphia, Pennsylvania.

1983 – Schwarzenegger becomes a naturalized citizen of the United States.

1989 – The television show *American Gladiators*, in which everyday people compete against physically gifted athletes, premieres with female bodybuilder Raye Hollitt starring as one of the gladiators, using the screen name Zap.

1991 – Schwarzenegger's film *Terminator 2*, directed by James Cameron, earns $515 million at the worldwide box office, making it the fifth most successful film in history up to that point.

1999 – Former bodybuilder Joan Laurer, a professional wrestler using the name Chyna, becomes the first woman to win World Wrestling Entertainment's intercontinental championship.

2003 – Schwarzenegger is elected governor of California.

2005 – Ronnie Coleman wins his eighth Mr. Olympia title, tying him for most all-time with Lee Haney.

2013 – Joe Weider dies.

2018 – Actor and retired bodybuilder Lou Ferrigno is named chairperson of the President's Council on Sports, Fitness, and Nutrition, joining a list of names that includes astronaut Jim Lovell, gold-medal-winning sprinter Florence Griffith Joyner, and Schwarzenegger.

See also: Cycling; Diving; Gymnastics.

Further Reading

Baines, D. (2014). *Charles Atlas: The Man, the Myth, and the Muscles*. Birch Tree Publishing: New York.

Coleman, R. (2019). *Yeah Buddy! My Incredible Story*. Poltergeist Publishing Company: Miami Beach, Florida.

Cotter, S. (2016). *Bodybuilding for Women*. CreateSpace Independent Publishing Platform: Scotts Valley, California.

Ferrigno, L. (1996). *Lou Ferrigno's Guide to Personal Power, Bodybuilding, and Fitness*. Contemporary Books: Chicago.

Gaines, C. (1982). *Yours in Perfect Manhood, Charles Atlas: The Most Effective Fitness Program Ever Devised*. Simon & Schuster: New York.

Geiger, E. (2003). "Austria Bursts with Pride Over Native Son 'Arnie': Schwarzenegger Possesses Rare Dual Citizenship." *San Francisco Chronicle*, Aug. 18, 2003. https://www.sfgate.com/politics/article/Austria-bursts-with-pride-over-native-son-Arnie-2595228.php.

Haney, L. (1987). *TotaLee Awesome: A Complete Guide to Bodybuilding Success*. Peachtree Publishers Ltd.: Atlanta, Georgia.

Schwarzenegger, A. (1993). *Arnold: The Education of a Bodybuilder*. Simon & Schuster: New York.

Schwarzenegger, A. (2012). *The Encyclopedia of Modern Bodybuilding*. Simon & Schuster: New York.

Vodrazka, M. (2019). *The Bodybuilding Meal Prep Cookbook: Macro-Friendly Meals to Prepare, Grab, and Go*. Rockridge Press: Emeryville, California.

Bowling

If only bowling's history were as simple as its rules: One ball, one bowler, and pins that need to be knocked down. The sport remains popular because it can be played competitively or recreationally by people of all ages and physical ability. Although the game takes skill, it also requires minimal physical exertion, which makes it ideal for wide ranges of people, from senior citizens looking to stay active to six-year-olds in search of a Saturday morning activity. Bowling alleys can be found in more than 90 countries. Some people have made the sport their profession, others use it to socialize, others for gambling, and still others as a background activity for a child's birthday party. But figuring out how bowling got to where it is today is far more complex a task than understanding the sport itself.

HISTORICAL CONTEXT

In Washington Irving's 1819 short story "Rip Van Winkle," the title character wanders into the woods to escape his nagging wife. There he encounters a group of men playing "nine pin," a precursor to modern bowling. They offer him something to drink, he accepts, and he promptly passes out and sleeps in the woods for the next 20 years. The nine-pin players, it turns out, were ghosts—former members of the crew of the sailor-explorer Henry Hudson. Indeed, it seems that from its earliest days bowling was associated with debauchery.

Except that the days of Irving and his creation Rip were not bowling's earliest. The game, which likely shares its roots with the game of bocce, goes back to at least 300 CE, when it was used as part of a religious ritual in Germany to secure eternal salvation. In that version of the game, the bowling pin represented the devil. While a member of the clergy watched, local parishioners rolled a stone at the pin. If they knocked over the pin, their sins were absolved.

From this, one can see how the sport naturally lent itself to gambling, albeit for stakes far less stressful than one's eternal soul. Martin Luther enjoyed the game so much that he had a lane built for his children. Bowling writer Mark Miller credited Luther for standardizing some of the rules—such as each lane having nine pins (one less than the modern game)—which helped the game's popularity spread. Luther was one of the most powerful, influential church figures in history, and ideas (or sports) that carried the blessing of the clergy during the Renaissance—Luther's time—had far more chance to spread geographically than those that did not. King Henry VIII of England, who lived at the same time as Luther, also loved bowling. He loved it so much, in fact, that he only let select others play alongside him. He banned commoners from taking part.

But bowling may have even older roots. Much, much older. In 1936 a British archaeologist uncovered a child's tomb in Egypt that included a bowling-like game. The artifacts in the tomb were dated to 3200 BCE. If the articles made up a form of bowling, that would date the origins of the sport to more than 5,000 years ago. This seems to be closer to the truth. The earliest precursors to modern bowling were played by ancient Egyptians and Romans, who used leather balls stuffed with corn.

The sport as it is most commonly played today developed during the early 20th century as the Industrial Revolution changed how equipment could be mass-produced and lanes constructed. It remains a sport popular among recreational participants, competitive bowlers, families, and gamblers.

GLOBALIZATION

Although the business of professional bowling tends to be led by the United States, the game itself has long held international appeal, with a version of the game dating back to ancient Egypt and the game as we know it today developing under the watchful eyes of such historical figures as Martin Luther and King Henry VIII of England. Indian bowlers formed the Bowling Federation of India—now called the Tenpin Bowling Federation (India)—in 1975.

As interest in the American version faded in the late 1980s, bowling appeared as an exhibition sport in the 1988 Summer Olympics in Seoul, South Korea. A new market for the sport exploded in eastern parts of Asia, including Korea and China. By 1997 more than 15,000 bowling alleys were built in China, whereas in 1993 there had been just a few hundred.

The European Bowling Tour, formed in 2000, has slowly but steadily gained traction as a professional league. It hosted only 12 events in 2018 but is notable for its coed competition; women and men are not separated into divided classes.

WHERE IT'S PLAYED TODAY

Hong Kong hosted the World Tenpin Bowling Championships for Men in 2018. The 2014 event was held in Abu Dhabi, United Arab Emirates. Germany hosted the championship for senior citizens in 2017. France hosted the first championships for juniors in 2019, while the United States has hosted the last two youth championships, first in Nebraska, then Michigan. Tokyo, Japan, hosted the singles championships, and in 2017 Wroclaw, Poland, hosted the World Games, which takes place every four years.

The Professional Bowlers Association held the bulk of its 2019 schedule in the United States, but it did host a small handful of events outside of the United States as well. It held tournaments in China, Japan, Kuwait, Sweden, and Thailand.

ECONOMICS AND MEDIA

To understand the economics of bowling, split the sport into two sides: professional bowlers and recreational bowlers. The Professional Bowlers Association (PBA) formed in 1958 and has grown into the world's largest and most successful professional bowling organization. It started with 33 original members and now comprises four separate leagues: the PBA Tour; PBA50, for professional bowlers who are at least 50 years old; PBA Women's Series; and the PBA Regional Tour, effectively a minor league for professionals and amateurs who aspire to reach the PBA Tour.

Interest in professional bowling peaked during the 1980s and early 1990s. The 1987 U.S. Open offered $500,000 in total prize money, including $100,000 to the winner. Bowlers were teased with $100,000 bonuses if they could bowl a perfect 300 game on national television. The American Broadcasting Company (ABC) broadcast tour events weekly from 1962 to 1997. By the early part of the 21st century, prize money for the winning bowler had dropped to as little as $20,000. Professional bowler Ryan Ciminelli earned $50,000 for winning the 2015 U.S. Open, half of what the winner of the same tournament earned nearly 30 years earlier.

Columbia Broadcasting System (CBS) decided to broadcast bowling starting in 1998 after ABC abandoned the sport, but CBS lasted just two years. Fox Sports carried it for two years, from 1999 to 2000. In 2000 ABC subsidiary ESPN—the American all-sports cable network that includes six different channels and more than 8,000 hours of programming per day—picked up coverage of the Pro Bowlers Tour and covered it until 2019, when Fox Sports and the Professional Bowlers Association agreed to a multiyear broadcast contract.

Recreationally, the sport remains popular, with more than 67 million Americans visiting a bowling alley at least once in 2014. Business analysts consider bowling a $6 billion industry that has found new success for two reasons. First, bowling-alley owners have updated their facilities. Second, many younger consumers have returned to the sport as a social activity.

DIMENSIONS OF THE SPORT

The U.S. Bowling Congress, the governing body of U.S. bowling, states that a regulation bowling lane should be 60 feet long and 41⅞ inches wide. A gutter must line each side of the lane. Each game consists of 10 frames, and each frame gives a bowler 2 rolls of the ball to knock down all 10 pins. A bowler who gets a strike or a spare in the 10th frame may earn a third roll.

Knocking down all 10 pins on the first roll is called a strike and is designated with an X on the score sheet. Using 2 rolls to knock down 10 pins is called a spare and is marked with "/." A bowler who fails to knock down all 10 pins after 2 rolls has bowled an "open frame." Three strikes in a row is called a turkey. A ball that rolls into the gutter is called a gutter ball and results in the bowler earning no points for the roll as well as "–," on the scoresheet.

Scoring in bowling goes as follows: A bowler who rolls a spare earns 10 points plus the amount of the next ball the bowler rolls. A spare earned in the first frame plus 8 pins knocked down on the first roll in the second frame earns the bowler 18 points in the first frame. A bowler who gets a strike earns 10 points plus the amount of the next 2 balls the bowler rolls, so a strike followed by 2 more strikes can earn the bowler up to 30 points in a single frame. A perfect game equals 300 points.

Bowling lanes are 2 inches thick and made either of wood—typically maple and pine for different parts of the lane—or a synthetic material. Both woods are strong, but maple is stronger and therefore is used to construct the front of the lane where bowlers toss or drop their ball. It holds up better against the balls, which weigh anywhere from 6 pounds for a young child up to 16 pounds for the stronger adults. Pine wood makes up the center part of a lane, where all a ball does is roll rather than slam into it. Wood lanes, however, while traditional, can be far more expensive over the long term because they need to be maintained, repaired, and replaced more often. Synthetic lanes are designed to look like wood. They include resistant aluminum in a fiber-reinforced formula of melamine resin. Both types of surfaces include an oil over the top to reduce friction and help prevent damage to the lanes.

Today's bowling balls are made from one of four types of materials: plastic, proactive particle (which gets the best traction over lane oil), resin, and urethane. The materials differ in cost production, which are costs passed down to consumers. The more friction a ball can generate, the more a bowler can hook the ball. A ball that is hooking upon making contact with the pins creates more action than a ball rolled straight down the alley, which makes getting strikes less difficult. Therefore, the better, more competitive bowlers pay for the more expensive balls, while the balls that bowling alleys provide for casual patrons are usually made from the cheapest materials that generate the least amount of friction. In bowling's earlier days, balls were made of lignum vitae wood, one of the types of woods that are so hard they are part of an informal family of woods called "ironwood." *Lignum vitae* is Latin for "wood of life."

IMPORTANT FIGURES

Well, it doesn't get more important than King Henry VIII and Martin Luther. But a close second might be John Moses Brunswick, who founded the J. M. Brunswick Manufacturing Company in Ohio in 1845. The company made many products but few with the lasting impact of its bowling pins and balls. Prior to Brunswick, bowling balls were made mostly of wood, but the company introduced manufactured balls made from vulcanized rubber. In the 1960s, a "vertical" of the Brunswick Corporation opened bowling centers in 14 countries across four continents: Australia, Europe, North America, and South America.

The Weber family, which includes father Dick and son Pete, remains one of the most successful, influential bowling families in U.S. history. Dick was a founding member of the Professional Bowlers Association and was one of the organization's first stars. He won 10 of the PBA's first 23 events and won tournaments in six different decades. He is a member of the United States Bowling Congress Hall of Fame, as is his son, Pete, who as of 2019 remains active and has won more tournaments than his father has won. Pete Weber became part of the backbone of the network ESPN's attempt to reinvigorate the game. The network highlighted Weber, who bowled in sunglasses and became especially animated during televised matches.

POP CULTURE

Cementing his legacy as an ambassador for the sport, Dick Weber periodically appeared on *Late Night with David Letterman* on the National Broadcasting Company (NBC) television network. In one segment, Letterman had Weber bowl outside in New York City in November.

Two movies from the late 1990s prominently featured bowling. The 1996 comedy *Kingpin*, starring Woody Harrelson, Bill Murray, and Randy Quaid, is about an Amish bowling prodigy who is mentored by a former bowler whose career was cut short after his hand was cut off in a bowling alley ball-return machine. In 1998's cult-classic film *The Big Lebowski*, actor Jeff Bridges's character, The

Dude, relaxes by bowling. Another character in the movie, Walter Sobchak, lashes out at others for not obeying the rules of bowling.

SCANDALS

Gambling and bowling hold deep ties, mostly on the recreational circuit. Some websites, for example, exist explicitly to teach people how to incorporate gambling into bowling. Professional bowling, however, which generates a small fraction of the revenue that other sporting leagues produce, has not found itself overtaken by scandal the way sports such as baseball, college basketball, and the NFL have been at various times throughout their history.

POLITICS

Robert Putnam's 2000 book, *Bowling Alone*, was received as an instant foundational, if imperfect, work of modern sociology. In the book Putnam used bowling to show how individuals in modern society have grown disconnected from one another. The book rocked academia and found its way into the mainstream. The *Houston Chronicle* referenced the book as recently as September 2018 in an article about a local historical bowling alley. The *New York Times* summed up conflicting reactions to Putnam's book when Margaret Talbot argued, "What Americans were experiencing was not the extinction of civic life but its reinvention" (Talbot 2000, 11). In other words, fewer people were bowling because they found something more interesting to do, not because individuals in society were drifting apart.

Timeline

3200 BCE – An Egyptian boy is buried with pins and a ball. Five thousand years later, anthropologist Flinders Petrie discovers the grave, which includes bowling's ancestor.

300 CE – Bowling, according to historian William Pehle, is born in Germany.

14th century – English King Edward III outlaws bowling.

16th century – English King Henry VIII allows bowling but only among elites.

16th century – German theologian Martin Luther falls so in love with bowling he builds a lane for his family.

1845 – John Moses Brunswick starts a manufacturing company that makes, among other things, bowling balls and pins, ending the era of wooden balls.

1895 – The American Bowling Congress is founded in New York City.

1952 – American Machine Foundry (AMF) begins selling automatic pin-setter machines for bowling alleys, ending the era of "pinboys," people whose job was to reset pins by hand after they were knocked down.

1962 – ABC television makes its first broadcast of the Professional Bowlers Tour.

1993 – The International Bowling Hall of Fame opens in St. Louis, Missouri.

1997 – ABC television makes its final broadcast of the Professional Bowlers Tour, ending a 35-year relationship.

2000 – Sociologist Robert Putnam releases his book, *Bowling Alone*, which becomes one of the most debated and influential academic books of its era.

2010 – The International Bowling Hall of Fame relocates to Arlington, Texas.

See also: Baseball; Basketball; Football.

Further Reading

Aulby, M. and Ferraro, D. (1989). *Bowling 200: Winning Strategies to Up Your Average and Improve Your Game.* Contemporary Books: Chicago.

Dregni, E. (2013). *Let's Go Bowling.* Crestline Books: Sarasota, Florida.

Hinitz, D. (2016). *Bowling Psychology: A Guide to Mental Mastery of the Lanes.* Human Kinetics: Champaign, Illinois.

Irving, W. and Neider, C. (1998). *The Complete Tales of Washington Irving.* Da Capo Press: Cambridge, Massachusetts.

Jowdy, J. (2009). *Bowling Execution: Master Technique, Maximize Your Score.* Human Kinetics: Champaign, Illinois.

Manzione, G. (2014). *Pin Action: Small-Time Gangsters, High-Stakes Gambling, and the Teenage Hustler Who Became a Bowling Champion.* Pegasus Books: New York.

Miller, M. (2013). *Bowling.* Shire Publications: London.

Putnam, R. (2000). *Bowling Alone: The Collapse and Revival of American Community.* Simon & Schuster: New York.

Schmidt, D. (2007). *They Came to Bowl: How Milwaukee Became America's Tenpin Capital.* Wisconsin Historical Society Press: Madison, Wisconsin.

Talbot, M. (2000). "Who Wants to Be a Legionnaire." *New York Times*, June 25, 2000, 11.

Boxing

Some sports require hundreds of words to explain, but not boxing. Boxing's concept is simple: put two people in front of each other and tell them to start punching. The person left standing is the winner, or if they have fought long enough and both are still standing, the one who hit the other person more is declared the winner by a group of judges.

Boxing's roots are nearly as old as civilized human society. As far back as 3000 BCE, people paid tribute to boxing through art. Boxing, also known as pugilism, prizefighting, and the "sweet science" is one of just a handful of sporting contests that appeared in both the ancient and modern Olympic Games, along with wrestling and track and field.

Modern boxing's popularity peaked during the first half of the 20th century but remains popular to varying degrees in different parts of the world. Champions in both women's and men's boxing have come from nearly every corner of the globe. Participation in the sport occurs most often among low-income people because the barrier to entry requires minimal financial resources—all that participants need are their fists and a pair of boxing gloves—and because boxing physically hurts a great deal.

The 1910 so-called "Fight of the Century" featured heavyweight champion Jack Johnson (right) and James J. Jeffries, dubbed "The Great White Hope." Johnson won, but the U.S. government harassed the African American Johnson, who had to flee the country for seven years. (Library of Congress)

Many of the 20th century's most popular international athletes were boxers, including American Muhammad Ali, Panamanian Roberto Durán, Swede Ingemar Johansson, and Briton Lennox Lewis.

Even as boxing's international popularity waned toward the end of the century, sports fans across the world remained infatuated with participants such as Filipino Manny Pacquiao, American Sugar Ray Leonard, and Mexican Julio César Chávez.

HISTORICAL CONTEXT

A lot has been said and written about boxing, but perhaps no one better encapsulated the nature of the sport and those who play it than Roberto Duran, the superstar from Panama who competed from 1968 to 2001: "Getting hit motivates me. It makes me punish the guy more. A fighter takes a punch, hits back with three punches" (Llaban 2017, 82).

Unlike many sports, whose origins can be traced to specific countries or regions of the world, boxing, because of its simplistic nature, started everywhere. Certain rules might have come to be in England or Rome or elsewhere, but the art of two people punching each other for the purpose of determining a victor should be credited to the human race. Evidence of boxing existed in ancient Egypt—and in Sumer, Greece, India, Rome, North America, South America.

Everywhere.

Spectators ranged across all class levels and, some evidence shows, interest from fans transcended lines of gender and race as well. Some boxers fought for glory and others for fortune. Others fought because they were forced to. Slaves from ancient Rome were forced to fight for the pleasure of their owners and other spectators. The fight sometimes would take place inside a circle drawn in the dirt, which some historians believe is why the spot where boxers fight is called a ring.

Modern boxing developed in the mid-18th century. British fighters engaged in bare-knuckles fighting, which is boxing without gloves on. Great Britain's James Figg earned recognition as the first boxing champion, winning the bare-knuckles championship in 1719. Administration of boxing remained chaotic and largely unregulated until the mid-19th century, when two organizations attempted—and succeeded—to bring order to the sport. Great Britain's Jack Broughton wrote down a set of rules around 1840 that remain a part of the common iteration of the sport, most notably the rules that kept the sport focused on punching and outlawed attacks such as biting and kicking. Then in 1867 John Douglas, the Ninth Marquess of Queensberry, endorsed an additional code of conduct that declared most of the rules of boxing still followed today, such as the definition of a knockout and a standing eight count. The Marquess of Queensberry rules continue to be regarded as boxing's guiding light.

Boxing exists as both an amateur and professional sport and as local, regional, and international competition. It has been featured at the amateur level at every Summer Olympics since 1904 except for 1912 in Stockholm, Sweden, where boxing was illegal. To ensure fair and interesting competition, boxing is broken down by weight classes, gender, and age, and it is overseen by private and sometimes governmental agencies. A match between a 135-pound woman and a 190-pound man could never get sanctioned, but a match between two 130-pound men or two 150-pound women could be. As of 2019 there were 17 separate weight classes in boxing.

GLOBALIZATION

People have boxed in every nation on every continent except for Antarctica for as long as there has been organized sport. British boxer Tyson Fury joked in 2018 that he would like to fight in Antarctica so that he could say he had a fight on every continent. Women, men, adults, kids, professionals, amateurs, and even fashion aficionados looking for new ways to stay fit take part in boxing. At the 2016 Olympics alone, boxers from 19 different countries earned a medal, and 76 separate countries sent at least one boxer to the Games.

ECONOMICS AND MEDIA

Boxing's top fighters and promoters earn among the most of any athletes in professional sports. American boxer Floyd Mayweather, who finished his formal career with a 50-0 record, is estimated to have earned more than $1 billion in his career. His purse for winning each of his fights has not added up to that amount. Rather, as part of his fight contract he earned percentages of pay-per view and television revenue. As his undefeated record climbed and he won championships, public interest in his fights climbed too. He could earn more than $50 million on one fight.

Yet most professional boxers earn less—far, far less, sometimes in the range of $50 a fight in boxing's lower levels, which are sometimes held in the back rooms of public theaters or recreation centers.

As for its media coverage, for decades professional boxing served as one of the staples of *Wide World of Sports*, the popular Saturday afternoon sports show on the American television network ABC. *Wide World of Sports* regularly hosted or showed highlights from championship fights. But boxing's Saturday afternoon appeal fell dramatically for one reason: the nature of boxing itself.

Fans still enjoyed it, but the network no longer found it a useful programming option. If ABC hosted a basketball game, it had a good idea that the game would last about two hours. However, a boxer such as American Mike Tyson could end a match with one mighty blow in as little as 30 seconds. If *Wide World of Sports* slotted two hours for the coverage of a match that lasted less than a minute, that created significant programming concerns. Those concerns, coupled with the perception that the sport was crooked, led to boxing's departure from prime-time television. It found a new home on late-night all-sports-programming networks, where a station could easily cut to a sports highlight show if a boxing match ended earlier than anticipated.

DIMENSIONS OF THE SPORT

Boxing takes place atop a 16-by-16-foot square or a 20-by-20-foot platform, surrounded by ropes made of fiber or steel on all four sides. Only three people are allowed inside the "ring" while the fight is going on: the two boxers and the referee. A boxer's corner people, including trainers and medical overseers, wait just outside of the ring near one of the corners while the fight is going on and are allowed in the ring before and after the fight and between rounds to tend to their boxer. Judges—usually three—also sit outside the ring so that they can observe the fight and, if necessary should one boxer not knock out the other, render a decision to determine a winner or, possibly, a draw.

Boxing gloves became mandatory in 1865 for fights fought under the Marquess of Queensbury rules. The original boxing gloves provided little protection either for the person being hit or the hands of the person doing the hitting. Today, boxing gloves weigh between 8 ounces and 16 ounces and are used to protect the wrists, thumbs, and knuckles of the puncher and, to some degree, the head and face of the person being hit. Professional boxers typically wear 8- or 10-ounce gloves for a fight, and heavier gloves for training. The two boxers agree on what size gloves to wear before the fight to make sure neither has an unfair advantage over the other.

Women's championship matches typically are scheduled for 10 two-minute rounds, with one minute of rest in between each round. A boxing match that ends with neither fighter knocked out is said to have "gone the distance." Men's championship matches are usually scheduled for 12 three-minute rounds with one minute of rest in between, while nonchampionship matches have a 10-round distance.

For safety, boxers are required to wear a custom-made, fitted mouthpiece, which provides some protection against head and mouth injuries. In amateur fighting such as Golden Gloves and the Olympics, headgear is required. The referee checks all fighters' gear at the start of the fight, including the boxing trunks, to make sure no one has tried to sneak in something that would give them an advantage. One way fighters might try to cheat is to remove some of the padding from their gloves. Although it might hurt their hands more, it also will increase the impact of their punches that land against their opponents.

IMPORTANT FIGURE

American boxer Muhammad Ali (born Cassius Clay), by any metric, was the most famous athlete in recorded human history. He won a gold medal at the 1960 Rome Olympics and went on to win the heavyweight championship of the world as a young professional, upsetting Sonny Liston. But that was just the beginning of Ali's move into the mainstream.

In the late 1960s the U.S. military drafted Ali for service in the Vietnam War. Ali refused to go on grounds of religious freedom—he had converted to Islam—and because he saw the war as unjust, famously declaring he had no quarrel with the Viet Cong. Boxing officials stripped him of his title and banned him from the sport. Not reporting for the draft was a federal crime, but the Supreme Court of the United States eventually found in favor of Ali because, based on his religious beliefs, he was a conscientious objector to the war. His conviction was overturned.

During his suspension Ali spoke across the country and fought matches in Europe and Canada. He returned to American boxing after a three-and-a-half-year hiatus, eventually regaining his championship. His international profile grew as he fought championship fights in Zaire, Africa, and in the Philippines, in Asia. By his retirement in 1981, Ali was a global icon.

However, Ali also suffered significant brain damage, the result of his "rope-a-dope" style (letting his opponents punch at him until they tired out and then defeating them with a barrage of punches while they were too exhausted to defend themselves) and of retiring too late. His penultimate fight against future heavyweight champion Larry Holmes left Holmes as both the victor and in tears, so distraught he was at the beating he had given his hero. Not long after his retirement, Ali was diagnosed with Parkinson's disease, which many attributed to his boxing career. He became an ambassador for those suffering from the disease. Ali also became an outspoken advocate for human rights. Upon his death in 2016, tens of thousands of people traveled to his hometown of Louisville, Kentucky, to pay tribute, while an estimated one billion people around the world tuned in to at least part of a broadcast memorial service.

POP CULTURE

Moviegoers around the world devour movies set around boxing, whether it's the 1997 British film *The Boxer* or Russia's popular 2005 movie *Shadowboxing*. Boxing movies are human, dramatic, and filled with close-ups of violence and triumphs in ways that other sports movies cannot replicate. As a result, it's common for boxing films to be nominated and sometimes win major film awards.

In 2005 actress Hilary Swank won the Academy Award for Best Actress for her portrayal of boxer Maggie Fitzgerald. Directed by Clint Eastwood, *Million Dollar Baby* captured Best Picture for the story of Fitzgerald, who suffers a paralyzing injury in the ring. In 1981 Robert De Niro earned Best Actor for his portrayal of boxer Jake La Motta, and Christian Bale won Best Supporting Actor in the 2010 boxing movie *The Fighter*. The independent American film *Girlfight* shocked major studios in 2000 by winning the Grand Jury Prize at the prestigious Sundance Film Festival. *Girlfight* told the story of a teenager who learns to box over the objections of her family.

Some of American film history's greatest actors—Marlon Brando, Buster Keaton, Paul Newman—have portrayed boxers. But if one film franchise has come to define the genre, it's the series of films about fictional prizefighter Rocky Balboa, starring the actor Sylvester Stallone. The first of the franchises' eight films, *Rocky*, debuted in 1976 and won the Academy Award for Best Picture. Stallone, who had been struggling in Hollywood, went on to become one of its biggest stars as he portrayed the character six times as a boxer between 1976 and 2006. In 2015 the franchise was reborn as *Creed* with Balboa as a trainer to the son, played by Michael B. Jordan, of one of his former opponents. *Creed* and *Creed II* earned Stallone and Jordan numerous acting nominations, including a Golden Globe win for Stallone in 2015. Through 2019, the eight Rocky Balboa-Creed movies have made a combined $1.5 billion worldwide at the box office.

SCANDALS

Boxing has been one of the most scandalized modern sports. Gamblers, crooked promoters, and cheating boxers are among the obstacles the sport has placed in front of itself in the battle for public respectability. Despite significant oversight by private and governmental officials, those in boxing wage a constant battle to maintain the public's trust.

POLITICS

U.S. federal prosecutors charged heavyweight boxing champion Jack Johnson in 1912 with violating the Mann Act in an act motivated by racism and insecurity. Johnson, the first African American heavyweight champ, defeated every opponent whom boxer promoters put in front of him. Most of them were white, including former champion John L. Sullivan in 1910 in what was dubbed the "Fight of the Century."

White politicians were further enraged because Johnson refused to play by the rules of white America. He opened a desegregated restaurant and dated white women. So in 1910 the U.S. Congress passed the Mann Act, which made it a felony to transport a woman across state lines for immoral purposes. Some historians believe the law was passed specifically to target Johnson. He was charged after crossing a state border with Lucille Cameron. It did not matter that Cameron and Johnson were dating or that the two later married. Johnson faced charges.

The charges had their intended effect. Johnson fled the country and did not return for seven years. He fought while in exile—in Cuba (where he lost his title in 1915), France, Spain, Mexico, and Argentina—but when he returned in 1920, he served his one-year prison sentence. He fought several times while in prison and returned overseas to fight after being released. By the time he fought his next fight in the United States, in 1926, he was 48 years old and well past his prime. The losses mounted. Johnson received a posthumous federal pardon for the Mann Act violation from U.S. president Donald Trump in 2018.

Timeline

3000 BCE – Civilizations in various parts of the world begin to document boxing.

1000 BCE – Boxing gloves are worn for the first time in the form of leather straps wrapped around boxers' hands to protect their knuckles.

1719 – Boxing's first champion, James Figg, is crowned.

1865 – Boxing gloves become mandatory for most professional fights.

1876 – The first recorded women's boxing match takes place in New York.

1904 – Boxing becomes part of the Summer Olympics.

1908 – Jack Johnson becomes the first African American heavyweight champion.

1936/1938 – African American Joe Louis and German Max Schmeling, falsely portrayed as a stooge of Adolf Hitler, engage in two fights that become more about nationalism and race than boxing. Schmeling won the first fight, Louis won the second, and later in life the two became friends.

1960 – Muhammad Ali wins a gold medal at the Rome Olympics.

1982 – Boxer Kim Duk-Koo dies from injuries suffered in a fight, which leads to reforms to help protect boxers, including reducing the number of rounds in a match.

1989 – Christy Martin begins her professional career with a draw. She goes on to become the most successful women's boxer to date, retiring in 2012 with a career record of 49-7-3.

2007 – Laila Ali, daughter of Muhammad Ali, retires with a perfect 24-0 career record and five championships.

2012 – Women's boxing debuts at the Olympics.

2017 – American Floyd Mayweather wins his 50th and final fight to retire 50-0, breaking Rocky Marciano's 60-year-old record of 49-0.

See also: Olympics; Track and Field; Wrestling.

Further Reading

Baldwin, J. (2011). *The Cross of Redemption: Uncollected Writings*. Vintage Books: New York.

Florio, J. and Shapiro, O. (2019). *War in the Ring: Joe Louis, Max Schmeling, and the Fight between America and Hitler*. Roaring Book Press: New York.

Klein, C. (2015). *Strong Boy: The Life and Times of John L. Sullivan, America's First Sports Hero*. Lyons Press: Lanham, Maryland.

Llaban, K. S. (2017). *The Fired-Up Life: Passion Principles to Motivate You for Work and Life*. Shepherd's Voice Publications: Quezon City, Philippines.

Margolick. D. (2005). *Beyond Glory: Joe Louis vs. Max Schmeling, and a World on the Brink*. Knopf Doubleday: New York.

Marqusee, M. (1999). *Redemption Song: Muhammad Ali and the Spirit of the Sixties*. Verso Books: Brooklyn, New York.

Remnick, D. (1999). *King of the World: Muhammad Ali and the Rise of an American Hero*. Random House: Crawfordsville, Indiana.

Schaap, J. (2005). *Cinderella Man: James J. Braddock, Max Baer, and the Greatest Upset in Boxing History*. Houghton Mifflin: Boston.

Smith, M. N. (2017). *A History of Women's Boxing*. Rowman & Littlefield: Lanham, Maryland.

Ward, G. C. (2006). *Unforgivable Blackness: The Rise and Fall of Jack Johnson*. Vintage Books: New York.

Bullfighting

Few sports have been as simultaneously romanticized and vilified as bullfighting. From one perspective, literary artists such as Ernest Hemingway write of the majesty of matadors and the beauty of the beasts. From another, activists detail the horrific mistreatment of the animals. In parts of the world, bullfighting represents the best of historic cultural values. In others, the worst of human nature. The one thing people tend to agree on, however, is that bullfighting is a spectacle: thinking humans squaring off versus massive, instinctual nature. With horns. Whatever one thinks of the results, bullfighting's roots grow deep in parts of the world, and the practice requires a closer look if one is to understand the cultures from which it originated and in which it survives to this day.

HISTORICAL CONTEXT

Human sport against bulls, and humanity's fascination with bulls, dates to ancient civilizations. The ancient Greeks created Minotaur, the mythical half man, half bull who lived at the center of elaborate mazes called labyrinths. The Mesopotamian epic poem, *The Epic of Gilgamesh* includes the Bull of Heaven, against

Spain's Manuel Sánchez, known around the world as Manolete and immortalized in this statue, became one of the most famous matadors in history during the first half of the 20th century. He died at age 30 after being gored by a bull. (Felipe Caparros Cruz/Dreamstime.com)

which the poem's hero must do battle. The ancient Romans, who reveled in sporting contests that included people versus animals, battled bulls, and during their conquests exported contests against bulls to Hispania, a region that today includes Spain and Portugal.

Around 700 CE colonists from North Africa made their way into what is now Spain and there discovered bullfighting. They altered the sport's strategy and meaning. Before their arrival bullfighting took on a brutish feel, with battlers killing bulls by any—often vulgar—means. The North Africans tied bullfights to festivals and other contests and helped to grow showmanship within the sport. Matadors—the bullfighters—went beyond merely killing the animal. Death was still involved, but it now incorporated different skills and elements of performance art.

Religious festivals included forms of bullfighting, such as a fighter mounting a steed while carrying a lance to kill the bull. Charlemagne attended at least one bullfight. By the 12th century in Spain, it was common for royal weddings, which could be large, multiday events, to include bullfighting among the festivities. There is some question whether bullfighting is a sport or a morbid activity, since the bull presumably thinks of it as a fight for survival, not a game. (Is it really a game when only one side knows it is playing?) Nevertheless, by the mid-18th century, bullfighting assumed its modern form after matadors made two important changes. First, they abandoned their horses and fought the bulls on equal footing—while standing. Second, they introduced the traditional small red cape, called a muleta, to help direct and manipulate the bull, and a sword called an *estoque* to kill the bull.

Throughout the centuries, countries where there has been bullfighting, including Spain, Argentina, Cuba, and the United States, have periodically imposed bans on the sport, sometimes because of potential dangers to the bullfighters but mostly because of the cruelty committed against the bulls. Catalonia, a region of Spain, banned bullfighting, prompting communities in other parts of the world, including regions in France, to pass legislation explicitly intended to protect bullfighting.

GLOBALIZATION

Spanish imperialism, primarily from the late 15th century through the late 18th century, spread bullfighting to other parts of the world, while regional proximity also contributed. Spanish conquistadores helped bring bullfighting to South America—mostly Argentina and Ecuador—as well as Cuba, Mexico, and other regions that today help make up parts of the Spanish-speaking world.

The Spanish presence in Mexico led to bullfighting's migration into what is now parts of the southwestern and western United States. Most of that growth took place before the United States took possession of those territories, and California remains the last American state to regularly host bullfights (see "Where It's Played Today").

The history of bullfighting in France is less understood and occurred gradually late in the sport's expansion. It grew in southern France in the 19th century, centering on religious traditions. The rest of the country has shown little interest in the sport.

WHERE IT'S PLAYED TODAY

Bullfighting still takes place in Spain, Portugal, parts of Mexico, and other regions of former Spanish colonies where the sport is not banned, as well as parts of France and India, where citizens enjoy a variation of traditional bullfighting that ensures the bull's survival. Most notably, in 2010 the Ecuadorian government held a referendum on whether to continue bullfighting. They voted to keep it but not commit the final bull kill in front of the crowd, instead moving it elsewhere. In other words, they still wanted bullfighting that called for the matador to slay the bull—they just did not want to see the death.

Bullfighting has been banned in several Mexican states but still occasionally appears in other parts of the country. Mexico City boasts the Plaza Mexico, the largest bullfighting arena in the world, with about 50,000 seats for spectators. From November through April, Mexico's drier months, thousands of bullfights take place, although not as many as Mexico used to have since the states of Quintana Roo, Coahuila, Guerrero, and Sonora banned bullfighting. All state action has taken place since 2013 as local citizens have lost their taste for the blood sport.

Various efforts have attempted to ban bullfighting in parts of Portugal. Many government officials and citizens are sympathetic to the cause, but the activism has failed to get much traction because it has not addressed ways for the country to simultaneously protect bulls while maintaining centuries-old traditions. Bullfighting also continues in southern France, where bullfighting's popularity has grown in recent years, contrary to public opinion around much of the world. Many events in that region take place around religious holidays in ancient venues.

The only place bullfighting exists today in the United States is in parts of the state of California, but local laws exist to protect the safety of the bulls and matadors. Matadors are not allowed to slay bulls, and bulls' horns are shaved down to have blunt ends rather than sharp points. Matadors and bulls can still get hurt, but deaths are rare. Forms of bullfighting also exist in the American and Canadian spectacle known as rodeo.

ECONOMICS AND MEDIA

The most celebrated and successful matadors do more than provide entertainment. They fulfill cultural and religious expectations, which enables them to request and receive high salaries. Depending on the event and the individual matadors, a single appearance can earn them between $75,000 and $500,000. They can increase their income further through popular media and artistic appearances, such as film and television.

Beginning matadors earn next to nothing and will need to hold jobs outside of bullfighting to earn enough income to live. It is common for low-level matadors to travel to an event and not make enough money to cover their meals and transportation costs. Beyond regional coverage, bullfighting receives almost no media coverage except in the case of a grotesque event, such as the goring of a matador. Bullfighting accidents draw far more interest on streaming services such as YouTube and Dailymotion, similar to what happens in the regionalized American motorsport of stock-car racing.

DIMENSIONS OF THE SPORT

Ceremony and tradition dominate bullfighting. Other than laws passed to protect bulls or ban the sport, it has remained relatively unchanged for centuries, with the entire spectacle lasting about three hours. Competitions take place in a ring in front of spectators. The event begins with a parade. Matadors walk out with their assistants known as banderilleros, picadors, and *mozos de espada* (sword carriers). Once they are introduced, the bull enters the arena and the competition begins.

The cape stage is what most casual observers recognize as bullfighting. The matador waves his red cape, antagonizing the bull in a tradition presented as allowing the bull to showcase his strength and agility. As the bull charges, the matador moves out of its way, and the crowd yells, "Olé!" Hundreds of years of Islamic occupancy of Spain, including during the 8th century when bullfighting was refined, have led some historians to believe that *olé* is a variation on "Allah."

After the cape stage comes the picador stage, which is what begins to anger activists and other opponents of bullfighting while thrilling the sport's fans. Matadors on horseback, called picadors, ride around the bull, angering it. When it gets close, they stab it in the shoulders. Sometimes bulls gore the horses. The banderilleros run around the bulls on foot, hurling darts into its back.

The final stage—the kill stage—occurs when the matador plunges his sword into the back of the bull to kill it. The bull is still angry and strong but not at full strength because of the previous attacks. Once the bull falls, a matador's assistant cuts the bull's throat to secure the kill.

IMPORTANT FIGURES

Manuel Sánchez, better known as Manolete, came to represent the best and worst of Spanish bullfighting. Considered by many the greatest matador of the modern era, Manolete achieved his fame through the prolific killing of bulls. He became so famous throughout the world that he was referenced in an episode of the American television series *The Twilight Zone*, and film director George Romero named one of his characters Manolete in the 2005 film *Land of the Dead*. He died in 1947 at the age of 30, gored in the upper leg by a bull. Bullfighting fans in Spain, Mexico, and elsewhere mourned his death.

Luis Miguel Domínguín, who debuted in 1941, picked up where Manolete left off. Although Domínguín was not considered as skilled as Manolete, his ability to stay alive allowed him to achieve a level of international fame that exceeded even Manolete's. Domínguín dated American actress Ava Gardner, appeared on game shows and films, and had one of his bullfighting outfits designed by his good friend, artist and fellow Spaniard, Pablo Picasso. One book written about Domínguín was called *Luis Miguel Domínguín: El Numero Uno*, which according to urban legend is what Domínguín called himself after learning of Manolete's death.

The novelist Ernest Hemingway loved bullfighting. He wrote about it in both his fiction and nonfiction books writings. *Death in the Afternoon*, written in 1932, highlighted Hemingway's journalistic side. It included a glossary of terms and images. Notably, *Death* is considered one of Hemingway's more autobiographical works, not because he wrote directly about himself, which he did not, but because he used bullfighting to meditate on emotions such as fear, leading students of Hemingway's work to more profound understanding of the author's own emotional inner workings.

POP CULTURE

Antibullfighting activism received a boost in 1936 with the publishing of *The Story of Ferdinand*, a children's book about a bull who would rather smell flowers than fight matadors. Ferdinand preferred peace to violence. In the book's climax, he is led into the ring to fight but gets distracted by the flowers in women's hair. The matador and his assistant become so mad that they start crying, but they cannot attack a pacifist bull. Ferdinand is not forced to fight and is instead rewarded with a long life in a pasture where he can smell flowers and be free. The book proved so popular for so long that by 1938, two years after its publication, it became the best-selling book in the United States. According to the *Washington Post*, Ferdinand has been translated into more than 60 languages and sold more than 2 million copies. Its pop-cultural influence has never wavered: Hemingway, ever the bullfighting fan, wrote a children's story called *The Faithful Bull* in response to Ferdinand; Marvel Comics named a character known for its peaceful nature after Ferdinand; and in 2017 an animated film that expanded on the Ferdinand story earned an Academy Award nomination.

In 1953 Warner Brothers, the American entertainment studio, produced *Bully for Bugs*, a comedic seven-minute animated short starring the popular cartoon rabbit Bugs Bunny. Bugs accidentally takes a wrong turn and ends up in a bullfighting ring with a terrified matador, who flees the arena and leaves Bugs alone with the bull. After temporarily feeling the bull's rage, Bugs tricks the bull with a combination of machine grease, glue, a matchstick, and dynamite, appearing to have killed the bull. The words "The End" appear on his muleta. Director Chuck Jones used actual sound from a bullfight recorded in Spain to make the cartoon sound realistic. It turned out to be one of the most popular Bugs Bunny shorts ever made and has been included in numerous Warner Brother collectors' editions.

From 1976 to 1991, professional wrestler Merced Solis, better known by his screen name of Tito Santana, portrayed a fan favorite, a wrestler so beloved in the United States and Mexico that he received cheers and drew fans wherever he went. But in the early 1990s Santana's promotors, the World Wrestling Federation (WWF), shifted strategy from promoting individuals to promoting characters, many of which ended up as vicious cultural stereotypes. WWF rebranded Santana as "El Matador" and had him walk to the ring in a traditional matador costume. The move backfired, and by 1993, unable to draw fan interest, Santana left the organization, returning only occasionally for special appearances. Santana was inducted into the World Wrestling Entertainment (WWF's new name) Hall of Fame in 2004.

SCANDALS

Depending on one's personal views, the whole sport might be considered a scandal. Similar to horse racing, some ask (as noted earlier) whether it can be classified a sport at all when one of the key competitors—the bull—does not know what is going on. Then, of course, there is the killing of the bull, an act that thrills some but infuriates others, even those who are not animal-rights activists but recognize the inhumanity and unfairness of the competition.

POLITICS

Even in the countries where bullfighting is most popular—Spain, Portugal, and Mexico—it is common for government officials, supported by citizens, to introduce legislation to ban the sport. Most effective antibullfighting legislation has happened at local levels but rarely at the national level.

PATRIOTISM AND NATIONAL PRIDE

The countries of Spain, Portugal, and Mexico take great pride in bullfighting although, as evidenced by antibullfighting activists, the good feelings are not universal. It is common for government officials to take visiting dignitaries—those who are willing to watch bullfighting—to major bullfighting events.

Timeline

2000 BCE – Cretans create art that depicts people performing athletic feats against bulls.

711 CE – Although competitions against and involving bulls have been taking place for thousands of years, the first official bullfight—as we recognize it today—takes place, but this date is in dispute. Some historians say the first official fight does not take place for close to another 400 years.

c. 800 – Charlemagne, emperor of the Holy Roman Empire and considered a pivotal figure in the creation of modern Europe, observes a bullfight.

c. 1065 – Spaniard Ruy Díaz de Vivar, a famous and powerful knight better known as "El Cid," who briefly ruled a community and commanded both Christian and Islamic forces, dazzles during an exhibition bullfight.

1128 – Bullfights are included in festivities to honor a Spanish royal marriage.

1730 – The muleta, the traditional red cape of bullfighting, and *estoque*, the sword used to kill the bull at the end of a fight, are introduced into mainstream bullfighting.

1926 – Ernest Hemingway's novel *The Sun Also Rises*, which emphasizes bullfighting and helps popularize the sport, is published.

1932 – Hemingway writes in *Death in the Afternoon* that bullfighting "is the only art in which the artist is in danger of death." Antibullfighting activists over the decades have added on to Hemingway's passage with, "or the art itself requires the death of the canvas."

1936   Munro Leaf and Robert Lawson's book about a bull, *The Story of Ferdinand*, is published, becoming one of the best-selling children's books in history.

1953 – Warner Brothers entertainment studio produces the animated cartoon short *Bully for Bugs*, starring the popular animated character Bugs Bunny.

2013 – The Mexican state of Sonora bans bullfighting, as do three more states over the next few years, although bullfighting still takes place through much of the country, including in Mexico City, home to the largest bullfighting arena in the world.

See also: Horse Racing; Rodeo.

Further Reading

Conrad, B. (2007). *The Death of Manolete*. Phoenix Books: Essex Junction, Vermont.

Fiske-Harrison, A. (2011). *Into the Arena: The World of the Spanish Bullfight*. Profile Books: London.

Hardouin-Fugier, E. and Rose, S. (2010). *Bullfighting: A Troubled History*. Reaktion Books: London; Routledge: Abingdon, England.

Hedrick, B. (2018). *Spain and the Bulls: A Memoir*. Self-published.

Hemingway, E. (1926). *The Sun Also Rises*. Scribner: New York.

Hemingway, E. (1932). *Death in the Afternoon*. Scribner: New York.

Kennedy, A. L. (2001). *On Bullfighting*. Anchor Books: New York.

Leaf, M. (1936). *The Story of Ferdinand*. Viking Books for Young Readers: New York.

McCormick, J. (1999). *Bullfighting: Art, Technique & Spanish Society*. Routledge: Abingdon, England.

Salcedo, L. F. and Bonet, E. (1970). *Bulls & Bullfighting: History, Technique, Spectacle*. Crown Publishers: New York.

Cricket

Cricket, the world's second most popular spectator sport after soccer, is played by an estimated 265 million people. More than two billion people tuned in globally to watch at least one match during the 2015 Cricket World Cup, which saw Australia defeat New Zealand for the championship. Cricket is played on nearly every continent, but it finds its greatest popularity in South Asia, the United Kingdom, and Australia.

Each team employs 11 players. All 11 may play in the field, but while batting, only two players per team—the batsmen—can be on the field at once. Similar to baseball and softball, each of which owe significant parts of their history to cricket, the purpose of cricket is to score more runs than your opponent. Each team gets a turn at bat within an innings (in cricket, the term *innings* is used in both singular and plural). Depending on the level of the players and event (e.g., age, professional vs. amateur, local vs. international), a cricket match can last between a few hours and five days.

Cricket's signature event, the Cricket World Cup, takes place every four years and is organized by the International Cricket Council. It deliberately is held on years when the Summer Olympics and Men's FIFA World Cup are not held in order to maximize audience, media attention, and marketing opportunities. For example, the Summer Olympics were scheduled to take place in 2020 (moved to 2021 because of the COVID-19 pandemic), the FIFA Men's World Cup in 2022, and the Cricket World Cup in 2023. In 1844 in New York City, Canada played the United States in cricket in what was billed as the first-ever international sporting event. Journalist Jon Harris wrote that a little more than $100,000 in wagers were placed on the event—nearly $3 million in today's money. Cricket appeared in the Olympics just once, in 1900, but that did not stop the game's enormous growth during the remainder of the century.

HISTORICAL CONTEXT

The first recorded cricket match took place in 1646 in Kent, England, but the game's origins go back at least 300 years earlier, to the days of King Edward II, and perhaps even earlier than that. Oliver Cromwell, lord protector of much of what today is the United Kingdom, is alleged to have played too. Mythologies surround the game's foundation, including: the game developed in the southeast of England because of the area's short grass; the gate was always defended with a bat made from a shepherd's crooked staff; and the game was always played between

More than two billion people watched the Cricket World Cup, making it the second most popular spectator sport in the world, behind soccer. The first known cricket match took place in the mid-17th century. (Shutterstock)

gentlepeople without any ambition to earn money through the sport. In reality, cricket likely is the amalgamation of numerous bat-related sports that formed over time; those various sports took place across the island, not just in southeastern England; and financial gain and gambling own deep roots within the sport.

Others have dated the first reference of cricket to 1597, in a court case over disputed land. Whenever the game actually began, its pivotal developmental period occurred during the 18th and 19th centuries, when it evolved in England into the game most recognizable today. During that period numerous cricket clubs emerged, including the Marylebone Cricket Club, which became the stewards of the Laws of Cricket: essentially the game's rules and standards. New laws became introduced in the 19th century, most notably rules for the bowler—the defensive player who pitches the ball—being altered so that bowlers could throw overhanded instead of underhanded.

From its earliest days cricket joined boxing and horse racing as sources of revenue for its participants and spectators. While some participants received compensation for competing, spectators quickly realized there was money to be made in gambling on cricket. This occurred as early as the 17th century—and the money to be made was significant indeed. Spectators could bet on a match's outcome, individual performance, or a team's or individual's performance within innings or even specific turns at bat. Now in its 4th century of existence, gambling on cricket sees billions of dollars change hands annually, not all of them legally.

The 2019 Cricket World Cup featured squads from the following 10 countries from across five continents: Afghanistan, Australia, Bangladesh, England, India, New Zealand, Pakistan, South Africa, Sri Lanka, and West Indies.

GLOBALIZATION

It is no coincidence that 9 of the 10 countries in the 2019 Cricket World Cup were once British colonies, which allowed the game to spread from its first home to across the globe. Even the only country that was not officially a British colony, Afghanistan, fought numerous wars alongside the British during the 19th and early 20th centuries.

As the British empire expanded, so did cricket. Indians played their first cricket match on home soil in 1721. A little more than 200 years later—in 1932—India's cricket squad was elevated to the level of "test" country, which meant it played matches at the highest level, the ones that last five days, against some of the best competition in the world. In 1983 India won its first Cricket World Cup.

Great Britain did more than spread cricket through colonization. It cultivated the game and used it as a form of laying the seeds of British homogeneity. In 1909 it formed the Imperial Cricket Conference (ICC), an organization that survives to this day and oversees, among other things, the Cricket World Cup. England, Australia, and South Africa made up the original ICC lineup. West Indies, New Zealand, and India were added in 1926. Pakistan joined in 1952, five years after gaining its formation as a country.

The global layout had changed by the 1960s. Great Britain still held global influence, but the form of its colonialism had mostly, but not entirely, shifted away from territorial conquest. Nevertheless, cricket's popularity continued to grow, so the ICC, now rebranded as the International Cricket Conference, began to admit other countries, including but not limited to: Fiji and the United States in 1964; Denmark, Bermuda, and the Netherlands in 1968; Israel and Singapore in 1974; Bangladesh in 1977; Papua-New Guinea in 1978; United Arab Emirates in 1990; and Namibia and Austria in 1992. Some countries are admitted as full members, others as associate members. The last two full members admitted, as of the writing of this book, were Afghanistan and Ireland in 2017.

WHERE IT'S PLAYED TODAY

The game is played all over the world but is most popular in Great Britain—primarily England and Ireland—and South Asia, most notably Bangladesh, India, Pakistan, and Sri Lanka. Although the United States had been affiliated with the ICC, the organization expelled the United States in 2017 over concerns about the sport's regional governance. U.S. cricket leadership currently is working to address the ICC's concerns, although even if it is readmitted, it remains highly unlikely that cricket in the United States ever will reach the heights it did during the mid-19th century, before it was replaced in popularity by its distant cousin, baseball.

North America's strongest cricket presence has for decades been the West Indies, which has made 11 World Cup appearances. South America traditionally has not been a cricket hotbed, but the sport is growing there. Various South American countries have taken turns hosting the South American Cricket Championship since the event was first held in 1995. Argentina has won nine championships, the most by any South American nation, while Mexico has won twice; the fact that Mexico has to play in the South American championship to find good competition speaks as much about South America's growing cricket presence as it does about the sport's dwindling North American presence.

ECONOMICS AND MEDIA

How much professional cricket players get paid comes down to two factors: how good they are, and what team or country they play for. For example, the top earner in Australia, according to *Cricket Monthly*, earns nearly $1.5 million annually, and the top Indian players receive nearly $1 million. However, the top Zimbabwean player earns just less than $100,000 per year. Additionally, players may earn money through advertising and marketing, appearing in commercials and endorsing products.

The most valuable cricket club in the world is the Board of Cricket Control in India, with a market value of nearly $300 million. The Australian Cricket Board comes in second, with revenues of just more than $100 million. Some of that revenue comes from television contracts. Regional and sports networks throughout South Asia and Europe typically broadcast the sport. U.S. fans of cricket often have to go online to watch live cricket, although American networks periodically will show a match or its highlights.

DIMENSIONS OF THE SPORT

Cricket is played on an oval-shaped field with a rectangular box, called a pitch, in the middle. The pitch, from which the bowler bowls the ball to the opposing team's batsman, is 20.1 meters long by 3 meters wide, although those dimensions can sometimes vary depending on various circumstances.

On both sides of the pitch sits a wicket, three stumps driven into the ground connected on top by two bails. The batsman's job is to protect the wicket using a bat. The bowler bowls the ball from the pitch, and the batsman tries to hit the ball, the result of which could lead to runs. A team's score is determined by the number of wickets lost and runs scored.

The longest, most competitive cricket matches are known as "test matches." The ICC determines which nations earn test-match status. Once earned, they compete against other nations in matches that usually last five days for men and four for women. Even World Cup cricket does not engage in test matches because of the length of the matches. In 2019 the ICC began hosting its first World Test Championship, but it was not concluded until 2021.

IMPORTANT FIGURES

Many consider India's Sunil Gavaskar to be the greatest batsman in cricket history. Gavaskar played test matches between 1971 and 1987 and became the first person to score 10,000 test runs. His record of 34 test centuries—scoring at least 100 runs in a single innings—held for nearly 20 years. In 2012 Indian cricket awarded Gavaskar its lifetime achievement award.

Few players were as influential to or as famous for the game of cricket than W. G. Grace, the British cricketer who batted, bowled, and fielded from 1865 to 1908. Known as an "all arounder" because of competencies at every position, Grace was most well known for his bat and ability to make money—despite being classified as an amateur (Grace was also a doctor).

One of Grace's biographers, Simon Rae, wrote that at Grace's peak, his fame in England was surpassed only by Queen Victoria and former prime minister William Ewart Gladstone. Great Britain commemorated Grace's career on a series of postage stamps in the 1970s. Beyond his success as a cricketer, Grace also stood out for his height of 6 feet, 2 inches and weight that pushed well past 200 pounds, which was large for his era. By comparison King Edward VIII, who was born in the twilight of Grace's life and met the cricketer, stood 5 feet, 7 inches.

POP CULTURE

The 2002 British film *Bend It Like Beckham*, which is about soccer, features an impassioned speech by the main character's father, a person of Indian descent who works at a London airport. In the speech, the man shares with his daughter the heartbreak he felt when he gave up playing his favorite sport, cricket, because of the discrimination he faced against native Brits. At the movie's conclusion, a scene shows that the father has finally returned to playing cricket after decades of self-exile, and he has been joined in the sport by his daughter's boyfriend.

In 2014 Walt Disney Pictures released *Million Dollar Arm*, a film about an American baseball scout who travels to India to find untapped talent. The film's lead character is aware of baseball's historical ties to cricket, but he soon learns that cricket bowling and baseball pitching are two completely different athletic feats. Although he eventually finds two players to sign to baseball contracts, he also learns that similarities between the two games are few and far between.

In the *Hitchhiker* series, Douglas Adams's legendary farcical book series of science fiction, the book *Life, the Universe, and Everything* includes a subplot in which cricket is revealed as an interspecies, universal vessel for "unconscious memory." Unfortunately, humans have loused it up by turning cricket into little more than just another game.

SCANDALS

During the 1932–1933 season, England's national team traveled to Australia for a series of tests. The Australian squad featured some dominant bats, so the English team devised the tactic of bodylining: bowling the ball at the body of

Australian batters in the hopes of forcing them to use the bats to defend themselves, with the balls therefore rolling harmlessly into the playing field instead of in positions to allow the Australians to score runs.

This legal but dirty tactic infuriated Australian fans, and when a ball struck favorite player Bill Woodfull near the heart, a riot nearly broke out. Woodfull, known for his calm demeanor and steadying influence, did not retaliate, but when the English manager later went to apologize, Woodfull spurned the attempt and declared that whatever the English squad might have been playing, it wasn't cricket.

Cricket's gambling influence has led to dozens of players over the decades taking bribes and other payments to alter the outcomes of games and give away insider information to benefit gamblers and themselves. The results for players discovered to have fixed matches ranges from suspensions to lifetime bans, depending on the severity of the crimes. One of the more critical scandals involved three members of the Pakistani national cricket team taking bribes in 2010. The players each received bans from the ICC, and each player as well as a bookmaker were found guilty in British criminal court of fixing the match and received prison sentences.

POLITICS

For nearly a quarter-century, South Africa's policy of apartheid—its official governmental approach to segregating and discriminating against Black people—prevented it from playing competitive international cricket. On September 24, 1968, Britain's Marylebone Cricket Club canceled the English team's tour of South Africa after South African officials refused to let Briton Basil D'Olivera take part.

D'Olivera was of Indian and Portuguese ancestry, which left him on the victim's side of South Africa's apartheid laws. Countries across the world had already started to boycott sporting contests against South Africa because of apartheid, but the D'Olivera Affair, as it came to be known, accelerated South Africa's seclusion. No country played formal international cricket against South Africa from 1971 into the 1980s. South Africa was finally allowed to return to international cricket in 1991, once its apartheid initiative had significantly fallen apart.

Timeline

Late 16th century – Cricket begins to shape into the sport we know today.

1646 – The first recorded cricket match takes place in Kent, England.

1694 – The first instance of a wager being made on a cricket match is documented.

1721 – A cricket match is played on Indian soil for the first time.

1744 – The first known version of the Laws of Cricket is issued by the London Club.

1844 – The United States hosts Canada in the first international cricket match.

1873 – W. G. Grace becomes the first cricketer to record 1,000 and 100 wickets in a season.

1877 – England and Australia engage in the first test match, a match that routinely lasts five days.

1900 – Cricket appears in the Olympics for the first and only time.

1909 – The Imperial Cricket Conference (ICC), which later becomes the International Cricket Conference, is formed.

1970 – The ICC suspends South Africa from international cricket competition because of the South African policy of apartheid. South Africa does not return until 1991, once the government begins to do away with apartheid.

1973 – The first Women's Cricket World Cup is held.

1975 – The first Cricket World Cup for men is held.

1979 – England and Australia engage in the first women's test match 102 years after the same nations played the first men's test match.

1983 – India wins its first Cricket World Cup.

2010 – A bookmaker and three members of the Pakistani national team are jailed for their roles in a cricket gambling scandal.

2019 – The ICC hosts the beginning of its first World Test Championship.

See also: Baseball; Boxing; Olympics.

Further Reading
Cotterill, S. and Barker, J. (2013). *The Psychology of Cricket: Developing Mental Toughness.* Bennion Kearny Limited: Oakamoor, United Kingdom.

Dutta, A. (2017). *A Gentleman's Game: Reflections on Cricket History.* Independent.

Eastaway, R. (1993). *Cricket Explained.* St. Martin's Press: New York.

James, C. L. R. (2013). *Beyond & Boundary: 50th Anniversary Edition.* Duke University Press Books: Durham, North Carolina.

Levison, B. (2016). *Remarkable Cricket Grounds.* Pavilion Books: London.

Majumdar, B. (2018). *Eleven Gods and a Billion Indians: The On and Off the Field Story of Cricket in India and Beyond.* S&S India: New York.

Murray, P. (2019). *World Cup Cricket: A Complete History.* G2 Entertainment: East Sussex, United Kingdom.

Prabhu-Paseband, A. (2019). *An Illustrated Guide to Cricket.* Self-published.

Roberts, A. (2019). *A History & Guide to the Cricket World Cup.* White Owl Books: South Yorkshire, United Kingdom.

Samiudden, O. (2014). *The Unquiet Ones: A History of Pakistan Cricket.* Harper Collins India: Noida, India.

Cross-Country Skiing

The biathlon represents the ultimate test of cold-weather survival: cross-country skiing and shooting. The ability to swiftly and safely navigate snowy, icy terrain combined with the marksmanship to hunt for food is more than a chance to win cash prizes and medals. It is a way of life with both civilian and military roots.

Whether it is in the Arctic conditions of Russia and Northern Europe or an artificially constructed Olympic course, cross-country skiing requires endurance. It is the marathon of winter sports. Some cross-country ski events push their athletes to go farther than a marathon. Speed matters but not like it does in downhill skiing. In cross-country skiing, weather and course conditions push athletes to levels few can comprehend. Imagine 15-degree weather, a blast of arctic wind in your face, with 50 kilometers (about 31 miles) of snowy hills in front of you. In most of the world's races, finishing first is the goal. In cross-country skiing, sometimes the goal is simply being able to finish at all.

HISTORICAL CONTEXT

Cross-country skiing the activity—not the sport—has a long history. Historians once found a ski in Northern Europe they dated to about 4,500 years old. Ancient Scandinavians had to be entrepreneurial if they were going to navigate the region's cold temperatures and great amounts of snow. Cross-country skiing as a military exercise—again, not the sport—also has a centuries-long history. Dutch, Norwegian, and Russian officers enlisted cross-country skiing as a training exercise to increase their troops' strength and endurance. To increase the soldiers' effectiveness, they incorporated shooting into cross-country skiing, laying the groundwork for what would become the biathlon, the Winter Olympic event that tests an athlete's ability to ski and shoot. Endurance skiing, now called cross-country skiing, and an early version of the biathlon were born about the same time in 1766, when a Dutch military officer helped organize a series of skiing contests.

Northern Europe's decision to connect cross-country skiing to military service remained for another 200 years—Norway finally ended the relationship in 1984—but during the interim, skiing also became a popular recreational and competitive activity. Sondre Norheim, born in Norway in the early 1800s, proved one of the most influential figures in the sport's history. He developed a number of skiing techniques that today are considered basic for learning how to ski. Toward the end of his life he immigrated to the United States, to wintry North Dakota, to be closer to his family at a time when Northern Europeans' migration to the United States and Canada was planting the seeds of skiing in North America as well. Norheim died in 1897.

Ski clubs began to form in Europe in the 1860s. In 1892 Norway hosted the first Holmenkollen Ski Festival, an event that continues to this day. Skiing made its way into other parts of Europe with access to mountains and wintry terrain. Germany hosted a skiing competition in 1900 (won by a Norwegian, naturally) and cross-country skiing was by this point both a form of transportation and competition in Austria, Russia, Finland, Switzerland, and other European nations. In 1912 the Netherlands organized what would be the first modern biathlon, with competitors challenged to ski long distances while stopping to shoot along the way, two skills with cultural and military applications.

The International Olympic Committee (IOC) recognized cross-country skiing's popularity among cold-weather nations and included it at the inaugural

Winter Olympics in 1924 in Chamonix, France. The IOC also included a sport called military patrol, which required individuals and teams to combine cross-country skiing, mountaineering, and rifle shooting. Military patrol lacked cross-country skiing's staying power. Its appearance at the 1924 Games would be its first and last at the Olympics, although it did reemerge as an exhibition sport. Nonetheless, it lay the groundwork for the biathlon, which became an Olympic sport in 1960. Biathlon captured fans' attention more than basic cross-country skiing, partially because of its novelty: ski, then shoot, and then continue to ski. By the 1980s the IOC had expanded the number of events under the biathlon umbrella.

GLOBALIZATION

Because athletes need mountains, hills, and enough snow to cross-country ski, not much globalization has occurred in the sport. You are either born in or near a region with the condition, in which case you can participate, or you are not, so you learn a different sport. A quick look up and down the list of all winners of Olympic medals in cross-country skiing might make one think there are just a small handful of countries on the planet. Finland, Norway, Russia/Soviet Union, and Sweden have won more than 75 percent of all medals ever awarded in the sport.

A few other countries have had fleeting moments of glory, including Estonia, Germany, Italy, and Switzerland. Since 1924 the IOC has handed out 508 medals for cross-country skiing. All but five have gone to European nations with access to mountains or other snowy regions. The other five medals have gone to Canada, which has won three, and the United States, which has won two. Biathlon tells a similar story. Since 1960 the IOC has awarded 256 biathlon medals, with European nations winning 253 of them. Canada won the other three.

WHERE IT'S PLAYED TODAY

Although the same nations consistently have produced the most successful cross-country skiers and biathletes, the sports themselves invite competitors from all over the world. Countries from six continents sent representatives to the Olympics, including numerous nations from South America (Argentina, Bolivia, Brazil, Chile, Colombia, and Ecuador), Africa (Togo and Morocco), and Asia (China, India, Japan, Lebanon, Mongolia, North Korea, and South Korea), as well as Australia. None of these has ever medaled in cross-country skiing or biathlon.

ECONOMICS AND MEDIA

Cross-country skiers and biathletes usually make living expenses from their national Olympic organizations and occasionally money through product endorsements. Additionally, professional media do not pay to broadcast the sports beyond what they acquire through Olympic broadcast contracts. In other words, these are not sports in which athletes will become wealthy even though meal expenses might be considerable since they are known to go through as many as 8,000 calories per day while training.

DIMENSIONS OF THE SPORT

On paper biathlon is simple and straightforward: skiing and shooting. The details show that is slightly more complicated. Biathlon courses take skiers along trails or circular routes that consist of either two or four rounds of shooting, depending on the event. Each round requires the skier to hit five targets, which means that in a two-round race, skiers must fire at 10 targets, and in a four-round race, they must fire at 20 targets.

For every shot they miss they are assessed a penalty in one of two ways, depending on the event. The more common penalty, which is used at the Winter Olympics, is they must ski a lap around a 150-meter penalty loop for every target they miss. Usually this lap adds 25 to 30 seconds to their time. Other biathlons, rather than make skiers ski a penalty lap, will instead add a predetermined penalty—30 or 60 seconds—to their overall finishing time. The biathlete who finishes in the quickest amount of time once all penalties have been assessed is the winner.

Cross-country skiing events are organized similar to running races. Distances and conditions differentiate the events. The International Ski Federation currently sanctions the following events, not all of which are competed in by both women and men: 5-kilometer, 10-kilometer, 15-kilometer, 30-kilometer, and 50-kilometer races; 4-by-10-kilometer and 4-by-5-kilometer relays; and individual and team sprints (1.4 kilometers).

IMPORTANT FIGURES

In 1766 Dutchman Carl Schack Rantzau was on top of the military world after being named commander-in-chief of the Norwegian Army. The honor did not last long. By the end of the year, he had lost the position. With more time on his hands, he turned his attention to skiing and its applications to military training. He organized skiing into four separate disciplines, taught skills, and held contests. In doing so, he laid the groundwork for four of the world's most popular cold-weather sports: downhill racing; hurling, which evolved into slalom; long racing, which became cross-country skiing; and shooting while skiing, which today we call biathlon. James Naismith's name will always be remembered as the inventor of basketball. But Rantzau? He gets credit for four sports.

Sometimes we read about history, and sometimes we get to live through it. As of the writing of this book, Switzerland's Dario Cologna is in the midst of what might be the most successful competitive cross-country skiing career the world has ever seen. To date he has won four gold medals across three Olympic Games—2010 in Vancouver, Canada; 2014 in Sochi, Russia; and 2018 in PyeongChang, South Korea—to go along with a World Championship and four World Cup titles.

Although one of his gold medals came at the 30-kilometer distance, his specialty is 15 kilometers. Two of his golds are in 15-kilometer freestyle, and one is in 15-kilometer classical.

POP CULTURE

Neither cross-country skiing nor biathlon has inspired many novels, films, or other art. There are some that toil in obscurity, but it is usually downhill racing that makes for more pop-culture drama, like the downhill chase scene in the 1977 James Bond movie, *The Spy Who Loved Me*, or the 1969 film starring Robert Redford and Gene Hackman, *Downhill Racer*.

The writers who consistently appear most enamored with cross-country skiing and biathlon are journalists at the Olympics, many of whom are seeing them for the first time. First, they note how few fans the sports have and how boring it can be. Then they describe how they become interested and that more people should give the sport a spectating opportunity. "The sport essentially asks you to get yourself all sweaty and worked up and ready to collapse," wrote an American journalist, "and then you have to stop and hit a teeny-tiny target" (Holmes 2010). Although it is clear that some journalists do not understand the sports' military roots, watching them learn more about the sports is almost as fun as watching the sports themselves.

SCANDALS

At the Nordic World Ski Championships in Austria in 2019, five competitors were arrested on-site for blood doping. The scandal rocked the event and the sport when a photo of one of the competitors, taken while he allegedly was in the actual process of doping, leaked to the public. In total, local law enforcement officers arrested nine people. Blood doping is the process of increasing the amount of oxygen that can be carried by red blood cells, which increases a person's stamina. Physical endurance is crucial to success in cross-country skiing.

POLITICS

In the mid-1990s American fitness company Nike threw its money and marketing behind a new generation of athletes. One of its initiatives included sponsoring two Kenyan athletes who hoped to become their country's first-ever entrants into the Winter Olympics. With Nike's backing, both traveled to Finland to train in cross-country skiing. Their training began in winter 1996, just two years before the 1998 Games in Nagano, Japan, and decades behind some of the more experienced cross-country skiers who grew up in Northern Europe.

In the end Kenya was allowed to send just one athlete to the Winter Games—it is unclear whether that was because of qualification rules or other obstacles—and the spot went to Philip Boit. Boit competed in the 10-kilometer classic race, finishing dead last out of 92 competitors. However, in a show of sportsmanship and camaraderie, Norway's Bjørn Dæhlie, who won the race, refused to take the stand to accept his gold medal until Boit finished. The two embraced when Boit crossed the finish line, and years later Boit named his son Dæhlie. Boit continued to ski. He qualified for the 2002 and the 2006 Games, and while he never came close to medaling, he never finished last again after that first race in 1998.

PATRIOTISM AND NATIONAL PRIDE

In 2018, with the Winter Olympic Games in PyeongChang, South Korea, approaching, the most read paper in the United States, the *New York Times*, went deep on cross-country skiing with its article, "What Cross-Country Skiing Reveals about the Human Condition." It asked why anyone would bother to watch or compete in what it called the most boring, unwatchable, grueling event at the Winter Olympics. The paper had a point. If you are there in person, you might catch just a glimpse of the athletes going by; if you are watching on TV, you have no sense of perspective for the size or scope of the course; and if you are competing, the physical toll on your body is more taxing than even the toll absorbed by a marathon runner.

Then the *Times* answered its own question. It was a matter of pride, of defiance—not national pride or the right to hear one's national anthem played, but the pride the human race feels collectively by achieving something physically that seems impossible. "Cross-country skiers are existential heroes in goggles and tights," the author wrote. "Instead of offering us distraction . . . cross-country skiers lean right into a bleak truth: We are stranded on a planet that is largely indifferent to us. . . . Cross-country skiing expresses something deep about the human condition: the absolute, nonnegotiable necessity of the grind" (Anderson 2018).

Timeline

2500 BCE – Ancient Scandinavians build what some archaeologists believe to be the first skis.

1767 CE – Dutch military officer Carl Schack Rantzau classifies four types of skiing contests, including a distance race that evolves into cross-country skiing.

1767 – The first unofficial biathlon is held between platoons of Norwegian soldiers.

1825 – Sondre Norheim, considered the father of modern skiing, is born in Norway.

1843 – Norway hosts one of the first official distance skiing competitions.

1861 – The Trysil Rifle and Ski Club forms in Norway.

1892 – The first Holmenkollen Ski Festival, which continues today, is held in Norway.

1897 – Norheim dies in North Dakota, United States, during a wave of Norwegian immigration that helps spark an interest for skiing in the United States.

1900 – Germany hosts its first distance skiing competition, won by Norwegian Bjame Nilssen.

Early 1900s – Skate skiing is introduced to the sport. The motion eventually becomes the standard for how cross-country skiers compete, but not for decades.

1912 – The Norwegian military organizes the first modern biathlon.

1924 – Cross-country skiing debuts during the first Winter Olympics. Also included for the only time as an official Olympic sport: military patrol, a sport that combines cross-country skiing, mountaineering, and rifle shooting.

1952 – Women's Nordic skiing debuts at the Olympics in Oslo, Norway.

1958 – Austria hosts the first biathlon world-championship event.

1960 – The IOC includes biathlon in the Olympics for the first time.

1970s – The skate style of skiing begins to regain popularity.

1975 – Carbon fiber poles become the sport standard.

1976 – Cross-country skiing first appears at the Paralympics.

1980 – A second individual biathlon event is added to the Winter Olympics.

1982 – American Bill Koch wins the World Cup of cross-country skiing in Norway using the skate step after he observed it in Sweden, sparking a period of controversy about the legitimacy of the approach, which eventually revolutionizes how events, contests, and awards are organized.

1984 – After more than a century, Norway no longer administers biathlon as a tool for national self-defense. Biathlons are still popular but for sport and fitness only.

1992 – Women's biathlon is held in the Olympics for the first time.

1993 – The International Biathlon Union, headquartered in Austria, is formed. Five years later it becomes independent from the International Modern Pentathlon Union.

1998 – Cross-country skier Philip Boit becomes the first Kenyan to compete in the Winter Olympics.

1998 – Three members of the Russia's 4-by-5-kilometer Olympic relay team win their third consecutive gold medal in the event.

2011 – Ski Classic, an eight-event cross-country competition in Europe, debuts.

2018 – Switzerland's Dario Cologna wins gold in the 15-kilometer race at the Winter Olympics in PyeongChang, his third consecutive Olympic gold in the event.

See also: Basketball; Speed Skating.

Further Reading
Anderson, S. (2018). "What Cross-Country Skiing Reveals about the Human Condition." *New York Times*, March 6, 2018. https://www.nytimes.com/interactive/2018/01/31/magazine/winter-olympics-cross-country-skiing.html.

Burns, K. (2009). *Biathlon, Cross Country Skiing, and Nordic Combined*. Crabtree Publishing: St. Catharines, Ontario, Canada.

Diggins, J. (2020). *Brave Enough*. University of Minnesota Press: Minneapolis.

Frank, William D. (2013). *Everyone to Skis! Skiing in Russia and the Rise of Soviet Biathlon*. Northern Illinois University Press: DeKalb, Illinois.

Hindman, S. (2005). *Cross Country Skiing: Building Skills for Fun and Fitness*. The Mountaineers: Seattle, Washington.

Holmes, L. (2010). "Biathlon: The Greatest, Slushiest, Shoot-Em-Uppiest Sport You're Not Watching." National Public Radio, Feb. 16, 2010. https://www.npr.org/2010/02/16/114529431/biathlon-the-greatest-slushiest-shoot-em-uppiest-sport-youre-not-watching.

Liebner, A. (2011). *Wild Shot: Struggles and Successes in Biathlon and Cross Country Skiing*. Xlibris Publishing: Bloomington, Indiana.

McKibben, B. (2010). *Long Distance: Testing the Limits of Body and Spirit in a Year of Living Strenuously*. Rodale Press: Emmaus, Pennsylvania.

Morton, J. (1998). *A Medal of Honor: An Insider Unveils the Agony and Ecstasy of the Olympic Dream*. Book Partners: Manchester, Indiana.

Shinn, P. (2018). *World Class: The Making of the U.S. Women's Cross-Country Ski Team*. ForeEdge: Lebanon, New Hampshire.

Curling

Curling has been called "bocce on ice." "Frozen shuffleboard." It has been made fun of, revered, imitated, and disparaged. Yet since the end of the 20th century, few sports have so quickly captured international attention on the level of curling. Its players and fans championed it so rabidly that in 1924 the International Olympic Committee (IOC) felt compelled to include it in the inaugural Winter Games. But it quickly became clear that other sports created far more buzz than curling, and the IOC removed it from the Games for the next 70 years. The game persevered. It built its fanbase and recruited recreational players; although top-level curling advances physical fitness, it does not require the kinetic fundamentals—strength, speed, power, hand-eye coordination—required by many other sports. So how did curling make its comeback? Drama. It is an easy sport to understand, and it plays at a rate of speed slow enough to build drama. Everyone in the ice arena can see the situation as it develops, then tension builds, and the crowds begin to roar.

HISTORICAL CONTEXT

Curling is a game of stones and ice, two objects found in nature. Sports not dependent upon the Industrial Revolution typically hold origins that run thousands of years deep, such as track and field, wrestling, and swimming. Curling, however, falls somewhere in between. The game appears to have been invented during the early 16th century, a quarter of a millennium before the Industrial Revolution yet well after ancient times. Its invention is more about intelligent, creative people making do with the objects around them: rocks, ice, and broomsticks.

Scottish locals invented curling around 1511, to which the earliest-known curling stone is dated, as a way to pass time during bitterly cold winter months. From the beginning curling was a team sport, making it one of the world's first to emphasize individual cooperation as much as head-to-head competition. Today's curling stones include handles for easier travel, movement, and storage, but in the game's earliest days, since stones do not typically form naturally with their own handles, players sought stones of a proper weight with at least one flat, relatively smooth side. Curlers began to carve handles into stones during the 17th century, about a century after the game's invention.

Curling caught up to the modern era at a predictable time: the mid-1800s. As curling's birth occurred in the United Kingdom, it joined many other UK sports that came of age during this period, including soccer, tennis, cricket, and rugby. No longer were people content to meet nonchalantly at a frozen pond to play on some random day, adjusting rules according to local or regional customs. It was time to get serious. In 1838 a group of curling supporters in Scotland formed the Grand Caledonian Curling Club. They demonstrated curling for England's Queen Victoria, who enjoyed the exhibition and gave it her blessing, which led to a name change in 1843 to the Royal Caledonian Curling Club.

Although it had already existed for 300 years before the royal demonstration, there was room for improvement. For one, the sport was dependent on weather. Two local teams could schedule an important match, but if the weather unexpectedly warmed, the ice over the pond might be too weak to host the match, so it would have to be canceled. Advances in refrigeration during the Industrial Revolution made indoor ice rinks sustainable. That enabled the Royal Caledonian Curling Club to be able to sponsor matches with less fear of whether the weather would cooperate. Another development that benefited curling was standardization of the rules, including delivery, which is the process by which the stone is slid ("delivered") down the ice by one of the players before that player's teammates begin the process of "sweeping," or manipulating the stone to the desired location. Both of these advances occurred during the mid-19th century, although outdoor curling at that point was still more popular—and far more available because of lack of access to new technologies—than indoor curling. In fact, curling's first appearance at the Winter Olympics, in 1924, took place at an outside facility.

GLOBALIZATION

Although Scotland is the indisputable home to curling, today the country most associated with it is Canada. This, too, should be credited to the Scots, who brought curling to Canada when they immigrated in the early 1800s. The first curling club in North America, the Royal Montreal Curling Club, was founded in 1807, and by the end of the century, curling had found homes in Sweden, Switzerland, and Canada's southern neighbor, the United States.

That it took place in the first Winter Olympics should be considered a minor miracle, given its lack of international support at that time. One reason for its inclusion might have been its popularity in Canada, the United Kingdom, and the northern United States, all of whom held some sway within the IOC. That first appearance was probably too soon for the sport, which was not ready for that level of exposure. For example, the first curling world championship did not even take place until 1959, 35 years after it attempted to become an Olympic sport. By contrast, figure skating had started holding its world championships decades before the first Winter Olympics, not afterward.

Because of the lack of initial interest, the IOC removed curling from the winter program for decades. It did not return to the Olympic stage until the 1998 Winter Games in Nagano, Japan. By then, curling had been able to grow up internationally. More countries developed curling programs, including Brazil, China, Japan, and New Zealand. Whereas criteria for Olympic inclusion a century ago meant someone lobbied hard enough for a sport, today a sport must meet certain markers, including oversight and administration on national and regional levels. Since 1998 the following 10 countries have won medals in Olympic curling: Canada, China, Denmark, Finland, Great Britain, Japan, Norway, South Korea, Switzerland, and the United States.

WHERE IT'S PLAYED TODAY

Curling takes place all over the world, although it is more popular in cold-weather regions such as Northern Europe and Canada than in warmer-weather climates, such as Brazil. Curling can return to its roots and be played recreationally. For example, curling lessons were offered in the midwestern American state of Iowa, typically known for its massive agricultural production and devotion to the niche, ancient sport of amateur wrestling. Competitive curling is mostly reserved to countries with strong economies, such as China and Japan, and a tradition of enjoying outdoor winter sports, such as Canada and Finland.

ECONOMICS AND MEDIA

Curling can be a tough way to earn a living. According to various curling organizations, only the 10 best curlers in the world (women and men) are likely to make more than $40,000 a year, with the top two or three earning as much as $100,000. Money is made through curling tours across the world, a way of generating revenue for the sport and showing appreciation to the sport's hard-core fans. Most curlers outside the top 10 earn between $100 and $39,000 a year, which means most curlers compete in the sport as a hobby or side job while holding down full-time jobs in careers outside of curling.

Just because earning potential remains humble does not mean the sport has lost popularity. To the contrary, it has become one of the world's most recognizable cold-weather sports, along with figure skating, skiing, ice hockey, and a few others. The problem for those looking to make a living in curling is that, outside of the Olympics, it is a niche sport. Networks that broadcast the Olympics have begun to show curling because audiences demanded it. That is the good news for curling. The bad news is that polling firms that track the popularity of winter sports consistently report that once the Olympics are over, curling finishes near the bottom of the world's most popular winter sports.

DIMENSIONS OF THE SPORT

The goal of curling is to get your team's stone closer to the button (target) than the other team's. Teams are 4 per side, and matches consist of 10 ends, which are like innings in baseball. Each team gets to deliver 16 stones per end, which means each of the 4 players on each team gets to deliver, or push, the stone twice per end, for a total of 20 deliveries per player per match. Teams can consist of all women, all men, or mixed genders.

The first team member to deliver their stones is called the lead. The second is just called the "second," the third is what is known as the vice skip, and the fourth, or anchor, is known as the skip. Often the skip is like the captain, who calls out directions throughout the match about stone placement and other matters. The button is at the center of the 12-foot "house," which other sports might refer to as bull's-eye. Two players have brooms they use to control friction on the ice. The more vigorously the sweepers sweep, the less friction between the ice and the stone. Each throw is performed to complete one of two purposes: to get as close to the button as possible, or to knock an opponent's stone out of the way.

Score is determined at the conclusion of each end based on which team has more stones closer to the button than the other team. Points from each of the 10 ends are totaled to determine the winner. Games can take place on their own (e.g., Canada vs. Denmark), or they can be part of a larger tournament of teams known as a bonspiel, which can take place over multiple days. The largest bonspiel takes place annually in Winnipeg, Manitoba, Canada. It has been hosted by the Manitoba Curling Association (MCA) since 1888 and has been known to draw more than 1,000 teams from around the world to a single event.

IMPORTANT FIGURES

Few curlers in history have had as much local and international success as Canada's Jennifer Jones. Jones, a native of Manitoba, Canada, has been part of 11 Manitoba provincial championship teams and 6 Canadian national championship teams, tied for most among any Canadian curler. In 2014 she represented Canada's women's team at the Winter Olympics in Sochi, Russia, where she served as skip. Canada won gold without losing a single game, the first time a women's Olympic team had accomplished that feat.

Norwegian curler Thomas Ulsrud is known for his success on the ice. He is a two-time European champion, owns an Olympic silver medal, and holds the curling world record for most wins while playing skip at the World Curling Championships. But in 2010 at the Vancouver Winter Olympics, Ulsrud turned heads for something else altogether. He wore bright, gaudy pants that stood out from the rest of the sport's conservative sportswear, most of which could pass for business casual or relaxed attire, depending on the team's preferences. The pants were made by a little-known company called Loudmouth Golf LLC. The pants proved so attention-grabbing that the American news company ABC even did a story, which in itself was a big deal since it was not the American broadcast rights holder to the Olympics. ABC producers realized the pants had created such a stir that it was time to do a story for its viewers.

POP CULTURE

In 2002 Canadian-based Serendipity Point Films tried to capitalize on its country's interest in curling. In the two Olympics since curling had returned from obscurity, Canada teams had medaled four out of a possible four times: a gold and a bronze in women's events and two silvers in the men's. Enter *Men with Brooms*, a film about four down-on-their luck men reuniting their curling team. The movie performed poorly, earning $3 million less worldwide than the meager $7.5 million it cost to make. The film remains notable for two of its actors: Leslie Nielsen, the legendary Canadian actor who reinvented his career as a comedic actor in the 1980s, and Molly Parker, the character actor who won praise for television roles in such critically acclaimed shows as *Deadwood* and the U.S. version of *House of Cards*.

Curling also made a cameo in the Beatles' 1965 film *Help!* The film centers loosely around the legendary band's attempt to protect its drummer, Ringo Starr, from thieves. In one scene Starr and bandmates George Harrison, John Lennon, and Paul McCartney play curling but have to run because one of the stones is a bomb. According to Starr in a documentary about the band years later, he and McCartney kept running long after the director called "Cut" until they felt they were far enough away to smoke marijuana without getting caught.

SCANDALS

"I think most people will laugh" (Keating 2018). Those were the words of a Danish curler when she learned in 2018 that a Russian curler had tested positive for performance-enhancing drugs (PEDs). The joke was not lost on Madeleine Dupont, the Danish curler. Most Olympic athletes caught using PEDs use them to enhance strength, speed, or biological recovery time. Curlers do not particularly need any of those enhancements since their sport involves precision and—for the sweepers—endurance.

The doping violation proved problematic for two reasons. First, it was embarrassing. Curlers are keenly aware that some see their sport as a joke. Second, and more significantly, Russia was already deep in a multiyear doping scandal that had the world's attention. Athletes across numerous sports, now including—it seemed—curling, were caught for putting illegal substances in their body. The Russian curler was just the latest example. In December 2019 the World Anti-Doping Agency finally had enough. It banned Russia from all international sports for four years. Some Russian athletes would be able to compete, but the scope of the infractions was so wide and so deep that the country itself could not be represented, meaning Russian athletes allowed to compete in the Olympics and other international events would have to do so as individuals, not as representatives of their country.

POLITICS

In 2019 the British and Norwegian curling teams found themselves embroiled in controversy—low-stakes curling controversy—when Norway's team thought it had won, only to be disqualified because one of its players used the wrong broom. According to curling rules, an alternate entering the game must use the broom of the sweeper the alternate has replaced, but in this case the Norwegian sweeper used his own broom. Norwegian curling fans were irate, but the ruling stood. Rules are rules.

PATRIOTISM AND NATIONAL PRIDE

Canadian curling has led the nation's sports in the acceptance and championing of the LGBTQ community. The nation for decades has led the world in LGBTQ causes. As of 2016, Canada included 12 LGBTQ curling leagues that featured hundreds of teams, the first of which debuted and was out to the public during the 1960s. There is even an annual Canadian Gay Curling Championships. Although leagues are billed as being LGBTQ, people of all sexualities are encouraged to take part.

Timeline

1511 – Scots create what are believed to be the earliest-known curling stones.

1600s – Stones with handles are introduced.

1838 – The first official curling club, the Grand Caledonian Curling Club, is formed in Scotland. It is credited with creating the official rules of the sport.

1843 – Queen Victoria renames the club the Royal Caledonian Curling Club after a curling demonstration.

1924 – Curling is introduced internationally during the first Winter Olympics. It does not return to the Olympics until 1998.

1959 – Scotland and Canada launch the Scotch Cup series.

1961–1967 – The United States, Sweden, Norway, Switzerland, France, and Germany join the Scotch Cup, in that order.

1966 – The International Curling Federation is created.

1967 – The United States joins the International Curling Federation.

1979 – The Ladies' Curling Championship is created.

1989 – The World Curling Championships debut. Women's and men's championships and junior championships for each are held.

1990 – The International Curling Federation is renamed the World Curling Federation.

1992 – Curling is granted official medal status for the 2002 Olympics, with possible inclusion in the 1998 Games.

1998 – Curling returns to the Winter Olympics.

2002 – The first World Wheelchair Curling Championship takes place.

2005 – The Men's and Women's Championships are separated and held in different parts of the world.

2008 – The first World Mixed Doubles Curling Championship is held.

2012 – Curling takes place in the inaugural Youth Olympic Winter Games.

2014 – A curling sculpture, *Curling: Pure Emotion*, is unveiled in the Olympic Museum Park in Lausanne, Switzerland.

See also: Figure Skating; Ice Hockey.

Further Reading

Chick, B. (2018). *Written in Stone: A Modern History of Curling*. CreateSpace Independent Publishing Platform: Scotts Valley, California.

Gutman, D. (2018). *My Weird School: Teamwork Trouble*. HarperCollins: New York.

Howard, R. (2014). *Curl to Win: Expert Advice to Improve Your Game*. HarperCollins: New York.

Jones, C. (2015). *Throwing Rocks at Houses: My Life in and out of Curling*. Viking Books: New York.

Keating, S. (2018). "Bemused Curlers Ask 'Why Would Anyone Dope in Our Sport?'" Reuters, Feb. 18, 2018. https://www.reuters.com/article/us-olympics-2018-doping-curling/bemused-curlers-ask-why-would-anyone-dope-in-our-sport-idUSKCN1G30AN.

Mitchell, W. O. (1993). *The Black Bonspiel of Willie MacCrimmon*. McClelland & Stewart: Toronto, Ontario, Canada.

Richardson, E. (1962). *Curling: An Authoritative Handbook of the Techniques and Strategy of the Ancient Game of Curling*. Thomas Allan: London.

Russell, S. (2003). *Open House: Canada and the Magic of Curling*. Doubleday: New York.

Turriff, S. (2016). *Curling: Steps to Success*. Human Kinetics: Champaign, Illinois.

Weeks, B. (2008). *Curling, Etcetera: A Whole Bunch of Stuff about the Roaring Game*. Wiley: Hoboken, New Jersey.

Cycling

Cycling is one of the world's most popular activities. It's also an exciting sport because of its speed, danger, technological innovation, and beautiful scenery. Whereas many sports take place inside an arena and on a court or a field, cycling might take place along a scenic countryside, next to a pristine beach, or through treacherous mountains.

It's hard to imagine a world without bicycles, but they are a relatively new invention, coming along in the 19th century. They became so popular by the turn of the 20th century that they crashed the horse-sale industry. Everyone wanted a

Cycling races can take place in velodromes, indoor facilities designed specifically for the sport, or outdoors on closed-off streets, such as this race in Canada (pictured). Off-road races also exist and require different types of bicycles and tires. (Sergei Bachlakov/Shutterstock)

bike. The enthusiasm never completely waned, but the advent and proliferation of automobiles did cut into the market. By the mid-20th century, however, interest in cycling returned.

Competitive racers and fans found plenty of outlets for their passion, and their options were diverse. Some racing took place on roads—even as cars whipped by. Other races took place on closed road courses. Some took place in specially designed arenas called velodromes, while others still took place among dirt, trees, and hills.

Cycling tests a rider's endurance, power, balance, and speed. Crashes can be vicious, bloody spectacles. Imagine a five-car pileup in which none of the drivers could wear seatbelts. For spectators, cycling represents an exhilarating thrill ride. Riders pedaling downhill can accelerate past 60 miles per hour, and they can come through in large packs. Most key to the sport is how relatable it is. Spectators of auto racing would get arrested if they tried to go as fast as auto racers; baseball spectators will never get to throw a baseball 100 miles per hour—if they did, they would be players, not spectators. But in cycling, spectators fuel the sport because once the race is over, they can go home to their own bikes and imagine what it must feel like to reach unimaginable speeds on a bicycle.

HISTORICAL CONTEXT

Long before fitness culture enveloped the 21st century, before the aerobics and jazzercise fads swept the 1980s, before the Cold War pushed average citizens across the globe to address their physical conditioning, and even before U.S. president Theodore Roosevelt implored his constituents to undertake competitive sports and calisthenics to improve their quality of life, cycling was all the rage.

Bicycles came along in the early 19th century. They were interesting but clunky at first. By the end of the century, technological advancements had made them lighter and easier to control, and once the average person was able to buy and operate one, it was only a matter of time before cycling moved from recreational activity and means of transportation into a full-blown sport. The first cycling race took place in 1868, but the sport really took off in the 1890s and was part of the first modern Olympic Games in 1896.

The sport proved popular for both men and women—in fact, it was so alluring to the latter that it changed the United States' fashion sensibilities. Women began buying bloomers in droves because they allowed them to ride bicycles more comfortably. Suffragist Susan B. Anthony said the bicycle "has done more to emancipate women than anything else in the world" (Dawson 2011). The League of American Wheelmen consisted of 40 members in 1880 and 200,000 in 1898. According to the magazine *Mental Floss*, it was around this time that the *New York Journal of Commerce* estimated that cycling's popularity cost America's entertainment industries, such as movie theaters, more than $100 million annually in revenue, which in today's dollars comes to a little more than $3 billion.

Cycling's popularity included East Asian and Western European markets. To help boost revenue, a French newspaper in 1903 created a long bicycle race. That race—the Tour de France—has evolved into the most prestigious cycling race in the world. The annual 21-day event draws spectators from all over the world and broadcasts in multiple languages. Oddly, even though cycling represented one of the first sports that women eagerly competed in, and even though the Tour de France has been held for more than a century, it remains open exclusively to men.

GLOBALIZATION

Cycling spread because of bicycles' practical use in everyday life. As a form of transportation, they were useful—life-changing, even—across the world. That some chose to race with their bikes proved secondary to the commercial side of cycling. There was money to be made, and bicycle manufacturers and repair people found they could generate revenue whether they operated out of China, India, Brazil, France, the United States, or anywhere else where having a bike would make someone's life easier.

To understand the global expansion of cycling is to understand business manufacturing and finance, not sport. An understanding of human nature also helps. People like to go fast, and they like to see who can go faster, whether it's by running, driving, riding a horse—or pedaling a bicycle.

WHERE IT'S PLAYED TODAY

Cycling races take place all over the world, but they have their strongest professional presence in Europe. Races annually take place in Belgium, Germany, Great Britain, Ireland, Netherlands, Spain, and Turkey. Races also take place in Hong Kong, Australia, Puerto Rico, and other points across the world.

In the early 21st century, many countries have returned to cycling as a cost-effective means of public transportation. Some countries and cities have made bicycles available to the general public, which boosts fitness and might reduce pollution caused by automobiles. Additionally, tourism bureaus across the world estimate that cycling opportunities generate tens of billions of dollars annually to the global tourism industry.

ECONOMICS AND MEDIA

One reason bicycles for recreational use or for basic transportation are so popular around the world is that they are relatively low cost. A good road bike, however, one that can be used for competitive racing, comes with a hefty price tag and serves as a barrier to entry to many who may want to enter the sport. The most low-end road bike costs about $500, while a high-end bike can cost north of $15,000. That does not include regular maintenance costs, tire replacement, and other expenses. The average cost of a Tour de France bike, according to *Fortune* magazine, is about $12,000.

The Tour de France winner will earn about 500,000 Euros, and all combined the event hands out about 2.5 million Euros in prize money. Professional cyclists earn money at events around the world, but they can earn far more in endorsements. Many of their expenses are paid by sponsors—companies that pay for the riders and their crews' salaries, travel, and equipment.

Most media coverage of cycling occurs during one of two events: the Tour de France and the Summer Olympics. Various Olympic trials and other professional events periodically appear on networks throughout the world. The National Broadcasting Company (NBC) in the United States pays about $10 million a year for the rights to broadcast the Tour de France, and each day about 200,000 people watch part of a stage. That number nearly doubled when American Lance Armstrong took part. NBC also offered an online, commercial-free Tour experience, charging diehard cycling fans $50 for access.

DIMENSIONS OF THE SPORT

There are a number of different types of cycling races, each with its own rules and parameters.

Road racing takes place on public roads and divides into three categories: road races, criteriums, and time trials. They can take place over one day or multiple days, as individual or team events. A criterium takes place on a closed circuit, meaning the riders complete laps of varying lengths. Road races typically are point to point.

Track races take place on tracks made specifically for cycling called velodromes. Velodromes vary in length, from 150 to 500 meters per cycle. Like road racing, track racing can be an individual or team event. Velodromes consist of two steep banked turns and two longer straightaways.

Motocross racing, sometimes called BMX, is known for riders going head-to-head on dirt, hilly tracks. Cyclo-cross combines BMX traits with mountain biking and road races. In cyclo-cross, riders brave a mix of paved and dirt roads, plus hills, stairs, and other obstacles.

IMPORTANT FIGURES

In Indianapolis, Indiana, one can find a velodrome named after Major Taylor, an Indianapolis native. Taylor, an African American, faced racism his entire career as a racing cyclist. Despite that, he won the sprint event at the 1899 Track Cycling World Championships in Montreal. He won again in 1900. From 1896 to 1907, Taylor was one of the sport's most dominant competitors, racing all over the world. His life story since has become the subject of numerous biographies. Despite his success, he faced racial discrimination throughout his career and life. Jim Crow laws throughout the United States prevented him from competing in some locations. He died at age 53 in 1932 in poverty.

Today, those who work in marketing talk about "branding" and entrepreneurship, but in the late 19th century, Annie Kopchovsky, who sold advertising in the local newspaper to help support her husband and three children, became the first person to bicycle around the world. She left Chicago at the end of September 1894 with the motivation to complete her journey in less than 12 months, and if she did so while earning money along the way, she would win $10,000 as part of a wager. She returned to Chicago mid-September 1895, two weeks ahead of the deadline, and collected her money. She made her trip not as Annie Kopchovsky but as Annie Londonderry because of a marketing deal she struck with Londonderry Lithia Spring Water Company.

Denise Mueller-Koronek is the fastest cyclist who ever lived. In September 2018 she rode her custom-built carbon bicycle 183.932 miles per hour, shattering the previous record by 16 mph. She received a tow up to 90 miles per hour, then rode in the slipstream of the car in front of her until she reached the new record mark.

POP CULTURE

The premise of the 1979 movie *Breaking Away* might sound absurd: a young Indiana man obsessed with the Italian cycling team tries to win over his crush. It starred a young Dennis Quaid and Daniel Stern and burst onto the scene in the wake of film powerhouses such as *Star Wars* and *Apocalypse Now*, and with a small fraction of their budget. But the movie was a hit, eventually earning nearly eight times its small budget and becoming a favorite rewatch during the early days of cable television and videocassette recorders (VCRs).

> **From Seven Titles Down to None**
>
> Greg LeMond in 1989 became the first American to win the Tour de France since its 1903 inception. When he again won the following year, it appeared U.S. competitive cycling had finally arrived, and when a decade later Lance Armstrong became the second American to win—and subsequently won seven straight Tour championships—American cycling was on top of the world.
>
> However, rather than take his place atop cycling's all-time greats, Armstrong took the lead role in one of the ugliest scandals in sports. Armstrong, it turned out, had been cheating through what in cycling is known as doping, a sophisticated, coordinated process of using performance-enhancing drugs and other methods to gain an unfair competitive advantage. After years of whispers and allegations, the sport's officials finally accumulated enough evidence to strip Armstrong of his Tour de France titles and ban him from the sport permanently, even though he was already near retirement age.
>
> The scandal rocked the cycling world and disappointed Armstrong's legions of fans, who for years had defended him against the accusations. Many felt inspired by Armstrong's back story: early in his cycling career, Armstrong developed, and then defeated, a potentially fatal form of cancer. His recovery earned him hero status in cycling, throughout the sports world and in mainstream culture.
>
> That is why Armstrong's fall from grace left so many feeling disappointed. The U.S. Anti-Doping Agency said Armstrong led the "most sophisticated, professionalized, and successful doping program that sport has ever seen" (Boren 2012). He even chose to resign from the Livestrong Foundation, his hugely successful nonprofit designed to help people affected by cancer. The Tour de France record books now say that from 1999 to 2005, there was no winner.
>
> And the only American to win the event? Greg LeMond.

Believe it or not, since 1986 there have been not one but two major motion pictures made about bike messengers who run into trouble with criminals. Actor Kevin Bacon portrayed a stock trader turned delivery rider who squares off against a criminal in 1986's *Quicksilver*, a box-office disappointment. In 2012 actor Joseph Gordon-Levitt starred in *Premium Rush* as a delivery rider pursued by a dirty police officer. That, too, performed poorly in front of audiences.

Competitive cycling's most successful venture into pop culture occurred not in fictional movies, but in real life. Academy Award–winning actor and comedian Robin Williams adored cycling and regularly attended the Tour de France before his death in 2014. Williams, himself an avid cyclist and a good friend to American rider Lance Armstrong, championed the sport, speaking on its behalf to share his passion and interest.

SCANDALS

Four riders have won five Tour de France events. They are tied for the record. American Lance Armstrong won seven in a row. So why isn't he considered the record holder? Because technically, he won zero. He was stripped of his victories. For more details, see the sidebar.

PATRIOTISM AND NATIONAL PRIDE

One of the most beautiful components of the Tour de France—other than racing—is the spectators who turn fan-watching into part of the event. One way they do this is by waving flags of the home countries of the riders whom they support. Waves of flags from Finland, Argentina, Germany, the United States, Italy, France, and others dot the viewing landscape with numerous flowing colors.

Winners become heroes in their home countries, meet celebrities, become celebrities, and often go on riding and speaking tours throughout their respective countries. In the United States, Lance Armstrong, before having his victories vacated, received the prestigious accolade of appearing on the front of a Wheaties cereal box, an honor previously reserved for American sports legends such as track and field star Jesse Owens, baseball player Lou Gehrig, and Olympic gold-medal gymnast Mary Lou Retton. Armstrong also headlined RAGBRAI, an annual bicycle trek across the state of Iowa, made a cameo in the popular comedy film *Dodgeball*, dated singer Sheryl Crow, and was honored by former U.S. president George W. Bush.

Timeline

1817 – German Karl Drais invents the "Hobby Horse," or "Draisine," a feat of engineering that plants the seeds of what becomes the bicycle.

1868 – Briton James Moore wins what is alleged to be the first bicycle race, in St. Cloud, in the suburbs of Paris, although there is some dispute as to whether his race was actually the first.

1869 – The term *bicycle* is first used.

1880 – As cycling's popularity begins to grow, a group comes together to lobby for better quality roads. They're known as the League of American Wheelmen.

1895 – Annie Londonderry completes her 11-month bike trip around the world.

1895–1902 – The success of women's cycling races across the United States challenges misconceptions of women's athletics.

1896 – Cycling is part of the first modern Olympics.

1899 – The first subminute mile on a bike is ridden.

1903 – Bicycle builders and mechanics Orville and Wilbur Wright fly the first airplane.

1903 – The Tour de France, the world's premier cycling race, is held for the first time. As of 2019, women still were not allowed to compete.

1919 – The legendary "yellow jersey," ridden each stage by the Tour de France's front-runner, is introduced.

1966 – Tour de France competitors go on strike to protest midroute drug tests.

1984 – Women compete in Olympic cycling for the first time.

1995 – Spain's Miguel Indurain wins his fifth consecutive Tour de France. He is one of only four people to win the event five times and the only cyclist to win it five consecutive years.

2005 – American Lance Armstrong wins the last of seven consecutive Tour de France titles. He later is stripped of all of them because of doping.

2008 – BMX racing becomes an Olympic sport.

2018 – Denise Mueller-Koronek reaches a world-record 183 miles per hour on her bike.

See also: Horse Racing; Track and Field.

Further Reading

Albergotti, R. and O'Connell, V. (2014). *Wheelmen: Lance Armstrong, the Tour de France, and the Greatest Sports Conspiracy Ever.* Avery Publishing: New York.

Armstrong, L. and Jenkins, S. (2001). *It's Not about the Bike: My Journey Back to Life.* Berkley Trade: New York.

Boren, C. (2012). "Lance Armstrong Was at Center of Doping Program, USADA Says." *Washington Post*, Oct. 10, 2012. https://www.washingtonpost.com/news/early-lead/wp/2012/10/10/lance-armstrong-was-at-center-of-doping-program-usada-says.

Dawson, L. (2011). "How the Bicycle Became a Symbol of Women's Emancipation." *The Guardian*, Nov. 4, 2011. https://www.theguardian.com/environment/bike-blog/2011/nov/04/bicycle-symbol-womens-emancipation.

Gilles, R. (2018). *Women on the Move: The Forgotten Era of Women's Bicycle Racing.* University of Nebraska Press: Lincoln.

Hamilton, T. (2013). *The Secret Race: Inside the Hidden World of the Tour de France.* Bantam Books: New York.

Holl, J. (2017). *Downhills Don't Come Free: One Man's Bike Ride from Alaska to Mexico.* Wise Ink Creative Publishing: Minneapolis, Minnesota.

Kranish, M. (2019). *The World's Fastest Man: The Extraordinary Life of Cyclist Major Taylor, America's First Black Sports Hero.* Scribner: New York.

Moore, R. (2012). *Slaying the Badger: Greg LeMond, Bernard Hinault, and the Greatest Tour de France.* VeloPress: Boulder, Colorado.

Veltkamp, M. (2016). *The Hidden Motor: The Psychology of Cycling.* Dark River Publishing: Farwell, Michigan.

Diving

Imagine if someone said, "I wonder what would happen if we combined two sports like, say, gymnastics and swimming." You could respond that someone already did, and that sport is called diving. In the sport of diving, rosters are littered with competitors who began their careers as gymnasts—athletes with unparalleled control over the movement of their bodies. They came to diving after establishing a gymnastics base; perhaps they switched to diving because of the thrill of jumping headfirst off a 10-meter platform, or because the swimming pool was more forgiving to their ankle and knee joints than a gymnastics mat. Either way, diving is a sport of strength, finesse, and bodily control, and definitely not for the faint of heart. What many overlook, however, is that despite the sport's requirement to harness the power of the human body, it ultimately is about grace. The way to impress judges is not a thunderous splash, but to jump from high above and enter the water far below as quietly and delicately as possible, disturbing as little as possible.

HISTORICAL CONTEXT

Cliff diving and recreational diving go back hundreds of years, but diving as competitive sport—or training for competitive sport—dates to the late 18th century, when gymnasts used diving to help train. Diving, or in those days performing gymnastics over water, allowed gymnasts to try new, complicated moves with less fear of suffering injury. Landing awkwardly on one's head on a gymnastics mat is potentially paralyzing, while landing awkwardly on one's head in the water is little more than embarrassing. German and Norwegian gymnasts are believed to be the first competitive divers. By the mid- to late 19th century, diving and a similar sport called plunging were their own sports. Each had the goal of performing gymnastics in midair while producing as little splash as possible upon entry into water.

Swedish divers toured Great Britain in the late 19th century. As was the case often during the Victorian era, the British became smitten with the sport and quickly bureaucratized it. Training became regimented, an organized body was formed (the American Diving Association in 1901), and the sport was transmitted throughout the British Empire. It was also during this period that it became apparent Europeans did not have exclusive rights with regard to diving history. Hawaiians, for example, trace their cliff-diving roots to the mid- to late 1700s. At first diving existed as a military exercise. Soldiers plunged off high cliffs to show their loyalty to the king or to prove their bravery. Within a couple of decades, they were diving off cliffs to see who could dive off cliffs the best—in other words, it became a competition.

Because diving came of age during the early years of the modern Olympics, what fans see today resembles what they would have seen during the early 20th century. Not all events remain the same—there no longer exists a separate category for professional sailors—but there remain uniform heights and surfaces from which to plunge. Dives from lower heights, about 3 meters, take place on a springboard, or what recreational swimmers might recognize as a traditional diving board. Dives from higher heights, typically 10 meters, happen off platforms made of concrete or other materials, the thought being that because of wind and greater potential for danger, a wider, sturdier surface was needed. Still, early diving officials did tinker a little with events. Plain high diving disappeared after the 1924 Olympics, although it has made a bit of a comeback in the early 21st century, just not in the Olympics. Plunge for distance, an event that measured how far divers could travel underwater without coming up for air after diving in, was featured only in the 1904 Games in St. Louis.

Diving's newest adopted event is synchronized diving, in which two people spring off side-by-side diving boards, perform the same acrobatic maneuvers, and attempt to enter the water at the same moment, having completed identical routines. Casual sports fans became aware of synchronized diving when it debuted at the 2000 Olympics in Australia.

GLOBALIZATION

Again, because of the Olympics, competitive diving spread almost all at once. Popular in Western Europe, Hawaii and other Polynesian areas, and parts of the continental United States, once diving debuted at the Olympics, its popularity dispersed around the globe, mostly in countries with warmer climates and access to water and, later, countries with enough economic infrastructure to build indoor facilities.

Diving's most significant global shift occurred in 1984, when China was finally allowed to compete. China has dominated since entering the sport. In 1984, its first year, Zhou Jihong won Olympic gold in the women's 10-meter platform, while China also earned silver in the men's 3 meters and bronze in men's 10 meters. That was just the beginning. Chinese divers have won gold in the 3-meter women's springboard in every Olympics since then, beginning in 1988, and in five of those eight games, China has won both gold and silver. Chinese divers have been almost equally as dominant in the 10-meter women's platform, winning six of the last eight gold medals.

On the men's side, Chinese divers have earned four of the last five 3-meter gold medals and four of the last seven 10-meter gold medals. The last five Olympic Games have included synchronized diving. China's women's team has won all five gold medals at 10 meters, and the men's team has won four of the five gold medals awarded in the same event. Over the nine Olympic Summer Games in which China has been allowed to compete in diving, a total of 177 diving medals have been awarded; China has won 69 of those medals (39 percent), including 40 of a possible 72 gold medals (56 percent).

WHERE IT'S PLAYED TODAY

Diving today takes place across the world on all continents. The proliferation of indoor swimming and diving facilities has removed the weather barrier for many countries, although warm-weather nations own an inherent advantage because children become acclimated to water from a young age. Consider Olympic medals awarded during just the 21st century. In the men's 10-meter platform, medalists have come from China, Russia, Australia, Great Britain, Mexico, and the United States, while in the women's 10 meter, medalists have come from China, Canada, Australia, Malaysia, and the United States.

Meanwhile, 21st century 3-meter medalists in both women's and men's have come from China, Germany, Russia, Mexico, and Italy, Canada, Great Britain, and the United States. Throw in synchronized medalists, which includes Ukraine, and in just this new millennium already 11 countries on four continents have earned Olympic medals. In the previous century other countries that earned medals included Egypt, Sweden, Denmark, Czechoslovakia, and France.

ECONOMICS AND MEDIA

Divers who are not able to strike an endorsement deal are not going to make much money. Their training, lodging, and meals will be supported by their nation's sports authority or Olympic training committee, but beyond that nearly all of their income will come from endorsements or winning Olympic medals. Even winning Olympic gold, however, does not guarantee financial success. Gold medal bonuses for diving fall somewhere between $35,000 and $75,000, and since the Summer Olympics come around only once every four years, that bonus does not last long.

Even more striking is how little media buzz divers generate. American Greg Louganis (see "Important Figures"), who has not competed since 1988, remains the only diver most Americans can name. The only international diver in the last 30 years whose stature has approached Louganis's is Great Britain's Tom Daley, who to date has won just two bronze medals but nevertheless captured attention as a teen idol. He does have three world championships and a book to his name. Years after his retirement, Louganis was asked whether his status as a gay athlete blocked endorsement opportunities. Louganis said perhaps, but it was more likely that he was overshadowed by American Olympians from more popular sports, such as gymnastics.

DIMENSIONS OF THE SPORT

Competitive cliff diving is what it sounds like: diving off a cliff. A cliff might be 25 feet, 50 feet, or 100 feet high—there is no telling. Cliffs were formed by millions of years of geological and meteorological phenomena. Both platform and springboard diving are more controllable. Today, nearly all competitive diving takes place on either a 3-meter springboard—or diving board—or a 10-meter platform. Even the synchronized competitions take place at 3- and 10-meter heights.

Similar to figure skating and gymnastics, diving is considered an artistic sport. It is won by completing challenges that require mastery over one's own body, not over another's. Judges, therefore, play a pivotal role in who wins or loses. Judges score dives using several uniform criteria, including proper use of the body while performing certain moves, including pointing the toes at all times; the height a diver achieves above the springboard or platform; the diver's ability to leap a proper distance from the board (about two feet is considered ideal); the coordinated number of rotations performed during a dive before entering the water; how little splash a diver generates; angle of entry—meaning whether the diver enters the water in a straight vertical position, which is ideal, or enters at an angle.

Types of dives typically include four different positions achieved in one of six dive groups: forward dives, back dives, reverse dives, inward dives, dives with a twist, and dives that begin with the diver doing a handstand. The four basic dive positions are the straight position (knees and hips), pike (straight knees, but a bend at the hips), free (a combination of positions usually achieved when a diver transitions between other positions), and tuck (body rolled into a ball with the toes pointed).

IMPORTANT FIGURES

China's Wu Minxia's success, longevity, and versatility are unrivaled. The winner of eight world championships, Wu earned gold medals in four consecutive Olympics as both an individual and synchronized competitor. In all she has earned seven Olympic medals, and she dominated the Asian Games through the first two decades of the 21st century. Chinese divers have dominated the sport since being admitted to the Olympic Games in 1984, but out of the many Chinese divers who have achieved international success, none stand as tall as Wu.

In 1988, at the Olympic Games in Seoul, South Korea, Greg Louganis sprang off a 3-meter springboard, ready to attempt a reverse 2½ pike. He came down too close to the board and hit his head. The crowd gasped in horror as Louganis, a two-time gold medalist during the 1984 Olympics, fell into the water, bleeding from the top of his head. He needed stitches but returned about 40 minutes later. Not only did he complete his next dive successfully, he did so nearly perfectly. It helped earn him a gold medal, and he earned another later in the Games, in the 10-meter event, making him only the second diver in Olympic history to sweep the 3-meter and 10-meter events in consecutive Olympics. The other was Pat McCormick. She completed the sweeps in 1952 and 1956.

POP CULTURE

After Louganis's postdisaster dive in 1988, the most famous dive in history is not from the Olympics but from a slapstick comedy starring late comedian

Rodney Dangerfield. In 1986 Dangerfield starred in *Back to School*, a film about a late-middle-aged businessman who decides to attend college with his son. The college diving coach learns that Dangerfield, in his youth, completed a famous dive called the Triple Lindy, a dive so complex that it called for the diver to jump off a high platform onto a springboard below, then from that springboard perform a tuck with a double roll to the right onto another springboard, which had to be specially installed for the dive, followed by another backflip on the final board, into a tuck with 2½ rotations into the dive.

In the movie's climax, Dangerfield's character agrees to perform the dive, which, of course, he pulls off successfully. In 2013 an anonymous internet commenter on a sports website claimed to be one of Dangerfield's movie stunt doubles for the dive. The commenter, replying to someone's question about whether the Triple Lindy was real, explained that it was not. It was performed and filmed with a strategic combination of trampolines placed in and around the diving pool and professional camerawork, and it was filmed in four separately shot sequences.

SCANDALS

In 2015 Filipino divers John Fabriga and John Pahoyo, competing in the Southeast Asian Games, each performed dives so poorly that they scored zeros. One entered the water flat on his back, the other on his bended knees. Pahoyo later explained that it was the first time either had competed at such a high level and, in a candid moment, admitted the pressure got to them. Yet that was not the scandal. The real problem was how they were treated after the dives, when American cable network ESPN made fun of them on the air and an Australian YouTuber created a video that mocked the pair.

To date, the video has received more than seven million views. The pair handled their poor dives with class, even laughing at themselves. Most impressively, two days after the dives, they competed together in a synchronized event. They did not earn medals, but they did just fine, entering the water in unison, heads first, toes pointed.

PATRIOTISM AND NATIONAL PRIDE

Chinese divers have achieved great heights not just because of their training and dedication but also because of the divers that have come before them. Chinese divers who achieved early success in the late 1980s and early 1990s inspired the current generation of divers. Said a Chinese diving administrator, "An athlete without a sense of patriotism can't go too far" (Beech 2016).

Diving has become more than an athletic activity with potential medals as a reward. It has become a point of national pride. Only the South Koreans in archery, Americans in basketball and softball, and Cubans in baseball come close to China's international success in diving (and table tennis).

Timeline

Ancient civilizations – People across the ancient world dive to hunt and for fun and recreation.

c. 1770 – Cliff diving debuts in the Hawaiian Islands as a way to test the bravery and loyalty of its soldiers. It will become a sporting competition two or three decades later.

Late 18th century – German and Swedish gymnasts practice tumbling by jumping off boards and platforms into water.

1845 – In a sport later dubbed "plunging," reports surface in England of a swimmer diving 16 meters, or 52 feet, into water.

1901 – The Amateur Diving Association forms in Great Britain after a visit from Swedish divers generates enthusiasm for the sport.

1904 – The Olympics, held in St. Louis, allow men's diving for the first time. The "plunge for distance," an event in which competitors see how far they can travel underwater without moving their limbs after diving in, is held for the first and only time during Olympic competition.

1912 – The Olympics allow women's diving for the first time.

1928 – Diving as we understand it today takes place during the Amsterdam Olympics, which include 3-meter and 10-meter events.

1937 – The final plunging championships are held after diving's popularity overwhelms the more ancient sport.

1956 – Pat McCormick becomes the first Olympic diver to win 3-meter and 10-meter gold medals in consecutive Olympic Games. She remains the only person to do so for another 32 years.

1956 – Joaquín Capilla becomes the first—and, to date, only—Mexican gold medalist in diving when he wins the 10 meters.

1988 – Greg Louganis sweeps Olympic gold medals in 3-meter springboard and 10-meter platform for a second consecutive Olympics.

2000 – The International Olympic Committee welcomes synchronized diving into the Games.

2000 – Aileen Riggin, the first-ever women's 3-meter Olympic gold medal winner, who won in Antwerp, Belgium, in 1920, attends the Sydney, Australia, Olympics as a spectator.

2016 – China's Wu Minxia makes her case as the greatest competitive diver in history by earning a gold medal in a fourth consecutive Olympic Games.

See also: Figure Skating; Gymnastics; Swimming.

Further Reading

Beech, H. (2016). "Inside the System That Turned China into the Most Dominant Divers in the World." *Time*, Aug. 9, 2016. https://time.com/4442329/china-diving-rio-2016-olympics.

Billingsley, H. S. (2017). *Challenge: How to Succeed beyond Your Wildest Dreams*. Trius Publishing: La Mesa, California.

Billingsley, H. and Anderson, P. (2018). *Competitive Diving Illustrated: Coaching Strategies to Perform 134 Dives*. Trius Publishing: La Mesa, California.

Daley, T. (2012). *Tom Daley: My Story*. Michael Joseph: London.

Huber, J. J. (2015). *Springboard and Platform Diving*. Human Kinetics: Champaign, Illinois.

Lanser, A. (2016). *The Science behind Swimming, Diving, and Other Water Sports*. Capstone Press: North Mankato, Minnesota.

Louganis, G. (1995). *Breaking the Surface*. Random House: New York.

Miller, D. I. (2007). *Biomechanics of Competitive Diving*. USA Diving: Indianapolis, Indiana.

O'Brien, R. (2002). *Springboard and Platform Diving*. Human Kinetics: Champaign, Illinois.

Upper, S. and Upper, J. (2013). *The Cartwheel Kid*. CreateSpace Independent Publishing Platform: Scotts Valley, California.

E

E-Sports

E-sports represent the fastest growing sport in the world. E-sports, or electronic sports, bring together video game players from across the world for massive, multiplayer contests across various genres of games. Participants compete in arena games, sports games, war games, and games of skill. In 2013 the United States recognized e-sports as a legitimate competitive profession, which opened the door for players from around the world to apply for a U.S. visa so that they could travel to the states and practice alongside teammates. E-sports competitions offer hundreds of millions of dollars each year in prize money, while the video game industry itself is worth tens of billions, with revenues in the hundreds of billions expected by the end of the current decade. Although barely 40 years old, e-sports already have produced their share of celebrities, highlights, and scandals. Media companies are scrambling to find ways to get involved, having identified e-sports as one of the biggest opportunities for growth in sports coverage in this century.

HISTORICAL CONTEXT

Computer scientists began creating and playing around with computer games in the late 1960s and early 1970s. The games would look primitive by today's standards, even unrecognizable—dots on a screen. In 1972 the electronics company Atari released Pong, two lines and a dot that mimicked a tennis or table tennis (Ping-Pong) match. Although proportionately expensive compared with income of the day, Pong proved a hit. Other electronics companies saw potential and entered the video game market, but Atari, with its head start, prevailed. Its 1976 release of the Atari 2600 kickstarted the era of play-at-home video games, and in November 1980 Atari used its video game Space Invaders as the centerpiece for the first video game competition, the National Space Invaders Championship.

Other consoles made their mark, most notably Coleco, Odyssey, and Intellivision, but Atari continued to lead the way until 1983 and 1984, when the video game market collapsed and tech analysts wondered whether games were better suited for video arcades or personal computers made by IBM and Apple than consoles attached to home television screens. That line of thinking held until early 1987 with the wide release of the Nintendo Entertainment System. Nintendo's console made a giant leap forward in the quality of graphics and sophistication of game play, and Nintendo, which learned from Atari's mistakes, achieved a long-term industry stability that survives to this day. In 1990 the company

E-sports are one of the world's newest sports and connect players digitally from across the world. Some events, such as this Counter-Strike game competition held in Russia, take place on site and draw hundreds of fans. (Roman Kosolapov/Dreamstime.com)

established the Nintendo World Championships, which brought together thousands of competitors to compete for cash and other prizes.

Mainstream internet access helped e-sports take its next step. By the mid- to late 1990s, college students and their parents could connect online from their dorms and houses. The world shrank. The days of people having to be in the same room to play games against or with one another were over. Now, as long as internet dialup speed could sustain it, players from across the world could log into a game and occupy the same online space. They could compete as warlocks and ogres, make up a World War II infantry unit, or line up as teammates on the basketball court.

That proved to be the final step in e-sports' evolution. Graphics, the quality of game play and design, connectivity speeds, and hardware all continue to improve—even to the extent that a gamer from 1997 might not recognize today's equipment and capabilities—but the ability to play together, with and against one another, launched e-sports. Before global interactivity, video games were solitary activities. Afterward, they constituted a billion-dollar market with millions of participants working in unison.

GLOBALIZATION

The e-sports market grew up in two primary markets: East Asia, primarily South Korea and Japan, and the United States. E-sports are one of the world's newest sports. They developed within—and because of—the global capitalist marketplace, wherever there was interest and technological privilege. They lacked the colonialist, imperialist roots of many sports, such as cricket and soccer.

Some find the term itself—*e-sports*—misleading, since "sports" implies some sort of physical skill or requirement: cardiovascular conditioning, physical strength, running, and jumping. E-sports, while demanding of hand-eye coordination, take place mostly in chairs or some other seated position. Nevertheless, the International Olympic Committee has voted to admit e-sports as a demonstration sport during the 2024 Summer Olympics in Paris.

WHERE THEY'RE PLAYED TODAY

E-sports are played on every continent in nearly every country. Competitive, professional e-sports competitions occur everywhere from Singapore to South Africa, from London to Brazil, while recreational players can be found in all corners of the globe because of the abundance of gaming systems and increased online access.

By the end of 2019, Sony had sold 450 million units of its various PlayStation consoles. Microsoft had sold 126 million units of its Xbox systems. Nintendo had sold nearly three-quarters of a billion units, including 52 million units of its Switch, a portable device that came out in 2017.

ECONOMICS AND MEDIA

Video game revenue reached $120 billion in 2019, the most in industry history. The industry also set records in 2018 and 2017 and is expected to continue to break records every year in the foreseeable future so long as the world's economy is healthy. Those figures represent the entire industry. E-sports continue to grow as well, especially as media companies become more involved.

American-based, Walt Disney–owned ESPN, the most valuable cable and media channel in the world, dedicates a full section of its website, ESPN.com, to e-sports. It also has its own Twitch channel, ESPN Esports, and has attempted to start its own events, similar to what it did in the 1990s and 2000s with action sports like skateboarding and BMX. Overall, Twitch welcomes 15 million daily active users and is valued in the billions. The Amazon-owned platform is for viewers as much as for players, with 355 billion minutes of gaming watched through 2020.

Championships and tournaments are held throughout the world on multiple platforms for all genres of video games. EA Sports has held the Madden Championship series, an American football video game series, since the early 2000s. Epic Games, creator of Fortnite, began the Fortnite World Cup in 2018. The event grew so big the company hosted it in Arthur Ashe Stadium, site of the annual U.S. Open Tennis Championships in New York. As of 2018, the highest-rated e-sports event on traditional television was neither an arena game nor a sports game. It was Candy Crush, the hugely addictive mobile phone game. Candy Crush drew four million viewers when it aired on the American television network CBS.

DIMENSIONS OF THE SPORT

Video games historically take place on one of five types of machines. The most common in e-sports, home gaming consoles, attach to the internet and a home monitor or television. Past and present home-console companies include Atari, Colecovision, Odyssey, Intellivision, Nintendo, Sega, Sony PlayStation, and Microsoft. Nintendo and other companies have also created mobile consoles, at first created to keep kids busy on long trips yet now part of the e-sports universe.

Arcade games were all the rage in the 1980s and 1990s. Alongside pinball machines, which date back to the early to mid-20th century, arcade games filled social spaces in malls, restaurants, and bowling alleys. For the cost of 25 or 50 cents per game, patrons visited arcades and bade farewell to their allowance money. Some of the most popular console games first appeared as arcade games, including Donkey Kong from Nintendo's Mario universe, and the fighting game Mortal Kombat, with popularity that extended to feature films.

Computer games, built for personal computers, first were known for their stacks of floppy disks. They became the first hub of online, multiplayer gaming that evolved into e-sports because of their connectivity. One of today's fastest-growing markets for e-sports and online game are mobile phones, including iPhones and Samsung Galaxy phones. In previous decades, some games could be found in arcades, some on computers, and some on consoles, but today the most popular games can sometimes be found across multiple platforms, including mobile phones.

IMPORTANT FIGURES

By the age of 16 in 2007, Richard Blevins, just a teenager from the Chicago suburbs, was one of the top Halo gamers in the world. Although he enjoyed playing soccer in the physical world, Halo was where he made his name—not as Richard but as his online handle, Ninja. He had some fans, but when he switched to competitive Fortnite Battle Royale in 2017, his fame skyrocketed. Ninja became one of the most famous American e-sports competitors, streaming on both YouTube and Twitch. His net worth soared to around $10 million as gamers flocked to his channels.

Another fan of Fortnite? Korg, the fictional alien sidekick to the Asgardian Thor in the Marvel cinematic universe. Movie fans who watched the worldwide sensation *Avengers: Endgame* howled with laughter when Korg, hanging out in Thor's house, was shown playing Fortnite. He encounters an online player who continually harasses him, Noobmaster69, whom Thor threatens by phone to get him to stop.

POP CULTURE

Ready Player One, published in 2011 and written by Ernest Cline, tells the story of teenager Wade Watts, who lives in a dystopian futuristic United States in which happiness can only be found inside a massive multiplayer online game. The game was built by a deceased computer genius, and whoever can win the game presumably inherits riches. No one has ever won, but Watts and his companions stumble onto the right path. They are, of course, pursued by an evil corporation. The book became an instant cross-generational hit, appealing to younger readers because of the gaming component and older readers because the book's online world is inhabited with nostalgia. Players use weapons, vehicles, and locations originally set around 1970s and 1980s movies. The book caught the attention of movie director Steven Spielberg, who helped adapt it into a film, which came out in 2018 and earned nearly $600 million worldwide.

A quarter century before *Ready Player One*, upstart cable television network TBS, owned by businessman Ted Turner, suspected that people would watch others play video games. From 1982 to 1984 the station aired *Starcade*, a game show where young contestants competed against each other in popular arcade video games. It was not a runaway hit, but it found a niche audience, airing a total of 123 episodes before going off the air. It included some of the era's most iconic video games, including BurgerTime, Donkey Kong, Dragon's Lair, Ms. Pac-Man, and Q*bert, a number of which were later included in the Walt Disney movie *Wreck-It Ralph*, about a 1980s-era video game whose characters look for meaning in the modern world.

SCANDALS

In 2010, 11 South Korean gamers, including the wildly popular Ma Jae-yoon, were implicated in game-fixing scandals and banned for life. Ma, who played under the name sAviOr and was nicknamed The Maestro, was alleged to have conspired with gamblers and lost games on purpose, therefore benefiting financially from intentionally losing.

Ma received bans from multiple organizations on multiple platforms. He grew to fame playing StarCraft, a real-time science fiction strategy game. Ma resurfaced in 2013 to play a StarCraft-related tournament in Shanghai, China. His team won, but the host organization earned criticism for its decision to let Ma compete. Gaming fans so dislike Ma for his game fixing that they have given him the nickname Maregi, which combines his name with the Korean word for trash.

POLITICS

In 2013 designer Zoë Quinn released Depression Quest, a game designed to explain the challenges of depression. She created it to spread awareness, compassion, and empathy. For many, Depression Quest hit the mark. Viewed as educational gaming, some proceeds from its sales went to the International Foundation for Research and Education.

The game also accomplished something it never intended. It lured the darkest impulses of male players into the mainstream. Online male gamers, many using pseudonyms, unleashed coordinated attacks on Quinn and other female designers and journalists. They threatened them with physical violence and doxed them—the act of revealing personal information, such as home address and other private information, online. Quinn fled her home because it became unsafe.

Reporting later showed that male gamers attacked Quinn because they did not like her game format and feared a feminization of the video game industry. Numerous male gamers, according to the *New Yorker* magazine, received training from far-right activists in the coordination and execution of cyberharassment that they used in their attacks on Quinn and others. Female game designers for years had called on the industry to address its inherent misogyny; "Gamergate," as the attacks came to be known, finally helped turn a spotlight on gaming's dirty secret.

PATRIOTISM AND NATIONAL PRIDE

Overwatch, one of the world's most popular competitive games, embarked on a world tour in 2018 en route to its world championship. Stages of the event took place in South Korea, Paris, Thailand, and the United States. At each stop fans gathered to root on teams from their home countries. It looked like something out of basketball or soccer, with fans showing up dressed in their nation's colors and carrying their flags. Fans even traveled from afar to cheer on their team. "When you see Italy vs. the Netherlands, it immediately makes sense and you also get to play on the national pride," Overwatch league commissioner Nate Nanzer said (Castello 2018).

Timeline

1980 – Atari hosts the first-ever open-invitational video game tournament. The game: Space Invaders.

1982 – American cable television station TBS debuts *Starcade*, a game show in which contestants compete against each other in video games.

1990 – Taking a cue from its gaming predecessor, Atari, Nintendo hosts the Nintendo World Championships. It offers a $10,000 cash prize.

1994 – The Interactive Digital Software Association is founded and is later rebranded the Entertainment Software Association, the most popular gaming trade organization in the world.

1997 – The Cyberathlete Professional League is founded. It runs in its original form through 2008, at which time it enters partnerships with other organizations.

1998 – StarCraft, considered by many to be the original e-sports game, is released.

2000 – KeSPA, the Korea e-Sports Association, is founded and becomes one of the most influential organizations in the sport's short history.

2000 – The first World Cyber Games are held in South Korea.

2002 – Major League Gaming is founded in New York City.

2009 – The League of Legends begins.

2009 – Richard Blevins, better known by his gaming handle "Ninja," turns professional at the age of 16. He becomes known for playing the Halo series of games.

2011 – The video game streaming service Twitch goes live.

2011 – Ernest Cline's dystopian novel, *Ready Player One*, about a society where many take refuge inside a virtual online gaming world, is published to major success.

2013 – Game designer Zoë Quinn releases Depression Quest, a game to help people learn about depression and how it affects people.

2014 – Amazon acquires Twitch for just less than $1 billion.

2014 – Angered by Depression Quest, Gamergate, the online, male-coordinated harassment of women in the video game industry, rattles the industry and reveals its misogynistic culture.

2019 – The total prize money for the arena-battle game Dota 2 exceeds a series total of $200 million, most among any e-sports title.

See also: Action Sports; Basketball; Olympics.

Further Reading

Andrejkovics, Z. (2016). *The Invisible Game: Mindset of a Winning Team.* CreateSpace Independent Publishing Platform: Scotts Valley, California.

Andrejkovics, Z. (2018). *A Newborn Business: E-Sports.* Self-published.

Castello, J. (2018). "'Playing on National Pride': E-Sports Is Coming Home at the Overwatch World Cup." *The Guardian*, Oct. 12, 2018. https://www.theguardian.com/games/2018/oct/12/playing-on-national-pride-on-the-road-at-the-overwatch-e-sports-world-cup.

Cline, E. (2011). *Ready Player One.* Crown Publishing Group: New York.

H3CZ, NaDeSHot, Scump, BigTymer, and Midnite. (2016). *OpTic Gaming: The Making of E-Sports Champions.* Dey Street Books: New York.

Li, Ronald (2017). *Good Luck Have Fun: The Rise of E-Sports.* Skyhorse: New York.

Rogers, R., ed. (2019). *Understanding E-Sports: An Introduction to the Global Phenomenon.* Lexington Books, Rowman & Littlefield Publishers: Lanham, Maryland.

Scholz, T. M. (2019). *E-Sports Is Business: Management in the World of Competitive Gaming.* Palgrave Pivot: London.

Taylor, T. L. (2015). *Raising the Stakes: E-Sports and the Professionalization of Computer Gaming.* MIT Press: Cambridge, Massachusetts.

Taylor, T. L. (2018). *Watch Me Play: Twitch and the Rise of Game Live Streaming.* Princeton University Press: Princeton, New Jersey.

Field Hockey

To a newcomer, field hockey might look like a grab bag of other sports. It has dribbling, but it is not basketball. It has tackling and takes place on a 100-yard field, but it is not American football. The players carry sticks and run around on a grass field, but it is not lacrosse. Players shoot the ball and cannot touch it with their hands, but it is not soccer, although soccer is the sport it mostly closely resembles. People unfamiliar with field hockey sometimes express confusion about how the sport is played, but once they see it, it takes just minutes to understand. Each team has 11 players, including a goalkeeper, who try to score the ball in the other team's net. The team that scores the most goals wins. It can be fast, exciting, and highly skilled, all reasons why the game has become so popular in South Asia, North America, and Western Europe, and yet to other parts of the world, field hockey ranges from a nonentity to a niche curiosity.

HISTORICAL CONTEXT

Games resembling field hockey—or just "hockey" as it is known through most of the world since ice hockey by comparison is played in fewer countries—appeared in the ancient world and the first post-year-zero millennium in countries and regions including East Asia, Egypt, Greece, India, and Mongolia. A game called choule found popularity in parts of the United Kingdom and France in the early 13th century. It resembled rugby but sometimes included sticks, and because American football, which is played on a 100-yard field, grew out of rugby, and field hockey is played on a 100-yard field with sticks, some historians view choule as field hockey's most direct ancestor.

As with many games traced to have Western European origins, hockey-type games originated among royals and the aristocracy before working their way toward the masses. Western imperialism also aided hockey's global spread. The game as it looks today grew out of the United Kingdom school system in the early 19th century. Blackheath Proprietary School organized the world's first formal field hockey club team in the 1860s, and from there other clubs formed and began to play one another. Eventually the school children grew up, but they did not leave behind their love of hockey, making it acceptable for adults to play at varying skill levels. By 1895 Ireland and Wales engaged in the first official international hockey competition. Ireland won, 3-0, but it is important to note that countries playing hockey-like games had squared off prior to 1895.

Ireland also was home to the first national women's hockey organization, the Irish Ladies Hockey Union, founded in 1894. As the sport grew during the United Kingdom's Victorian era, the era's misogyny made it difficult for women to get equal opportunities, but over time hockey grew more quickly in women's circles than men's, and today the sport is closely associated with women's athletics across multiple continents, especially North America.

GLOBALIZATION

India, which learned the game while suffering the oppression of colonial British rule, was hockey's first global power. From 1928 to 1956 the Indian men's field hockey team won every Olympic gold medal, six straight in total (the 1940 and 1944 Olympics were canceled because of World War II). For much of the 1900s, India and Pakistan, which gained independence from India in 1947, dominated international men's field hockey, which is overseen by the Fédération Internationale de Hockey (FIH).

Founded in 1924, the FIH oversees administration and rules for field hockey. It also oversees the World Cup and other tournaments. It was started in France by founding nations Austria, Belgium, Czechoslovakia, France, Hungary, Spain, and Switzerland—that the United Kingdom was not included signifies how quickly the game's popularity spread through Europe—then moved to Belgium and in 2005 moved to Switzerland. Since the World Cup began in 1971, nations from every continent except Antarctica have competed. Some countries that have finished near the top of the standings include Argentina, Australia, Germany, Kenya, Malaysia, and Pakistan, none of which was a founding member of the FIH and all of which discovered the game later in its global growth.

The Federation of Women's Hockey Associations started the women's World Cup in 1974. Recent World Cups include high finishes from nations including the Netherlands, Ireland, Argentina, China, Australia, Canada, and Spain. The International Olympic Committee did not admit women's field hockey into the Games until 1980, when it was hosted by Moscow. Zimbabwe won the inaugural women's gold medal.

Although international women's field hockey across the world followed a similar trajectory as other sports—delayed organized and recognized activity despite thousands of competing athletes—in the United States women's field hockey grew at a far brisker pace than men's did. Today nearly 80 American colleges and universities fund women's field hockey teams, while none supports men's field hockey. Despite success at the college level, the United States' national field hockey team has never finished higher than the bronze medal it earned at the 1984 Games in Los Angeles, California, when the Soviet Union declined to compete.

WHERE IT'S PLAYED TODAY

International women's and men's field hockey remains most popular in Europe and South Asia but has grown to include heavy pockets of participation in East Asia, parts of South America—most notably Argentina—North and Central

> ### Field Hockey? In Iowa?
>
> Field hockey is a sport that attracts players—both women and men—all over the world. It's especially popular in India, Australia, and the Netherlands, as well as the eastern United States and part of the West Coast, particularly as a college sport. In fact, between 1981 and 2018, of the 38 college champions in field hockey, 37 came from what would be considered an East Coast school.
>
> The one exception? The University of Iowa's women's field hockey team in 1986. Iowa's championship was exceptional for a number of reasons. First, field hockey is not popular in Iowa. Not a single public elementary or secondary school in the midwestern state offered field hockey as a varsity student activity. The team, even as it compiled victories, struggled to draw an audience, because not many people cared for the sport and those who did show up did not always understand the game's nuances. Second, the university had only been playing field hockey for nine years, whereas other institutions' field-hockey presence reached back decades. Third, none of the University of Iowa players came from the state of Iowa, which meant the coaches had to recruit the entire team from other states.
>
> In 1986 the University of Iowa, known as the Hawkeyes, finished their season with 19 victories, just 2 losses, and a tie. They won their college conference, the Big Ten, for the second consecutive season amid what would be part of a streak in which they won 7 conference championships over 8 seasons. As of 2019, Iowa's 1986 squad remains the only college from the Midwest to win a national championship in field hockey. To win the championship, Iowa defeated the University of New Hampshire 2-1 in double overtime.

Africa, and parts of North America, most notably the women's collegiate game in the United States.

In the United States, field hockey officials have tried, with little success, to grow beyond the East Coast. Field hockey programs throughout New England and the rest of the Eastern Seaboard have become a multimillion-dollar industry. They also supply nearly all of the country's college field-hockey athletes. However, the farther west and inland you travel into the United States, the less likely it is that you will find competitive field hockey.

ECONOMICS AND MEDIA

Even in countries where field hockey is popular, with the exception of the world's top athletes, field hockey players usually do not make salaries comparable with other professional sports. A player would be fortunate to make the annual equivalent of $40,000. The bigger events, such as the World Cup and Olympics, occasionally are broadcast internationally, but most events receive only regional or online coverage. Still, the largest viewership ever for a women's sporting event other than soccer is held by field hockey. The gold-medal match between the Netherlands and Great Britain at the 2016 Olympics in Rio drew 5.5 million viewers across the world.

DIMENSIONS OF THE SPORT

Field hockey calls for 11 players per side, the same as soccer and American football, with near-identical alignment to soccer: one goalkeeper, who is the only team member allowed to touch the ball with the body, plus some combination of attackers, defenders, and midfielders. Games take place on fields 100 yards in length and 60 yards in width. Games throughout the world take place on manicured grass fields, while more affluent leagues and clubs as well as American universities build fields with synthetic surfaces that bring down long-term maintenance costs.

Field hockey officials have in recent years tinkered with changing the length of matches. Olympic and college matches had been two 35-minute halves; now Olympic matches consist of four 15-minute quarters with a short break after the first and third quarters plus a halftime.

Sticks must weigh no more than 23 ounces and, per tradition, be able to pass through a ring two inches in diameter. All players hold the sticks in their left hands—even right-handed players—because of the stick's peculiar design of flat on one side and rounded on the other. The sticks are dense, made of composite materials such as carbon and Kevlar, the same base material associated with bulletproof vests, so many of the game's fouls focus on misuse of the stick to deter players from using them dangerously. Fouls include wielding the stick in an uncontrolled manner, playing with the wrong (rounded) side of the stick, and interfering with an opponent's stick.

Teams attempt to score goals by putting the ball in the other team's net. Field hockey employs the term "tackling," which in this sport means using your stick to try to steal the ball from the opponent. Players dribble the ball with the stick through and around opponents then hit the ball, again using only the stick, to pass or shoot.

IMPORTANT FIGURES

No one influenced the game of field hockey more than Great Britain's Constance M. K. Applebee, who, while she took a course at Harvard University in the United States in the early 1900s, ended up introducing field hockey to women's universities. The sport spread quickly. One of her Harvard classmates asked Applebee to teach field hockey at Vassar. Soon the game migrated to Bryn Mawr, Mount Holyoke, Radcliffe, Wellesley, and others, including public universities, and today the U.S. collegiate women's field hockey presence is unparalleled internationally. Applebee was nearly 28 years old when she attended Harvard in 1901. Remarkably, she lived nearly another 80 years, dying in 1981 at age 107. She is credited as being one of the founders of the organization that would eventually become USA Field Hockey.

Even when Dr. Christine Grant became the first director of athletics for the University of Iowa in 1973, one year after the U.S. federal government passed Title IX, a law that requires—among other things—equal funding for women's and men's sports at publication institutions, she never let go of her love for field hockey. Born in Scotland, Grant moved to Canada after graduating college to teach and coach field hockey, which she did for a decade in British Columbia, Ottawa, and Toronto. In 1977 Grant added field hockey to the list of women's sports offered by the University of Iowa, a peculiar choice since in the United States it was almost exclusively an East Coast sport and Iowa is in the Midwest. Nearly every player had to be recruited from out of state since the sport was not played at the high school level in Iowa or any surrounding state. The experiment, however, worked. In 1986 Iowa won the NCAA national field hockey championship to become the only U.S. school in the American Midwest to win the title. Grant retired in 2000, with the field hockey championship counting as just one of the 12 national championships won by Iowa under her leadership.

POP CULTURE

Field hockey does not get a lot of play in popular culture. When it does appear, it does so in a tertiary or background role, such as when George Orwell's lead character in the novel *1984*, Winston Smith, expresses dislike for another character partially because of her interest in field hockey. The American television show *Gossip Girl* once included a scene where two characters took their anger out on each other during a field hockey match, culminating in numerous fouls and eventually a fight. Another American program, *Switched at Birth*, featured field hockey more prominently as a recurring activity of one of the characters, but the show, although it lasted several seasons, did not appear on a major American television network. The pilot episode of the American television program *Black-ish* in 2014 included a main character joining his school's boys field hockey team, for which he is mocked by his father, who had hoped his son would play basketball.

The 2007 Indian film *Chak de! India* is considered by many the best art ever made about the sport of field hockey, with fans around the world and near universal praise among film critics. *Chak de! India* stars Shah Rukh Khan as Kabir Khan, coach of India's women's hockey team. The film is loosely based on the team's 2002 victory at the Commonwealth Games. It explores issues of religious bigotry and feminism, earned numerous local and regional awards, and the United States' Academy of Motion Picture Arts and Sciences, which oversees the prestigious annual Academy Awards, requested a copy of *Chak de! India* for its library of historic and worthy films.

SCANDALS

In 2019 U.S. federal investigators began to crack down on colleges and families involved in illegal college admissions practices. Behavior by a number of the country's top universities and numerous celebrities uncovered patterns of abuse. One of the more common tactics involved athletes from nonrevenue sports (ruling out football, basketball, baseball, and volleyball) receiving backdoor favoritism in the college-recruiting process.

The scandal shone a light on class, racial, and cultural tension in the U.S. education system. One of the sports most commonly used to admit nondeserving, affluent white athletes was field hockey. Academic researchers later found that rather than admit academically high-achieving, low-income students in need of financial assistance to attend college, the school would admit academically low-achieving students as long as their parents promised to pay the full cost of tuition.

PATRIOTISM AND NATIONAL PRIDE

Many in India were shocked to learn a number of years ago that, contrary to popular belief, field hockey is not the national sport. Given India's rich history of field hockey success, coupled with cricket not becoming popular until after hockey already had taken hold, it seemed like a given that hockey would have at some point received the honorary designation.

It turned out that India does not have an official sport because it never got around to naming one. This came to light after a school-age child wrote to the government to ask for a list of official designations for a school report: official flower, tree, song, sport, and so forth. The public reaction was more surprise than anger, since Indian field hockey has fallen on hard times the last couple of decades while cricket has come to dominate the recreational landscape. It is worth noting, however, that Pakistan, which split from India just after World War II, did name a national sport: field hockey.

Timeline

500 BCE – Using animal horns as sticks, Greeks play a game that historians determine looks like field hockey.

c. 1850 – Field hockey as it exists today appears in the United Kingdom.

1861 – Blackheath Football and Hockey Club forms in England at Blackheath Proprietary School.

1894 – The Irish Senior Cup—the oldest surviving trophy in field hockey—is awarded for the first time.

1895 – Ireland defeats Wales, 3-0, in what is regarded as the first international field hockey competition.

Late 1890s – Club teams begin appearing in Western Canada.

1901 – Briton Constance M. K. Applebee brings field hockey to the United States, introducing it at numerous East Coast colleges including Vassar, Holyoke, and Wellesley.

1903 – The first recorded match between a girls' team and a boys' team takes place in Vancouver, Canada.

1908 – Men's field hockey included in the Olympics for the first time.

1920 – The United States sends a field hockey team to tour the United Kingdom.

1922 – The governing body of American women's field hockey, the U.S. Field Hockey Association (USFHA), is formed.

1924 – The Fédération Internationale de Hockey (FIH) is founded.

1928 – India wins the field hockey gold medal at the Olympics, its first of six consecutive Olympic golds, through 1956.

1930 – The Field Hockey Association of America forms to oversee the men's game. It merges with the USFHA in 1993.

1980 – Women's field hockey is included in the Olympics for the first time.

1986 – The University of Iowa wins the NCAA women's field hockey championship, the only time to date the championship has been won by an American university outside the Eastern time zone.

2002 – Argentina wins the men's world championship, then wins again in 2010.

See also: Football; Ice Hockey; Rugby.

Further Reading

Anders, E. R. and Myers, S. (2008). *Field Hockey: Steps to Success*. Human Kinetics: Champaign, Illinois.

Connolly, H. (2004). *Field Hockey: Rules, Tips, Strategy, and Safety*. Rosen Publishing: New York.

Gilmour, G. and MacDougall, T. (2018). *Seoul Glow: The Story Behind Britain's First Olympic Hockey Gold*. Pitch Publishing: Sussex, United Kingdom.

Johnson-Crell, E. (2007). *Mastering the Net: Field Hockey Goalkeeping Basics*. Wish Publishing: Johannesburg, South Africa.

Maddox, J. (2014). Field Hockey Firsts. Stone Arch Books: North Mankato, Minnesota.

Maloney, C. (2013). *Field Hockey: Understanding the Game*. CreateSpace Independent Publishing Platform: Scotts Valley, California.

Maloney, C. (2018). *Field Hockey: The Beginner's Guide*. Full color edition. CreateSpace Independent Publishing Platform: Scotts Valley, California.

Misra, S. (2007). *Forgive Me Amma*. Wisdom Tree: New Delhi, India.

Speck, N. (2001). *Freedom Trail Mystery: Going to Boston*. Four Corners Books: London.

Uribe, D. (2017). *The Field Hockey Psychology Workbook: How to Use Advanced Sports Psychology to Succeed on the Hockey Field*. CreateSpace Independent Publishing Platform: Scotts Valley, California.

Figure Skating

Figure skating, like its fellow ice-skating sports of ice hockey and speed skating, originated in Northern Europe. Where it separated itself was in its opportunity. Sports are a social institution, and most social institutions carry misogynistic histories. The Olympics illustrate that history. Men's basketball became an Olympic sport before women's basketball did, as did men's speed skating before women's speed skating and men's track and field before women's track and field. Figure skating holds a unique position: it became an Olympic sport in 1908 for both women and men, who could compete individually or as pairs. Figure skating was not the first Olympic sport for women—it was sailing in 1900—but it was the first to be introduced during the same year as the men's equivalent, and over the 100-plus years since figure skating's international arrival, women's figure skating has far surpassed men's in terms of popularity and athletic recognition. Television ratings in the United States for the ladies' free skate portion of the U.S. championships routinely draw more viewers than regular-season, nationally broadcast Major League Baseball games. Known for its strength, skill, and artistry, figure skating ranks among the world's most popular Olympic sports.

HISTORICAL CONTEXT

Credit a British army lieutenant for elevating figure skating to a sport and art form. Robert Jones's 1772 book, *A Treatise for Skating*, described such early moves as the figure eight. Just as soccer had its pivotal moment when rugby and soccer split into different sports, many consider Jones's book to be the moment when figure skating and speed skating went their separate ways. As of 2020 *Treatise* was still in print, albeit more as novelty than instructive text.

Although Jones excluded women, the sport integrated far

Women's figure skating regularly draws the largest television audience among sports at the Winter Olympics. Broadcast networks build their Winter Olympics coverage around the event. (Corel)

quicker by the era's standards than most other sports did. By the mid-19th century, a public skating rink in New York's Central Park opened to men and women. According to historians, despite the mingling of genders, the city required no chaperones, another oddity for its day. American ballet dancer Jackson Haines pushed Jones's ideas of figure skating to new heights by mingling ballet and ice skating. No longer was figure skating confined to a skater making smooth, fancy maneuvers on the ice. Now skaters could leap in the air and spin at great velocity. The Skating Club of New York, founded in 1863 during the American Civil War, became a breeding ground for figure-skating enthusiasts and a test kitchen for element innovation. Haines is credited for the sit spin, one of figure skating's foundational elements.

The International Skating Union (ISU) formed in the Netherlands in 1892 and helped to produce the first set of competition rules. It drew much of its inspiration from Haines's willingness to push the limits of what the human body was capable of doing even though he had died 15 years earlier. Haines was American, but leadership in American figure skating preferred Jones's more grounded approach. Haines found more enthusiasm in Northern and Eastern Europe. Hence just four years after the Haines-influenced ISU's formation, the first World Figure Skating

Championships were held in St. Petersburg, Russia, in 1896. With some exceptions, most notably during the two World Wars, the world championships have been held every year since.

GLOBALIZATION

To date, the World Championships have been held on just three continents: Asia, Europe, and North America. No competitor outside of those three regions has medaled at the championships, a common trait among ice-based sports. As figure-skating officials have noted, it is tough to learn ice sports in regions where ice is naturally scarce or nonexistent, as is the case in many parts of Africa, Australia, and South America. For example, it took a freak occurrence at the 1994 Winter Olympics for Australian speed skater Steven Bradbury to win a medal. He won each of his races because his competitors kept crashing (see the "Speed Skating" sidebar).

Thus, whether it is the World Championships or the Olympics, the top competitors and nearly every medalist come from Europe, Eastern Asia, or North America, from Canada or the United States. Since the early 20th century, the sport has experienced minimal global migration in terms of participation. Most growth has occurred through popularity and spectatorship. Broadcast media brought figure skating into homes across the world. Women's figure skating consistently ranks as the highest-rated television event during the Winter Olympics.

Outshining the Athletes

Tara Lipinski and Johnny Weir each achieved individual success as figure skaters. Lipinski won Olympic gold as a singles skater at the 1998 games in Nagano, Japan. She also earned gold at the World Championships in 1997. Although Weir qualified for two Olympic Games, medaling in neither appearance, from 2004 to 2006 he won three consecutive U.S. Championships and won bronze at the 2008 World Championships.

Each achieved relative levels of fame for their accomplishments, but when the American television network NBC put them together in 2014 as broadcasters for the network's figure skating coverage, a spark was lit. The two showed instant chemistry, and a cultural phenomenon was born. Skating fans talking online during and after major events, such as the Olympics, talked more about Lipinski and Weir than about the skaters. Known for their brutal honesty, candid insight, hilarious commentary, and eccentric fashion choices, the pair became a breakout story at the 2014 Winter Olympics in Sochi, Russia.

Prior to the 2018 Olympics in PyeongChang, South Korea, mainstream media covered Lipinski and Weir as much as they did some of the athletes. "Through some cocktail of flash, chemistry, and pure energy, Weir and Lipinski became the Internet's darlings," wrote *GQ* magazine (Skipper 2018). "And, most importantly, each other's best friend." They started a joint Instagram account, traveled and dined together, and coordinated outfits. Lipinski even later revealed that it was their idea—not NBC's—to pair them together on commentary. The network had planned on using them separately, Lipinski for women's figure skating and Weir for men's. But NBC took a chance and paired them together as the sport's backup broadcast team. It did not take long for them to become number one.

WHERE IT'S PLAYED TODAY

Recreational athletes throughout the world figure skate, with participation numbers in the tens of millions. They can indulge their hobby at either indoor ice rinks or frozen outdoor bodies of water. Competitive figure skating also takes place throughout the world, with regional competitions taking place across the globe.

The most successful international competitors, however, originate almost exclusively from Europe, from Eastern Asia, or from Canada or the United States in North America, as noted earlier with regard to medalists. One reason for this is economics. Ice skates are inexpensive compared with equipment in other sports such as golf or auto racing, but to become successful, figure skaters also need to hire a coach and rent time on an ice rink. These economic factors therefore limit who has access to the sport.

ECONOMICS AND MEDIA

Women's figure skating regularly draws the highest ratings of any Winter Olympic event. The International Olympic Committee (IOC) schedules the finals of the women's short and long programs for evening performances to accommodate the demands of fans and maximize viewership. Television networks broadcasting in a similar time zone as the host country will carry the event live. Broadcasters in other parts of the world often choose to show the event on a delay (not live) to increase viewership.

The world's top figure skaters earn millions of dollars annually, mostly through product endorsements, a common track of income for athletes who complete in Olympic sports with little following outside of the Games. Noncompetitive professional figure skaters earn their livings a few ways, most notably performing in traveling shows. One example was the Ice Capades, a traveling performance group that put on theatrical skating shows between 1940 and 1997. Theatrical ice skaters earn between $18,000 and $50,000 a year, with a select few earning more.

DIMENSIONS OF THE SPORT

The results of figure-skating competitions are determined by judges who closely watch an individual's or pair's routine. Judges watch for technical precision and level of difficulty as skaters complete required movements within their choreographed routines. Smaller, less consequential competitions might have as few as five judges, while national and international competitions have nine judges who score the different elements of a skater's routine. Bigger competitions also have a technical panel of five people who look at a skater's routine in real time for signs of stumbles or falls.

Figure skating consists of edge jumps and toe jumps. Edge jumps are more complicated. They involve bending the knee a certain way and can generate enormous power. Toe jumps are what they sound like: pushing off the toe from the free foot. The six most widely executed jumps in figure skating include three types of toe jumps (the flip, the Lutz, and the toe loop) and three types of edge jumps (the Salchow, the loop, and the most widely known jump in figure skating, the axel). Jumps are not allowed in ice dancing. In figure skating they are broken down into three categories for judging, according to skating association handbooks: an individual jump, a jump combination, and a jump sequence.

Individual short routines last about 2 minutes, 40 seconds. Free-skating routines, which are part of the long program, last 4 minutes for both pairs and individuals. All routines are set to music. Figure skating's theatricality leads skaters to coordinate three elements of their performance: music, wardrobe, and how they present their required elements on the ice. Nearly all events are held at both the adult and junior levels.

IMPORTANT FIGURES

Norway's Sonja Henie became the world's first international figure skating superstar, but her fame also came with complications. Before retiring from formal competition in 1936, Henie won three Olympic gold medals, six European championships, and a staggering 10 world championships between 1928 and 1936. She later became an international movie star and one of the wealthiest nonroyal women in the world.

Henie also struggled to separate herself from connections to Nazis—specifically, Adolf Hitler. She met Hitler with a Nazi salute at the 1936 Winter Olympics and dined with him after the games. German troops destroyed homes and other property during their World War II occupation of Norway, but according to historians they left alone the Henie family home when they found a signed photo of Hitler inside personally inscribed to the figure skater. Ultimately, she became a naturalized U.S. citizen who supported American troops during World War II, but she did not return to perform in her native Norway until the 1950s. She later said she made the Nazi salute in 1936 to help her chances of earning success at the Olympic Games, which were held in Germany.

POP CULTURE

Few figure skaters achieve pop-culture fame beyond skating to the level reached by American Dorothy Hamill. Hamill owned 1976, winning both Olympic and World Championship gold. With nothing left to prove, Hamill retired from international competition. In those days, the IOC and U.S. Olympic Committee enforced tight restrictions on amateurism and how athletes could earn money, but Hamill was so popular that her notoriety continued to soar. Her bob haircut became the most sought-after hairstyle among women in the United States. She joined the traveling Ice Capades as its featured performer. In the early 1990s the international news service Associated Press surveyed Americans about their favorite and most recognizable athletes. Hamill, who had not competed in nearly 20 years, finished second in the survey.

Not many Hollywood studies make films about figure skating. What few movies are made earn little money. The 2007 comedy *Blades of Glory* broke the mold in multiple ways and became a box office smash, earning nearly $150 million worldwide. *Blades* starred comedians Will Ferrell (portraying Chazz Michael Michaels) and Jon Heder (as Jimmy MacElroy) as rival men's figure skaters forced to team up and compete in pairs. Their success depends on whether they can complete a dangerous move called the "Iron Lotus," which when done wrong results in the decapitation of one of the skaters. "What do you say?" says Michaels and MacElroy's trainer. "Let's give it a try!"

SCANDALS

American Nancy Kerrigan had just finished a practice session at the 1994 U.S. Figure Skating Championships when a man ambushed her, striking her just above the right knee with a club. Television cameras caught the aftermath: Kerrigan in pain as officials and her team tended to her. She could not complete her attempt to qualify for the Olympics—to the potential benefit of fellow competitor Tonya Harding. The attacker, it turned out, was an associate of Harding's ex-husband, and Harding was alleged to have held some awareness of the attack; she later pleaded guilty to obstructing prosecutors.

Harding qualified for the Olympics, but even though Kerrigan did not, her fellow skaters voted to let her have the second qualifying spot. The injury caused by the attack was emotionally traumatic, but it was not physically debilitating. Kerrigan earned the silver medal. Harding placed eighth. Years after the attack, Harding maintained she did not know in advance that it would happen but that she nevertheless felt guilty because of her association to the conspirators. Her life and the attack became the subject of the 2017 biopic *I, Tonya*.

POLITICS

Something peculiar began popping up in the song choices of the world's top figure skaters in the mid-1990s. Figure skaters mingle basic elements with their more artistic moves and then bring it all together with coordinated wardrobes and music. For the song choice, many began selecting music from the film *Schindler's List*. The film is considered by many to be American director Steven Spielberg's masterpiece. It is common for skaters to use film scores in their performances. What raised the curiosity and discomfort of some fans, however, is that *Schindler's List* tells the story of Nazi Holocaust victims and survivors and features graphic scenes of mass genocide. Why do skaters keep wrapping their act in a robe of genocide? For its emotional impact and inspirational message of hope, skaters say.

Music from the emotionally powerful film lends itself well to the pageantry of figure skating, so much so that it has become routine at top-level figure-skating competitions to see skaters gliding on the ice to the composer John Williams's haunting score. Still, audiences and media notice. Every four years, when the Winter Olympics come around, some of the world's largest media organizations make it a point to let their audiences know why music from a movie about the Nazi Holocaust is in the background while figures leap and twirl through the air.

PATRIOTISM AND NATIONAL PRIDE

In the early part of the 20th century, Russia and then the Soviet Union were conspicuously absent from the competitive figure-skating scene. The first World Championships were held in Russia, which had built a tradition of excellence in the sport. Then for decades their program drifted from the national spotlight. But as the middle part of the 20th century approached, World War II ended and the Soviets emerged as a global power. They chose sports as one way to showcase cultural dominance.

Two married Soviet skaters, Ludmila Belousova and Oleg Protopopov, won a gold medal in pairs figure skating at the 1964 Winter Olympics in Innsbruck, Austria. The Soviets dominated many of the speed and power sports at the summer games, and now they were winning the grace and agility events as well. Soviet Premier Nikita Khrushchev could not have been more proud. In 1968 Belousova and Protopopov won again. While the couple made their government proud, they were unhappy living under communist rule. They defected to Switzerland in the 1970s and continued to skate public exhibitions as a couple into the early 2000s.

Timeline

3000 BCE – The first ice skates, made from animal bones, are made. Scientists believe they were first developed by the Finns and also used in Russia.

1610 CE – Holy Roman Emperor Rudolf II orders the construction of an ice carnival, partially to showcase ice skating.

1742 – The Edinburgh Skating Club is formed in Scotland and is believed to be the first formal skating organization.

1850 – American Edward Bushnell invents steel blades, which revolutionizes the types of moves skaters can accomplish.

1858 – Figure skating takes off in the United States when a skating pond opens in New York City. Five years later, the Skating Club of New York is founded, and a year after that—1864—Jackson Haines wins the Championships of America, held in Troy, New York.

1896 – St. Petersburg, Russia, hosts the first World Figure Skating Championships, which continue to take place annually.

1901 – Swede Ulrich Salchow wins his first of 10 world championships.

1908 – Figure skating becomes the first winter event held during an Olympic Games. Women and men are both allowed to compete individually and in pairs.

1922 – The World Figure Skating Championships take place for the first time since 1914, before the outbreak of World War I.

1952 – Ice dancing is added to the World Championships.

1964 – Soviet pair skaters Ludmila Belousova and Oleg Protopopov, a married couple, wins gold in pair skating at the Winter Olympics. They win gold again in 1968 and, remarkably, Soviet/Russian skaters win gold in the event at every Olympics through 2006.

1976 – American Dorothy Hamill wins gold medals at the Olympics and World Championships, while her haircut becomes a national fad.

2017 – *I, Tonya,* the film about American figure skater Tonya Harding, who was involved in a plot to injure a competitor, debuts and earns three Academy Award nominations.

See also: Ice Hockey; Olympics; Speed Skating.

Further Reading
Brennan, C. (1998). *Edge of Glory: The Inside Story of the Quest for Figure Skating's Olympic Gold Medals.* Scribner: New York.
Fleming, P. (1999). *The Long Program: Skating Toward Life's Victories.* Atria: New York.
Goodwin, J. (2007). *The Second Mark: Courage, Corruption, and the Battle for Olympic Gold.* Simon & Schuster: New York.
Hamill, D. (2007). *A Skating Life: My Story.* Hyperion: Glendale, California.
Hamilton, S. (2018). *Finish First: Winning Changes Everything.* Thomas Nelson: New York.
Poe, C. (2002). *Conditioning for Figure Skating: Off-Ice Techniques for On-Ice Performance.* McGraw-Hill: New York.
Rippon, A. (2019). *Beautiful on the Outside: A Memoir.* Grand Central Publishing: New York.
Russell, R.R. (2012). *Tales from a Not-So-Graceful-Ice Princess.* Aladdin: New York.
Ryan, J. (2018). *Little Girls in Pretty Boxes: The Making and Breaking of Elite Gymnasts and Figure Skaters.* Grand Central Publishing: New York.
Skipper, C. (2018). "How Johnny Weir and Tara Lipinski Became the Most Iconic Duo in Figure Skating." *GQ,* Feb. 12, 2018. https://www.gq.com/story/name-a-more-iconic-duo-johnny-weir-tara-lipinski-interview.

Football

American football is the United States' most popular spectator sport, and there is no close second. Forty of the 50 most watched sporting events in 2018 were National Football League (NFL) games, while of the remaining 10 events, two were college football games. "In life, as in football," said one of the game's earliest fans, former U.S. president Theodore Roosevelt, "the principle to follow is to hit the line hard" (Roosevelt 1900, 574).

Popular both as a college sport and professional sport, American football primarily takes place on Saturdays and Sundays during the fall. With some minor exceptions, a football game includes 11 players per side with the ultimate goal of moving the ball across the end zone to score a touchdown. Its roots lie in rugby and soccer. Pieces of each were taken to create football, with more of rugby's principles edging out soccer's as the game developed.

American football is the most popular sport in the United States. A fall and winter sport, it began as a college game but evolved into a professional enterprise by the early 20th century. (Courtesy of DePauw University)

American football dominates much of American culture, whether through advertising, marketing, spectating, or pop culture. A dangerous game, football is as noteworthy for its violence as its excitement. Players wear heavy padding to protect themselves, though padding can only save players for so long when they are being tackled or run into on nearly every play. It is common for retired players to experience long-term neurological and orthopedic problems. Multiple scientific studies have suggested that the average lifespan of an NFL player is 15 to 20 years shorter than that of men who did not play professional football.

The sport primarily was and is played by men, as opposed to most other sports around the world that have grown to become more inclusive.

HISTORICAL CONTEXT

Rutgers University and Princeton University played in 1869 what is recognized as the first American football game, although if people watched that first game today, they would not think of it as football. Football had an identity crisis in its earliest years: Would it be more heavily influenced by rugby or by soccer? In the end it was more rugby, because football requires players to use their hands, but it does owe its 11 players per side to soccer.

Yale University player and coach Walter Camp is credited as the "Father of American Football." In 1876 Camp and others attended what is known as the Massasoit Convention in Springfield, Massachusetts, to hammer out football's rules.

Most were written by Camp, including such basics as what the names of the positions were and how the field would be laid out. Camp served as an ambassador of the game as well, popularizing it first on the United States' East Coast, as head coach of Yale; then on the West Coast, as head coach of Stanford University; then to the rest of the country, as the originator of college football's popular All-American team, which to this day recognizes annually the best college players in the country; and lastly, as the author of numerous books.

Football's professional presence took a big step in 1920 with the formation of the American Professional Football Association, which two years later rebranded as the NFL. While college football flourished, the professional game succeeded or failed to varying degrees before finally finding real traction with the success of the 1958 NFL Championship Game. It was broadcast nationally and, by sheer luck, also happened to be the first championship game to go into overtime. Nicknamed "the Greatest Game Ever Played," the 1958 championship won over new fans and gave sportswriters a lot to write about. In part because of this game, football less than 10 years later would become the United States' most popular sport.

In 1967 the NFL and upstart American Football League (AFL) played a championship game that soon would be rebranded the Super Bowl. The NFL absorbed the AFL in 1970 to form one larger, more popular league, and over the decades the Super Bowl became an American phenomenon. Twenty-four of the 30 most watched television programs in American history are Super Bowls, with the game routinely exceeding 100 million viewers, because people use the game as a reason to host parties or go out to bars to watch it.

GLOBALIZATION

Two of the United States' more popular sports, baseball and basketball, have become popular around the world. It is interesting, then, that football, America's most popular sport domestically, has not had the same success abroad, despite numerous attempts to export the game. American football has a minor presence in Europe and Australia, but it is far from extraordinary. The World League of American Football debuted across Europe in 1991 and was rebranded as NFL Europe in 1998, but by 2007 the league ceased operations.

Perhaps not surprising because of its proximity to the United States, Canada boasts the second largest professional American football league in the world. The Canadian Football League, formed in 1958, plays on a 110-yard field, and the field is wider as well, which means each team gets 12 players per side instead of 11. Teams get three downs to move 10 yards instead of four. As a result, passing has become a larger part of the game, because CFL offenses have fewer opportunities to move the ball a farther distance. The CFL season ends with the Grey Cup, which was named after the Fourth Earl Grey, Canada's governor general from 1904 to 1911, and was originally awarded to amateur football teams. The governor general, as legend has it, had hoped the Cup would be awarded in the sport of hockey, not American football.

> *Doing It Their Way*
>
> In the late 1970s the University of Miami football team had become so ineffectual and interest in the community had dwindled so low that the college's administrators considered dropping the team down from Division I, the sport's largest college division, to Division II, in order to save money and put their priorities elsewhere. Instead, they decided to give the program one last chance. The school hired Howard Schnellenberger as its new coach, and he boasted that he had a five-year plan to win the national championship. In his fifth year, Miami won the championship, and a two-decade college football dynasty was born.
>
> But admiration did not follow success. Until the Miami Hurricanes came around, college football championed a modest, workmanlike attitude. Players were to be seen, not heard, while coaches did all the talking. At Miami, the players took center stage. They openly celebrated after big plays, scored so many points against their opponents that they did not care when they earned unsportsmanlike-conduct penalties, and refused to engage in the clichés and pleasantries spoken so often by college football players of the past.
>
> Between 1983 and 2001, Miami won five national championships, but it was its attitude that earned national attention. The magazine *Sports Illustrated* asked on the cover of one issue whether Miami should get rid of football altogether because of all the rules violations going on behind the scenes. Documentary filmmaker Billy Corben made not one but two films about the Miami football program. Old-time football broadcasters lectured their audiences about why Miami wasn't worthy of their respect. Despite all of this, the Miami players and the coaches who followed Schnellenberger did not care about public response. They had charted a new course for college football.

WHERE IT'S PLAYED TODAY

American football is played in the United States, Canada, Mexico, Australia, and parts of Europe. Small pockets of the sport exist in other parts of the world, but the participation numbers are too low and erratic to tabulate.

Within the United States, recent medical studies that shown the health risks of playing football have slightly reduced the number of youth participants. In the early 21st century former professional football players began to tell stories of long-term side effects from playing, including memory loss, uncontrollable erratic behavior, and extreme sensitivity to light. Multiple high-profile players committed suicide. *Forbes* magazine reported that in a single year youth participation in football dropped in the United States by 3 percent (Cook 2019).

ECONOMICS AND MEDIA

In the early 1960s, America's broadcast networks approached Major League Baseball about televising more games. The MLB balked, worried that if people could watch on television, no one would go to games anymore. Pete Rozelle, then the commissioner of the NFL, saw an opportunity and immediately agreed to a partnership with the networks that almost changed the course of televised sport and American culture. By fall of 1965 the NFL's TV ratings had surpassed the MLB's, and baseball, once "America's pastime," never regained its status as America's top sport.

DIMENSIONS OF THE SPORT

American football is played on a 100-yard-long field with 10-yard-deep end zones on each end. The goal for the offensive team is to get the ball into the end zone, either by a player holding the ball and running it in or by throwing the ball to a player who catches it in the end zone. The field is 160 feet wide.

Each team gets four tries, called downs, to move the ball 10 yards. If players are able to accomplish that, they get another four tries to move the ball another 10 yards. A team's offensive possession can end one of five ways:

1. Scoring a touchdown, which is worth six points and includes a chance after the touchdown to kick the ball through uprights for an extra point.
2. Scoring a field goal—which is done by kicking the ball through the upright that is positioned at the back of the end zone—without having first scored a touchdown.
3. Turning the ball over to the other team on downs, which is what happens when a team does not move the ball 10 yards following its four attempts.
4. Punting the ball, which takes place on fourth down when a team decides it likely cannot achieve a first down. A punt occurs when one player boots the ball downfield toward the other team.
5. Completing a turnover in which the defensive team either causes the offensive team to fumble (drop the ball while running with it) or makes an interception (catches a pass thrown by the other team).

Professional and college football games are split into four 15-minute quarters, with a halftime declared between the second and third quarters. Football games for younger players might consist of 8-, 10-, or 12-minute quarters. Although football games supposedly should last little more than an hour, they often last much longer because of television commercials used to generate revenue for team owners and league officials. Professional and college games routinely last at least three hours, but there is only about 11 minutes of actual game action.

More than 20 positions exist in football. Most visible is the quarterback, the offensive player responsible for running a team's offense. The quarterback has the option to throw the ball or to hand off to a teammate who will run with the ball.

IMPORTANT FIGURES

In 1963 the NFL included in its inaugural Hall of Fame class Jim Thorpe, whom the Associated Press once named the greatest American athlete of the first half of the 20th century. In addition to winning Olympic medals in track and field, Thorpe excelled at football, which he learned from legendary coach Glenn "Pop" Warner. Thorpe, of Native American descent, was recognized by some as the first president of the American Professional Football Association before it became the NFL. He played 52 NFL games between 1920 and 1928.

All sports have star players, but it's rare to find one so dominant that he makes other stars look paltry by comparison. When NFL wide receiver Jerry Rice retired in 2004, he had nearly 8,000 more yards receiving than anyone in league history, 400 more catches than anyone else, and 30 more touchdowns than any player at any position.

POP CULTURE

The 1985 Chicago Bears won the NFL's Super Bowl, but they accomplished far more than just that. Led by running back Walter Payton and quarterback Jim McMahon, the Bears accelerated the NFL's move into mainstream culture with a song and music video called the "Super Bowl Shuffle," in which they sang about how good they were and showed supreme confidence by releasing the song *before* they won the Super Bowl. The album sold more than 500,000 copies and received regular airplay on radio stations across the country.

The video game series Madden NFL has generated nearly $5 billion in sales and sold more than 150 million copies since the first game came out in 1993. Named for former NFL coach and broadcaster John Madden, Madden NFL lets users simulate professional football games, control game action, make personnel moves, and design plays. NFL players openly lobby to be on the game's cover, while retailers routinely sell out of the game on the day each year that the new version is released.

SCANDALS

In 2013 two investigate journalists published the book *League of Denial*, which detailed the NFL's decades-long choice to ignore brain damage being caused to its players directly by the game of football. The book was thorough and incriminating, detailing, among other things, false scientific evidence provided by the NFL to medical journals, and players being lied to about their own condition. The scandal grew when the sports network ESPN, a partner of the NFL's, backed out of an agreement to show a documentary based on the book, presumably because of its relationship with the league.

Ex-NFL players, many who suffered debilitating injuries during their careers, sued the league, which eventually settled out of court for nearly $700 million. As part of the agreement the league did not have to admit any guilt. The NFL also agreed to fund further research into chronic traumatic encephalopathy (CTE), the football-caused brain condition that gives some players symptoms the rest of their lives, including severe depression that sometimes leads to suicide.

POLITICS

NFL team owners were incensed during the 2016 season when sports media focused their cameras on San Francisco 49ers quarterback Colin Kaepernick. Kaepernick, frustrated by police violence against African Americans, took the suggestion of a military veteran and began to kneel during the American national anthem, which was played before each game.

Some fans supported Kaepernick while others did not. When other players around the league began to follow Kaepernick's lead, some team owners ordered their players not to do so and threatened to cut them from the team. A couple of team owners actually showed solidarity with their players by joining them on the field to support Kaepernick's cause.

Kaepernick faced backlash. No team was willing to sign him after the 2016 season. The president of the United States called him a vulgar name to a national audience. The NFL, it turned out, colluded to keep Kaepernick out of the league and awarded him an undisclosed cash settlement in 2019.

PATRIOTISM AND NATIONAL PRIDE

American football has grown its audience by connecting football to three American institutions: the military, Judeo-Christian traditions, and patriotism. This became most evident in 2015 when two U.S. congressmen revealed that the military had paid the NFL millions of dollars in sports marketing contracts to include military content in and around its games, including the pregame flyovers of jet fighters. YouTube had become full of videos from football games that showed returning soldiers surprising their families before and during games. Many of these videos, it turned out, were a result of the marketing dollars paid by the military to football leagues.

Timeline

1869 – Rutgers University and Princeton University play the first football game, although it looks little like the game of today.

1876 – Football begins to take its modern shape at the Massasoit Convention, where Walter Camp leads a group to determine the sport's first rules and regulations.

1893 – The Pittsburgh Athletic Club gives a football player a contract, turning football into a professional sport.

1899 – The Morgan Athletic Club, known today as the Arizona Cardinals of the National Football League, forms. It is the longest-tenured active professional football team in the United States.

1906 – The first legal forward pass is thrown by St. Louis University.

1906 – Following a combined 37 deaths caused by football between 1904 and 1905, President Theodore Roosevelt encourages football's custodians to make the game safer and threatens to get the government involved. Rules are added by the newly formed National Collegiate Athletic Association (NCAA) to curb the game's violence.

1912 – The touchdown is determined to be worth six points.

1922 – The American Professional Football Association changes its name to the National Football League.

1935 – The first Heisman Trophy, awarded to college football's top player, is awarded to the University of Chicago's Jay Berwanger.

1943 – The University of Iowa's Nile Kinnick, who won the 1939 Heisman Trophy, dies during a Navy pilot training flight during World War II.

1950 – The plastic football helmet becomes commonplace in the NFL, replacing leather.

1957 – Jim Brown, considered the greatest running back ever, debuts for the NFL's Cleveland Browns.

1958 – At the age of 96, Amos Alonzo Stagg coaches his final college football game. To put his tenure into context, Stagg (who lived another seven years) once coached a game against Walter Camp, the "Father of American Football," on Christmas Day 1884, which by then was already his fifth season as a coach.

1960 – Pete Rozelle is elected commissioner of the NFL.

1965 – The television ratings for football surpass baseball. As of 2020, football remains the most popular televised sport in the United States.

1966 – Author George Plimpton publishes *Paper Lion*, his first-person account of trying out for the NFL's Detroit Lions.

1967 – The first AFL-NFL Championship Game is held and won by the Green Bay Packers. The game soon would be rebranded as the Super Bowl.

1968 – The University of Southern California's O.J. Simpson wins the Heisman Trophy. He goes on to a successful career as a professional player, actor, and broadcaster, but in 1995 he becomes the defendant in one of the most infamous murder trials of the 20th century. He is found not guilty in criminal court but liable in civil court.

1993 – Alan Page, the first defensive player to win the NFL's Most Valuable Player award, is elected to the Minnesota Supreme Court.

2015 – 114.4 million viewers tune in to watch the New England Patriots beat the Seattle Seahawks in the Super Bowl—a record for an American television audience.

2019 – At $5 billion, *Forbes* magazine names the NFL's Dallas Cowboys the most valuable franchise in all of professional sports.

See also: Baseball; Rugby; Soccer.

Further Reading

Bissinger, H. G. (1990). *Friday Night Lights: A Town, a Team, and a Dream.* Addison-Wesley: Boston.

Camp, W. (2010). *The Book of Football* (1910): Reprint. Kessinger Publishing LLC: Whitefish, Montana.

Cook, B. (2019). "High School Football Participation is On a Decade-Long Decline." *Forbes*, Aug. 29, 2019. https://www.forbes.com/sites/bobcook/2019/08/29/high-school-football-participation-is-on-a-decade-long-decline/#695e026e33de.

Fainaru-Wada, M. and Fainaru, S. (2013). *League of Denial: The NFL, Concussions, and the Battle for Truth.* Three Rivers Press: New York.

Gallagher, R. C. (2008). *The Express: The Ernie Davis Story.* Ballantine Books: New York.

MacCambridge, M. (2004). *America's Game: The Epic Story of How Pro Football Captured a Nation*. Random House: New York.

Maraniss, D. (2000). *When Pride Still Mattered: A Life of Vince Lombardi*. Simon & Schuster: New York.

Pearlman, J. (2018). *Football for a Buck: The Crazy Rise and Crazier Demise of the USFL*. Houghton Mifflin Harcourt: Boston.

Plimpton, G. (1966). *Paper Lion*. Harper & Row: New York.

Roosevelt, T. (1900). "What We Can Expect of the American Boy." *St. Nicholas Magazine*, May 1900, 574.

Vogan, T. (2014). *Keepers of the Flame: NFL Films and the Rise of Sports Media*. University of Illinois Press: Champaign.

G

Golf

Many strands of golf make it a unique sport, but its most distinguishing quality might be that it is one of the few sports ever created in which the lowest score wins. In golf, a game predicated on how few strokes one can take to hit a ball into a hole, 68 beats 75. It is played around the world, on every continent, by amateurs and professionals, recreational and competitive players. Golf also is hundreds of years older than other sports, with origins that might reach even deeper than that. Today, because of the time and money needed to play, wealthier and upper-middle-class people tend to dominate the game's participation numbers. It is a game with a complex history, associated with leisure, classism, bigotry of all sorts, immense skill, personal honor, and a requisite patience that few have been able to master.

HISTORICAL CONTEXT

Golf has experienced several boom periods in its long, complicated, murky history, but the game as we know it today grew to popularity in mid-1800s Scotland. As was the case in many of today's popular international sports, such as tennis, cricket, and rugby, the game first spread through the United Kingdom and then to the rest of the world through the United Kingdom's imperialist ambitions.

Golf's etymology rests in the old Dutch word *kolf*, which means "club" or "bat." The old course at St. Andrews in Scotland is considered the oldest continuously played golf course. Golfers first played it in the early 15th century; The Open Championship (also known as the British Open), considered one of professional golf's four premier events (known as "majors") took place at St. Andrews as recently as 2021. The Royal & Ancient, the governing body of golf throughout much of the world, is headquartered at St. Andrews.

Scottish and British slave traders opened a course on Bunce Island in Sierra Leone around 1775, which brought the game to the African continent. In 1829 the British opened the first golf club outside of the United Kingdom when it established the Royal Calcutta Golf Club in India, which brought golf to Asia. During this time the game became more widespread throughout the United Kingdom and the rest of Europe as well. According to historian John Lowerson, England had 12 golf courses in 1880, 50 by 1887, and more than 1,000 by 1914. During this boom period British imperialists also brought golf to other parts of its empire, including Canada, Singapore, South Africa, and Oceania.

A golf-like game might have been played in what is now the Netherlands in the late 13th century, but that story is more legend than factual—similar to baseball's Abner Doubleday origin story. Evidence also exists that golf first came to North America and the American colonies in the mid-17th century. As in the rest of the world, however, golf in the United States experienced its most significant growth in the 19th century. The U.S. Golf Association was formed near the end of the 19th century in part to bring together competing organizations and to help stabilize a growing game. America's post–World War I cultural explosion of the 1920s saw the number of golf courses grow to more than a 1,000. Today, there are about 15,000.

The modern form of golf evolved mostly in Scotland, including Kirkcaldy on the nation's eastern coast (pictured in this 1898 image). The sport has wrestled with issues of class and race over the last century. (The Illustrated London News Picture Library)

GLOBALIZATION

Improved transportation and media have helped unify global interest in golf, despite a 20-year lull spurred by the global depression of the 1930s and World War II into the mid-1940s. American Walter Hagan in 1922 became the first American-born player to win the Open Championship, which had been played annually most years since 1860. Golf became hugely popular in Japan during the early 20th century. Following a dormant period during World War II, followed by foreign occupation right after it, golf's popularity within the country was so insatiable, and so many golf courses were built, that some considered it an environmental hazard. Today there are nearly 2,500 courses in Japan. To compare, about 8 percent of Americans golf regularly, while in Japan about 13 percent golf.

Television's growth further fueled golf's expansion. Three golfers from the mid-20th century in particular helped drive popularity as television as a medium took off. Most notable was American Arnold Palmer, who, contrary to many other golfers, came from working-class roots and public golf courses. Born in a steel-mill town, Palmer learned the game from his father, a groundskeeper, and then honed it while in the military. He turned professional in the 1950s and became an instant sensation: charismatic, handsome, and funny. Americans, many of whom considered themselves part of "Arnie's Army," took up recreational golf because of Palmer.

Palmer was part of golf's "Big Three," along with South African Gary Player (see "Important Figures") and American Jack Nicklaus. Each won more majors than Palmer did—Nicklaus has won more majors than any other golfer has—but Palmer's popularity remained unmatched. In 1964 he won the first World Match Play Championship, an annual event in Europe. Palmer, Player, and Nicklaus won 8 of the first 10 Match Play Championships, furthering their friendly rivalry while growing the game.

As an example of golf's global popularity, consider that between 2004 and 2014, the prestigious U.S. Open golf tournament was won by golfers from South Africa, New Zealand, Australia, Argentina, Northern Ireland, the United States, England, and Germany.

WHERE IT'S PLAYED TODAY

Golfers tee off on every continent—Antarctica included, although the ice makes for odd bounces. Professional players cross the globe each year in search of the best competition and mightiest paychecks. Recreational players never have to look too far for a course. The game itself is played on a golf course, a mass of land that on average ranges from 100 to 200 acres.

In many communities the land was gifted decades ago, tax-free, to course owners, which means that course owners earn money from greens fees while local communities earn nothing in tax revenue on massive chunks of land. Such public-private partnerships are said to exploit local communities, many of which include low-income people in their residential area who are unable to afford to play golf. This results in low-income people unable to partake in recreational opportunities within their own community, and the golf course, which is tax-exempt, offering nothing back to local low-income residents.

ECONOMICS AND MEDIA

Golf requires significant financial and social resources, which limits the number of recreational golfers who are able to play. A single, 18-hole round takes, on average, about 4½ hours to complete and, on a public course, costs anywhere from $25 to $300. Additionally, golfers must bring their own golf clubs, the full set of which might cost $200 to $2,000. Proper golf shoes and attire also are required. On many courses, a comfortable pair of shorts and T-shirt are not allowed. To become good at golf takes practice, and the only way to practice is by gaining access to hundreds of rounds of golf—hence, the financial barriers.

Professional golf exists around the world. The highest levels include the European Tour, the Professional Golf Association (PGA), and the Ladies Professional Golf Association (LPGA) in the United States; the Asian Tour; and the PGA of Australia. Winning a single event can earn a top professional golfer between $250,000 and $2 million. On the PGA Tour, the total purse from which all golfers get paid can run between $9 million and $12 million per event.

Lower-level professional golfers who are trying to work their way up earn significantly less money and hope to have their travel expenses paid by sponsors. The world's top professional golfers earn more from sponsorships than from golf. Tiger

Woods has earned the most sponsorship money among professional golfers, or any athlete, coming in at about $1.5 billion since 1996.

DIMENSIONS OF THE SPORT

The goal of golf is to hit a ball into a hole in as few strokes as possible. Golfers use several types of clubs to strike a spherical ball that is 5.28 inches in circumference: woods, which are used for longer distances, including off the tee (first shot on a hole); irons, which are used for middle-range distances; a putter, to roll the ball along the ground once it is close to the hole; a sand wedge to get out of a course's sand trap; and a pitching wedge for when the ball is too far to putt but too close to use an iron.

The typical golf course is 18 holes. To play them all is to play a "round" of golf. Each of the 18 holes earns a par score, or the number of strokes it should take to finish the hole. Par can be 3, 4, or 5 strokes, depending on the distance from the tee, where the first shot is made, to the hole. A typical par 3 hole might be 180 yards, while a par 5 might be 530 yards, and a par 4, which is most common, is somewhere in between.

The scoring on a hole goes as such:

Par = The golfer used exactly the number of strokes to finish the hole as was prescribed (e.g., four strokes on a par 4 hole).

Birdie = The golfer finished a hole in one stroke under par (e.g., three strokes on a par 4 hole).

Eagle = The golfer finished a hole in two strokes under par (e.g., three strokes on a par 5 hole).

Double eagle = The golfer finished a hole in three strokes under par (e.g., two strokes on a par 5 hole). This is the rarest single-hole result in all of golf.

Ace = The golfer finished a hole in just one stroke, also known as a "hole in one." This happens almost exclusively on a par 3 hole.

Bogey = The golfer finished a hole in one stroke over par (e.g., five strokes on a par 4 hole).

Double bogey, triple bogey, etc. = The golfer finished a hole in two strokes, three strokes, etc., over par.

Following a round of golf, the player who scored the lowest total score over 18 holes wins. Some events cover multiple rounds. In a four-round event, the golfer who scored the lowest over 72 holes wins.

IMPORTANT FIGURES

Nothing Gary Player did qualified as normal. Player, of South Africa, not only built a career as one of the best golfers of his era but also became a fitness icon before fitness became trendy and big business. He earned the nickname "Mr. Fitness" and, in 2015 at the age of 80, shared his fitness tips with the prestigious magazine *Sports Illustrated*. He also became a champion of civil rights after first signaling support early in his career for South Africa's system of apartheid—the governmental initiative of creating legal discrimination against people of color. He later rejected that view, acknowledged his error in judgment, and defied the South African government.

In 2000 Michelle Wie qualified for the U.S. Women's Amateur at age 10, becoming at that time the youngest person ever to qualify for that event. Three years later, she became the youngest person ever to make the cut at an LPGA event. She was an overnight celebrity, with expectations heaped upon her before she even had time to enjoy being a teenager. Wie never fulfilled those unrealistic expectations, but she still found professional success, winning five professional tournaments before the age of 30.

Tiger Woods, like Wie, was a child golf prodigy. He appeared on American television at the age of 2 to show off his golf swing alongside celebrity Bob Hope. Upon turning professional Woods became one of the most successful men's professional golfers of all time, winning 15 majors, second only to Jack Nicklaus's 18. At age 22 in 1997, Woods won the United States' premier golf event, the Masters, by a record 12 strokes. He went on to become the most famous athlete of his generation. Sports apparel company Nike even expanded its golf presence specifically to capitalize on its relationship with Woods, whose career prime was limited by back and leg injuries.

POP CULTURE

Movies come and go, but *Caddyshack*, the 1980 golf-centered comedy starring Bill Murray, Rodney Dangerfield, and other comedy legends, became a permanent part of American pop culture because of its repeatable quotes, prominence on cable

---

Ben Hogan Barely Survives, but Then Returns

Ben Hogan's pelvis was crushed. So was the entire left side of his body: shoulder, collarbone, knee, ribs, ankle. So were his left eye and internal organs. In 1949, while driving back from the Phoenix Open with his wife, Valerie, on a foggy night, Hogan noticed a Greyhound bus coming straight at them in their lane. Ben stretched to his right to protect Valerie when the bus struck their car head on. Somehow they both survived, but barely. Hogan had served in and survived World War II, but somehow the transport to and from a golf tournament had proved more dangerous.

Hogan was one of his era's top golfers before the accident, but his ability to come back from it—after a one-year hiatus to recover—made him a golfing legend. Not only did Hogan return, he found success. He finished tied for the lead in his very first tournament before losing in an 18-hole playoff. Hogan never fully regained his strength, while his left eye grew progressively worse as he aged. Still, in 1953 Hogan had a season for the ages. He entered six tournaments (he could not play a full PGA schedule because of his injuries) and won five, including all three majors that he entered: the Masters, the British Open, and the U.S. Open, the latter of which he also won in 1950 and 1951 after the accident.

Hogan later cowrote the book, *Ben Hogan's Five Lessons: The Modern Fundamentals of Golf*, which, more than 60 years since it was published, remains one of the most read books about an approach to golf by young, novice, and experienced golfers. He died in 1997 at the age of 84. Valerie died two years later.

television, and extensive DVD sales. The Internet Movie Database ranked *Caddyshack* as the fourth-greatest comedy film of all time. Largely without a recognizable plot, *Caddyshack* followed the exploits of golf caddies, rich country club members, and a greenskeeper desperate to keep gophers away from the course.

In 1996 Kevin Costner, nicknamed "King of the Sports Movie," starred in *Tin Cup*, a film about a brilliant but self-destructive golfer named Roy McAvoy. A fairly typical romance about an underdog trying to make a comeback, *Tin Cup* became famous for one of its final lines. In the film's climax, McAvoy again self-destructs, this time on the 18th hole of the U.S. Open, when he continually hits the ball into the water. He ultimately earns a 12 on the hole when the ball goes in the hole off the tee, sending the crowd into a frenzy. Molly Griswold, played by Rene Russo, then declares that years from now nobody will remember who won or lost, but they will remember McAvoy's 12.

SCANDALS

Golf's exclusivity has long caused it to inflict bigotry among select groups of people on the basis of race, gender, and class. Much of this occurred in the United States at institutions called country clubs—private clubs used to socialize, conduct business, and recreate at sports such as golf and tennis. For decades country clubs, because they were private, could restrict membership to, for example, just men or just white people. Augusta National Golf Club, which opened in 1932, did not admit its first African American member until 1990 or its first female member until 2012.

Bigotry extended to the players as well. Tiger Woods, who is of Thai and African American descent, faced taunts from fellow players after winning the 1997 Masters (which, perhaps not coincidentally, takes place at Augusta National). When Woods fired his caddy in 2011, the caddy made public racist comment about Woods to the press. As of the writing of this book, country clubs still exist in the United States that refuse to admit women.

POLITICS

Several U.S. presidents held golf in high regard, none more than the 34th president, Dwight D. Eisenhower (1953–1961). Eisenhower so loved the game that he had a putting green installed on the White House lawn. He belonged to four country clubs, including Augusta National, which he visited 29 times during his presidency. Eisenhower did so much to promote golf in the United States that in 2009, 40 years after his death, he was inducted into the World Golf Hall of Fame. Other presidents who enjoyed golf included William Taft (1909–1913), John F. Kennedy (1961–1963), and Donald Trump (2017–2021).

PATRIOTISM AND NATIONAL PRIDE

In 1927 the Worcester Country Club in Massachusetts hosted a golf competition between teams from the United States and Great Britain, with the winner receiving a trophy donated by businessperson Samuel Ryder. The event, which came to be known as the Ryder Cup, now takes place biennially and has become one of the most heated rivalries and sought-after trophies in sports.

In 1979 the UK team was expanded to allow other European countries, partially due to the Americans' dominance in the event but also because of Spain's growing presence as a golfing power. Since the expansion, the European squad has won 11 times to the United States' 8 victories.

The event was created to be a friendly rivalry, and golf advocates preach the game's "gentlemanly" roots, but the Ryder Cup owns a history of bad feelings and poor sportsmanship brought on by patriotism and fierce tempers. A shouting match erupted between the teams in 1969 over putting etiquette. In 1999 heckling of Europe's Colin Montgomerie by American fans became so severe that his father left the course rather than listen to it.

Timeline

Early 15th century – Golf is first played in Scotland.

1759 – Stroke play is introduced.

1764 – The first 18-hole golf course is constructed, and it later becomes the standard.

1775 – British slave traders open the first golf course on the African continent.

1834 – British royals dub St. Andrews "Royal & Ancient" St. Andrews. Today the Royal & Ancient serves as golf's governing body to much of the world.

1895 – St. Andrews becomes home to the first women's golf club.

1927 – The first Ryder Cup is played between Great Britain and the United States.

1932 – The Augusta National Golf Club, designed by Bobby Jones, opens. Two years later it hosts the first Masters Tournament.

1956 – Babe Didrikson Zaharias, a two-time Olympic gold medalist in track and field and winner of 82 golf tournaments, including 10 women's major championships, dies from cancer at age 45.

1962 – Jack Nicklaus wins his first of a professional-record 18 major championships.

1974 – Francis Ouimet, considered the "Father of Amateur Golf," is elected to the World Golf Hall of Fame.

1978 – Nancy Lopez, a rookie on the LPGA Tour, wins 5 consecutive events and 9 overall and appears on the cover of *Sports Illustrated*.

1997 – American Tiger Woods wins the Masters by a record 12 strokes at age 22.

2008 – Swede Annika Sörenstam retires at the young age of 38 as the most successful women's golfer in history, with 93 professional wins.

See also: Baseball; Cricket; Tennis.

Further Reading

Browning, R. (1955). *A History of Golf: The Royal and Ancient Game*. Papamoa Press: Chicago.

Demas, L. (2017). *Game of Privilege: An African-American History of Golf.* University of North Carolina Press: Chapel Hill.

Feinstein, J. (1996). *A Good Walk Spoiled: Days and Nights on the PGA Tour.* Little, Brown and Company: New York.

Frost, M. (2004). *The Greatest Game Ever Played: Harry Vardon, Francis Ouimet, and the Birth of Modern Golf.* Hachette Books: New York.

Frost, M. (2009). *The Match: The Day the Game of Golf Changed Forever.* Hachette Books: New York.

Hogan, B. and Wind, H. W. (1985). *Ben Hogan's Five Lessons: The Modern Fundamentals of Golf.* Touchstone: New York.

Lopez, N. and Schwed, P. (1979). *The Education of a Woman Golfer.* Simon & Schuster: New York.

Sorenstam, A. (2004). *Golf Annika's Way: How I Elevated My Game to Be the Best—and How You Can Too.* Gotham: New York.

Starn, O. (2011). *The Passion of Tiger Woods: An Anthropologist Reports on Golf, Race, and Celebrity Scandal.* Duke University Press: Durham, North Carolina.

Williamson, J. (2018). *Born on the Links: A Concise History of Golf.* Rowman & Littlefield Publishers: Lanham, Maryland.

Gymnastics

Gymnastics, one of the world's oldest sports, literally means "skilled in bodily exercise" and "to train naked," depending on the preferred etymology. Although today it involves human-made devices such as balance beams, pommel horses, and uneven bars, it can also be done naturally on tree branches, tree stumps, or by jumping off big rocks. Gymnastics is all about bodily control: balance, strength, and agility. It might be an individual, noncontact sport, but because of the abuse it lays on the human body, it also is one of the most taxing. Each year high school gymnasts in the United States suffer more injuries than athletes who compete in wrestling, ice hockey, softball, volleyball, or track and field. Gymnastics' roots reach deep into ancient human civilization. It began with our most basic curiosity about how to push our bodies to do new and impressive feats.

HISTORICAL CONTEXT

The ancient Greeks developed gymnastics to develop their bodies and help prepare for warfare. Key skills included jumping, throwing, running, and wrestling. The Greeks valued physical fitness and passed that love along to the Romans after they conquered ancient Greece. Whereas Greek culture focused heavily on fitness, the Romans used it almost exclusively as training for warfare. They included tumbling within gymnastics. But as Rome declined, so did its interest in gymnastics, and in 393 CE Roman emperor Theodosius banned the Olympics. Gymnastics remained as an obscure form of entertainment, but for the most part the skills faded from developing cultures.

Gymnastics, one of the world's most ancient sports, was developed by the Ancient Greeks and later passed along to Ancient Rome. Simone Biles (pictured) won 14 World Championships by the age of 22. (Zhukovsky/Dreamstime.com)

Then in 1811 German Friedrich Ludwig Jahn, embarrassed by how easily France and its emperor, Napoleon Bonaparte, had defeated his country, opened a gymnasium in Berlin. A staunch nationalist, Jahn intended to use gymnastics to empower Germans. However, he tried to extend his power beyond just being the state head of gymnastics training by moving into political endeavors. He received a prison sentence that was overturned, but he was also banned from Berlin. Nevertheless, he had succeeded at one thing: he resurrected gymnastics. Jahn had a hand in the invention of the parallel bars, rings, pommel horse, and high bar—all staples of men's gymnastics to this day.

The Federation of International Gymnastics (FIG) was founded in 1881. Fifteen years later, men's gymnastics was included in the first modern Olympic Games in Athens.

GLOBALIZATION

Gymnastics in its most pure form never needed to globalize. Kids tumbled and played all over the world. But its Olympic popularity, combined with standards determined by FIG and apparatuses influenced by Jahn, helped spread a more uniform idea of what organized, formal gymnastics could be. FIG had just three member countries—Belgium, France, and the Netherlands—until 1921, when it began to admit non-European countries. Today membership stands at around 150 countries.

Still, modern gymnastics did not totally crystalize until the 1950s, during the start of the Cold War. Then, the Soviet Union showed unparalleled dominance, winning team gold at the Olympics in 1952 and 1956. Soviet gymnasts won both the gold and silver individual men's medals in 1952, and Soviet gymnasts won all-around gold in 1952, 1956, 1960, 1976, 1980, and 1988. The Soviet Union collapsed before the 1992 Olympics, but Vitaly Scherbo, competing for a block of former Soviet states known as the Unified Team, won gold that year. Soviet women were even more dominant, winning team gold in the 1952, 1956, 1960, 1964, 1968, 1972, 1976, 1980, and 1988 games. They won gold at nine out of 10 Olympics; the only year within that time span that they did not win, 1984, was the year the Soviets boycotted the games in Los Angeles.

Gymnastics grew in the United States in large part due to the country's college athletics programs, a phenomenon unique to the country. As of 2018 there were 63 Division I colleges with women's gymnastics teams and 16 men's teams. Although, like most sports, gymnastics started as primarily a men's activity, gymnastics, especially in the United States, sees far higher participation among girls than boys at the youth and recreational levels.

WHERE IT'S PLAYED TODAY

Wherever there are children, there is gymnastics. A two-year-old attempting a somersault, an adolescent trying to balance across a log straddling a stream, a teenager jumping off a large tree branch—these display the origins of gymnastics. Beyond that, countries across the world offer gymnastics classes for children. The sport is everywhere.

On a more competitive level, the world's top gymnastics programs generally reside in China, Japan, Romania, Russia, and the United States. The last time a country other than one of those five won a team Olympic medal in women's gymnastics was when East Germany earned bronze in 1988—and East Germany is not even a country anymore. The situation is similar for men's gymnastics, although Great Britain did manage to sneak a bronze medal at the 2012 London Games. Ukraine also used to have some success on the world stage.

ECONOMICS AND MEDIA

As in many Olympic sports, most earnings by high-level competitors come from endorsements. American Simone Biles is one of the most decorated gymnasts in history (see "Important Figures"). Because of that, brands such as Nike, Kellogg's, Procter & Gamble, and others pay big money to attach their names to her. For those Olympic athletes who don't have many professional prospects beyond the Olympics, such as swimmer Michael Phelps and skier Lindsey Vonn, endorsement deals are critical to financial well-being.

Meanwhile, gymnastics remains the biggest draw among Olympics television viewers. In 2012 nearly two-thirds of all Americans watched at least some Olympics coverage, making it the most watched multiday event in American television history. Of those approximately 210 million people, the most watched sport was women's gymnastics. Men's gymnastics also placed high on the list. This allows television networks to charge more for brands to advertise during gymnastics telecasts. Networks periodically broadcast other gymnastics events, such as the U.S. and World Championships and some college meets, but for the most part, finding gymnastics on television is rare during non-Olympic seasons.

DIMENSIONS OF THE SPORT

Women compete in four events, and men compete in six. The four women's events are balance beam, floor exercise, uneven bars, and vault. Men compete in floor exercise, horizontal bar, parallel bars, pommel horse, still rings, and vault.

The floor exercise sometimes confuses audiences who do not understand how it is scored. In both women's and men's floor exercise, gymnasts compete on a 12-meter by 12-meter spring floor. The springs are covered by plywood, which is covered by gym mats. Women's floor exercise lasts up to 90 seconds and is accompanied by music, while men's typically lasts 60 to 70 seconds and takes place without music. In each version, gymnasts are required to showcase certain required skills while at the same time infusing their performance with creativity.

Scoring is even more complicated and has changed in recent years. It also varies depending on the level of gymnastics, individual versus team, and sometimes regionally. For individual events in American college gymnastics, athletes start off with a 10 and then have points deducted if they make a mistake. A perfect 10, therefore, would be a perfect routine. However, under some scoring systems, the starting score is 9.5, and even a gymnast who performed a flawless event would not earn a perfect 10 unless the judges decided that the athlete strung together or successfully attempted certain exercises, at which point the additional 0.5 could be added to the score to create a potential perfect 10.

IMPORTANT FIGURES

Gymnastics would not be as popular as it is today if it had not been for the success of Romanian Nadia Comaneci at the 1976 and 1980 Olympic games. In 1976 she became the first gymnast ever to earn a perfect 10 at the Olympics, doing so on the uneven bars. To show her performance was not a fluke, she eventually earned seven perfect 10s at the 1976 games: four on the uneven bars and the other three on the balance beam. At the 1980 games in Moscow, she earned two more perfect 10s. In all, she earned five gold medals and nine medals overall. She was inducted into the International Women's Sports Hall of Fame in 1990.

Li Ning won six Olympic medals at the 1984 games in Los Angeles while representing China. By the time he retired in 1988, he had won 14 world championships, earning him the nickname "Prince of Gymnastics." China shocked the gymnastics world by cutting him from the team before the 1988 games, but he recovered: the following year he started Li Ning Company Limited, one of the most financially successful sporting brands in the world, regularly totaling more than a billion dollars in annual revenue.

Simone Biles earned the title of greatest gymnast of all time before her career even ended. By the age of 22, she had earned four Olympic gold medals, 14 World Championships, and two FIG All-Around World Cups. She is likely to add to that count since, as of the writing of this book, she remains an active competitor. Biles also is an innovator. In 2019 she became the first female gymnast ever to successfully complete a triple-twisting double somersault on the floor exercise. After she hit it, the broadcasters just laughed in amazement.

POP CULTURE

Sports' dramatic nature naturally lends itself to pop culture, particularly film and television. Gymnastics, however, never has found its way around pop culture the way other sports have. One reason for this is the challenge of finding actors who can successfully pull off gymnastics exercises. There have been just a few mainstream examples.

Academy-Award-winning actor Jeff Bridges starred as a gymnastics coach in the 2006 film *Stick It*, about a rebellious teen, played by Missy Peregrym, who turns to the world of gymnastics. The film turned a modest profit at the box office. In 1985 three-time World Champion Kurt Thomas appeared in *Gymkata*, a film about a gymnast who combines gymnastics with martial arts in an international fighting competition. *Maxim* magazine in 2007 named *Gymkata* the 17th-worst movie of all time. A year later, in 1986, Mitch Gaylord, a member of the United States' 1984 gold-medal-winning Olympic team, starred in *American Anthem*, which told the story of a football player who became a gymnast and strove to make the Olympics. The film grossed less than $5 million—a paltry sum by any metric.

Gymnastics' deepest footprint in pop culture has come in the form of parody and humor. After American Keri Strug became a national hero for successfully performing a vault on a heavily damaged ankle during the 1996 Olympics in Atlanta—an accomplishment that secured the Americans the team gold—the sketch comedy television show *Saturday Night Live* created the character Kippy Strug. Kippy, played by Chris Kattan, was supposed to be Keri's brother, and he shared Keri's high-pitched voice and bubbly personality. In one episode, the two appeared alongside each other. Then in 2003 the comedy *Old School*, a film about grown men starting a college fraternity, turned to gymnastics for laughs. Tasked with having to demonstrate their physical prowess, the character Frank the Tank, played by Will Ferrell, performs a rhythmic gymnastics routine, while his friend Beanie, played by Vince Vaughn, does his still-rings exercise while puffing on a lit cigarette. *Old School* was one of the best-performing comedies of the year.

> **One Leg Was All She Needed**
>
> "Do we need to do this?" American gymnast Keri Strug asked her coach, Béla Károlyi, after she badly injured her left ankle on the vault at the 1996 Summer Olympics in Atlanta, Georgia (Leavy 1997, 60). The answer, unfortunately for Strug, was yes. The U.S. women's gymnastics team, nicknamed the "Magnificent Seven," was locked in a battle with the Russian squad for the team gold medal, and it all came down to Strug.
>
> She did not need a perfect 10. She did, however, need to perform a competent vault on her bad ankle, on which the pain was getting worse. All she had to do was perform a vault that was good enough, which is easier said than done when one can barely walk, much less run. Károlyi replied to Strug's question that the team needed her to make one more attempt. So Strug did what she had done hundreds of times in practice. She walked to the front of her approach and began her sprint toward the vault.
>
> If someone did not know she was injured, they might not have ever found out if they watched only the approach. She sprinted—left foot, right foot, left foot, right foot—as if she were at full strength. Then she leapt, tumbled, and sprang backward off both legs, off the pommel horse, and onto the mat, landing again on both feet, which she planted together for just a fraction of a second until she could not hold it any longer. With the pain too great, and with her face strained, she yanked up her left foot and balanced on her healthy right leg. Then she hopped in a semicircle before falling to her knees, her pain laid bare to the world. The judges scored Strug's vault a 9.712, easily good enough for the United States to win the team gold.

SCANDALS

In 1986 USA Gymnastics hired Larry Nassar to join its athletic training staff. Not long after that, he entered medical school at Michigan State University, during which time he began to sexually assault minors as he was supposedly treating them. Nassar, a serial rapist, continued his assaults on minors for nearly 30 years, even as he became the team physician for USA Gymnastics and a professor at Michigan State in 1997. Some of his victims came forward, but they were either dismissed or discredited.

Using "treatment" as his ruse, he assaulted hundreds of people as USA Gymnastics and Michigan State University did nothing. Finally, in 2016 the *Indianapolis Star* newspaper published its investigation into Nassar and the USA Gymnastics program. Although there were some stories before, and his assaults were hardly a secret within the U.S. gymnastics community, the newspaper's investigative journalism alerted the general public to the allegations. From there, it was only a matter of time before Nassar faced justice.

The day after the report, the U.S. Congress got involved; then federal law enforcement did as well. Later that month, one of his victims, who 16 years earlier had tried to tell officials about Nassar's assaults while she was being treated for a back injury, filed charges. A day later he resigned some of his duties from Michigan State. More accusers came forward. By September Michigan State had fired Nassar, and by November, more than 50 accusers had filed complaints. Charges piled up, including sexual assault and possession of child pornography.

Between 2017 and 2018, Nassar pleaded guilty to charges of child pornography, sexual assault of minors, and sexual assault, resulting in prison sentences of up to 360 years. Former Michigan State women's gymnastics coach Kathie Klages retired and was then found guilty of lying to police about the Nassar case. Michigan State University's president and athletic director both resigned, as did every board member of USA Gymnastics.

POLITICS

Similar to how Jahn used gymnastics to bolster German pride in the 19th century, Eastern Bloc communist countries of the mid- to late 20th century employed gymnastics as a symbol of societal discipline and strength. The scholar Petr Roubal noted that the communist traditions of gymnastics very much echoed the path of Jahn's intent. Gymnastics became a reflection of how governments wanted their countries to be perceived. The mechanization of the gymnast's body, Roubal wrote, served as an avatar for the modernization and mechanization of a country's ambitions.

PATRIOTISM AND NATIONAL PRIDE

As noted earlier, only five countries have achieved sustained success in gymnastics on the world stage over the last several decades: China, Japan, Romania, Russia, and the United States, with a few other countries making an occasional cameo on the medal stand. This has driven those five countries to compete even harder against one another for the honor of being named best in the world. To achieve that goal, national programs have been ruthless in determining which gymnasts get to continue to remain on the team, such as when China cut Li Ning before the 1988 Olympic Games. It is common for athletes such as American Shawn Johnson to win audience favor by earning gold, as she did in 2008, and not be on the team just one Olympic Games later.

Timeline

800–500 BCE – Ancient Greeks develop gymnastics as a means to achieve physical fitness and prepare for war.

393 CE – Ancient Olympics are outlawed by Roman emperor Theodosius. Gymnastics fades from popular culture.

1774 – Prussian Johann Bernhard Basedow begins the modern gymnastics movement by including exercises alongside academic work.

1811 – Germany's Ludwig Jahn opens a gymnastics school that includes balance beam, parallel bars, and jumps.

1896 – Men's gymnastics is included in the first modern Olympic Games.

Late 18th century – U.S. military adopts gymnastics as a training exercise, growing the sport's popularity.

1936 – Women's gymnastics receives inclusion in the Olympics.

1954 – The International Olympic Committee finalizes gymnastics' scoring system and rules. Although some tweaks have been made, today's events are rooted in that foundation.

1976 – Romanian Nadia Comaneci earns the first perfect 10 in women's gymnastics, on the uneven bars at the Montreal Olympics.

1984 – Rhythmic gymnastics joins the Olympics.

1984 – American Mary Lou Retton scores perfect 10s in vault and floor exercise at the Los Angeles Olympics and earns the all-around gold medal.

1984 – China's Li Ning wins six gymnastics medals at the Olympic Games, including three golds in individual events.

1984 – The U.S. men's team wins its first and, to date, only team gold medal at the Olympics, led by Mitch Gaylord, whose innovative style led to two moves being named after him, including the Gaylord Flip.

1996 – At the Atlanta Olympics, American Keri Strug performs the vault with a badly damaged ankle, but doing so without falling guarantees her team the gold medal.

2006 – A new scoring system is adopted to score artistic gymnastics.

2008 – China's Cheng Fei leads her country to its first Olympics all-around gold medal.

2019 – Simone Biles, a four-time Olympic gold-medal winner, wins her unprecedented sixth U.S. all-around championship, during which she became the first woman to hit a triple-twisting double somersault on the floor exercise.

See also: Olympics; Swimming.

Further Reading

Biles, S. (2016). *Courage to Soar: A Body in Motion, a Life in Balance.* Zondervan: Grand Rapids, Michigan.

George, G. S. (2014). *Championship Gymnastics: Biomechanical Techniques for Shaping Winners.* Designs for Wellness Press: Carlsbad, California.

Goodbody, J. (1983). *The Illustrated History of Gymnastics.* Beaufort Books: New York.

Gray, K. (2016). *Nadia: The Girl Who Couldn't Sit Still.* HMH Books for Young Readers: Boston.

Haines, R. (2019). *Abused: Surviving Sexual Assault and a Toxic Gymnastics Culture.* Rowman & Littlefield: Lanham, Maryland.

Jemni, M. (2011). *The Science of Gymnastics.* Routledge: Abingdon, United Kingdom.

Leavy, J. (1997). "Happy Landing." *Sports Illustrated*, Aug. 11, 1997, 54–60. https://vault.si.com/vault/1997/08/11/happy-landing-a-year-after-her-olympic-vault-to-fame-kerri-strug-is-in-college-learning-to-live-like-an-ordinary-kid.

Loken, N. C. (1977). *The Complete Book of Gymnastics.* Prentice-Hall: Upper Saddle River, New Jersey.

Meyers, D. (2017). *The End of the Perfect 10: The Making and Breaking of Gymnastics' Top Score—from Nadia to Now.* Atria Books: New York.

Ryan, J. (2018). *Little Girls in Pretty Boxes: The Making and Breaking of Elite Gymnasts and Figure Skaters.* Grand Central Publishing: New York.

Handball

Handball has a specificity problem. There are four games called handball, and each is its own version. The differences are not merely regional—if you play handball in Wales, then in Denmark, and then in the United States, you will not find the games to be familiar with subtle local flavors. There are four sporting games in the world called "handball," and they all are unique. Welsh handball exists in the same family tree as rugby, Australian rules football, and even squash, with roots dating to the 9th century. Outdoor handball, a team game, was popular in the early 20th century and had a brief fling with the Olympics. Today, it is a niche sport played because it ties people to their regional histories. Indoor team handball emerged in the mid-20th century as a better alternative to the outdoor game. It has become one of the 10 most popular sports in Europe. Lastly, there is recreational handball, sometimes called American handball, which plays a lot like racquetball or squash, but with players using their hands instead of a racket. It mostly is played in a racquetball court. All four are popular in their own ways, and the fact that all four are played in the 21st century helps explain the cultural currency each one carries.

HISTORICAL CONTEXT

The version of handball that today thrills audiences at the Olympics and many parts of the world began as an outdoor game in Denmark in the late 19th century. As the game built momentum and locals figured out how they wanted handball played, it spread to other parts of Northern Europe before moving south. Participants finally decided on a uniform set of rules in 1917 in Berlin, Germany. By December 1917 the sport we today recognize as team handball could be played across Europe under a standard set of rules. Local organizations adopted the rules, which allowed for the formation of clubs. One club could play another from across a city, or even from another country, and there would be no confusion about the game's format.

Outdoor team handball was played with 11 players per side. By 1925 the first international men's matches began to take place, while women's international matches began in 1930. Although the game proved popular in Europe, it was slow to spread to other parts of the world. This is partly because handball was born just a little outside of the window for when many sports were showcased in other countries on goodwill tours or spread through colonialism. Football-based sports, such as soccer, rugby, American football, and Australian rules football, as well as sports including basketball, volleyball, and various racket sports, found their champions in the back half of the 19th century, and as the calendar turned to the 20th century, they were finding new fans around the world. As other sports were going global, handball was just getting started.

Handball also faced a different significant timing challenge. Although the game was almost exclusively Eurocentric, it won inclusion from the International Olympic Committee (IOC) into the 1936 Berlin Olympics. Handball may have been gaining momentum, but the world was on the cusp of its second world war in 25 years. The 1940 and 1944 Olympics were both canceled because of World War II. By the time the Olympics restarted with the 1948 Games in London, the ground had shifted under handball. Northern Europe, the very region where handball was born and found its first competitors, began to prefer a seven-on-seven, indoor version of team handball. The IOC omitted handball at the 1948 Games, partially to let the sport sort itself out.

It took decades for handball to figure out what it wanted to be. Would it stick with the traditions of the larger outdoor game or the new and exciting indoor version? For years separate world championships for indoor and outdoor were held (see "Scandals"). By the mid-1960s it became clear that the indoor game had become more popular. It retained the excitement of outdoor handball, but the indoor version gave Northern European countries an exciting sports options for colder months. As with the outdoor version a half-century earlier, Europeans again fell in love, this time with indoor team handball. The IOC again took notice of the sport and readmitted it to the regular Olympic rotation. As it had in 1936, handball made its Olympic debut in Germany, this time in Munich at the 1972 Games, except this time it was played seven-on-seven indoors. It has been a part of the Olympics ever since.

GLOBALIZATION

Countries around the world have adopted indoor handball more than they ever took to outdoor team handball. Still, in the men's game, the balance of power rests in Europe. European nations have won all but one men's handball Olympic medal since the sport reemerged in 1972; South Korea won a silver medal in 1988.

True handball globalization has occurred in the women's division, where South Korea has won two Olympic gold medals. China also has earned an Olympic medal, earning bronze at the 1984 Games in Los Angeles. Brazil won the 2013 Women's World Championship, held in Serbia, which marked the first time a South American nation won one of handball's most prestigious championships. South Korea won in 1995. But other than Brazil and South Korea, no non-European country has ever even finished in the top four at the Women's World Championship.

WHERE IT'S PLAYED TODAY

The world's most successful handball programs exist in Europe, but the game itself is played throughout the world. Southeast Asia and North Africa represent some of handball's fastest growing areas. Qatar and Tunisia both qualified for the 2016 Summer Olympics in handball, as did Angola, along Africa's western coast. Argentina and Brazil from South Africa as well as perennial power South Korea also qualified.

Founded in 1991, the European Handball Federation helps guide the most high-profile, significant, and lucrative handball competitions in the world. The most prestigious event, the EHF Champions League, takes place annually and includes some of the best-paid professional athletes in the world. The event welcomes club teams from across Europe, similar to European soccer and basketball competitions. One of the most successful handball nations remains Denmark, the inventor of the sport. It has the only women's team to win three consecutive Olympic gold medals, and its men's team finally won gold in 2016.

ECONOMICS AND MEDIA

Handball players are among the highest-paid professional athletes in Europe. Their salaries do not compare favorably to those of soccer players (no other European athletes' salaries can compare to those of soccer players), but as team sports go, top-level professional handball athletes make a good living. Paris Saint-Germain, a professional club based in France, pays its top player, Denmark's Mikkel Hansen, a base salary of 2.5 million Euros. His teammate, France's Luc Abalo, earns 1.25 million Euros in annual salary. Dozens of other players earn at least six figures per year, far more than athletes in sports such as diving, cross-country skiing, and weightlifting earn in basic income.

Professional and European handball competitions can draw big ratings. Networks routinely try to lock the sport into multiyear contracts to maximize profits. It also is one of the few sports in which ratings for Olympic handball might be less than regional events because interest in the sport outside of Europe is far less than inside of it. Twenty-two different television companies from 20 countries broadcast at least part of the 2020 European Men's Handball Championship. It turned out to be one of the most lucrative sporting events of the year; the event took place in January, before the COVID-19 pandemic prevented the occurrence of many other professional sports events during 2020.

DIMENSIONS OF THE SPORT

The goal of handball, as in so many sports, is to score more points than your opponent. As there are many different forms of handball, this section will choose to focus on the world's most popular version: 7-on-7 indoor team handball. In team handball, rosters consist of 14 players. Seven act as substitutes while 7 are on the court at all times. One is a goalkeeper and the other 6 are called outfielders. Historically the ball was made from leather but today is of a synthetic material. It ranges in size from 50 to 60 centimeters in circumference depending on the age group of the players.

Scoring is simple: as in water polo, soccer, and field hockey, a team earns a point by putting the ball into the other team's goal. Games last 60 minutes, split into two 30-minute halves (youth matches might play less time). The handball court is 40 meters long by 20 meters wide. Outfielders may not touch the ball below their knee and can keep the ball for no more than three seconds before they are required to dribble, as in basketball. Violations of game rules, including stripping the opposing team of the ball instead of blocking a pass or shot attempt, result in a free throw.

IMPORTANT FIGURES

Romania's Cristina Neagu was just 22 years old when she was named the International Handball Federation's top player in 2010, but over the next four years other players won, which seemed to indicate that while Neagu was an excellent player, her award might have been an aberration, the result of a young player playing above her skill level. But in 2015 Neagu won her second top honor, then she won a third, and in 2018 she won her fourth, making her the first IHF player—women's or men's—to win the award four times. Now in her 30s, with her career still going, Neagu already is considered one of the greatest team-handball players who ever lived.

By the time Mikkel Hansen was just 30 years old, he had already been named the best team-handball player in the world three times. In addition to being the highest-paid professional handball player in the world, with an annual salary of 2.5 million Euros, Hansen has won every major team championship one can win. As part of Denmark's national team, he has won the European Championship, World Championship, and an Olympic gold medal at the 2016 Summer Olympics in Rio de Janeiro, Brazil. Hansen's game no doubt came partially from his father, who represented Denmark's team-handball squad at the 1984 Olympics in Los Angeles, California.

POP CULTURE

The 2001 film about mobsters, *Knockaround Guys*, performed poorly at the box office despite having a cast that included well-known actors such as Dennis Hopper, John Malkovich, Vin Diesel, and Seth Green. In one scene the film's lead character, played by Barry Pepper, finds the characters played by Hopper and Malkovich, two well-known Hollywood actors, engaged in a competitive game of the American version of handball. The scene includes a short monologue on handball strategy.

SCANDALS

In what should be considered more of an identity crisis than a scandal, from 1938 to 1966 the outdoor, 11-on-11 team handball game and the indoor, 7-on-7 version of the game held separate world championships. They were played in different locations on different dates, with the two sides refusing to come together. Outdoor handball looked poised for global liftoff after the IOC included it at the 1936 Olympic Games in Berlin. Instead, the IOC dropped handball and refused to readmit it to the Olympic rotation except for an occasional appearance at exhibition status.

Around the same time period, Northern European nations began to fall in love with the indoor game. It was an ideal sport for cold-weather climates, something they could play indoors and still break a serious sweat. The two groups—indoor and outdoor—believed their versions superior. It became clear by the 1950s that participants preferred the indoor version, which could be played year-round and required fewer people. Indoor handball had won. In 1972, after 36 years on the Olympic sidelines, handball returned to the Games, this time as an indoor sport.

PATRIOTISM AND NATIONAL PRIDE

The old phrase that everything old is new again is playing out in Wales with the resurgence of handball. This version of handball does not relate to the indoor or outdoor team handball made popular in Northern Europe and now finding appreciation in areas of the world that include East Asia, Northern Africa, and parts of South America. Welsh handball dates back more than 1,000 years before team handball, with one historian raising the possibility that the sport has ancient ties to the Roman Empire's occupation of what is now the United Kingdom.

Called *chwarae pêl*, loosely translated to "playing ball," Welsh handball traces back to the 9th century. It bears a resemblance to the modern-day games of squash and rackets, as well as the American version of handball, which is played inside a racquetball court. It also holds some similarities to games played in ancient South America. A player serves the leather-wrapped ball against a wall and tries to keep it out of the opponent's hands. Points are scored by the serving player. If that player loses control of the ball, the opponent takes over serving and can then score points.

The 9th-century Welsh monk Nennius, known as one of the most important historians not just of his era but in all of UK history, included handball in his writings. During the Middle Ages, British royalty tried to forbid the Welsh from playing handball because it was seen as a distraction from duties to the crown, which included another skill: archery. Later, religious forces tried to exorcise handball because it was preached to be an un-Christian activity. Handball persevered throughout the centuries at varying levels of interest but has roared back in recent years. It was even the subject of a well-regarded history book, Kevin Dicks's 2017 *Handball: The Story of Wales' First National Sport*.

Timeline

9th century – The game of Welsh handball develops during the Middle Ages. It resembles the current American version of the game more closely than the popular international version does. Although rugby and soccer now rule Wales, Welsh handball is considered its first national sport.

Late 1800s – An early version of the modern game emerges in Northern Europe, including Denmark and Sweden.

1906 – Danish gym teacher Holger Nielsen publishes the first set of handball rules. Nielsen was a two-sport Olympic athlete, but neither sport was handball. He competed in fencing and shooting at the first modern Olympic Games, in Athens in 1896.

1917 – With Nielsen's rules followed by some but not others, three Germans publish a new set of handball rules that create the modern version of the game in October. Two months later, in December 1917, the first match under the new rules takes place.

1927 – Ireland's John Joseph Keane proposes handball to the IOC, but the IOC rejects the proposal.

1928 – The International Amateur Handball Federation is formed in Amsterdam while the Olympics are being held.

1936 – Field handball takes place at the 1936 Munich Olympics but is dropped right afterward. It never makes another appearance as an official Olympic sport, although it does reappear as an exhibition event during the 1952 Games.

1938 – The first Field Handball World Championships are held, also in Germany.

1946 – The International Handball Federation is founded in Basel, Switzerland.

1957 – The first Handball Women's World Championship is held.

1965 – The IOC votes during a meeting in Madrid, Spain, to expand the number of sports offered during the Summer Olympic Games, which finally opens the door for handball's inclusion, but this time it is the indoor version.

1966 – Indoor and outdoor, or field, handball hold separate world championships for the final time.

1972 – Indoor handball, the version of the game more commonly recognized today, is contested for the first time as an official Olympic sport. As they had been during handball's exhibition debut 36 years earlier, the Games are held in Germany, this time in Munich.

1976 – Women's handball debuts at the Montreal Olympics.

1988 – South Korea wins gold in women's handball at the Summer Olympics and again in 1992, marking the only times a non-European country has won gold in women's or men's.

2008 – For the first time at the Olympics, the IOC grants entry to an equal number of nations fielding women's teams as men's. Both genders are allowed a 12-nation field.

2016 – Denmark wins men's gold at the Summer Olympics in Rio de Janeiro, Brazil. The victory shows yet again the popularity and competitiveness of the sport, as Denmark is the ninth different country to win gold in the event's 14 Olympic appearances.

2017 – Returning handball to its Middle Ages roots, author Kevin Dicks writes *Handball: The Story of Wales' First National Sport*.

See also: Soccer; Squash; Water Polo.

Further Reading

Dicks, K. (2017). *Handball: The Story of Wales' First National Sport*. Y Lolfa: Ceredigion, Wales.

Estriga, L. (2019). *Team Handball: Teaching and Learning Step-By-Step*. Agência Nacional: Lisbon, Portugal.

Flickstein, D. (2017). *The Perfect Game: New York Handball Stories*. CreateSpace Independent Publishing Platform: Scotts Valley, California.

Lowry, L. (2000). *Handball Handbook: Strategies and Techniques*. American Press: Boston.

McElligott, T. (1997). *The Story of Handball: The Game, the Players, the History*. Wolfhound Press: Dublin, Ireland.

Medina, M. (2016). *The Girl from Brooklyn: My Story of Living with Depression*. CreateSpace Independent Publishing Platform: Scotts Valley, California.

Phillips, B. E. (2010). *Fundamental Handball*. Kessinger Publishing LLC: Whitefish, Montana.

Radu, F. L. and Abalasei, B. A. (2015). *Team Handball 101*. Bloomsbury Publishing: London.

Turman, J. and Tyson, P. (1983). *The Handball Book*. Leisure Books: New York.

Uribe, D. (2019). *The Handball Psychology Workbook: How to Use Advanced Sports Psychology to Succeed on the Handball Field*. Self-published.

Horse Racing

Only one sport, horse racing, has earned the nickname "the Sport of Kings." Its label came honestly, most likely from King Charles II of the United Kingdom, who enjoyed racing horses during the mid-17th century. Horse racing draws a unique mix of crowds: rich and poor, high and low society, royalty and scoundrels—and sometimes royal scoundrels. Humans have always been obsessed with who can move from one place to another the fastest, whether by foot, horse, automobile, or air. Remarkably, horse racing has survived the test of time as many of its contemporary sports lost public interest or developed into new sports. Perhaps this is because of our obsession with speed, but it also can be attributed to humanity's long relationship with horses, domesticated in parts of Asia and Europe about 6,000 years ago. They are one of earth's most beloved animals, appreciated as much for their spirit as for their physicality.

HISTORICAL CONTEXT

Hundreds of books have been written about the history of horses and horse racing. A few paragraphs simply cannot do. Because horses have been domesticated for thousands of years and have been used for transportation, agricultural work, and entertainment, and because they have been part of the global social fabric for so long, historians have learned that, similar to wrestling, horse racing grew at different places throughout different parts of the world.

Horse racing takes place all over the world. One of the countries in which the sport continues to find a growing audience is China (pictured). (Gan Hui/Dreamstime.com)

No single mass movement or exportation of horse racing ever took place. It grew and evolved over time, from the Mongols of Asia to the royals of Europe, from the indigenous people of North America to the citizens of northern Africa.

GLOBALIZATION

It is best to think of globalization in horse racing not in terms of the sport itself but from the perspective of gambling and wagering. Countries and regions such as India, China, the United Kingdom, the Middle East, Eastern Europe, and the United States, among others, came to horse racing on their own or through ancient human migration. Testing the speed of horses came as naturally as testing the speed of human beings. Imperialism somewhat spread—then altered—the forms of horse racing seen throughout the world, but the idea that humanity would compete to see who could ride horses the fastest is not exclusive to any one part of the world.

Gambling gives us a better gauge to understand migration patterns, and in this case, imperialism once again provides us with the tools, whether it was the Moorish influence on Spain and other parts of Southern Europe, Great Britain's push into countries such as Australia and the United States, or the extension of Mongolian rule into what is now China. Even today horse racing remains a contested symbol: entertainment and excess, seediness and crime, good-natured fun and addiction. In 2018 China announced plans to increase tourism in the Hainan

Province by opening, among other things, facilities for horse racing. Not to be outdone, in 2019 Saudi Arabia announced it would host the Saudi Cup, a new horse race that would offer a $20 million purse, the sport's largest ever, to help attract tourists and major sporting events to the country.

WHERE IT'S PLAYED TODAY

Horse racing takes place in many countries around the world on nearly every continent—just as it has for centuries. Because horse racing does not muster the support it did a half century ago, horse tracks that exist today do so in older, more developed regions. Populations searching for new residential developments and activities rarely count horse racing among their top priorities.

Horse racing's most rapid growth is taking place in North Africa and East Asia, while there is almost no growth in Western Europe and North America. In the United States and Great Britain, a few events each year still draw community attention, but much of that is based on tradition and not a surge in the sport's popularity, which means that once the traditional annual events are over, common interest subsides until the following year.

ECONOMICS AND MEDIA

Horse racing is big money. Some owners invest tens, if not hundreds, of millions of dollars into their investments over the course of a lifetime, which means horse owners need to be wealthy to be competitive. There is no one concentrated region of the world from which horse owners tend to come. Owners live in United Arab Emirates, China, Japan, the United States, Australia—basically, everywhere.

In 2014 the American-based National Broadcasting Company signed a 10-year deal with Churchill Downs Incorporated to be the exclusive carrier of the Kentucky Derby, which draws between 15 and 20 million viewers each year. Neither the network nor Churchill Downs disclosed the amount of the contract, which some horse racing reporters estimate to be worth several hundred million dollars.

DIMENSIONS OF THE SPORT

One might think that horse racing can best be described as horses running as fast as they can around a track while mounted by people who are dubbed "jockeys." However, there are different types of horse racing, each with unique properties.

The most common form of horse racing is flat racing, which is, in fact, horses running as fast as they can around a track while mounted by jockeys. Media outlets most often show flat racing when they show horse racing. The Kentucky Derby in the United States is an example of flat racing. Flat-race tracks typically are one to three miles in circumference. Grass turf makes up the most flat-race surfaces. Some use dirt. European flat racing breaks down into two categories: conditions racing, which might split horses into similar age or gender categories;

and handicap racing. Handicap racing, common in the United States, employs handicappers to generate odds about how likely a horse is to win its race.

Harness racing, popular in France, calls for the horse to pull its jockey in a type of carriage called a sulky. Achieving top speed is not the goal in harness racing, which requires horses to maintain a specific speed determined before the start of the race. Horses that break the speed limit are penalized, often by being forced to the back of the pack. Paris's Prix d'Amerique, the world's premier harness-racing event, has taken place each year since 1920 except for two years during World War II.

National Hunt, a form of track-and-field steeplechase event, is popular in parts of Europe, including the United Kingdom. Jockeys direct their horses around and over obstacles, with jumping serving as the showcased skill.

Other forms of horse racing include maiden racing, which is restricted to horses that have never won a race; claiming racing, a sometimes unsavory form of racing in which horses are run for the purpose of showing them off so that they can be sold to the highest bidder; and endurance racing, popular in Mongolia and a few other countries, which calls for horses to win long-distance races rather than speed events. The Mongol Derby tests horses to run 1,000 kilometers and is believed to have been inspired by Genghis Khan, whose kingdom used horses to carry messages over long distances.

IMPORTANT FIGURES

In the late-18th century, a British horse called Diomed finished a successful racing career. He won numerous championships, yet his career as a stud, serving as a sire for future generations of horses, failed. He was sold to an American military officer in 1798 for a paltry sum and went on to become known as the most successful horse stud of the second millennium.

Diomed's offspring live into the modern era. In 2015 American Pharoah won the first Triple Crown since 1978. American Pharoah is a direct descendant of Diomed—not bad for Diomed's selling price of $250. The name Diomed derives from Greek mythology, a character known for aligning with Greece in its battle against Troy.

POP CULTURE

In 1989 Richard Dreyfuss, an Academy Award–winning actor known for appearing in some of the United States' most culturally important movies, including *Jaws* and *Close Encounters of the Third Kind*, decided to have a little fun and made *Let It Ride*. The comedy starred Dreyfuss as a loser who wasted his life betting horses at the track. His gambling threatened his marriage and affected his professional life and friendships. Finally, one day he finds he cannot lose. He wins race after race while encountering obstacle after obstacle, and just when it is time for the final race and the movie audience braces for his inevitable loss, the story flips conventional narrative on its head and lets him win the big one. He goes the entire movie, which takes place in a single day, without losing a race and avoids the bad guys. *Let It Ride* tanked at the box office, making a little less than $5 million worldwide, but it found new life on cable television, becoming a staple of movie channels throughout the 1990s, thanks to audiences who loved the movie far more than professional movie critics did.

On the heels of *Seabiscuit*, the wildly successful 2003 film about a racehorse who captivated the United States during the Great Depression (see more in "Patriotism and National Pride"), Walt Disney Pictures decided to make the movie *Secretariat*, perhaps the most popular American horse of the 20th century. Secretariat won the Triple Crown in 1973; its Belmont Stakes win was by 31 lengths (approximately 250 feet). Secretariat resonated so deeply with American sporting culture that in 1999 ESPN, the sports cable network, named Secretariat the 35th greatest athlete of the 20th century—the only nonhuman to make the list. Unfortunately for Disney, audience reception for its 2010 release did not match the country's enthusiasm for the horse. The film did not flop, but it came nowhere near Seabiscuit's $150 million haul, earning nearly $100 less.

That horses are faster than humans over short distances cannot be disputed, but humans—in their never-ending quest to determine who is faster than whom—long wondered whether they could outlast horses over long distances. The thought process went that eventually horses need to stop for sleep, water, and rest, while humans can pace themselves and overtake the horse as long as the human runs a certain pace. It is a tortoise-and-the-hare scenario with humans as the tortoise and horses as the hare. The first documented effort of a human trying to win was England's J Barnett, who supposed in 1818 that he could run farther than a horse over a 48-hour period. He came close, losing 179 miles to 158 miles (the horse also had to carry 168-pound load, while Barnett did not). Human versus horse competitions continue today. Scotland and New Zealand host annual races between the species, while numerous television shows around the world pit the two against one another.

SCANDALS

Australian thoroughbred Fine Cotton might have been a pretty horse, but it was not a winning horse. A perennial middle-of-the-packer who occasionally dipped to the bottom of the field, Fine Cotton's owners had grown tired of losing and wanted a win—at any cost, apparently. In 1984, before a race in Queensland, the owners decided to engage in ringing, a horse-racing scam in which a similar-looking, faster horse is brought in to run as the slower horse, with the hope that nobody will notice.

The second horse, Bold Personality, held a similar brown color to Fine Cotton, but it lacked Fine Cotton's white spots on the back of its legs, so those in on the ruse bought over-the-counter hair-coloring product to color the corresponding locations on the back of Bold Personality's legs. On race day, however, someone forgot the hair coloring, so the conspirators instead went with basic white paint. The conspirators, looking for a big pay day, bet heavily on their own horse, thinking they would get away with it. Their wages shifted the betting lines, which raised suspicions. Those suspicions were confirmed after the race when race officials and fans noticed the white paint, which had not settled, dripping down the back of Bold Personality's legs. With the ruse obvious, six conspirators were banned from horse racing for life.

POLITICS

Traditionally, horse-racing powers that be do not like change. They like control. They prefer that classes do not mix: owners mingle with owners, two-dollar bettors stay away from the high rollers, and genders know their roles. So imagine their dismay when British model Jean Shrimpton showed up to the 1968 Victoria Derby in Melbourne, Australia, wearing a skirt a full five inches above her knee without stockings or gloves to hide the rest of her body.

News media and race officials went into a tizzy. Matters got worse when they noticed Shrimpton was wearing . . . gasp! . . . a men's watch. Shrimpton's boldness became the biggest story out of that year's Victoria Derby. Shrimpton said she did not think her outfit would cause such a stir. She attended the event as part of a promotional tour to fulfill an endorsement deal.

PATRIOTISM AND NATIONAL PRIDE

No one expected much out of Seabiscuit when he debuted in the 1930s. He won no races over his first 40 starts, appeared undersized, and attracted little fanfare as the United States slogged through the global Great Depression.

Seabiscuit found a new owner in the late 1930s, and the new owner handed him off to a new trainer, Tom Smith. Smith looked at Seabiscuit's unorthodox body, and he thought alternative training methods might give the horse a chance at success. Smith was right. Seabiscuit's career took off in 1936 with a series of victories, and Americans began to see themselves in Seabiscuit: a horse everyone had written off who refused to give up and eventually found his way to the winner's circle.

Seabiscuit's story climaxed in 1938. He won 11 starts before challenging the far larger War Admiral, winner of the Triple Crown, in November of that year in a head-to-head race. More than 40,000 fans packed Pimlico Race Course in Baltimore to watch the race and cheer on the small but resilient Seabiscuit. Seabiscuit won, chasing down War Admiral over the final 250 yards to win by four lengths. And just in case anyone thinks War Admiral may have had a bad day and Seabiscuit just got lucky, that idea was put to rest when timers showed that War Admiral had run its fastest-ever race at that distance.

Timeline

4000 BCE – Humans in Asia and Europe begin to domesticate horses.

644 BCE – Forms of horse racing take part in the ancient Greek Olympics.

Late 1600s – King Charles II, through his fandom, popularizes horse racing across what is now the United Kingdom and parts of Western Europe.

1160 – Discussions of horse racing take place during the reign of King Henry II of England.

1778 – In the city of Madras, located in the state of Tamil Nadu, the first horse track is built in India.

1798 – Diomed, a champion racehorse but failed stud from England, is sold to a U.S. military officer for $250. Diomed goes on to become the most successful stud in American horse-racing history, with descendants reaching into the 21st century.

1861 – The American Civil War leads to the destruction of horse-breeding facilities, and horses of all breeds are brought into military service, setting back the horse-racing industry.

1866 – The Negishi Racecourse, the first modern horse-racing facility in Japan, is built. It stays open until 1942.

1875 – Churchill Downs, home to the Kentucky Derby in the United States, opens. The first Kentucky Derby is held the same year and has been held annually, without missing a year, ever since.

1894 – The Jockey Club forms to track, log, and register thoroughbreds in the United States and Canada.

1919 – Sir Barton wins the first American "Triple Crown," the term for winning the Kentucky Derby, Preakness Stakes, and Belmont Stakes in the same year.

1920 – The first Prix d'Amerique, the world's premier harness-racing event, debuts in Paris.

1933 – Betting on horse races becomes legal in California for the first time since 1909.

1948 – Diane Crump, the first female jockey to ride in sanctioned betting races, is born.

1970 – Author Hunter S. Thompson writes "The Kentucky Derby is Decadent and Depraved" for *Scanlan's Monthly* magazine. Thompson's signature "gonzo journalism" brings a new perspective to the legendary race, previously framed as distinguished and traditional.

1973 – Secretariat becomes the first triple-crown winner since 1948.

2003 – Willie Shoemaker, a jockey who retired as the sport's leader in victories, dies at 72. He was immortalized in the 1970s through a series of paintings by the artist Andy Warhol.

2015 – American Pharoah wins the first triple crown since 1978.

See also: Bullfighting; Rodeo; Track and Field

Further Reading
Askwith, R. (2019). *Unbreakable: The Woman Who Defied the Nazis in the World's Most Dangerous Horse Race.* Pegasus Books: New York.
Beyer, A. (1994). *Picking Winners: A Horseplayer's Guide.* Mariner Books: Boston.
Carroll, L. (2018). *Out of the Clouds: The Unlikely Horseman and the Unwanted Colt Who Conquered the Sport of Kings.* Hachette Books: New York.

Ende, B. (2018). *Lady Long Rider: Alone Across America on Horseback*. Farcountry Press: Helena, Montana.

Hillenbrand, L. (2002). *Seabiscuit: An American Legend*. Ballantine Books: New York.

Letts, E. (2012). *The Eighty-Dollar Champion: Snowman, the Horse that Inspired a Nation*. Ballantine Books: New York.

Morgan, C. E. (2016). *The Sport of Kings*. Farrar, Straus and Giroux: New York.

Morpurgo, M. (2010). *War Horse*. Scholastic Press: New York.

Nack, W. (2010). *Secretariat*. Hyperion: Glendale, California.

Townsend, N. (2015). *The Sure Thing: The Greatest Coup in Horse Racing History*. Random House: London.

I

Ice Hockey

Ice hockey is one of the fastest, most popular team sports in the world, with amateur and professional leagues across North America, Northern Europe, and Russia that complete for international glory and professional dollars. Hockey has been the stage for political drama. It has held the hopes and pride of nations. Children as young as 13 and 14 years old leave home for the privilege of training with the right club in the hope of someday wearing their nation's colors. The game is unique: players pass around an object called a puck, which is not used in any other sport. It also has been measured as the fastest team sport in the world. Game play does not even stop for substitutions—new players jump on the ice as tired ones skate off, and a rotation might last just a couple of minutes because of how quickly the sport wears down a player's endurance. Hockey is played by young and old, women and men, amateurs and professionals.

HISTORICAL CONTEXT

As sports go, ice hockey is on the younger side. King Edward III of England banned field hockey—among other games—in 1363. But ice hockey did not begin to thrive until the late 19th century. The first organized indoor ice hockey game took place in Montreal, Canada, in 1875. McGill University in Montreal organized the first hockey club in 1877, and the first World Championships were held at Montreal's "Winter Carnival" in 1883.

The game was born and developed around the same period as basketball and, like basketball, its rules were first published in a newspaper: *The Gazette*, in Montreal. The game's rules mirrored the rules of field hockey, with the notable exception of one game being played on ice and the other on grass.

The sixth World Championships were held at Montreal's 1888 Winter Games. Lord Stanley of Preston, the governor general of Canada, attended the tournament at the encouragement of his children. He enjoyed the game. A few years later he bought a large silver cup, and in 1892 the Stanley Cup was awarded for the first time. The trophy originally went to the champion of the Amateur Hockey Association of Canada but has been awarded to the champion of the National Hockey League (NHL) since 1926.

The cup, considered the most famous sports trophy in North American athletics, today stands nearly three feet tall and weighs 34.5 pounds, whereas the original cup was just a cup. Tiers were added below the original cup to allow for the inscription

Although lacrosse is the official sport of Canada, ice hockey became so popular that the government named it the official "winter sport" of Canada. Today the sport thrives in North America, Russia, and Northern Europe. (Igor Mojzes/Dreamstime.com)

of names of everyone who was part of a championship-winning team.

Hockey joined the Olympic Games in 1920. Canada won six of the first seven Olympic gold medals for men's ice hockey between 1920 and 1952 but would not win again until 2002.

Since they played for the first time in February 1987, there has been no fiercer rivalry in hockey than between Canada's and the United States' women's hockey teams.

The International Ice Hockey Federation has held 18 women's world championships. Canada and the United States have met in the finals of all 18, with the United States winning 8 out of the last 10. The Winter Olympics have hosted women's hockey six times; Canada and the United States have played against each other for the gold medal five times, with Canada winning head-to-head three times and the United States winning twice. The two countries have been so dominant that it's been tough for other squads to crack the national conversation. Sweden, in 2006, is the only other program to ever play for Olympic gold.

GLOBALIZATION

Canada developed ice hockey and served as its ambassador across the world. Today the sport is popular in Russia, the United States, and much of Northern and Eastern Europe. Canadians introduced hockey to each of the regions.

As a sign of the sport's global popularity, consider the diversity of countries that have won medals in ice hockey at the Olympic Games: Canada, United States, Czechoslovakia/Czech Republic, Great Britain, Switzerland, Sweden, Germany/West Germany, Russia/Soviet Union, and Finland. Other countries that have competed in recent years include Italy, Latvia, Kazakhstan, Norway, Slovakia, and Belarus.

Professional leagues exist across the world. One of the newest is the Champions Hockey League in Europe, which began play in 2014. The league recruits the best teams from individual countries' leagues across Europe. In 2008 the Kontinental Hockey League began play in Russia and parts of Eastern and Northern Europe. It is considered the second-best professional hockey league in the world after the NHL.

WHERE IT'S PLAYED TODAY

It's played everywhere, but those who are looking for the most competitive hockey will begin with North America (Canada and the United States) and Russia. Hockey is growing in popularity as a youth sport. Since 2012, for instance, USA Hockey has experienced annual growth in membership. It announced membership of just more than 562,000 people during the 2017–2018 enrollment period. Twenty years earlier (1997–1998), membership stood at just more than 400,000.

Canada, which has one-tenth the population of the United States, has between 600,000 and 700,000 registered hockey players. Because of the sport's popularity, some Canadian Parliament members proposed in the mid-1990s to name ice hockey the country's national sport, but the government faced blowback because lacrosse had already been named the national sport and changing it to hockey would be disrespectful to Canada's First Nations people, who invented lacrosse. As a result, the parliament passed the National Sports of Canada Act, which named lacrosse Canada's official summer sport and hockey its official winter sport.

ECONOMICS AND MEDIA

The NHL is considered one of the "Big 4" professional sports of the United States, joining the National Basketball Association, Major League Baseball, and the National Football League. It draws its income from selling television and radio broadcast rights, ticket sales, and other revenue streams, such as merchandise sales. The most valuable franchise is the New York Rangers, with a franchise value of $1.55 billion.

The league itself earns at least $700 million annually from national television deals, or roughly $23 million per team per year. That total does not include local television deals. Each NHL team has its own contract with local broadcasters. Although that might sound like a lot of money, each team is required to spend at least $70 million annually on player salaries. Not all teams are able to meet their financial obligations, so they end up moving cities to try to find new revenue streams. This was the case with the Winnipeg Jets (formerly the Phoenix Coyotes), Carolina Hurricanes (formerly the Hartford Whalers), Colorado Avalanche (formerly the Quebec Nordiques), and Calgary Flames (formerly the Atlanta Flames).

The NHL owns its own television network, the NHL Network. Over the years its national broadcast partners have included nearly all of the United States' major broadcasting networks, including ESPN, the all-sports cable network that launched in the late 1970s.

DIMENSIONS OF THE SPORT

Hockey is played on a rectangle with rounded edges called an ice rink. Rinks might differ slightly in size, but generally in North America, where the game was founded, a rink is 200 feet by 80 feet. Goal lines typically sit 11 feet from the end of the boards.

The international dimensions of a hockey rink differ from North American rinks. They are slightly shorter (197 feet) but significantly wider (98 feet). Both international and North American rinks are divided in half by a center line. The game's opening face-off—when one player from each team battles for a puck that is dropped by an on-ice official—takes place on the center line.

In all, there are nine face-off areas. The ice as a whole is divided into three zones by two blue lines. They are used by referees to determine whether a player is offsides, which is against the rules and occurs when a player tries to skate too close toward the opposing team's goal without possession of the puck.

The opening of a goal is 6 feet wide by 4 feet tall by 40 inches deep. The hockey puck is made from vulcanized rubber. It appeared around the same time historically that wooden balls in bowling were replaced by vulcanized rubber balls. In order for a goal to count, the entirety of the puck must cross the entirety of the goal line.

Each team keeps six players on the ice at all times: five players who skate around the ice, and the goaltender, who guards the team's net. A team will lose a player on the ice for a determined number of minutes when a player commits a penalty and is banished by a referee to the penalty box.

IMPORTANT FIGURES

In many sports, fans can spend hours debating who is the greatest of all time. In hockey, this argument can be settled in two words: Wayne Gretzky. There are players who did specific things better than Gretzky, but no player in the game's 150 years put together the type of career that Gretzky had. Gretzky, from Ontario, Canada, amassed 2,857 points (goals plus assisted goals) in 1,487 professional games, an average of nearly two points per game. Only Mario Lemieux (1,723 points in 915 games) even remotely approached Gretzky's record. Gretzky led the Edmonton Oilers of the NHL to four Stanley Cup championships and was named the league's most valuable player nine times.

Gordie Howe laid the groundwork for Gretzky as one of the NHL's first crossover stars. He managed to gain popularity outside of hockey circles because of his success and longevity. Howe's full-time career lasted an astounding 36 years (1946–1980). Howe, from Saskatchewan, Canada, won four Stanley Cups with the Detroit Pistons of the NHL and earned the league's most valuable player award six times.

Mike "Doc" Emrick began his career as an NHL broadcaster in the early 1980s and retired in 2020, generally regarded as the best broadcaster of any team sport in the United States. For sports broadcasting, Emrick has won six Emmys—the highest honor a U.S. television broadcaster can receive. He is the only hockey announcer to ever win even one Emmy.

POP CULTURE

In 1977 Paul Newman, one of only four actors in history to be nominated for an Academy Award in five different decades, made the peculiar choice to star in *Slap Shot*, a vulgar, rough-around-the-edges comedy about a minor-league hockey team that resorts to on-ice violence to reverse its losing ways. Noting the movie's copious amount of foul language, one movie critic wrote, "People are more likely to be upset by the movie's dialogue than its split personality" (Arnold 1977). As it turned out, Newman knew what he was doing. Audiences enjoyed it, and in 2015, *Rolling Stone* magazine named *Slap Shot* the seventh-best sports movie of all time.

The American sportscaster Al Michaels made one of the most famous calls in sports-broadcast history in 1980, when the U.S. Men's Olympic Hockey Team upset the heavily favored Soviet Union, winning four to three. Michael hollered, "Do you believe in miracles? Yes!" (Leahy 2020). The 2004 movie *Miracle* told the story of the 1980 U.S. team. Starring Kurt Russell as Herb Brooks, the team's coach, *Miracle* cost just $28 million to make but earned nearly $65 million. Michaels even reprised his role as the game's broadcaster, but when it came time for his final famous line, he couldn't duplicate the natural excitement of the original, so the filmmakers decided instead to dub his original call into the film.

The Other Side of a Miracle

In the United States and some other Western countries, the U.S. men's hockey team's "miracle" upset of the Soviet Union in the 1980 Lake Placid games stands as a legendary Olympic moment.

But what of the Soviet team, the heavy favorite that expected victory? For them, the Olympic semifinal against the United States created the worst of memories. Defensive player Viacheslav Fetisov, shown a tape of the game more than 30 years later, could barely watch. He kept averting his eyes from the television screen. Head coach Viktor Tikhonov, known for his dictatorial style, further tightened his grip on the players, requiring them to practice 10 to 11 months a year and live in barracks, unable to see their families. He left some of the best Soviet players off the team if he suspected they might defect during international play, including Pavel Bure, who went on to become a member of the Hockey Hall of Fame.

Soviet forward Sergei Makarov told author Wayne Coffey that Soviet politicians were furious with the team when it returned from the Olympics (Coffey and Craig 2005, 259). The most remarkable thing, Fetisov and others said, was that Tikhonov kept his job. It proved to be the right move for the Soviets. Under Tikhonov's leadership, the Soviet Union regained its top spot in the world by winning gold at the 1984 and 1988 Olympics. Tikhonov also coached the Unified Team, a compilation of players from Russia and other Soviet Bloc countries, to gold in 1992 following the collapse of the Soviet Union.

Gabe Polsky's illuminating 2015 documentary *Red Army* talked with players from the famed Soviet hockey program. Their success from the 1960s through the 1980s was unparalleled, but the one loss to the United States during the 1980 Olympics was never too far from their minds.

SCANDALS

Since so many sports scandals deal with the dark side of games, let's enjoy one with a little less drama.

During the 1996 NHL All-Star Game, broadcaster Fox Sports introduced "Fox-Trax," an augmented-reality technology that made the puck appear to "glow" on the television screen, in theory making it easier for viewers at home to follow the game. Viewers did not respond kindly. One sportswriter wrote that the puck resembled a blueberry soaked in toxic waste.

Fox Sports meant well. This was before the days of high-definition, wide-screen televisions and retina-display computer screens. Televisions were smaller and squarer, and small details, such as fast-moving hockey pucks, could be difficult to see. But hockey fans, among the most diehard of any sport, prided themselves on being able to follow the game without technological enhancement. In short, they hated it. Fox ended the FoxTrax experiment in 1998, the same year HDTV sets became available in the United States.

POLITICS

Hockey players exhibit speed, power, grace, and coordination. However, another aspect of the game has both boosted and damaged its reputation: fighting. In the world's most talented and financially lucrative hockey league—the NHL—fighting is not only encouraged by players and fans but is explicitly allowed in the rulebook within certain parameters. This characteristic of hockey has come increasingly under scrutiny as the game continues to modernize, causing the amount of fighting in games to decline in recent years.

Hockey fights are not gladiatorial matches; there is a method to the madness. Typically, each team has one "enforcer" or "goon," a taller and stronger but less-skilled player who is part of the team to protect the team's best players. When a team's best player is targeted by the opposing team, the enforcer will confront the opposing player, and the two will throw punches. When one player loses his footing on the ice and falls down, the fight is considered over and the two players are separated.

On one level the practice sounds honorable. However, sometimes enforcers bloody or injure an opposing player, leading to calls from athletes, fans, and politicians that the practice is outdated and needs to be removed from the game. For example, for two different franchises Marty McSorley served as an enforcer for Wayne Gretzky. In 2000 McSorley, then playing for a different team, deliberately swung his stick and knocked an opposing player unconscious. McSorley was suspended by the NHL, found guilty of assault in a court of law, and never played another NHL game.

PATRIOTISM AND NATIONAL PRIDE

When the United States won the gold medal in hockey at the 1980s Winter Olympics, it immediately became considered one of the greatest upsets in modern sports history. It provided a lifetime of memories for the American players, but for the Soviet players, it sparked a completely different experience. For more on the 1980 Soviet hockey team, see the sidebar.

Timeline

1877 – *The Gazette*, a Montreal newspaper, publishes the first rules of ice hockey.

1888 – The governor general of Canada, Lord Stanley of Preston, sees his first hockey game. He takes an immediate liking to it. Several years later he donates a cup to be given to the game's champion. It becomes known as the Stanley Cup.

1892 – First women's hockey game is played in Canada.

Early 20th century – Canadians introduce ice hockey to Europe, where it becomes popular in the United Kingdom as well as Northern and Eastern Europe.

1894 – The first artificial ice rink is built in Baltimore, Maryland.

1896 – The Montreal Victorias win their first of three straight Stanley Cups.

1904 – A small band of teams from Ontario, Canada, and the United States form the first professional hockey league, the International Hockey League.

1917 – Out of the remnants of other leagues, the National Hockey League is formed.

1942–1967 – The NHL remains a six-team league of the Boston Bruins, Chicago Blackhawks, Detroit Red Wings, Montreal Canadians, New York Rangers, and Toronto Maple Leafs. They come to be known as the "Original Six."

1946 – Gordie Howe plays his first professional hockey game. He'll play his final game in 1997 at age 69, taking part in one shift for the Detroit Vipers of the International Hockey League.

1946 – Referees begin using hand signals to call penalties, which speeds up the game and helps keep fans engaged.

1956 – The Soviet Union wins the first of seven Olympic gold medals in ice hockey over the period of nine Winter Olympics (1956–1988).

1958 – Willie O'Ree is the NHL's first Black player.

1967 – The NHL doubles in size by expanding to six new cities.

1998 – The Olympics hosts women's ice hockey for the first time.

2010 – The Hockey Hall of Fame inducts Cammi Granato, a starring player for the 1998 gold-medal-winning U.S. Women's Hockey team.

See also: Field Hockey; Lacrosse; Olympics.

Further Reading

Arnold, G. (1977). "'Slap Shot': Vulgar, Rowdy, Mixed-Up and Commercial Mischief." *Washington Post*, April 1, 1977. https://www.washingtonpost.com/archive/lifestyle/1977/04/01/slap-shot-vulgar-rowdy-mixed-up-and-commercial-mischief/ebb68deb-c72e-4639-94ef-ace79822cc0e.

Branch, J. (2014). *Boys on Ice: The Life and Death of Derek Boogaard*. W. W. Norton & Company: New York.

Cermak, I. (2017). *The Cinema of Hockey: Four Decades of the Game on Screen.* McFarland & Company: Jefferson, North Carolina.

Coffey, W. and Craig, J. (2005*). The Boys of Winter: The Untold Story of a Coach, a Dream, and the 1980 U.S. Olympic Hockey Team.* Crown Publishers: New York.

Dryden, K. (2009). *The Game.* Wiley: Hoboken, New Jersey.

Etue, E. and Williams, M. K. (1996). *On the Edge: Women Making Hockey History.* Second Story Press: Toronto, Ontario, Canada.

Gave, K. (2018). *The Russian Five: A Story of Espionage, Defection, Bribery and Courage.* Gold Star Publishing: Ann Arbor, Michigan.

Harper, S. J. (2014). *A Great Game: The Forgotten Leafs & the Rise of Professional Hockey.* Simon & Schuster: New York.

Leahy, S. (2020). "How Al Michaels Ended Up Calling the 'Miracle on Ice.'" *NBC Sports*, Feb. 22, 2020. https://nhl.nbcsports.com/2020/02/22/how-al-michaels-ended-up-calling-the-miracle-on-ice.

Loverro, T. (2000). *Cammi Granato: Hockey Pioneer.* Lerner Publishing Group: Minneapolis, Minnesota.

Ruggiero, A. (2005). *Breaking the Ice: My Journey to Olympic Hockey, the Ivy League, and Beyond.* Drummond Publishing Company: New York.

J

Jai Alai

The fastest sprinter in human history, Jamaica's Usain Bolt, once ran 27.8 miles per hour. The fastest softball pitch hit 77 miles per hour, and the fastest recorded baseball pitch reached 105 miles per hour. In 2017, according to the *Guinness Book of World Records*, Spain's Ibon Aldazabal threw a pelota, or ball, 190 miles per hour, breaking the previous record by 2 miles per hour. It was a remarkable feat completely in line with jai alai's mystique: fast, powerful, unique, and achieved in near anonymity. Jai alai resides in the same family of sports as handball, squash, and racquetball, but it is played at a much faster pace and in a bigger venue. Tourists to the few parts of the world where jai alai is played flock to the spectacle, while locals attend mostly to take part in the gambling. Its athletes are big, strong, and fast, with some of the quickest reflexes of any athletes in any sport in the world. Those who get the chance to see jai alai never forget it. The real challenge is finding it in the first place.

HISTORICAL CONTEXT

Jai Alai originated in the early 1600s in the Basque area of Spain. It originally looked like a version of a game called handball, with leather used to wrap hands to protect players. It remained that way for more than 200 years, minus a few occasional tweaks. In the late 1800s, the game underwent a major change when players replaced leather with baskets, which enabled the players to whip the ball against a wall at high speeds. That represented the birth of what today people around the world recognize as jai alai. To some, the speed of the ball was the attraction to the sport. To others, it was the gambling.

Most sports attract gamblers. Jai alai goes to another level, existing primarily to satisfy gamblers. In the late 19th century, Spanish colonization helped spread jai alai to the Philippines and Cuba. The Spanish American War cost Spain many of its overseas colonies, but interest in jai alai remained. Cuba remained an American territory until 1902, but its proximity to the state of Florida—the two are about 100 miles apart—enabled American and Cuban cultures to mingle. Jai alai received an enormous boost in popularity in the United States when it appeared in St. Louis, Missouri, in 1904, at the same time as the World's Fair. Conflicting historical evidence exists as to whether jai alai was included as part of the fair or just happened to be an attraction near the fair. Either way, it found enough fans to drum up interest, although the St. Louis fronton—the name for the building where jai alai is played—closed before the end of 1904.

By the 1920s frontons had been built in Miami, Florida, New Orleans, Louisiana, and Chicago, Illinois, three of the largest cities in the United States as well as tourist destinations. Part of jai alai's allure was a specific type of betting called parimutuel betting. In parimutuel betting, everyone who bets on the same thing (e.g., a certain team to win) has their money put into one pot. The house takes a percentage, and the gamblers split the rest if their team wins. As a result, not only are they excited about the possibility of winning money but the collaborative nature of parimutuel betting creates a rooting atmosphere most commonly found in many team sports. Gamblers supporting one team cheer when something good happens for their bet, and gamblers supporting the other team cheer when something positive occurs for theirs.

Gambling also creates problems, and some governments have sought to eliminate it. In the 1980s the Filipino government temporarily banned jai alai in the Philippines because of rampant match fixing, which is the act of one team losing on purpose to help gamblers who bet on the "winning" team, an illegal act made famous in 1919 by the Chicago White Sox baseball team and in the early 1950s in college basketball. Jai alai eventually returned to the Philippines. The sport has also been banned in parts of China. During the back half of the 20th century, jai alai lost its presence in much of the United States but for a different reason: Americans found other things to gamble on. The expansion of casinos across the United States, coupled with a disastrous two-and-a-half-year labor strike that began in 1988, made jai alai frontons obsolete. The state of Connecticut, once one of the most popular northern states for jai alai, in the early 2000s converted one of its frontons into a dog-racing track and another into a casino. Today, forms of jai alai are mostly played in parts of Spain, the Philippines, Cuba, and Florida in the southeastern United States.

GLOBALIZATION

Unfortunately for fans of jai alai and the sport's administrators, jai alai has experienced no global boom over the last century. As sports such as soccer, basketball, baseball, track and field, and even mixed martial arts have become international endeavors worth billions of dollars, jai alai stalled. In the 1920s most of the world's jai alai could be found in Spain, Mexico, the Philippines, and parts of the United States. That remains the same in the 2020s. The good news for jai alai is that its small fan base remains a devoted fan base, which means there is a chance the modest sport will continue to chug along for the foreseeable future.

WHERE IT'S PLAYED TODAY

Jai alai is played in regions of Spain, the Philippines (when not banned by the government for gambling infractions), Mexico, and the southeastern United States, mostly Florida. That answer would have been the same a half century ago, with some additional locations in the United States. Jai alai is neither popular nor attractive to nations that do not have a history with it. The game's recent history of corruption has soiled its reputation.

Unfortunately for fans of jai alai, that reputation has spread quickly. To many in the sports world familiar with jai alai, it is corruption that first comes to mind. In 2016, for example, American cable network ESPN, the most profitable network in the world, finally gave jai alai some coverage. Those hoping for some positive coverage must have been disappointed, because ESPN titled its documentary, *What the Hell Happened to Jai Alai?*

ECONOMICS AND MEDIA

Traditional mainstream media coverage of jai alai is virtually nonexistent in North America and most of Europe. The major networks do not negotiate against each other for the rights to broadcast jai alai. Websites and magazines rarely seek interviews with the players. Instead, the only regular media coverage given to jai alai is in what is known as the "agate" section of local and regional news organizations. The agate section is the small print in the back of a newspaper sports section that lists the results of the previous day's events. It exists primarily for gamblers, who will use the small-print results to help them determine which jai alai individuals and teams to bet on the next time they visit a fronton.

The *New York Times* reported in an article titled, "Jai Alai; A Sport Fighting for Survival," that jai alai players earn between $35,000 and $50,000 per year annually, adding, "provided a player does not sustain an injury, which happens frequently" (Gray 2004, D1). Such little income for a professional athlete must be considered paltry, especially since jai alai thrives in Spain, part of economically developed Western Europe, and the United States. By contrast, Barcelona, Spain, soccer star Lionel Messi earns the equivalent of nearly $650,000 per week.

DIMENSIONS OF THE SPORT

Jai alai is played on a *cancha*, or court, that is walled on three sides and requires all players to play right-handed, regardless of what their natural dominant hand might be. In can be played in singles (one-on-one) or doubles (two-on-two). In both versions the goal is the same: sling the ball against the wall at an angle and speed that makes it hard for your opponent to catch on the fly or right after the first bounce. A judge presides to ensure the game's rules are enforced. For example, no blocking or screening is allowed, which means that a player on one team cannot purposely get in the way when another team's player is trying to catch the ball. The opposing player must get out of the way. If the violation happens, however, it is called interference. Another violation is juggling, which is called against a player by a judge when the player does not cleanly field the ball or when the player holds onto it for too long.

Jai alai players are required to wear five pieces of equipment. Beginning in the 1960s they had to wear helmets. This rule came to life after star player Fernando Orbea got hit in the head with a ball, suffered a serious head injury, and was forced to retire. The other piece of required protective equipment is an elbow pad on the right (throwing) arm. The most recognizable piece of jai alai equipment is the cesta—the wicker basket used to catch and throw the ball. Until the late 1800s, jai alai participants wrapped leather around their hands. Introduction of the cesta increased the speed of the game exponentially, so much so that historians wrote that the cesta transformed jai alai from one sport into a different sport entirely. The last two required pieces of equipment are the cinta, which secures the cesta to the player's hand and arm, and the faja, a traditional sash (also worn by bullfighters) worn around the waist that traces to the game's earliest days.

There are numerous versions of jai alai. The most common is "spectacular seven scoring." These matches typically are played round-robin style, with up to eight teams being involved in a match but only two at a time on the cancha. A team that loses a point has to leave the cancha, and the team that wins the point gets to keep playing. The first team to reach seven points wins, but the match is not over. The second team to reach seven is said to "place," and the third team to seven "shows." This is identical to another gambling sport, horse racing, where in each race a horse wins (first place), places (second place), and shows (third place).

IMPORTANT FIGURES

One minute Fernando Maria Orbea Alcibararichuluaga—better known as jai alai star Fernando Orbea—was in the cancha, whipping the ball around and catching those that came toward him. The next thing he knew, it was a week later and he was in a hospital bed, his previous seven days spent in a coma. The year was 1966, and Orbea, one of the best players in the world, had been struck in the head. He had not worn a helmet; in 1966 helmets were not mandatory in jai alai. The injury, suffered during a match in Durango, Spain, did not mark the end of Orbea's life. He recovered. It did, however, end his career. Despite numerous comeback attempts, the head injury caused him to suffer seizures. He continued his jai alai career away from the cancha, managing frontons and becoming a jai alai administrator. Known for his class and welcoming personality, Orbea also enjoyed watching his son embark on a jai alai career. Although his career ended prematurely, Orbea did leave a lasting impression on the sport: his injury directly led to helmets becoming mandatory for all players. It is likely his injury and the sport's reaction to it saved the lives and protected the well-being of players who came after him.

Roger Wheeler and John B. Callahan both led World Jai Alai, and in the span of two years, from 1981 to 1982, both were murdered. Wheeler bought World Jai Alai in 1977 for its business potential. In 1980 he became concerned about illegal gambling connections to the sport in Connecticut and attempted to sell his Connecticut fronton. According to FBI records and various news outlets, Callahan, a former president of World Jai Alai, hired someone to kill Wheeler because Callahan wanted to regain control over the business. In May 1981, Wheeler was shot and killed outside of his country club. The story did not end happily for Callahan. While federal investigators and detectives from multiple states were on the case,

Callahan's dead body, full of bullet holes, was located in August 1982. A man pleaded guilty in 2001 to Wheeler's murder (and the murder of others), while Callahan's case was never officially solved.

POP CULTURE

In 1982 Walt Disney Company released the movie *Tron*, about a computer hacker caught inside a virtual world. The movie's special effects were ahead of its time, but audience reception was unenthusiastic. They found the effects interesting but the story boring. In one of the few memorable action scenes, two characters have to play each other in a game of digital jai alai.

SCANDALS

Where to begin? Jai alai's close association with gambling has inevitably led to whispers, allegations, and shenanigans. At least six frontons mysteriously burned down during the 20th century. Players have received threats. Administrators have been murdered. The Philippines have shut down jai alai twice to get the sport under control: first, for many years starting in the 1980s, because of out-of-control match fixing; and then briefly again in the early 21st century when the sport looked like it again would fall into the seedier side of illegal gambling.

American hubs of jai alai, most notably the states of Florida, Connecticut, and Rhode Island, have seen sea changes in the sport, from the gradual phasing out of jai alai altogether in some instances, to the minimization of it, to finally throwing up their hands and giving up their efforts to try to make it respectable. When this happens, they add more gambling into the equation, so that fronton patrons can gamble not only on jai alai but also play slot machines and card games. State governments have had to get involved to try to assure jai alai's integrity, and if that proves unsuccessful, or if fans simply lose interest, a fronton closes and is replaced by something more current and respectable, like a standard casino or a racetrack.

POLITICS

Politicians across the jai alai world occasionally find the sport on their radar but almost never in a good way. Filipino politicians have on multiple occasions needed to either ban or suspend the sport to get its gambling components in order. U.S. politicians, mostly in the states of Connecticut and Florida, have from time to time been briefed on jai alai corruption, which results in legislation. Other times, jai alai frontons are included in negotiations for the awarding of casino licenses.

PATRIOTISM AND NATIONAL PRIDE

Despite its history of problems, the state of Florida values its jai alai history. Still, only six frontons remain in Florida. The last fronton in Connecticut closed in 2001. The newest fronton in the United States opened in 2009 in Plano, Texas.

Timeline

1798 – The first fronton is built in Spain.

1898 – Cesta Punta is introduced in Cuba, then a U.S. territory.

1904 – The United States builds its first jai alai fronton at or near the St. Louis World's Fair. It closes in just two months.

1924 – New Orleans, Louisiana, builds a jai alai fronton.

1925 – Jai alai is first professionally played at the Miami fronton, which is later destroyed by a hurricane.

1929 – Mexico Fronton opens in Mexico City.

1938 – Jai alai takes place at the New York City Hippodrome. In an unrelated move, the building is razed a year later.

1966 – Helmets for players become mandatory after Fernando Orbea suffers a career-ending head injury.

1971 – Parimutuel gambling, the force behind modern jai alai spectating, is popularized.

1981 – World Jai Alai CEO Roger Wheeler is murdered.

1982 – Former World Jai Alai CEO John B. Callahan is murdered.

1988 – In the Philippines, jai alai is banned following a match-fixing scandal. The International Jai Alai Players Association (IJAPA) forms.

1988 – The International Jai Alai Players Association goes on a two-and-a-half-year strike, which proves disastrous for the sport. American interest in the game never recovers.

1992 – Jai alai's popularity in the United States continues to fade. More than half of the country's frontons close over the next decade.

2001 – The Philippines reinstate jai alai under stricter agency supervision.

2003 – The Newport fronton in Rhode Island closes.

2004 – Several frontons in Florida receive major damage after hurricanes.

2005 – Jasper, Florida, opens the Hamilton fronton, the first American fronton to be opened in 27 years.

2011 – The Filipino government institutes a 60-day suspension of all jai alai to help prevent off-fronton betting.

2016 – All-sports television network ESPN releases the documentary, *What the Hell Happened to Jai Alai?*

See also: Baseball; Basketball; Squash.

Further Reading

Codden, H. (1978). *Jai Alai: Walls and Balls*. Gamblers Book Club: Las Vegas, Nevada.

Goitia, J. M. (2015). *Jai Alai: The Other Side of the Screen*. BookBaby Publishing: Pennsauken, New Jersey.

Gray, G. (2004). "Jai Alai; A Sport Fighting for Survival." *New York Times*, June 12, 2004, D1.

Hill, K. (2020). *Abandoned Northwest Florida.* Arcadia Publishing: Mount Pleasant, South Carolina.

Hollander, Z. (1978). *Jai Alai Handbook.* Pinnacle Books: New York.

Humphreys, J. (1977). *Jai Alai: Put Your Money on the Swinging Baskets.* Self-published.

Lostritto, D. (1985). *Jai Alai Wagering to Win: The Complete Book for Jai Alai Wagering.* Fair Haven Press: Fair Haven, Connecticut.

Morton, P. E. (2019). *Jai Alai: A Cultural History of the Fastest Game in the World.* University of New Mexico Press: Albuquerque.

Phoenix, D. (2019). *The Jai Alai Coincidence.* Self-published.

Skiena, S. (2001). *Calculated Bets: Computers, Gambling, and Mathematical Modeling to Win.* Cambridge University Press: Cambridge, United Kingdom.

Kabaddi

Searching for a centuries-old history of documented kabaddi would be a disappointing activity. As sports go, kabaddi—at least competitive kabaddi—is relatively new, with formal organization having happened in the 20th century. In fact, the Asian Games, one of the largest organized sporting events in the world, did not add kabaddi until 1990. The sport, which has ancient roots, became popular in villages in southern parts of Asia, most notably India and what is now Bangladesh. Kabaddi is a contact sport that combines elements of rugby, wrestling, and the children's games tag and dodgeball, even though there is no ball. Fast paced and action packed, it does not appear that kabaddi caught up with the modern era but rather that the modern era is starting to catch up to kabaddi.

HISTORICAL CONTEXT

The exact history of kabaddi is disputed, a common trait of sports believed to have origins that date back 5,000 years—or 2,000 years, depending on which sources one trusts. Skills used for kabaddi may have been developed during the Kurukshetra War, which took place in India between 2,500 and 7,000 years ago, again, depending on sources. Kabaddi called on participants to move quickly, evade capture, and return to their home side with speed after knocking out an opponent. Those skills helped trained soldiers but eventually grew into a team game.

Members of Iran's kabaddi program also claim the sport, noting that the word *kabaddi* has Persian origins while citing 2,000 years of kabaddi history. Most likely, as with most sports, kabaddi's development draws on multiple cultures, similar to kickboxing, which developed similarly in East and Southeast Asian countries with subtle regional differences. There are stories and written documentation of kabaddi or forms of kabaddi being played throughout South Asia, mostly in rural villages before making its way toward larger communities.

The epic Indian poem *Mahabharata* includes details of a character leading an attack on his enemies. Methods used during the attack closely resemble skills used in kabaddi. The sport received its first international attention as a demonstration sport at the 1936 Olympic Games in Berlin, about 10 years after Indian authorities first published a written set of rules. The Kabaddi Federation of India formed in 1950 and soon afterward began to hold national championships for men and women (1952 and 1955, respectively). Bangladesh declared kabaddi its national sport in 1972, the same year it won its independence from Pakistan. By

Kabaddi, which is most popular in parts of South Asia, evolved from a regional recreational sport into a professional juggernaut. Observers will notice it combines elements of rugby and the child's game tag. (Shariff Che\' Lah/Dreamstime.com)

the early 1980s an organization for amateur Pan-Asian kabaddi players had emerged, and in 1990 it finally earned inclusion in the Asian Games.

GLOBALIZATION

In a sign not just of kabaddi's growth but also its competitiveness, South Korea earned a silver medal at the 2018 Asian Games. Even more impressive, before the games began, South Korea found itself in a seemingly impossible position: it was drawn to Group A along with India, a country so strong in kabaddi that it had not lost at the Asian Games in 28 years. Yet South Korea prevailed and went on to earn a silver medal after finishing the event with a 6–1 record, losing only to the World Cup champion, Iran.

South Korean athletes play in professional kabaddi leagues throughout southern Asia. India and Pakistan ended tied for third. Iran's women's team also won gold that year at the Asian Games, with India taking second and Chinese Taipei earning a bronze medal.

WHERE IT'S PLAYED TODAY

Participation in the sport's two biggest regional and international events—the Asian Games and kabaddi's World Cup—continues to grow steadily, while athletes come from across the continent to compete in professional leagues.

Nations with established or growing kabaddi programs now include Afghanistan, Argentina, Australia, Bangladesh, Canada, Chinese Taipei, Denmark, England, India, Indonesia, Iran, Iraq, Japan, Kenya, Malaysia, Nepal, New Zealand, Norway, Pakistan, Poland, Scotland, Sri Lanka, Thailand, Turkmenistan, and the United States, among others. All inhabitable continents now include at least one country that fields an international kabaddi program.

ECONOMICS AND MEDIA

Nielsen Media Research, which tracks television ratings throughout much of the world, reported that viewership of kabaddi increased by about 14 percent per year since 2015, making it one of the fastest-growing mediated sports in the world. That was one year after the Pro Kabaddi League (PKL) began play in India. From PKL's founding to the publishing of this book, PKL experienced a 33 percent increase in viewership. Most professional sports leagues would be ecstatic with an increase of even just 5 percent.

The top Indian kabaddi players earn the equivalent of nearly $250,000 U.S. annually, while the top Pakistani players make about $150,000. The 2016 Kabaddi World Cup drew a total of 114 million television viewers to watch 12 countries play a total of 33 matches over two weeks. The sport is televised both locally and regionally by various networks, with larger events receiving attention from transnational broadcast corporations.

International streaming services have helped longtime kabaddi fans follow the sport even when they leave southern Asia. Some highlight clips and matches are available over Google's YouTube platform, while live matches can be streamed live over services such as Hotstar and the Star Sports Network. Over the last decade, professional leagues of various sports have tried to retain control of their sports' broadcasts by creating their own networks—soccer and American football are two examples—and kabaddi has followed suit by giving its fans the ability to watch matches broadcast directly by an event host.

The most recent kabaddi World Cup featured broadcast networks from Australia, Canada, India, Saudi Arabia, and the United Kingdom, while ESPN, the American sports network that is the most profitable cable television network in the world, broadcast the event to Latin American countries.

DIMENSIONS OF THE SPORT

Kabaddi varies in form and format depending on region and historical regions as well as professional specifications. The most commonly played version of the game features seven players per team (plus five reserve players on the bench) on a 13- by 10-meter court. Matches last 40 minutes split into two equal 20-minute halves. Taking turns, one player from each team attempts to run across the midcourt line and tag as many players as possible before returning to the home side unimpeded. Teams get one point for each opposing player their teammate tags, but if the opposing team physically prevents the "raider" from returning to the raider's own side, no points are scored.

The raider scores the points. One of the unique features of the sport is how the raider, while on the opposing side, must repeatedly say "kabaddi." A raider who runs out of breath and can no longer say it must try to get back to the home side before being tackled. Opposing defenses train themselves to identify when the raider's kabaddi chant begins to slow down; then they try to tackle the tiring raider.

There are two main variations of kabaddi: standard style and circle style. Standard style is described in the preceding paragraphs. In circle style, which itself has varying styles of play, the court is a circle 72 feet in diameter. Instead of earning points for tagging players, a team earns a point when every player on the other team is tagged out. The first team to five or seven points, depending on the version of circle style being played, wins. In other words: if the teams are playing seven-on-seven, once one team tags all seven players from the other team, the team that wins that round gets one point, and then all seven players on both teams retake the court to begin round two.

IMPORTANT FIGURES

It marked the end of an era in 2018 when Anup Kumar, who had amassed nearly 600 raider points in his professional kabaddi career, retired just weeks after his 35th birthday. Kumar, winner of India's Arjuna Award for athletic achievement and sportsmanship, captained the Indian national team and was part of two squads that won gold at the Asian Games (2010 and 2014). Not bad for someone who picked up the game as a kid just to pass the time.

While some players, such as Kumar, put up statistics, others are known for the longevity. India's Dharmaraj Cheralathan, as of this writing, was in his third decade of elite-level kabaddi in both the professional and international divisions. Cheralathan plays left corner and right corner, each a position responsible for preventing opposing raiders from scoring points. So while Cheralathan may not score a lot of points, when he is on the court, his team's opponents don't score much either.

South Korea's Lee Jang-kun is the first East Asian player to score 400 raid points in India's Vivo Pro Kabaddi league, and he led South Korea to its upset over India in the 2018 Asian Games—an event in which the Indians had never lost a kabaddi match dating back to 1990, the first year the Asian Games included kabaddi. In addition to being the highest-scoring non-Indian in league history, Jang-kun learned the game while in college and was selected to South Korea's international team before he graduated.

POP CULTURE

Kabaddi's greatest popularity rests in Asia, but the sport—rather, the name of the sport—has developed a cult following around the world on the cover of standard, everyday notebooks. Although hundreds of millions of people know and love kabaddi, millions more in Western Europe and North America do not. Despite this, the term kabaddi has popped up within random sayings on the cover of notebooks sold throughout the world. Examples include:

"Eat, Sleep, Kabaddi, Repeat"

"Just a Boy Who Loves Kabaddi"

"Don't Waste Your Time on Therapy—Waste It on Kabaddi"

"King of Kabaddi"

"Kabaddi: It's like Football, but for Men"

"It's a Kabaddi Thing—You Wouldn't Understand"

"Warning: I Talk a Lot about Kabaddi"

"This Girl Runs on Jesus and Kabaddi"

"Life Is Better When You Play Kabaddi"

Depictions of kabaddi also frequently appear in Indian film. The 2012 film *Kabaddi* tells the story of Shingara, a rural boy who yearns to play professionally. As he grows, he struggles to overcome a sport wrapped in potential scandals that involve performance-enhancing drugs and "fixing," a practice used by gamblers and athletes to control the outcome of a game for moneymaking purposes. The 2016 film *Ka Bodyscapes* follows three men, including Vishnu, a rural kabaddi player, as they encounter community conservatism while searching for personal happiness.

SCANDALS

For as long as there have been sports, there have been athletes looking for unfair advantages. In 2011 a staggering 48 percent of Indian athletes tested for the second kabaddi World Cup came back positive for steroids and other illegal performative stimulants, according to India's National Anti-Doping Agency (NADA). Every player who tested positive received some level of suspension.

NADA officials noted that they see more cases of doping in kabaddi than in any other Indian sport. Although they were unsure exactly why kabaddi attracted so many performance-enhancing drugs, Indian news publications theorized that it might be because kabaddi relies solely on the physical skills of strength and quick bursts of speed, two traits boosted by performance-enhancing drugs. India's most popular sport, cricket, features more timing and hand-eye coordination. Cricket players who used steroids would not gain the same competitive advantage that they would in kabaddi.

POLITICS

In 2011 the Canadian House of Commons took a break from its usual work so that Member of Parliament Parm Gill could pay tribute to the Canadian kabaddi team, which was preparing to compete in the World Cup. The Canadian newspaper *Globe and Mail* suggested that local politicians were courting kabaddi fans and teams because of their intense loyalty and organizational capabilities; kabaddi clubs are known for being well run, and those that are not struggle to find traction.

After Gill's tribute, he and Cabinet Minister Tim Uppal flew to Pakistan to watch the Pakistan-Canada match, which Canada won in what was considered its biggest upset in program history.

PATRIOTISM AND NATIONAL PRIDE

The United States fielded its first World Cup kabaddi team at the 2016 games in Ahmedabad, India, lost all five of its matches, and was not particularly competitive. The Americans debuted alongside two other first-time participants: Australia and Great Britain, with all three countries filling their rosters with competitors from other sports. Although none of the teams experienced much success, their appearances marked another milestone in kabaddi's global growth, and their attempts to compete were met with near-universal appreciation by a heavily Indian crowd that wanted to show support more for the attempt than the final scores.

Australia's team was made up mostly of former Australian rules football and rugby players. Great Britain cobbled together its squad from athletic university students. The American team was represented almost entirely by students from Florida A&M University, one of the United States' famed HBCUs (historically Black college and universities). A Florida A&M student recruited fellow A&M student-athletes from track and field, football, and basketball to build the team.

According to various newspaper reports, Indian crowds chanted "U-S-A, U-S-A" to support the Americans during their matches, even though the United States finished the World Cup without a victory. More importantly for the sport's international growth, the entries from Australia, Great Britain, and the United States started to do for kabaddi what global exhibition tours did for sports such as ice hockey and baseball in the late 19th century. Traditional kabaddi-competing countries encourage the sport's growth by reaching out to athletes across the world.

Timeline

c. 3000 BCE – Athletic feats begin to take place in India as part of military training, which plants the seeds of kabaddi.

c. 100 CE – Games similar to kabaddi begin to appear in what is now Iran.

1936 – Kabaddi occurs as a demonstration sport during the 1936 Olympic Games in Munich.

1938 – Kabaddi makes its first appearance in the Indian Games.

1950 – The Kabaddi Federation of India is founded.

1951 – At the Asian Games, kabaddi debuts as a demonstration sport.

1972 – Bangladesh officials name kabaddi the country's official sport.

1990 – Kabaddi finally receives official admission to the Asian Games, moving beyond demonstration status.

1992 – Great Britain, a former colonizer of India and home to many citizens of Indian heritage, airs its first weekly kabaddi-centered television show. It does not last long, canceled because of low viewership.

1996 – Iran joins the Asian Kabaddi Federation. Iran, which claims some ownership over the sport, joins the International Kabaddi Federation five years later.

2014 – The Pro Kabaddi League is formed.

2016 – The United States fields its first team at the Kabaddi World Cup, held in Ahmedabad, India.

2018 – South Korea upsets India at the Asian Games, marking the first time India had lost at the Asian Games since kabaddi joined the games in 1990.

2019 – The first European Kabaddi Championship is held in Scotland.

2019 – Iran defeats Kenya to win the first Junior Kabaddi World Championships.

See also: Rugby; Wrestling.

Further Reading

Chaudhary, V. (2018). *Kabaddi by Nature.* Palimpsest Publishers: New Delhi, India.

Kirankumar, P. and Choudhary, R. (2011). *Characteristics of Indian Kabaddi Players: Incentive Motivation and Anthropometric Characteristics and Functions of Different Playing Positions.* LAP Lambert Academic Publishing: Staarbrücken, Germany.

Kishore, N. (2016). *How to Play Kabaddi.* Self-published.

Mishra, S. C. (2007). *Teach Yourself Kabaddi.* Sports Publication: Delhi, India.

Muniraju, S. (2015). *A Text Book on Kabaddi: Kabaddi Skills, Techniques, and Strategies.* LAP Lambert Academic Publishing: Saarbrücken, Germany.

Ninan, T. N. (2017). *Turn of the Tortoise: The Challenge and Promise of India's Future.* Oxford University Press: Oxford, United Kingdom.

Rasiyath, S. B. (2019). *Anthropometric Characteristics of Kabaddi Players: An Analytic Approach Based on the Playing Position.* LAP Lambert Academic Publishing: Staarbrücken, Germany.

Reddy, N. G. (2012). *Read & Play Kabaddi: With Latest Rules and Regulations.* Nava Ratna Book House: Vijaywada, India.

Tatla, D. S. (1998). *The Sikh Diaspora: The Search for Statehood.* Routledge: Abingdon, United Kingdom.

Yadav, J. S. and Agashe, C. D. (2016). *Coordinative and Skill Ability: The Effect of Clay and Mat Surface on Coordinative and Skill Ability of the Kabaddi Players.* LAP Lambert Academic Publishing: Staarbrücken, Germany.

Kickboxing

Kickboxing has religious and military roots. Centuries of history show that forms of kickboxing, such as the most popular form, muay Thai from Thailand, helped its followers achieve spiritual growth. In more modern times, as training became formalized, the sport has moved from the spiritual to the commercial. There is money to be made, medals and trophies to be won. Kickboxing has developed fans around the world, from Southeast Asia to Northern Europe, to South and North

Muay Thai kickboxing experienced its greatest growth in Japan, Southeast Asia, and the United States during the second half of the 20th century. Today it has become a popular form of recreational fitness. (Dmitry Kalinovsky/Dreamstime.com)

America, to North Africa, and to Oceania. It has spawned movies and fitness crazes. Its athletes, meanwhile, are recognized for their intelligence, ferocity, and flexibility. It is not enough to understand the moves in kickboxing. The key to becoming successful, coaches say, is discipline, a willingness to train right and understand the sport's history. In some parts of the world, it is common to drive down the street and see kickboxing gyms, but very few understand what the sport is actually about.

HISTORICAL CONTEXT

Muay Thai dates to the 13th century and is often called the science of the eight limbs because the point of contact comes from two fists, two elbows, two knees, and two feet. Thai soldiers practiced the form of martial arts to be used in combat. It looked more like boxing several hundred years ago, and it evolved into the art of using different forms of strikes. By the 1800s muay Thai also became a form of recreation and self-defense. By the 1920s it had become a sport with rules, gloves, and other safety measures. It was after that point that Noguchi discovered muay Thai and incorporated it into karate and boxing to create kickboxing.

Today, sports training facilities and fitness centers across the world offer kickboxing as a form of self-defense, athletic training, or fitness. In the 1970s, however, many martial arts participants came to the sport by chance as they trained in their own disciplines, such as karate or tae kwon do. Others discovered kickboxing on television, most notably on *Wide World of Sports* (1961–1998), the American Broadcasting Company's iconic weekend sports-television show.

As kickboxing became regulated in the early 20th century, the sport's leaders altered muay Thai to aid with safety and enhance the attractiveness of competition. Headbutts and ground fighting were eliminated. The second change in particular helped grow the sport's popularity. Without ground fighting, kickboxers could focus more on agility, speed, and skill instead of power and bulk, which are more useful in wrestling and boxing. Some fighters put objects such as shards of glasses in their gloves to try to gain an advantage, but as the need to conduct fair fights grew, that practice was regulated out of kickboxing in mainstream organizations.

GLOBALIZATION

Muay Thai grew in Thailand, but similar martial arts developed in countries near Thailand in South and Southeast Asia. Cambodia, for example, is home to kun khmer; Laos has muay Lao. Kickboxing, which could not have been created without muay Thai, developed in Japan. Today there are kickboxing organizations, training facilities, professional and amateur leagues, and physical-fitness companies across the world.

Some examples of kickboxing organizations include but are by no means limited to the World Kickboxing Network (founded in France); King of Kings (Lithuania); Kunlun Fight (China); K-1 (Hong Kong); World Kickboxing Association (Italy and Australia); World Version W5 (Russia); World Professional MuayThai Federation (Thailand); International Kickboxing Federation (United States); and International Wushu Federation (Switzerland and China).

The globalization of amateur and recreational kickboxing for fitness has grown significantly over the last three decades, especially among women. News outlets in Thailand, the United States, and many other countries attribute the sport's recreational growth to numerous benefits, including self-defense, toughness, body image and body shaping, and mental and emotional benefits. In Thailand, the fastest-grown area of competitive kickboxing is among women.

WHERE IT'S PLAYED TODAY

Over the last two decades, kickboxing has most often been found within the larger sport of mixed martial arts (MMA). Kickboxing, along with boxing, jujitsu, wrestling, and other martial arts, are considered essential skills within MMA, which has grown to become the world's most profitable combat sport. (Boxing, because of its easy access point—all one has to do is skillfully punch—remains the most popular.) The start of an MMA match often mirrors the start of a kickboxing match, with two competitors circling each other and throwing strikes with their hands and feet.

Kickboxers who compete at the highest levels travel the world to fight. Professional organizations exist on six continents, although South and Southeast Asia—where kickboxing has its roots—remains the home base for the sport. As a show of respect to its Thai roots, the sport of kickboxing is often referred to as muay Thai kickboxing, even though the method of fighting has evolved over centuries.

ECONOMICS AND MEDIA

If one wants to find the source of kickboxing's greatest economic impact, look not at kickboxing as a professional sport but instead at its worth to the industries of health and fitness. Professional fighters at the highest levels of success and exposure who incorporate kickboxing into their mixed martial arts (MMA) repertoires can earn more than $1 million per year. However, those who choose to participate exclusively as kickboxers in the sport of kickboxing often earn money only when they fight, and even then it is important that they fight for a promotion that does not try to cheat them out of their earnings.

The actual earnings of a kickboxer are hard to pin down because they vary country to country, promotion to promotion. The top kickboxers could earn anywhere from $100,000 to $250,000 a year, a paltry sum compared to other popular combat sports such as MMA and boxing. Less successful kickboxers can expect to earn far less. And no professional kickboxing organizations offer health or insurance benefits, which means fighters have to decide between buying their own health insurance (if they can afford it), paying out of pocket, or forgoing it altogether. The number of professional kickboxers varies by country and organization, as do the concepts of "professional" and "amateur."

As for the health and fitness components, multiple industry and health organizations have written that consumers' thirst for fitness has turned the fitness industry into a $3 trillion market globally. That is three times as large as the pharmaceutical industry. Kickboxing falls within that multitrillion-dollar global market. A simple Google search on the phrase "kickboxing workout" returns more than 60 million entries.

Some fitness facilities incorporate kickboxing into a regular schedule of classes that also includes yoga, Pilates, and aerobics, while other facilities are dedicated entirely to kickboxing. Fitness centers argue that kickboxing improves stamina, coordination, strength, speed, and mental health. Consumers in the United States typically pay $75 to $200 per month to attend kickboxing classes.

DIMENSIONS OF THE SPORT

Kickboxing rings come in two sizes: 18 feet by 18 feet or 20 feet by 20 feet. A space of at least 3 feet between the ring and what lies outside the ring (spectators, timekeepers, etc.) must exist. In less formal, less regulated pockets of the sport, rings might not adhere to any of the above dimensions. Underground kickboxing might take place in someone's backyard or in a building meant intended for other use.

The number of rounds per fight and the length of those rounds differ by promotion and fighters' ages and skill levels, as does other equipment, most notably the gloves and trunks. The recreational kickboxing market has grown in recent years so that gloves are sold at popular retailers across the world. In total, kickboxing equipment sales top $100 million annually.

IMPORTANT FIGURES

Osamu Noguchi loved nearly everything about karate. He loved its physicality and spirituality. He loved its discipline. The one thing he wished karate had more of, however, was full striking. Noguchi came across muay Thai in Thailand. Muay Thai, which translates in English to "Thai boxing" or "Thai combat," teaches its followers various stand-up strikes with the arms and legs.

Noguchi's mind stirred. He saw how muay Thai blended well with concepts of karate, so in the early 1960s he incorporated the two along with the sport of boxing, and all together the fighting form earned the nickname "kickboxing." The name stuck. Little did Noguchi realize at the time that the tweak he was looking to make to karate sparked one of the most revolutionizing martial arts movements of the 20th century.

The Japan Kickboxing Association debuted in 1966 and proved so popular that just 10 years later, when Howard Hanson and Arnold Urquidez founded the World Karate Association (now the World Karate and Kickboxing Association), it took just one year until the WKA champion went to Japan to take part in a fight and truly internationalize the sport. Today, kickboxing's popularity is so great that it has become one of the more popular sports for individuals in the world, and training for the sport is so intense that it has found additional life as a recreational activity and tool to improve cardiovascular and strength fitness. In 2017 in just the United States, more than 6.9 million people participated in cardio kickboxing.

How's this for a book title? *No Limits: The Powerful Story of Leah Goldstein—World Champion Kickboxer, Ultra Endurance Cyclist, Israeli Undercover Police Officer.* No one can ever accuse Leah Goldstein of not making the most out of her life. Now a motivational speaker and personal trainer based out of British Columbia, Canada, Goldstein first gained notoriety when she won the World Bantamweight Kickboxing Championship in 1989.

Goldstein also won the Race across American cycling event in 2011, a 3,000-mile, 12-state endurance race. She showed off her kickboxing toughness by cycling through "Shermer's neck," a condition that cyclists can develop after spending upward of 22 hours a day on their bicycles. Her supporters helped her hold her head up by braiding tape into her hair and attaching it to her bra to keep her head held back.

Toshio Fujiwara was one of the most successful, feared fighters in professional muay Thai kickboxing history. He fought 141 professional fights from 1969 to 1983. Of those 141, he won 126, including a staggering 99 by knockout. He continued to contribute to the sport in retirement, running a kickboxing gym that trained some of the sport's successful fighters. He also served as an official ambassador to help grow the sport in Japan while supporting its endeavors in Thailand.

POP CULTURE

In 1989 Kurt Sloane could only watch as his brother, Eric, the U.S. kickboxing champion, was paralyzed by a ruthless opponent while fighting in Thailand. Enraged, Kurt himself decided to learn and train in the martial art of muay Thai. Finally, as Kurt was about to fight the man who paralyzed Eric, Eric was kidnapped, and Kurt was ordered to lose on purpose if he ever wanted to see his brother again. Kurt complied, but just as the final fight was winding down, he learned that Eric had been rescued. Kurt rose to his feet, avenged his brother, and emerged victorious.

Thus went the plot for the movie *Kickboxer*, which helped launch the career of actor Jean-Claude Van Damme along with a film franchise. The film exploited East Asian stereotypes and painted Americans as noble warriors, but it proved a financial success across the world. The film cost about $2 million to make, but it brought in $50 million worldwide—including only $15 million from the United States, which meant the movie played well internationally despite its U.S.-centric message.

Producers of *Kickboxer* made four sequels that came out in 1991, 1992, 1994, and 1995. None came close to the popularity of the original, and none starred Van Damme, whose movies over the course of his career have grossed more than $1 billion. Filmmaker Headmon Entertainment rebooted the *Kickboxer* franchise in 2016 with Van Damme playing a supporting role—and a different character. A sequel to the reboot came out in 2018.

SCANDALS

In November 2018, Thai kickboxer Anucha Tasako died of a brain hemorrhage two days after a fight. As sad as any death might be, death in sports is not unprecedented. Athletes have died while training or competing in sports ranging from baseball to American football to skiing. What made Anucha's death so notable was his age. Anucha, who had competed in 174 kickboxing bouts before his death, was 13 years old.

Thai lawmakers had considered legislation raising the minimum age at which Thai kickboxers can compete even before Anucha's death but instead chose to push guidelines that advise young fighters to avoid too much head contact before the age of 13. They can turn professional at 15. Anucha's amateur career began at age 8, as it sometimes does for child kickboxers in Thailand. Local legislators wanted to raise the age to 12, although as of 2019 no laws have been passed. The death of Anucha brought the subject back into the national conversation.

How young is too young? Was Anucha's death a fluke? According to a study by Dr. Witaya Sungkarat, it might not have been. His study, completed before

Anucha's death, studied the brains of young kids who take part in kickboxing and compared them to children who did not. Similar to kids who play American football, in kickboxing children Sungkarat found irreparable damage done to the brain. If anything positive came from Anucha's death, it was increased attention being paid to other children who take up kickboxing at such a young age.

POLITICS

Muay Thai kickboxing enthusiasts have long hoped that the sport would be included in the Olympic Games, but there is no indication that the International Olympic Committee (IOC) has any interest. There are a number of reasons why the IOC including kickboxing must be considered a longshot.

First, there is no one governing body to work with the IOC. As noted earlier (see "Globalization"), there are numerous organizations that claim to be the "world" or "international" federation for kickboxing. Second, colleges and universities around the world need to show support for a sport, which indicates a stronger push for amateurism and regulated feeder programs. Third, the IOC says it looks for sports that have equitable gender representation, which kickboxing does not.

Nevertheless, kickboxing supporters continue to point to current Olympic sports such as boxing and wrestling as evidence that kickboxing belongs. The IOC is not opposed to combat sports. It even approved karate for the 2020 Games, but a kickboxing-Olympic union does not appear on the horizon until kickboxing first addresses several concerns.

Timeline

1774 – Burmese king Hsinbyushin organizes a seven-day festival of fighting to take place in front of his throne. Thai boxing was among the styles. It proved so successful that its popularity began to grow.

Early 20th century – Thai boxing becomes professionalized. Headbutting and other moves are banned from the sport in favor of strikes with the hand, feet, and knees.

1902 – Religious reforms in Bangkok, Thailand, move Muay teachings away from temples and into clubs and camps, setting up certain formalizations in training.

1921 – A permanent muay Thai ring is constructed at Suan Kulap College in Siam.

1928 – The idea of splitting kickboxing into weight divisions surfaces for the first time.

1937 – Thailand's education department creates a formal set of rules that focuses on apparel and dress, including standardizing boxing gloves.

1955 – The first televised muay Thai event is held.

1960 – Japan's Osamu Noguchi witnesses muay Thai and incorporates its moves into karate and traditional boxing, thus creating kickboxing.

1963 – Three Japanese karate fighters travel to Thailand for exhibition bouts against three muay Thai fighters.

1966 – The Japan Kickboxing Association debuts.

1968 – The World Thai Boxing Association, the oldest muay Thai organization, is formed.

1970 – Kickboxing becomes so popular in Japan that is broadcast three times per week on multiple television channels.

1976 – Japanese-style kickboxing is introduced in the Netherlands.

1983 – Toshio Fujiwara retires as one of the most successful professional kickboxers of all time, winning 126 of 141 matches, including 99 by knockout.

1989 – Jean-Claude Van Damme stars in the movie *Kickboxer*, which becomes a worldwide hit.

1993 – To oversee amateur muay Thai, the International Federation of Muaythai Amateur is formed, eventually growing in membership to more than 100 countries.

2018 – The business publication *MarketWatch*, owned by Dow Jones & Company, reports that the fitness industry, which includes recreational kickboxing, has grown to an aggregate value of more than $3 trillion.

See also: Boxing; Mixed Martial Arts; Wrestling.

Further Reading

Buller, D. and Lawler, J. (2011). *Kickboxing for Women.* Wish Publishing: Terre Haute, Indiana.

Chambers, V. (2007). *Kickboxing Geishas: How Modern Japanese Women Are Changing Their Nature.* Free Press: New York.

Christian, D. (2018). *Footwork Wins Fights: The Footwork of Boxing, Kickboxing, Martial Arts & MMA.* Self-published.

Cunningham, P. and Mickey, R. (1996). *Peter "Sugarfoot" Cunningham's Civilized Warring: Fundamental Kickboxing Techniques.* Galt Publishing: Chicago.

Delp, C. (2012). *Muay Thai Basics: Introductory Thai Boxing Techniques.* North Atlantic Books: Berkeley, California.

Goldstein, L. (2016). *No Limits: The Powerful True Story of Leah Goldstein—World Champion Kickboxer, Ultra Endurance Cyclist, Israeli Undercover Police Officer.* No Finish Line Living Adventures Ltd: Vernon, British Columbia, Canada.

Harinck, T. and Punch, J. (2016). *Thom Harinck: Godfather of Muay Thai in the West.* Amsterdam Publishers: Oegstgeest, Netherlands.

McGarry, L. (2017). *Take Me On.* Harlequin: Toronto, Ontario, Canada.

Miller, M. and Jones, S. (2014). *Pain Don't Hurt: Fighting Inside and Outside the Ring.* Ecco Press: New York.

Sprague, M. and Livingston, K. (2004). *Complete Kickboxing: The Fighter's Ultimate Guide to Techniques, Concepts, and Strategy for Sparring and Competition.* Turtle Press: Wethersfield, Connecticut.

L

Lacrosse

Many sports were spread around the globe because of British colonialism, but no sport more accurately captures the arrogance and dangers of that process than lacrosse. North America's First Nations and other Indigenous people invented the game and taught it to westerners. Westerners then changed the rules, formalized the game, and tried to ban Indigenous people from playing it. Over time all parties have come to play and appreciate lacrosse, but its dark history should not be forgotten. Today, lacrosse resembles many of the world's most popular sports. It is a team game that involves passing a ball back and forth, offense and defense, and scoring goals. Enormously popular in parts of North America, primarily Canada and the eastern United States, lacrosse is a game of speed and coordination. Lacrosse is also notable for its polarization. Sports fans either love it or they never think of it. In a poll of 1,000 U.S. sports fans conducted in 2016, about 12 percent listed lacrosse as one of their three favorite sports. The other 88 percent did not have lacrosse anywhere in their top 10.

HISTORICAL CONTEXT

Lacrosse developed in Canada by First Nations and Native American communities during the 17th century. It was altered during periods of white European imperialism into a game that more closely resembles what is played today. The original game included elements of athleticism, spirituality, ritual, vitality, and culture, as well as skill and engineering craftsmanship. The tribes who played spent centuries fine-tuning the game, including developing the playing racket that today is called the lacrosse stick.

White European imperialists were intrigued by the game but would not accept that "savages," as they sometimes called native people, could possibly develop a game as well as could white Christians. First, they learned the game from native people, then they changed the rules, then they created formally organized competitions and barred native people from playing in them, and finally they redesigned the stick, which among other changes switched from wood to plastic, which meant that the sticks would be made mostly in white-owned factories instead of by the tribes who invented the game.

Lacrosse most likely received its name from Jean de Brebeuf, a French missionary from the early 17th century who felt the stick looked like a crosier—a type of staff carried at the time by some members of the Roman Catholic and Lutheran churches. Europeans first found the game violent but soon became interested, first as observers and for gambling purposes and later as participants. Tribes including, but not limited to, the Huron and Mohawk taught the Europeans, who accepted their teachings before ultimately deciding to change the game and cut out the native tribes.

Physicality has long been part of the game, with players using their bodies and sticks against other players. Local governments around the turn of the 20th century banned some native tribes from playing when they believed gambling became too rampant and the violence too severe, declaring that native tribes should spend more time in church. White players, however, were allowed to continue to play. Lacrosse briefly became an Olympic sport (1904 and 1908). By the late 20th century, professional leagues began to form in North America.

GLOBALIZATION

Like most sports, one can find pockets of those who play it across the world, but most lacrosse is played in North America, primarily Canada and the United States. The Czech Republic represents Europe's most prolific lacrosse presence. The Federation of International Lacrosse (FIL), formed in 2008 and located in New York, was the result of a merger between the International Federation of Women's Lacrosse Associations (IFWLA) and the International Lacrosse Federation (ILF-Men). It oversees five world championships, the first of which took place in 1967. As of 2018 FIL included members from 60 countries. The five world championships are Men's, Women's, Women's U19, Men's U19, and Men's Indoor. Championships have been held in Israel, Czech Republic, England, Australia, and throughout North America.

WHERE IT'S PLAYED TODAY

Lacrosse is played recreationally across the world, but the game flourishes in Canada and in the American Northeast and Atlantic Coast. As of 2018, 47 of 48 American men's lacrosse college champions have come from one of these regions, with the lone exception being the University of Denver in 2015. The only team not from one of these regions to win the women's title is Northwestern University, near Chicago, which has won seven times.

The game has spread somewhat to other parts of the world. For example, in 1995 six countries formed the European Lacrosse Federation (ELF): Czech Republic, England, Germany, Scotland, Sweden, and Wales. Today the ELF has grown to 31 nations that field women's and men's teams. The European Lacrosse Championships are held every three or four years. England has won the most championships. Its women's team has won 7 championships and its men's team has won 9 out of the 10 that have been held, with Germany the only other team to win a title.

Israel, which technically is in Asia but joins a lot of European federations because of its proximity to the continent, also became a member of the ELF. In 2016, during just its second appearance at the men's championships, it took second to England. It also took second at the 2019 women's championships, which it also hosted in the city of Netanya. It was the first time the ELF held its championship outside of Europe, signaling it might be willing to expand its reach.

ECONOMICS AND MEDIA

Although the game was invented by people of First Nations and Native American heritage, today's lacrosse is known in North America as a game primarily played by people of upper-middle-class and upper-class privilege. There is only a modicum of truth to this stereotype; compared to other sports such as golf and hockey, the game requires minimal financial output. A basic stick might cost as little as 40 dollars American, compared to several hundred dollars, for example, for a set of golf clubs. A helmet costs slightly more than a stick, but the most expensive part of playing lacrosse isn't the equipment—it's the cost of travel to tournaments.

One reason some view lacrosse as a rich person's game is that in North America the game is portrayed by sports media as a college undertaking, and the colleges most successful in lacrosse are considered affluent institutions, such as Johns Hopkins University, Princeton University, and Duke University. There are numerous professional lacrosse leagues across Canada and the United States, including Major League Lacrosse, the Women's Professional Lacrosse League, and the National Lacrosse League, but they receive only minimal coverage from professional sports media, which choose to instead focus on college lacrosse.

However, even college lacrosse's television ratings pale compared to other North American sports. In 2016 the NCAA men's lacrosse championships averaged 306,000 viewers per game, compared with sports such as women's basketball (3.8 million) and football (more than 20 million).

DIMENSIONS OF THE SPORT

Standard lacrosse fields measure 110 yards long and 60 yards wide. Each team defends a goal. The goals, which are 6 feet wide by 6 feet tall, are 80 feet apart and surrounded by the "crease," an area dominated by the goalkeeper. Opposing players may not shoot the ball while the goalkeeper is in the crease.

In addition to a team uniform, players are equipped with a helmet and stick. Balls regularly are shot toward the goalkeeper at a speed of more than 100 miles per hour (hence the required helmets). Lacrosse matches generally are broken into quarters for varying lengths of time, depending on the age group of the players.

IMPORTANT FIGURES

From 1957 to 1965, Jim Brown played running back for the National Football League's Cleveland Browns. He retired at the top of his game, a player so dominant that 30 years later, as Barry Sanders pursued the NFL's all-time rushing record, Sanders's own father made a point of telling him that no matter what happened, he would never be as good as Brown. "From the moment [Brown] stepped onto a playing field, the operative emotion expressed in describing Jim Brown has been reverence," wrote Brown's biographer, Dave Zirin (Judge 2020). Brown is football royalty, yet from those who knew him while he attended college at Syracuse University in upstate New York, you might learn that football was not even Brown's best sport. Brown's best sport was lacrosse.

He once scored three goals in a game just hours after competing in a track meet. He finished second in the nation in scoring as a senior, totaling 43 goals in just 10 games. Brown said lacrosse was the best sport he ever played. That Brown so loved the sport could not be considered a surprise; with roots dating to the 17th century, lacrosse to this day inspires uncommon devotion in those who play and watch it.

Curt Styres has owned and served as general manager for professional lacrosse franchises. Styres, a Mohawk, is the first person of First Nations heritage to own a professional sports team. He bought a junior lacrosse team, the Six Nations Arrows Express, in 2002. In 2004 four of his players made it to college; by 2008, 15 players were able to make it to college.

Joyce Barry in 1931 became the first president of the U.S. Women's Lacrosse Association. She also founded CranBarry Equipment Company, a provider of equipment for lacrosse and field hockey, and she was among the first female inductees into the U.S. Lacrosse Hall of Fame.

Almost by accident, Thomas Vennum came to lacrosse. He wasn't one of the game's great players or even a coach. He was a historian who made it a mission to get Native Americans the credit they deserved for creating lacrosse. Vennum wrote two books about the sport, including *American Indian Lacrosse: Little Brother of War* in 1995, which became lacrosse's modern foundational text. Vennum's contributions to the sport proved incalculable, and he provided the sport an essential moral and ethical grounding. Vennum, a historian of music and other artistic endeavors of indigenous cultures, came to lacrosse through his interest in the intricate craftsmanship of lacrosse sticks.

Cyrus C. Miller, one of the first two people inducted into the U.S. National Lacrosse Hall of Fame in 1957, played and helped promote lacrosse across the world in the late 19th and early 20th centuries. He played for New York University and then for numerous clubs. He was known as a champion of amateurism, which kept money (and therefore, allegedly, corruption) out of lacrosse but also had the effect of keeping lower- and middle-class people out of the sport since they would have to pay all expenses on their own.

POP CULTURE

The 2012 movie *Crooked Arrows* is about a Native American lacrosse team that takes part in a prep-league tournament and addresses the appropriation of the sport by rich, white players. The movie is most notable for its inclusion of Lyle and Miles Thompson, brothers who are part of a large Native American family with deep lacrosse roots, and their cousin Ty Thompson.

Regina George (played by Rachel McAdams), the meanest girl in the 2004 movie *Mean Girls*, at the end turns to the sport of lacrosse as an outlet for her anger. Seemingly reformed and making peace with her past, George instead channels her rage into lacrosse. In one of the movie's final scenes, George is shown running down field and slamming into opposing players on her way to a goal, after which she receives a celebratory tackle from her teammates.

In the 1999 movie *American Pie*, Chris Ostreicher (played by Chris Klein) portrays a star high school lacrosse player who falls in love with a glee club singer. He skips the championship lacrosse game in order to sing with the club and win back his girlfriend.

SCANDALS

In 2006 three members of the Duke University lacrosse team were accused of sexual assaulting a woman at a team party. The charges, all later dropped without going to trial, set off an international debate about race, power, gender, class, and assault. The university suspended the players and the coach resigned, but most notable was the case's lead prosecutor eventually losing his license to practice law because of how recklessly he pursued the case.

Some members of the North Carolina government, Duke University, and the general public viciously verbally attacked the accuser based on her gender, race (she is African American), profession (exotic dancing), and perceived lack of credibility. Long after the charges against the men were dropped, the accuser maintained her version of what happened at the party. The party and ensuing legal case have been the subject of numerous books and articles.

POLITICS

It's impossible to discuss the invention, development, and modern state of lacrosse without acknowledging the virulent racism of the white Americans and Europeans toward Native Americans and First Nations, without whom the game would not exist. Vennum's books about the history of lacrosse did much to reestablish credit for the game to its rightful place, as have the efforts of First Nations and Native Americans to either reaffirm or reclaim their ties to the sport.

Various lacrosse organizations as well as scholars and historians have tried to do their part to ensure the history of the game is understood and shared as new generations pick up the sport, which continues to grow in popularity.

PATRIOTISM AND NATIONAL PRIDE

The First Nations Lacrosse Association (FNLA) governs lacrosse for First Nations people in Canada and Native Americans in the United States. The Federation of International Lacrosse recognizes women's and men's teams from the FNLA in international competition, making it the only professional sports league in the world that sanctions First Nations and Native American people in any sport. In international play, FNLA's women's teams are known as the Haudenosaunee Nationals. The men's team is known as the Iroquois Nationals.

Timeline

17th century – Versions of the game now known as lacrosse, played by Native Americans and First Nations, are witnessed for the first time by European imperialists.

1636 – Jean de Brebeuf likely becomes the first to name the sport "lacrosse" in writing.

1750 – Mohawks teach lacrosse to French Canadians in Montreal.

1794 – A lacrosse match between the Mohawks and the Seneca is believed to be one of the first using modern rules.

1805 – The city of La Crosse, Wisconsin, is given its name after a U.S. Army soldier observes Native Americans playing lacrosse nearby.

1856 – The Montreal Lacrosse Club is founded.

1857 – White Europeans rewrite lacrosse's rules, claiming they improved the game invented by First Nations and Native American people.

1867 – William George Beers finalizes a set of rules for parts of Montreal and other areas of Quebec.

1880 – With First Nations and Native Americans banned from playing, the United States beats Canada for the first time.

1881 – The first college lacrosse tournament in the United States is held.

1890s – Women's lacrosse is adopted in England.

1904 – Lacrosse becomes an Olympic sport.

1908 – Lacrosse ceases to be an Olympic sport.

1931 – The U.S. Women's Lacrosse Association is founded.

1937 – Robert Pool creates a double-walled stick made from wood. The prototype becomes the model for today's plastic sticks.

1957 – The U.S. National Lacrosse Hall of Fame is established.

1967 – The United States wins the first World Lacrosse Championship.

1972 – The International Federation of Women's Lacrosse Association is founded and helps coordinate lacrosse events for women across the world.

1990 – American Roy Simmons Jr. becomes the first college coach to win four championships.

1993 – Despite having played for decades, the first women receive induction into the U.S. Lacrosse Hall of Fame.

1995 – Six nations form the European Lacrosse Federation.

See also: Field Hockey; Football; Olympics.

Further Reading

Buck, C. K. (2016). *Thinking Inside the Crease: The Mental Secrets to Becoming a Dominant Lacrosse Goalie*. CreateSpace Independent Publishing Platform: Scotts Valley, California.

Cohan, W. D. (2014). *The Price of Silence: The Duke Lacrosse Scandal, the Power of the Elite, and the Corruption of our Great Universities*. Scribner: New York.

Downey, A. (2018). *The Creator's Game: Lacrosse, Identity, and Indigenous Nationhood.* UBC Press: Vancouver, British Columbia, Canada.

Judge, C. (2020). "Why 'Reverence' Is the Operative Emotion When Describing Jim Brown." *Sports Illustrated*, March 13, 2020. https://www.si.com/nfl/talkoffame/nfl/guest-column-why-reverence-is-the-operative-emotion-when-describing-jim-brown.

Kaley, J. B. and Donovan, R. (2015). *Lacrosse Essentials: Master the Basics and Compete with Confidence.* Human Kinetics: Champaign, Illinois.

Morris, D. (2006). *Confident Coach's Guide to Teaching Lacrosse: From Basic Fundamentals to Advanced Player Skills and Team Strategies.* Lyons Press: Guilford, Connecticut.

Tucker, J. and Yakutchik, M. (2014). *Women's Lacrosse: A Guide for Advanced Players and Coaches.* Johns Hopkins University Press: Baltimore, Maryland.

Vennum, T. (1994). *American Indian Lacrosse: Little Brother of War.* Johns Hopkins University Press: Baltimore, Maryland.

Vennum, T. (2007). *Lacrosse Legends of the First Americans.* Johns Hopkins University Press: Baltimore, Maryland.

Zirin, D. (2018). *Jim Brown: Last Man Standing.* Blue Rider Press: New York.

Marathon

The marathon is a 26.2-mile running race. For competitive and recreational distance runners, it represents the pinnacle of testing one's resolve. Most races are shorter in distance and a small handful are longer, but the marathon, with its millennia of history, carries a cultural currency unmatched by nearly any other sporting accomplishment. Tell someone that you have run a marathon, and it brings instant credibility: *This is someone who has accomplished something in life*. People who finish marathons adorn their cars with bumper stickers to note the accomplishment, a move that could devalue the resale value of their automobile by thousands of dollars, but to them it is worth it. Training takes months, but even when the day comes to run the first marathon, veteran runners say there is no way to mentally prepare for it. Legs will ache, feet will blister, wills will deteriorate. But when it is over, the runners will forever carry with them the satisfaction of knowing they finished a marathon.

HISTORICAL CONTEXT

Legend has it that the marathon's roots trace to 490 BCE, when the Greek soldier Pheidippides ran from the town of Marathon to the city of Athens to announce Greece's victory over the Persians. He ran 25 miles, declared victory by yelling, "Niki!" Then he collapsed and died.

How, then, did the modern marathon come to be a 26.2-mile race? It took another 2,400 years to lengthen the marathon by 1.2 miles. The International Olympic Committee (IOC) staged the first modern Olympics in 1896 in Athens to commemorate the ancient games. Even then, the marathon distance was about 25 miles.

In 1908 London hosted the Games. Organizers set up the marathon to start at Windsor Castle and end at White City Stadium. The distance was 26 miles, but that wasn't good enough for Great Britain's royal family, who wanted to see the runners cross the finish line. The royals' viewing box could not be moved, so race organizers had to extend the finish line an extra 385 yards—or 0.2 miles—so the royals could see. The distance of the race was 26.2 miles.

Yet even then, marathoners and the IOC bickered over the ideal length of a marathon. Finally in 1921 the International Amateur Athletic Federation set the official marathon length at 26.2 miles, where it has been ever since. The length of a marathon differed at each of the first six modern Olympics. Some sporting events have come and gone, but the marathon has endured, and if the Boston Marathon seemed out of touch for not giving women permission to run it until the early 1970s,

The winners of one of the world's oldest marathons, the Boston Marathon, stand to earn at least $150,000. The annual event began in 1897 and was canceled for the first time in 2020 because of the COVID-19 pandemic. (Teconley/Dreamstime.com)

consider the IOC. Marathoning didn't open up as an Olympic sport for women until 1984, when American Joan Benoit topped Germany's Grete Waitz for the gold.

GLOBALIZATION

People from Kenya have dominated marathon and long-distance running, winning nearly two-thirds of all major distance races since the mid-1980s, including a stretch of 20 out of 25 men's Boston Marathons beginning in 1988. Trying to explain the success of Kenyans often has led to racial profiling from people in Western nations. One false explanation attributed their success to having to run back and forth to school every day, when in reality most Kenyan students take school buses or live within walking distance of a school.

The actual explanation is far more simple: hard work, modern training techniques, a cultural love for running, and a country with high elevations—as great as 7,000 feet—that helps build endurance. Morocco, Ethiopia, the United Kingdom, and the United States also produce some of the world's top marathoners, but no country has come close to matching the long-term success of Kenya.

WHERE IT'S PLAYED TODAY

Here's the thing about running: it was a basic human action before it was ever an organized activity, and it can be done anywhere, anytime, by anyone who is physically able. Marathons take place all over the world and draw runners from all over the world. There is even a marathon in Antarctica, making it one of the few sporting events on earth that take place on all seven continents.

One fun thing about marathons is not where they take place but under what conditions. Most marathons follow the basic 26.2-mile template, but others throw in certain wrinkles. Some have themes, such as the Walt Disney World Marathon, in which some runners dress up as their favorite Disney characters. The Hatfield-McCoy Marathon in West Virginia celebrates the legendary feud between two 19th-century American families. And then there are the ultramarathoners, runners who look at the 26.2-mile distance as a mere starting point. An ultramarathon tests runners' ability to run up to 100 miles.

ECONOMICS AND MEDIA

Winning a major marathon comes with a good bit of prize money. The winner of the Boston Marathon stands to earn at least $150,000. The winners of the New York or Chicago marathons will earn more than $100,000, and the winner of London might earn $50,000. Again, that might seem like a good living until one realizes that there can only be one winner. There is prize money for runners-up, but it is nominal compared with the champion's, which means the life of a professional marathon runner might at times be filled with financial struggle.

That is where endorsements come in. Almost nobody would be able to afford to be a professional marathoner without the support of sponsors, whether they are sporting-goods companies or companies from outside the athletic realm, such as banks and apparel companies. For example, the company Adidas sponsored runner Dennis Kimetto of Kenya. The money he earned from Adidas enabled Kimetto to train the way he needed to train and still meet his financial responsibilities.

Most media coverage of marathons comes from local outlets. London's broadcast networks and newspapers cover the London Marathon, Chicago outlets cover the Chicago Marathon, and so forth. Specialty publications such as the magazine *Runner's World* provide coverage for the sport's most devoted fans. Otherwise, finding coverage can be challenging, with exceptions. The Boston Marathon, because of its history, sometimes earns national media attention. The most watched marathon is the Olympic marathon, largely because it traditionally is held on the last day of Olympic competition.

DIMENSIONS OF THE SPORT

A marathon course needs to be 26.2 miles long. Where courses differ is in the challenges along the way. The San Francisco Marathon, for example, has earned the nickname "The Race Even Marathoners Fear" because of all its hills, while the Athens Classic Marathon in Greece is considered a milder course, mostly flat with a few small hills.

In 2019 the petrochemical company INEOS sponsored longtime marathoner Eliud Kipchoge of Kenya to see if he could be the first marathoner in history to break two hours. Preparation took months, and the first step was to find a course with favorable running conditions. INEOS representatives decided on a marathon held in Vienna, Austria, to be held in October. Preparation included far more than endurance training. They looked over the course, used geometry to uncover the exact angles to take around turns to limit the total distance Kipchoge would have to run, and surrounded him with a legion of pacesetters.

Kipchoge succeeded. His time of 1 hour, 59 minutes, 40 seconds exceeded even INEOS's expectations. The crowd roared down the final stretch as it became apparent Kipchoge would make it. Alas, his time was not counted as a world record, mostly because of the abnormally high number of pacesetters. Still, it was a landmark achievement for Kipchoge, who will forever be known as the first person to run a marathon in less than 2 hours.

IMPORTANT FIGURES

Kenyan Eliud Kipchoge will go down in history as one of the greatest marathoners ever when he chooses to retire. As of 2019 he had won a record nine straight marathons. His record-breaking ninth came at the 2018 Berlin Marathon in Germany, where he also set the world record for a marathon by finishing in 2:01.39. He also won a gold medal at the 2016 Olympic Games in Rio de Janeiro, Brazil, by an astonishing 1 minute, 10 seconds over the second-place finisher. Kipchoge never tried to hide the secret to his success. He said he never pushed himself too hard in practice, saving his real effort for race day.

Joan Benoit Samuelson won the first women's marathon in the Olympics during the 1984 Games in Los Angeles, California, but her running career extended far beyond the Olympics, when she won gold just 17 days after undergoing a medical procedure on one of her knees. A year before the Olympics, she set a women's world record at the 1983 Boston Marathon with a time of 2:22.43—a record that stood for 11 years. Thirty years later she said she still ran often but introduced other sports into the training regimen, and in 2013 she set a goal to run within 30 minutes of her 1983 time. At 56 years old she succeeded, running about 28 minutes off of her 1983 pace.

Between 1978 and 1988, Norwegian Grete Waitz won the New York Marathon nine times. She set a marathon world record the first time she ever ran one in 1978, having previously been a long-distance track-and-field runner. She ran her first marathon as a challenge set forth by her husband, and as she crossed the finish line she said, "I'll never do this stupid thing again" (McDonald 2011, 412). Waitz won gold at the 1983 World Championships in Athletics and twice won the London Marathon, but the closest she ever got to Olympic gold was in 1984, when she took silver behind Benoit Samuelson.

POP CULTURE

"Is it safe?"

With those three words, novelist and screenwriter William Goldman turned a routine experience like going to the dentist into one of terror. His novel, *Marathon*

> ### Switzer's Half Century of Inspiration
>
> Kathrine Switzer's time in the 2017 Boston Marathon—4:44:31—was just 24 minutes slower than when she had run the race 50 years earlier. To finish a 26.2-mile endurance race takes will, discipline, and months of training. To do it at age 70 requires more than a few months of workouts. It takes a lifetime of fitness.
>
> But Switzer won't be remembered for her times. She will be remembered for running her first Boston Marathon in 1967 under the name K. V. Switzer. She used her initials because in 1967 the Boston Marathon did not admit women. To say her appearance caused a fuss would be an understatement. Male race officials freaked out. One darted onto the course as Switzer ran by and tried to physically force Switzer out of the race. Her boyfriend at the time, who was running alongside her, tackled the official. Switzer went on to finish the race.
>
> The men who administered the marathon finally agreed to admit women starting with the 1972 race. Switzer ran it again in 1976 but not again until 2017. She was given the same bib number in 2017 as in 1967, number 261, and after the race it was announced that in her honor nobody would ever wear bib 261 again.
>
> Switzer went on to win the 1974 New York Marathon in just over 3 hours. She became a television commentator. There are many ways Switzer's legacy has been secured. First, she entered the race. Second, she not only ran the race, but her ambition was immortalized in Paul Connell's iconic photograph of the race official trying to drag her off the course. Third, as of 2019 more than half the registered marathon runners in the United States were women. Years later Switzer wrote in the *New York Times*, "We learned that women are not deficient in endurance and stamina, and that running requires no fancy facilities or equipment" (Switzer 2007).

Man, was the story of a graduate student and aspiring marathoner, Babe, who unwittingly gets caught in a conspiracy involving an old Nazi dentist.

The dentist, trying to discover whether Babe knows his secret, drills into Babe's teeth without anesthesia, asking him over and over, "Is it safe?" as Babe screams in pain. Eventually Babe escapes and, thanks to his marathon training, is able to run from the Nazi dentist and his henchmen. The novel became a movie of the same name that starred Sir Laurence Olivier as the dentist and Dustin Hoffman as Babe. Olivier won a Golden Globe for his performance.

SCANDALS

Three people died, 16 lost limbs, and hundreds of others were injured in April 2013 when two bombs detonated near the finish line of the Boston Marathon. Two brothers, Tamerlan and Dzhokhar Tsarnaev, placed the bombs to cause maximum damage. As the race drew to a close and runners crossed the finish line, the bombs detonated 12 seconds apart from each other and created a scene of blood, chaos, and heroism as fellow runners, spectators, and first-response emergency workers rushed to tend to the wounded. The terrorist act sparked a citywide manhunt for the brothers, one of whom was killed and the other captured and sentenced to death following trial.

Numerous public events, including concerts and sporting events, were canceled in response to the attack and aftermath, including a Boston Celtics basketball game, Boston Bruins hockey game, Boston Red Sox baseball game, and a performance of Beethoven's music by the Boston Symphony. An outpouring of goodwill and charity inspired the Boston region and beyond. Even five years later, a local storage company collected many of the memorials left by visitors and stored them free of charge in a climate-controlled room in order to preserve them.

A million people showed up one year later to watch the 2014 Boston Marathon—twice the size of the usual crowd. The crowd roared as Meb Keflezighi, a down-on-his-professional-luck, 39-year-old American came down the final stretch to win the men's race. Not long before, he had lost his lucrative shoe-endorsement contract with Nike. Now he was the winner of the oldest, continuously run annual marathon in the world, its oldest winner in more than 80 years, and he was doing so wearing a brand of shoe known more for skateboarding than for running.

In the days and weeks following the bombing, Bostonians adopted the phrase "Boston Strong" to communicate their resiliency and defiance. The city's mayor, Thomas Menino, who had been suffering from various ailments, appeared at a press conference in a wheelchair to help reassure the city. Boston Red Sox baseball player David Ortiz, one of the franchise's most iconic players, delivered an impromptu speech before his team's game at Fenway Park. The speech was laced with colorful language and a call for hope that was so powerful that ESPN said it was Ortiz's finest moment. The brothers intended to shred the fabric of Boston by bombing its annual marathon celebration, but the marathon went on without missing even a year, stronger than ever.

POLITICS

British marathoner and distance runner Mo Farah was unsure how or when he would see his kids again when, in 2017, the president of the United States, Donald Trump, banned citizens from several countries from traveling to the United States. Farah was a British citizen who was born in Somalia, one of the countries on the list. He lived and trained in Oregon but was in Ethiopia when the ban was enacted. "It's deeply troubling that I will have to tell my children that Daddy might not be able to come home," Farah said (Griffiths 2017).

Farah did make it home. However, later that year Farah and his wife decided to leave Oregon and return to London to be able to raise their children in the United Kingdom. So Farah, a four-time Olympic gold medalist, left the United States. He returned about a year later to run the 2018 Chicago Marathon, which he won.

Timeline

490 BCE – Greek soldier Pheidippides runs 25 miles from the city of Marathon to Athens to announce the Greek army's victory.

1896 – The IOC reinstitutes the marathon as one of the showpieces of the first modern games in Athens. Only nine people are able to complete the endurance race.

1897 – Inspired by the games in Athens, the first Boston Marathon is held.

1908 – The marathon is lengthened to 26.2 miles to accommodate the course at the London Olympics, which includes the viewing box of the royal family.

1908 – American John Hayes sets the first-recognized world men's marathon record, finishing in 2:55:18.

1908 – The distance of a marathon is extended by 385 yards after Queen Alexandra, wife of British King Edward VII, asks that it be moved so that her children can better see the race.

1921 – After years of infighting and bickering, the International Amateur Athletic Federation finally agrees to formally set the length of a marathon to 26.2 miles.

1964 – Great Britain's Dale Greig sets the first undisputed women's marathon world record mark, running in 3:27:45.

1967 – Kathrine Switzer enters the Boston Marathon under the name "K.V. Switzer" and becomes the first woman to run the event.

1970 – The first New York Marathon is held.

1984 – Joan Benoit wins the first Olympic gold medal awarded to women's marathoners.

2003 – While running in London, Briton Paul Radcliffe sets the women's marathon world record, running in 2:15:25.

2018 – Kenya's Eliud Kipchoge runs the Berlin Marathon in 2:01:39, a world record, averaging about 4 minutes, 38 seconds per mile.

2019 – Kenya's Eliud Kipchoge in Austria runs the world's first sub-2-hour marathon. Although the accomplishment is celebrated across the world, it is not considered a world record because he used too many pacesetters.

2020 – The Boston Marathon, in response to the COVID-19 pandemic, is canceled for the first time in its history.

See also: Baseball; Olympics; Track and Field.

Further Reading
Bauman, J. and Witter, B. (2014). *Stronger*. Grand Central Publishing: New York.

Connelly, M. (2014). *26.2 Miles to Boston: A Journey into the Heart of the Boston Marathon*. Lyons Press: Guilford, Connecticut.

Griffiths, E. (2017). "Mo Farah Responds to Donald Trump's Travel Ban: 'It's Deeply Troubling That I Will Have to Tell My Children That Daddy Might Not Be Able to Come Home.'" *Hello Magazine*, Jan. 29, 2017. https://www.hellomagazine.com/celebrities/gallery/2017012936213/mo-farah-responds-to-donald-trump-travel-ban/1.

Higdon, H. (2011). *Marathon: The Ultimate Training Guide: Advice, Plans, and Programs for Half and Full Marathons*. Rodale Press: Emmaus, Pennsylvania.

Keflezighi, M. and Douglas, S. (2019). *26 Marathons: What I Learned about Faith, Identity, Running, and Life from My Marathon Career*. Rodale Press: Emmaus, Pennsylvania.

Krahe, D. (2018). *Be Ready on Race Day: How to Create a Custom Training Plan for Your Next Marathon or Half Marathon*. Let's Tell Your Story Publishing: Watford, England.

McDonald, W. (2011). *The Obits: Annual 2012*. Workman Publishing Company: New York.

McDougall, C. (2011). *Born to Run: A Hidden Tribe, Superathletes, and the Greatest Race the World Has Ever Seen*. Vintage: New York.

Murakami, H. (2009). *What I Talk about When I Talk about Running: A Memoir*. Vintage: New York.

Switzer, K. (2007). "First Woman's Strides in Boston Still Echoing." *New York Times*, April 15, 2007. https://www.nytimes.com/2007/04/15/sports/othersports/15switzer.html.

Switzer, K. (2017). *Marathon Woman: Running the Race to Revolutionize Women's Sports*. Hachette Books Group: New York.

Mixed Martial Arts

The sport of mixed martial arts (MMA) occupies a unique space in sporting culture because it is defined by both its violence and its restraint. Fighters try to knock each other unconscious or inflict pain so severe that their opponent quits. Fighters bleed, break bones, and do everything in their power to devastate another person's body. On the other hand, sport officials have recognized that their fans have a taste for combat that goes only so far. When the sport grew too violent, a certain type of fan stopped coming and governments took steps to keep MMA out of their countries, states, and cities. It was culture's way of saying they like the skills involved in combat sports, but they also respect the long-term safety of individuals. As a result, the moment that changed MMA forever was the moment when the referees became empowered to protect a fighter, to step in and declare one fighter the winner the moment it became obvious that someone could get fatally injured. More than most sports, MMA informs us about our cultural values. Toughness and combat skills matter in the 21st century, but so do compassion and restraint. We want to see who is stronger and fiercer but not at the expense of another's health. MMA brings together age-old instincts with modern perspectives.

HISTORICAL CONTEXT

Some skills used in MMA, such as boxing and wrestling, date back thousands of years. Others, such as kickboxing and Brazilian jujitsu, developed during the early part of the 20th century. Combined, these skills along with martial arts and other forms of hand-to-hand combat make up the athletic foundation of MMA. Put two people with these skills inside a ring with a referee, rounds, time limits, and a few rules, and you get the foundation of one of the 21st century's fastest-growing sports.

The sport entered the public consciousness in 1993 when Ultimate Fighting Championship (UFC), a professional MMA organization based out of the United

States, held its first event in Denver, Colorado. The sport, once known more commonly as cage fighting, made many strides toward mainstream acceptance during its first 25 years. For example, UFC in its earliest days let fighters pull hair, gouge eyes, and hit each other in the groin. Although the sport attracted some fans, others were appalled by its brutality. One of the sport's earliest, most infamous matches at UFC 4 saw Keith Hackney repeatedly punch Joe Son in the groin, then dig his fingers into Son's carotid artery.

The late U.S. senator John McCain called MMA "human cockfighting." Thirty-six states banned MMA. With Japan's Pride Fighting Championships MMA organization threatening to overtake UFC in mainstream attention, it became clear that UFC had to become less violent and more regulated if it wanted to survive. Attacks on an opponent's eyes, hair, and groin were banned, as were some holds formerly used to make opponents submit or pass out.

Brothers Frank and Lorenzo Fertitta purchased UFC in 2001 for $2 million and instilled Dana White as president. With better regulation in place, White overseeing operations, and fighters bringing more martial arts (and less street violence) to the ring, many states overturned their ban on MMA, and the sport flourished. Major television networks, seeing MMA as a more attractive alternative to boxing, which was perceived by some as boring or corrupt, paid UFC for weekly programming. MMA also returned as a viable pay-per view alternative after McCain had earlier led a fight to have it removed.

MMA still delivered competitive violence that some fans craved, but its slight moderation and emphasis on training and skill attracted a new fan base as well. By 2016, the struggling pariah purchased by the Fertitta brothers for $2 million and reconfigured by the brothers and White had grown in value to $4 billion. As a sign that MMA, and UFC, had made it big as a mainstream sport, in 2019 its broadcast rights were bought by ESPN, the American sports cable network—the most profitable cable network in the world.

GLOBALIZATION

There are too many MMA organizations across the world to list them all. The total number is tough to pin down because new ones open and old ones close regularly. Hundreds are active at any given moment. As of 2019 the United States housed 16 organizations, including UFC. Russia had six, England had two, Japan had five, Brazil had six, Germany had four, Philippines had two, Canada had eight, Poland had three, Kazakhstan and Wales each had two, and countries that had at least one included but were not limited to Suriname, Sweden, Belgium, Peru, France, Singapore, Argentina, and Ecuador.

Whereas the world's older sports spread over centuries, as countries went to war and introduced each other to their cultures, MMA's success is a product of the digital age. The sport grew with the launch of UFC, and UFC launched in 1993, when the internet as a public tool was in its infancy and startup companies such as America Online reached large audiences by bringing together people with similar interests, such as MMA. The Fertitta brothers bought UFC in 2001, brought along

Dana White, domesticated the sport for larger audiences, and reaped the benefits provided by companies such as YouTube, founded in 2005, which let fans share videos in seconds instead of the old-fashioned way: by mailing each other videotapes and DVDs, as pro-wrestling hobbyists used to do.

WHERE IT'S PLAYED TODAY

MMA competitions happen on every continent except Antarctica in regulated and unregulated environments. Competitors include both adults and children, although critics debate the merits of the latter's participation.

MMA's mainstream regulation and the willingness of some organizations, including UFC, Bellator, and Strikeforce, to adhere to regional health and wellness standards have helped the sport return to regions where it previously was banned. MMA is now more present than ever, from local organizations that agree to safety codes and hold fights in community centers to multinational organizations that are licensed to host fights on multiple continents in massive arenas.

During the 2020 COVID-19 pandemic, UFC even took the bold step of purchasing its own island to host fights, allegedly to promote safety when it became apparent it could not logistically meet social-distancing standards and other new gathering rules. The idea also helped spur interest in the sport during a time when very few sports were happening. Fans wanted to know the secret location of the so-called Fight Island. They wanted to know who was allowed to go. They wanted to know about legal jurisdiction, and they wanted to know what would happen to the island once the pandemic passed. UFC simultaneously accomplished two goals: they found a place to legally hold their fight card, and they kept fans interested.

ECONOMICS AND MEDIA

ESPN paid UFC $1.5 billion for its broadcast rights. UFC earns additional income through its popular pay-per-views, which are regular broadcasts that viewers have to pay extra for through their cable, satellite, or internet providers. Its major pay-per-view events are still the numbered events, such as the maligned UFC 4 back in the 1990s. As of 2020 UFC was putting on pay-per views in the 250 range. When Khabib Nurmagomedov fought Conor McGregor at UFC 229 in late 2018, fans who wanted to watch at home paid between $55 and $65 to watch the broadcast. An estimated three million people bought the pay-per-view.

Most professional MMA fighters get paid on a per-fight basis, and most do not make very much, working side jobs to make ends meet while they train and pick up fights where they can. Picture the fictional boxing character Rocky Balboa, who in the first movie of the franchise made a few bucks from boxing but the rest from a sideline.

There are numerous professional MMA organizations throughout the country, some that have been around for years but others that open and vanish before they can even host a couple of fight cards. UFC is the most lucrative professional MMA organization. In 2018 the average annual income of a UFC fighter was $138,250, which doesn't include endorsement money. Overall, 187 UFC fighters made at least six figures in 2018, while a small handful made at least a million.

DIMENSIONS OF THE SPORT

The dimensions of an eight-sided MMA ring—or cage, commonly called "the Octagon"—has a diameter of 32 feet. The chain-link fence around the cage stands between 62 and 68 inches high and has padding on top. The whole structure rests atop a platform between 3 and 5 feet high that allows the audience to see the fight. The cage includes two doors on opposite sides, one through which each fighter can enter and exit.

Depending on the level of fighters, the country, and the organization, fights are scheduled from anywhere between three and five rounds. Each around will last between three and five minutes. A fighter wins by knocking out an opponent or making an opponent submit or if the referee determines the opponent can no longer continue.

IMPORTANT FIGURES

Dana White has become synonymous with MMA, specifically UFC. Although the sport has produced many household names—Ronda Rousey, Daniel Cormier, Ken Shamrock, Conor McGregor, and Randy Couture, to name just a few—White, who became president of UFC in 2001, has been the constant. White, whose bald head and fit physique sometimes cause casual fans to mistake him for a fighter, marketed UFC into a global juggernaut. Although he has not been free from controversy—his own mother, June, wrote a tell-all book about him—it is hard to find anyone who has done more to turn the sport into what it is today.

Brazilian Anderson Silva held UFC's middleweight championship for nearly 2,500 days—by far the longest title reign in the UFC's quarter century. From 2006 to 2013 no one could beat Silva, who won his last fight in 2017 at age 41 against Derek Brunson, a fighter 8 years his junior. Many within the sport consider him the greatest fighter in UFC history.

Poland's Joanna Jedrzejczyk earned the moniker of the best pound-for-pound women's fighter on the planet when she won UFC's strawweight championship in 2015. She became the first women's champion from Europe. She successfully defended the championships five times before losing it. But UFC was not her first taste of success. Prior to joining MMA, Jedrzejczyk won multiple championships and more than 60 matches in muay Thai kickboxing. She started her UFC career 13–0.

POP CULTURE

MMA features real athletes competing against each other. When they square off, the outcome is in doubt until the match is over. Conversely, professional wrestling also features real athletes, but they are actors, and their results are scripted by writers and producers. On the surface, it looks as if MMA and pro wrestling operate in different universes. That, however, is not the case.

In MMA's early days—the late 1990s—its fighters discovered they could have longer careers and make more money as professional wrestlers. Professional wrestling promotions, meanwhile, discovered that hiring MMA fighters brought credibility, name recognition, and realism to their shows. As a result, some of MMA's earliest successful fighters, such as Ken Shamrock, Dan "The Beast" Severn, and Tank Abbott found new careers as pro wrestlers.

This did not always sit well with MMA leadership, including Dana White, who expressed frustration toward pro wrestling. He claimed among other things that professional wrestling promoters were threatened by UFC's success and that fans knew that no matter how tough pro wrestlers looked, they were not as tough as MMA athletes. White and Vince McMahon, chairman of World Wrestling Entertainment (WWE), a billion-dollar professional wrestling promotion, bickered publicly for years about the value of each other's product, but more recently they found that each could benefit financially from the other.

Here are some examples of MMA-pro wrestling crossover: WWE wrestler Brock Lesnar left the company and joined UFC, where he won its heavyweight championship, and then returned to WWE to work for both companies simultaneously; MMA fighter Shayna Baszler competed for an astounding 14 years before moving to WWE, where it turned out she had a knack for connecting with audiences and was given a championship; professional wrestler CM Punk (Phillip Brooks) was one of the most popular wrestlers in the business when he decided to quit and enter MMA—he badly lost his debut fight in UFC, but his name recognition helped UFC make millions on his appearance.

SCANDALS

Jon Jones arrived at the perfect time for UFC, a 23-year-old phenom whom the organization could market alongside Ronda Rousey as the future of MMA. He became the youngest championship holder in the promotion's short history, knew how to work a crowd, and looked unbeatable. Unfortunately for Jones and UFC, Jones kept making mistakes that ended with suspensions.

Through 2018 Jones never lost a championship fight. UFC stripped him of his first championship in 2015 after he was charged with hit-and-run. He returned, won another championship, and was stripped again for failing a drug test for performance-enhancing drugs. He later returned again, won another championship in 2017, but then failed another drug test and lost another championship. Despite Jones's conduct, as recently as 2019 Jones was ranked the number-two pound-for-pound fighter in UFC.

POLITICS

In the mid-1990s, U.S. senator John McCain called MMA "human cockfighting," but he started to come around to the sport 15 years later. By 2007 he acknowledged MMA had made changes that left it safer for the competitors and easier to digest for the audience. And by 2014 McCain was actively working with MMA

> ### When Holm Stunned Rousey—and the World
>
> One kick. That's all it took to forever change the trajectory of mixed martial arts. Ronda Rousey had fought 12 matches before stepping into the ring with respected but underrated Holly Holm, who was 9–0. Rousey had won all 12 matches, including 9 by submission. Even more impressive for Rousey, she had won 8 of her 12 fights in less than one minute, and 11 of the 12 had ended in the first round.
>
> Rousey, winner of the bronze medal in judo at the 2008 Summer Olympics while competing for the United States, came in as a prohibitive favorite; Holm was a 9-to-1 underdog. Fifty-nine seconds into the second round, following a vicious kick to the neck and some ground strikes, another Rousey match was over—except there was one key difference: the kick and strikes came from Holm. Rousey lost.
>
> Holm threw her arms out wide and celebrated as Rousey lay bloodied and unconscious. Holm's kick struck Rousey so hard that the greatest women's fighter in MMA history to that point received a 180-day medical suspension. Rousey did not fight again for another 13 months, when she lost again and received another medical suspension. In MMA, history shifts in an instant. Rousey, MMA's main attraction, never fought again. She moved on to a lucrative career in acting and professional wrestling. Said Rousey of the sudden end to her illusion of invincibility, "Maybe winning all the time isn't what's best for everybody. Maybe I had to be that example of picking myself up off the floor" (Guardian Sport 2016).
>
> And what of Holm, who will forever be known for knocking out Rousey? She lost her next three fights.

officials (along with American football and boxing representatives) and people in the medical community to help athletes affected by concussions.

PATRIOTISM AND NATIONAL PRIDE

The International Olympic Committee presently does not welcome MMA into the Games. It likely will not happen anytime soon. Despite this reality, fans and fight organizations have found ways to organically grow patriotic ties. One fighter who represents this initiative is Ireland's Conor McGregor, whose success first came from his dominance in the octagon and then from his willingness to tap into his Irish heritage.

McGregor hoists the Irish flag overhead after his victories. He enters the ring to a song called "The Foggy Dew," written by an Irish priest, Father Charles O'Neill, about the Easter Rising. Easter Rising, also known as the Easter Rebellion, was an uprising against England's dominance over Ireland that took place during World War I. The version McGregor uses was sung by Irish singer Sinead O'Connor. Some of the lyrics go:

> But the bravest fell, and the requiem bell
> Rang mournfully and clear
> For those who died that Eastertide
> In the springtime of the year

Timeline

Ancient Greece – Fighters square off one-on-one in combat sports with few rules in what is considered the ancestor to cage fighting.

1887 – In an overlap of combat sports, boxer John L. Sullivan competes against wrestler William Muldoon.

1993 – Ultimate Fighting Championships (UFC), a professional cage fighting organization, is founded. There are few rules, and the sport is rebranded as mixed martial arts. Competitors are allowed to attack each other's eyes, throat, groin, and hair.

1993 – Royce Gracie wins UFC 1, a tournament, by defeating Ken Shamrock.

1995 – Appalled by MMA, U.S. senator John McCain, a former amateur boxer, calls the sport "human cockfighting." More than 30 states ban MMA fighting.

2001 – Frank and Lorenzo Fertitta buy UFC for $2 million and install Dana White as president. They'll sell it in 2016 for $4 billion.

2008 – Bellator MMA is founded in California and later becomes one of the few legitimate business competitors of UFC.

2008 – Brock Lesnar, a professional wrestler, wins UFC's heavyweight championship against UFC legend Randy Couture. He successfully defends it twice before losing.

2015 – Holly Holm stuns previously undefeated Ronda Rousey to win the bantamweight championship.

2016 – In a rematch of UFC 1 from 23 years earlier, Royce Gracie defeats Ken Shamrock at Bellator 149.

2017 – UFC fighter Jon Jones is stripped of a championship for a third time and is suspended for a third time, this time for performance-enhancing drugs.

2017 – UFC's Conor McGregor faces undefeated boxer Floyd Mayweather in a boxing match. Mayweather wins easily, but promotion of the match is so successful that both fighters are believed to have earned at least $100 million.

See also: Boxing; Kickboxing; Olympics.

Further Reading

Guardian Sport. (2016). "Ronda Rousey: I Thought 'about Killing Myself' after Holm Knockout." *The Guardian*, Feb. 16, 2016. https://www.theguardian.com/sport/2016/feb/16/ronda-rousey-thought-about-killing-myself-immediately-after-holm-knockout.

Hughes, M. and Malice, M. (2008). *Made in America: The Most Dominant Champion in UFC History*. Simon Spotlight Entertainment: New York.

Kavanagh, J. (2016). *Win or Learn: MMA, Conor McGregor, and Me: A Trainer's Journey*. Penguin Books: New York.

Liddell, C. (2008). *Iceman: My Fighting Life*. Penguin Books: New York.

McCarthy, J., Rutten, B., and Hunt, L. (2011). *Let's Get It On! The Making of MMA and Its Ultimate Referee*. Medallion Press: Chicago.

Penn, B. J. (2007). *Mixed Martial Arts: The Book of Knowledge*. Victory Belt Publishing: Las Vegas, Nevada.

Rousey, R. and Ortiz, M. B. (2015). *My Fight/Your Fight*. Regan Arts: New York.

Sheridan, S. (2010). *The Fighter's Mind: Inside the Mental Game*. Grove Atlantic: Boston.

Sonnen, C. (2012). *The Voice of Reason: A V.I.P. Pass to Enlightenment*. Victory Belt Publishing: Las Vegas, Nevada.

St. Pierre, G. (2013). *The Way of the Fight*. William Morrow Paperbacks: New York.

Wertheim, L. J. (2010). *Blood in the Cage: Mixed Martial Arts, Pat Miletich, and the Furious Rise of the UFC*. Houghton Mifflin: Boston.

Olympics

Since the modern Olympics debuted in 1896, nearly 1,500 years after the final ancient Olympics, the event has grown into an international cultural phenomenon and a financial titan. Much of the mediated world stops during the few weeks every other year when there is a summer or winter Olympics, which command the world's attention. Heroes are made, flags are waved, hearts swell and are broken. Although the wealthiest, largest nations with historical infrastructures tend to dominate smaller, underfinanced nations, the stories of underdogs are what keep us coming back for more: Jamaica, a nation that never accumulates snow or ice, fielding a bobsled team; a gymnast sticking the perfect landing on an injured ankle; a horseback rider, paralyzed by polio, winning a silver medal, with the gold-medal winner helping her onto the podium in a show of sportsmanship. Countries spend—and sometimes lose—millions of dollars, just for the honor of hosting the world, but for some countries the chance to become a part of history is worth the enormous financial risks.

HISTORICAL CONTEXT

Although 776 BCE generally is regarded as the first ancient Olympic Games, based on written records, common thought holds that the Games had been held for some time before 776. Champions received olive leaves. Officials said they held games to honor the Greek god Zeus, but as time went on the festival, held every four years, became a gathering to celebrate athletes, culture, and art. As Greek culture became merged with Roman culture, the games began to fall into disarray. In 394 CE Roman Emperor Theodosius banned the Olympics, citing them as a pagan ritual.

Nevertheless, Olympic lore lived on through written tales and art. The 19th century marked a rebirth of interest in fitness. Many of the sports still played today have their origins in that time period. Individual skills also returned to form, such as running, jumping, gymnastics, and swimming. In 1859 Greek businessperson Evangelos Zappas, inspired by Greece's independence from the Ottoman Empire and by Greek heritage, funded a version of the first Olympic Games in nearly 1,500 years. The Games grew in popularity, with 30,000 attending during the 1870s. Moved by Zappas's success, France's Charles Pierre de Frédy in 1894 convened a meeting from which the International Olympic Committee (IOC) would be formed. The IOC determined two important things during their first round of

Beijing, China, hosted the 2008 Summer Olympics. It marked the first time the Olympic Games took place in China. (Etherled/Dreamstime,com)

meetings: the Olympics should be held in a different country every four years, and Greece should be the first host in 1896.

Although the Games did not run perfectly, they still went off better than anyone could have expected, which fueled excitement for future games. Competing in more than 40 different events were 240 athletes from 14 nations. The winners received olive leaves, as in the ancient games. Only men were permitted to compete in 1896; women began competing in 1900 at the Paris Games—the last games in which olive leaves were awarded. Beginning at the first Olympics held away from Europe, in 1904 in St. Louis, Missouri, United States, winners received medals: gold for first place, silver for second, and bronze for third. The number of competitors grew each year of competition until 1912, when about 2,500 competitors from nearly 30 countries took part in the Stockholm, Sweden, Games. Two years later, World War I broke out, forcing the cancellation of the 1916 Olympics, which were supposed to be held in Germany. The Olympics returned in 1920, and a year later the IOC, which had expanded in small increments since 1896, made its biggest move to date by creating the Winter Olympics, which debuted in 1924. The decision was made after the IOC determined that winter sports deserved a showcase, but obviously downhill skiing and figure skating could not coexist in weather used to hold track-and-field and swimming events.

Germany finally hosted the Olympics in 1936. Its leader, Adolf Hitler, transformed the Games from an event to showcase athletes into one of spectacle, designed to put a country's might and prosperity on display. Hitler's fascist, racist government intended to also use the Games to showcase the might of white,

> **Muhammad Ali Returns to the Olympics**
>
> American boxer Muhammad Ali won Olympic Gold at the 1960 Summer Games in Rome. The world did not know it at the time, but it was witnessing the birth of a global icon, an athlete who would transcend sport until his death in 2016. Ali wrote in his 1975 autobiography that he threw his medal off a bridge after, having returned to the United States, he was refused service in a restaurant because he was Black. He did not want a medal representing the United States if the United States was going to treat him so poorly. Friends later disputed the tale, saying it made for a good story but that Ali actually just lost the medal.
>
> In the years after the Olympics, Ali became a worldwide figure, first for becoming boxing's heavyweight champion, then for changing his name to Ali from Cassius Clay in a move that startled much of white America, and then for refusing to serve in the Vietnam War after he was drafted. Although beloved now, Ali was reviled at the time. He was stripped of his championship and exiled from his sport for years. He eventually returned and regained his championship, but because of bad financial management, he had to continue boxing to earn money long after he should have retired. He suffered significant brain damage and eventually developed Parkinson's disease.
>
> Walking became a challenge, and even standing could cause major strain. So imagine the world's surprise when Ali emerged at the opening ceremony of the 1996 Summer Olympics in Atlanta, Georgia, to light the Olympic torch. Standing with his left arm trembling, Ali received the torch, presented it to the crowd, and walked across the stage to light the torch. The crowd roared. As one final honor, while the International Olympic Committee had Ali on-site, they presented him with a replacement gold medal.

Aryan athletes, whom Hitler believed to be a superior "race" of humans. American Jesse Owens, an African American college sprinter who faced plenty of racism in his own country, quickly dismantled Hitler's laughable premise by winning four gold medals. Owens's success marked a turn at the Olympics, in which political moments became as memorable as athletic moments. Some of the Olympics' most historically significant and memorable moments—some good, some bad, some tragic—had little to do with how athletes competed against one another.

There was the Cold War rivalry between the Soviet Union and the United States (see "Patriotism and National Pride"); Americans Tommie Smith and John Carlos protesting for human rights from the medal stand during the 1968 Mexico City Olympics, their fists raised in what became one of the most iconic photos of the 20th century; the 1972 Games in Munich, Germany, in which terrorists killed 11 Israeli athletes; the 1992 Olympics in Atlanta, Georgia, United States, in which a pro-life activist detonated a bomb that injured more than 100 people; and multiple scandals during the early 21st century in which allegations of rampant bribery to secure Olympics hosting opportunities swept the Olympics community.

Despite off-the-field distractions—and partially because of them—the Olympics have become a worldwide phenomenon. Billions of fans around the world pay attention to the outcomes every other year (summer and winter Olympics alternate every even-numbered year). Countries struggle to not bankrupt themselves to build facilities capable of hosting an Olympics. Broadcast companies pay billions of dollars for the rights to broadcast the Olympics, from which they earn billions more in revenue. Athletes still use the Olympics to showcase their talents and become internationally famous. Nearly 3,000 years after the first Olympics, they remain as strong as ever.

GLOBALIZATION

It took 44 years for the IOC to award an Olympics Games to a non-European or non-North American nation. That happened when the IOC named Tokyo, Japan, host of the 1940 Games, but World War II forced the cancellation of the 1940 and 1944 Games. Thus Australia became the third continent to host the Olympics when Melbourne put on the 1956 Games. Tokyo finally got its chance to host in 1964, which expanded the Olympic experience to a fourth continent. Brazil hosted the 2016 Games, giving South America its first opportunity to welcome the world. Africa and Antarctica remain the only two continents to have not yet hosted an Olympics.

It was fitting that the number of nations competing in the Olympics surpassed 200 for the first time in 2004, when the Olympics returned to Athens. Medal winners hail from all over the globe. Athletes from 87 countries won medals at the 2016 Games in Rio de Janeiro, while 30 countries won medals at the 2018 Winter Olympics in PyeongChang, South Korea.

WHERE IT'S PLAYED TODAY

Olympics are held across the world. Recent games have been held in China, Japan, Russia, and South Korea, and upcoming games have been awarded to France and the United States. In the 21st century, as media companies have gone digital—and therefore global—interest in coverage of Olympic qualifying has skyrocketed.

As a result, fans of Olympic sports have come to learn that athletes train and compete year-round across the world. They might follow wrestling qualifiers in Mongolia, swimming events in South Africa, and soccer matches in South America. Because the Olympics involve so many sports, all nations have Olympic-level activity going on throughout the year, not just every four years.

ECONOMICS AND MEDIA

The Council on Foreign Relations reported that since 1960, every country that has hosted the Olympics has spent more to host than was originally planned. Hosting has become so expensive that financial revenues do not make up the cost. Countries now host expecting to lose money, but they continue to do so with other goals in mind, such as when China hosted in 2008 to showcase the country's development to the world. In 1976 Montreal, Canada, expected to spend $124 million to host, but costs ballooned, leaving local taxpayers with $1.5 billion in debt that was not paid off until the early 21st century. Brazil spent $20 billion to host the 2016 Rio de Janeiro Summer Olympics.

While taxpayers lose money, the IOC makes it. Although the IOC, according to its website, gives millions of dollars "every day" to help athletes train, it is worth billions. No one is sure just how much the IOC is worth because it is based in Switzerland, which is famous for protecting the privacy and security of business entities that do business within its borders. Most of its expenditures go toward national Olympic committees, such as the U.S. Olympic Committee, while other costs go to travel, salaries, and other expenses. The bulk of its revenue comes from broadcast rights. American broadcasting company NBC paid $1.2 billion to show the 2016 Games, and the IOC also receives fees from other broadcast companies around the world.

DIMENSIONS OF THE SPORT

The most recent Summer Olympics included nearly 340 events across 33 distinct sports. The Winter Olympics are somewhat smaller, with 102 events over just seven sports. The IOC holds regular meetings to discuss matters such as future host countries and which sports to include and exclude.

The IOC also keeps tabs on the governing bodies of sports across the world. Over the last few decades, the IOC has shown its willingness to eliminate sports from the Olympics that do not receive proper oversight at the national level. The IOC also defers to regional and sport-specific governing bodies. For example, when badminton players tried to lose on purpose during the 2012 Games to improve their gold-medal draw, an action that enraged spectators in attendance, the IOC let the governing body of badminton, the Badminton World Federation, handle sanctions against the players.

IMPORTANT FIGURES

Charles Pierre de Frédy adored rugby. He credited much of his own success to education he received about life through rugby and sport in general. A historian and educator, de Frédy devoted a good portion of his life to the support and spread of rugby so that others might receive enlightenment, as he believed he had. In 1889 he organized a successful conference on physical education—a discipline he helped revolutionize in France—and five years later led the proposal to bring back the Olympics. He championed globalization, pushing to spread Olympics around the world. He also held antiquated views about women in sport, urging their inclusion while limiting sports in which they could participate because he believed participation did not match feminine sensibilities.

"When I was a kid, my father used to say, 'Our greatest hopes and our worst fears are seldom realized.' Our worst fears have been realized tonight." Those were the words spoken by Jim McKay, the legendary sports broadcaster known for covering 12 Olympic Games, when he announced to the world that terrorists murdered 11 Israeli athletes and a security guard during the 1972 Olympics in Munich (Kiehl 2004). The tragedy marked McKay's finest moment as a broadcaster, who called his first Games in 1960 and his final Games in 2002. When he died in 2008, two months before the Beijing Games, the *New York Times* wrote that McKay's name was synonymous with the Olympics.

POP CULTURE

The world loves underdogs, even if most of the time the final results do not. Two movies have been made about athletes that had almost no chance to win but won over the hearts of fans. In 1993 Walt Disney Pictures released *Cool Runnings*, a film very loosely based on the 1988 Jamaican bobsled team. The team caught the attention of fans because its origin country, Jamaica, exists in a tropical climate with little to no ice. The team found creative ways to train. To date the Jamaican program has never medaled, but they are beloved by fans.

Another fan favorite, British ski jumper Michael Edwards, better known as "Eddie the Eagle," became the subject of his own biopic in 2015. In 1988 Edwards became the first Briton to qualify for the Olympic ski jump in 60 years. Although he finished dead last in both events in which he competed, television and on-site spectators adored him. He wore Coke-bottle-thick glasses because he was so farsighted, and as he sailed through the air at high altitudes, the glasses collected frost that gave him a look when he landed that was unique from other jumpers. He was played in the movie by Taron Egerton, who would go on to win a Golden Globe for playing another famous Briton, singer-songwriter Elton John.

SCANDALS

The IOC makes a big deal about the purity of sport, but its board members are as vulnerable as anyone else to financial corruption at the end of the 20th century. Numerous board members resigned in shame after investigators learned they had accepted bribes from the Salt Lake Olympic Committee when the SLOC was trying to land the 2002 Winter Olympics. That turned out to be just the beginning. During the investigation, evidence showed that IOC members also received gifts during the bidding process of the 1998 and 2000 Olympics. In 2020 French investigators learned of even more corruption, this time tied to the bidding process for the 2021 Games in Tokyo.

POLITICS

The Denver Olympic Organizing Committee rejoiced when the IOC named the Colorado city the host of the 1976 Winter Olympics. The DOOC had worked tirelessly on the city's—even the country's—behalf. The citizens of Colorado had other ideas. Citing the financial costs to the region and the potential environmental costs to the Rocky Mountains and other local areas—Colorado is among the most nature-conscious of states in the United States—voters rejected the IOC's award through government referendum. The DOOC was forced to notify the IOC that Denver would not host because there was no financial backing. The IOC instead awarded the 1976 Winter Games to Innsbruck, Austria.

PATRIOTISM AND NATIONAL PRIDE

In 1948 U.S. athletes earned 84 medals, 40 more than any other country. The Soviet Union did not compete. In 1952 the Soviet Union emerged as a world athletic power by winning 71 medals, just 5 shy of the Americans, whose 76 led all nations. It was the height of the Cold War, and the Soviets showed they were the physical equals of the Americans. Then came 1956, when the Soviets surpassed the Americans to lead all nations in total medals won, a feat they repeated in 1960, and again in 1964, although that year the Americans won more gold medals. The two nations used the Olympics as a safe canvas for their Cold War. In 1980 the United States refused to compete in the Moscow Olympics, and in 1984 the Soviet Union refused to compete in games held in the United States. It was a bitter rivalry, but nearly all in the world agreed that it was better for the Soviets and the United States to work out their frustrations in athletic arenas than in military battlefields.

Timeline

776 BCE – The first ancient Olympics for which there are written records is held in Olympia, Greece.

394 CE – Roman Emperor Theodosius bans the Olympics.

1894 – The IOC is formed in Paris.

1896 – The Olympic Games are revived and—to honor their history—are held in Athens, Greece. Only men are allowed to compete.

1900 – The Olympics expand to include some competitions for women.

1904 – The Olympics are held in the United States for the first time, in St. Louis, Missouri. James E. Sullivan, the founder of the American Athletic Union (AAU) is asked to oversee many aspects of the Games, during which he conducts an experiment in the marathon of putting just one water station along the route. Only 14 of the 32 entrants complete the race.

1904 – Medals are handed out for the first time. In 1896 and 1900 competitors received an olive leaf.

1916 – World War I leads to the first cancellation of the Games.

1920 – The Olympic flag debuts and features the five rings. The five colors were chosen to represent at least one color from the flag of every country competing in the Games.

1924 – The first Winter Olympics are held in Chamonix, France.

1928 – Women are allowed to compete for the first time in the 100 meters, considered by many the most famous event in the Olympics Games.

1936 – Foy Draper, Ralph Metcalfe, Jesse Owens, and Frank Wykoff win gold in the 4x100 meters at the Berlin Olympics, also known as "Hitler's Olympics." The success of Metcalfe and Owens, both African American, debunks Hitler's xenophobic, farcical myth of the superior Aryan athlete.

1940 – World War II leads to the second (and third in 1944) cancellation of the Games.

1960 – Ethiopia's Abebe Bikila wins the men's marathon while running barefoot. He discarded his shoes on race day when he realized they did not fit properly.

1968 – American sprinters Tommie Smith and John Carlos raise their fist, covered by black gloves, in the air during the medal ceremony, to bring attention to human-rights violations.

1972 – During the Munich, Germany, Olympics, terrorists take 11 Israeli athletes hostage. They murder all 11.

1972 – American swimmer Mark Spitz wins seven gold medals and sets seven world records.

1990 – Venezuela's Flor Isava-Fonseca becomes the first woman elected to the IOC's executive board.

1992 – After British runner Derek Redmond injures his hamstring during a race, his father somehow avoids security to get on the track and help Redmond cross the finish line to thunderous applause.

1996 – An American pro-life advocate sets off a bomb during the Atlanta, Georgia, Olympics, injuring 111 people and killing 1.

2012 – For the first time, every country competing at the Games features at least one female competitor.

2020 – The Summer Olympics in Japan are postponed because of the worldwide COVID-19 pandemic.

See also: Boxing; Swimming; Track and Field.

Further Reading

Boykoff, J. (2016). *Power Games: A Political History of the Olympics*. Verso Books: Brooklyn, New York.

Goldblatt, D. (2018). *The Games: A Global History of the Olympics*. W. W. Norton & Company: New York.

Kiehl, S. (2004). "A Terror Retold." *Baltimore Sun*, Aug. 13, 2004. https://www.baltimoresun.com/sports/horse-racing/bal-kiehl0607-story.html.

Klein, A. (2007). *Striking Back: The 1972 Munich Olympics Massacre and Israel's Deadly Response*. Random House: New York.

Maraniss, D. (2008). *Rome 1960: The Olympics That Changed the World*. Simon & Schuster: New York.

Perrottet, T. (2004). *The Naked Olympics: The True Story of the Ancient Games*. Random House: New York.

Rider, T. C. (2016). *Cold War Games: Propaganda, the Olympics, and U.S. Foreign Policy*. University of Illinois Press: Champaign.

Schaap, J. (2007). *Triumph: The Untold Story of Jesse Owens and Hitler's Olympics*. Houghton Mifflin: Boston.

Sweet, D. A. F. (2019). *Three Seconds in Munich: The Controversial 1972 Olympic Basketball Final*. University of Nebraska Press: Lincoln.

Tomizawa, R. (2019). *1964—The Greatest Year in the History of Japan: How the Tokyo Olympics Symbolized Japan's Miraculous Rise from the Ashes*. Lioncrest Publishing: Austin, Texas.

P

Ping-Pong

Ping-Pong, also called table tennis, came into fashion because British people wanted to play lawn tennis indoors during the winter, but indoor tennis facilities were far more challenging to build in the late 19th century than they are today. So the size of the court shrank, the balls shrank, and the rackets became paddles. Ping-Pong was born.

Today the sport is as popular among competitive players as it is among families who have Ping-Pong tables in their basements. And it still looks like tennis—only smaller. With one player on each side (two if it's a doubles match), a ball is hit back and forth until one player is unable to return it according to the rules. When that happens, the other player receives a point.

This popular recreational sport entertains hundreds of millions of people annually, while at the most competitive levels it leads to international competition that reaches all the way to the Summer Olympics. The game has had a complicated and winding history, whether being used by world governments to break down diplomatic walls or evolving into a three-way spectacle known as triples in which the table becomes a circle divided into three parts, with three players winging the ball around it at breakneck speeds.

HISTORICAL CONTEXT

There has been much confusion over the years about the differences between Ping-Pong and table tennis. In truth, they are the same thing. Table tennis was the first official name, named literally in the 1880s because it was tennis played on top of a table. In 1901 the company Jacques London trademarked the name "Ping-Pong" because it was the sound the ball made when struck by the paddle. That name stuck, too, just as Kleenex came to be known for all nose tissue and Google for all internet searches. Table tennis *is* Ping-Pong.

The game first became a recreational hit before it took off as a competitive sport. Ping-Pong began in Great Britain similar to other paddle or bat games, such as cricket, lawn tennis, and rounders. The formation of the Table Tennis Association in 1921 helped bring together those who were serious about the game, standardized rules, and incentivized motivated players to increase their level of competition. Within two years a nationwide table tennis tournament drew nearly 40,000 competitors. The creation of the International Table Tennis Association five years later, in 1926, helped grow the sport even more, and by 1927 the first international competition was held in London.

Aside from minor changes, Ping-Pong's dynamics remained consistent until the 1950s. Then everything changed with the introduction of sandwich rubber. Sandwich rubber is the rubbery, padded part of the Ping-Pong paddle (also called a blade). It was stickier than the original paddle surface, which was made from a thin layer of a more basic rubber. Sandwich rubber, popularized by Japanese players, allowed players to start experimenting with new ideas, like putting spin on the ball. The International Table Tennis Federation (ITTF), established in 1946 as the new governing body of table tennis, tried to limit the new surface, but it proved too late. Players had become fascinated with new ways to steer the ball. The game was changed.

Today's game remains an echo of the changes made during the 1950s, minus a few other technical tweaks. By the 1980s the game had become so popular across the world that it became an Olympic sport at the 1988 Summer Games in Seoul, South Korea. Recreationally, Ping-Pong also remains popular, with the table tennis market expected to generate $650 million in revenue in the year 2020.

GLOBALIZATION

Although table tennis remains present around the world, it is most popular in the Asia Pacific region. The region counted 350 million recreational players in 2015. During that same period the United States boasted 17 million players, which was up from 15 million just a decade earlier. The United Kingdom, home to table tennis, included 2 million recreational players.

A Japanese professor brought Ping-Pong to the Asia Pacific region in the early 1900s after a visit to Great Britain. The sport flourished in Japan, Korea, China, and other East Asian countries. China, especially, fell in love with Ping-Pong. Igor Montagu, a British banker and communist who helped form the ITTF, helped grow Ping-Pong in China as its communist government secured control. Even as China become exiled from much of the world during the mid-20th century, Montagu viewed Ping-Pong as a way to support Chinese people, who could play matches against teams from other countries.

Ping-Pong experienced its period of growth in the United States during the 1920s. It was featured often in "speakeasies," bars and pubs that illegally sold alcohol during the 1920s, the United States' Prohibition period, in which alcohol was deemed illegal. Since then, Ping-Pong has remained a popular recreational activity among Americans. Legendary American writer Henry Miller declared Ping-Pong "a game of endless fascination" (Syed 2012).

WHERE IT'S PLAYED TODAY

Because Ping-Pong is so popular and readily available as a recreational activity, it is played around the world. Competitively, the best Ping-Pong players traditionally come from East Asia. Of the 24 Olympic medals (gold, silver, and bronze) awarded in women's Ping-Pong since it joined the Games in 1988, 17 were earned by Chinese players, 2 each by Chinese Taipei, South Korean, and North Korean players, and 1 from Singapore. The only non-Asian country to win a team Olympic medal in Ping-Pong since 1988 is Germany, which has won a silver and two bronzes.

The sport's equipment is made across the world, and there is a subindustry among Ping-Pong insiders that rates and sells paddles and tables. This matters less to casual players, who care less about high-performance equipment than getting something reliable and affordable. To competitive players, however, understanding manufacturing and price point is key.

DIMENSIONS OF THE SPORT

A standard Ping-Pong table sits 152.5 centimeters wide by 274 centimeters long with a 15.25-centimeter-high net dividing its length in two. In official competitions, a table must stand 76 centimeters off the ground. Tables mostly come in dark colors in order to make the ball more visible, with green, gray, black, and blue as the most popular choices. Each player holds a paddle that can vary slightly in size; a typical paddle is 5.9 inches wide by 6.7 inches long.

Competitors play a game to 11 and must win by at least 2 points. If the players are tied at 10, a player must win consecutive points to win the game 12 to 10; if they're still tied at 25-25, the first player to 27 wins; and so on. The server must make sure the opponent can see the ball before serving, and then the serve must bounce once on the server's side before going over the net. The receiver must let the ball bounce once before returning the ball, and from that point on balls must always bounce once before being hit and bounce again before going back over the net.

A full match dictates the winner is the first to win three games.

IMPORTANT FIGURES

When talking about the greatest table tennis players ever, Zhang Yining has to be at the front of the line. She held the world's number-one ranking for an unprecedented six consecutive years, from 2003 to 2009 except for one brief, two-month period. Notably, she walked away from professional table tennis in 2009 as the defending world champion and two-time defending Olympic gold medalist.

Sweden's Jan-Ove Waldner collects nicknames. He's been called the "Evergreen Tree" for his sustained success, as well as the "Mozart of Table Tennis." He won the gold medal at the 1992 Olympic Games in Barcelona and bronze at the 2000 games in Sydney. Having earned yet another nickname, "Old Waldner," he finally retired from competitive professional play in 2016 at the age of 50.

POP CULTURE

Forrest Gump still wanted to serve his country after taking a bullet in the Vietnam War. During his recovery he discovered Ping-Pong. He was a fast study, quickly becoming one of the best players in all of the United States. He earned a spot on the U.S. national Ping-Pong team and became part of the delegation that traveled to China on a goodwill tour in in 1971. Gump, a fictional character in the 1986 novel of the same name, captured America's attention when Tom Hanks portrayed him in the wildly successful 1994 film, also called *Forrest Gump*. The movie, which cost $55 million to make, earned $675 million worldwide, six Academy Awards, including Best Picture, and its soundtrack remains one of the best sellers of all time.

Far less acclaimed was the 2007 comedy *Balls of Fury*, about a disgraced former Ping-Pong player recruited by the American government for a secret mission. Critics panned the film, but audiences enjoyed it. Most notably, or perhaps most infamously, was the screen presence of Academy Award–winning actor Christopher Walken, who is of Scottish and German ancestry, as Feng, an evil criminal mastermind who dresses in traditional, historical Chinese clothing.

And if that wasn't obscure enough, the American version of the television show *The Office* once included a shout-out to some of Ping-Pong's greatest players. The character Dwight Schrute, played by Rainn Wilson, declared, "All of my heroes are table tennis players: Zoran Primorac, Jan-Ove Waldner, Wang Tao, Jorg Rosskopf, and, of course, Ashraf Helmy. I even have a life-size poster of Hugo Hoyama on my wall. And the first time I ever left Pennsylvania was to go to the Hall of Fame induction ceremony of Andrzej Grubba."

SCANDALS

As scandals go, this is tame compared to some of the things that have happened in other sports: in 2014 Zhang Jike enthusiastically celebrated his World Cup victory by kicking over advertising signage around the playing area and removing his shirt and tossing it into the crowd. Tournament officials, displeased with Jike's outburst, let him keep the championship but stripped him of his entire winnings: about $55,000.

POLITICS

Between 1949 and early 1971, no American diplomat or official legally set foot in the People's Republic of China. The United States cut off all economic ties with China, which had become a communist-run country, upon its involvement in the Korean War. The decision was made first by President Harry Truman, then carried forward by Presidents Dwight Eisenhower, John F. Kennedy, and Lyndon Johnson. The policy continued into the administration of Richard Nixon, but China was growing and wanted an opportunity to reintroduce itself to parts of the world. Nixon was listening but needed a less formal way reestablish relations.

Finally, the two countries found their olive branch.

Ping-Pong.

Japan hosted the 1971 World Table Tennis Championships. Teams from all over the world competed, including the United States and China. According to historians, a chance meeting occurred when American player Glenn Cowan missed his bus and had to ride back on the shuttle to the Olympic Village with the Chinese Ping-Pong delegation. Cowan was nervous until a Chinese player, Zhuang Zedong, who later admitted that he, too, was nervous, introduced himself. The two conversed, and Zedong presented Cowan with a gift as a sign of goodwill.

From there the diplomatic ball began to roll. Cowan responded yes to a reporter's question about whether he would like to visit China, although he made sure to add that he'd like to visit any country he had not been to. Word of the discussion reached officials from both countries. Eventually, China extended an invitation to the United States to have its Ping-Pong team visit for a goodwill tour and a series of matches. The United States agreed, and on April 10, 1971, the United States-China stalemate ended when the U.S. national Ping-Pong team crossed the border into the People's Republic of China.

The relationship generated a new term: Ping-Pong diplomacy. Ten months after the goodwill tour, Nixon himself visited China, opening the door for an economic relationship between the countries that proved one of the most lucrative in the world. It opened a market of a billion people to U.S. manufacturers and jump-started China's global economic expansion. To commemorate Nixon's 100th birthday in 2013, ABC News noted that if it weren't for the Watergate scandal that led to Nixon's shaming and resignation of the presidency, his greatest legacy might have been welcoming China back into the global community.

PATRIOTISM AND NATIONAL PRIDE

The World Table Tennis Championships take place at rotating sites. Budapest, Hungary, hosted in 2019; other past host cities include Halmstad, Sweden; Kuala Lumpur, Malaysia; Suzhou, China; and Doha, Qatar, as well as Paris and Moscow, among others.

Permanent, rotating trophies are presented to the winners, who at subsequent events have to bring them back so that they can be awarded to the new champions. Numerous categories of competition take place, including women's and men's singles, women's and men's doubles, and mixed doubles. China's women's team has won all but two championships since 1975. Hungary and Japan led the early years of the men's divisions. China—and for a brief period, Sweden—has over the last couple of decades dominated on the men's side.

Timeline

1880s – Lawn tennis players bring a version of their game indoors to play during colder months. Although not yet called Ping-Pong, it sets the stage for what would become table tennis.

1901 – Jacques London trademarks the game as "Ping-Pong," based on the sound made when the ball hit the paddles. Though most people at the time came to call it table tennis, the game's earliest adopters stuck with Ping-Pong, which is why today the two terms—table tennis and Ping-Pong—can be used interchangeably.

1902 – A professor visiting England from Japan learns of Ping-Pong and brings it back to Japan.

1921 – The Table Tennis Association is established.

1927 – Hungarian Roland Jacobi wins the first table tennis world championship.

1930 – The Soviet Union bans table tennis because officials believed focusing on such a small ball damaged players' eyesight.

1930s – The popularity of Ping-Pong begins to spread through China.

1933 – USA Table Tennis is formed.

1946 – The International Table Tennis Federation (ITTF) is established.

1971 – The United States' table tennis team members become the first Americans to enter China since its communist takeover. The sides engage in a series of matches and goodwill.

1980 – The first ITTF Men's World Cup is held.

1988 – Table tennis becomes an Olympic sport.

1996 – The first ITTF Women's World Cup is held.

2000 – The ITTF increases the size of Ping-Pong balls from 38 mm to 40 mm to slow down the game so that fans could more easily follow along.

2011 – China's Zhang Yining retires as the women's world champion and an Olympic gold medalist.

2016 – Swede Jan-Ove Waldner, considered by some the greatest men's table tennis player of all time, retires.

See also: Cricket; Olympics; Tennis.

Further Reading

Bennett, R. (2010). *Everything You Know Is Pong: How Mighty Table Tennis Shapes Our World*. It Books: New York.

Boggan, T. (2014). *History of U.S. Table Tennis, Volume I*. CreateSpace Independent Publishing Platform: Scotts Valley, California.

Church, C. (2008). *Ping-Pong Pig*. Holiday House: New York.

Groom, W. (1986). *Forrest Gump*. Doubleday: New York.

Hodges, L. (2013). *Table Tennis Tactics for Thinkers*. CreateSpace Independent Publishing Platform: Scotts Valley, California.

Jacobson, H. (1999). *The Mighty Walzer*. Jonathan Cape: London.

Priestly, S. and Larcombe, B. (2015). *Expert in a Year: The Ultimate Table Tennis Challenge*. CreateSpace Independent Publishing Platform: Scotts Valley, California.

Seemiller, D. and Holowchak, M. (1996). *Winning Table Tennis: Skills, Drills, and Strategies*. Human Kinetics: Champaign, Illinois.

Syed, M. (2012). "Finding Salvation at the Ping-Pong Table." *Times of London*, July 6, 2012. https://www.thetimes.co.uk/article/finding-salvation-at-the-ping-pong-table-gllq5gfsg8f.

Winkler, H. and Oliver, L. (2005). *My Secret Life as a Ping-Pong Wizard*. Grosset & Dunlap: New York.

R

Rodeo

Rodeo is a tall tale come to life. It is pure ego: find the biggest, strongest, fastest beast and survive it. Ride it. Wrestle it to the ground. Its athletes sometimes dress like cowboys out of the old American Wild West. They tame angry bulls. Mount horses that do not want to be tamed. It is the past come to life, a tradition rooted in the spirit of individuals who both respect nature and seek to dominate it. To witness rodeo is to witness a truly unique event. Imagine a 180-pound person voluntarily mounting an angry bull that weighs 10 times that much. Imagine that bull bucking and flailing and doing everything in its power to throw the rider from its back, but the rider stays on, unwilling to give in to the beast—unwilling to give in to nature. That is rodeo, viewed by some as brave and others as cruel, but understood by all for its danger.

HISTORICAL CONTEXT

Born in Mexico and commercialized in the United States, rodeo's history traces to the same Spaniards who came to popularize bullfighting. The skills are different, but both sports involve the conquering of large animals—either bulls or horses. Bullfighting never gained its footing in the United States except in small regional pockets, but it became popular in Mexico. What eventually became American rodeo started in what is now the American West and Southwest. In the early 1800s, Spanish influence over Mexico, which controlled much of the region at the time, included feats of showmanship with horses. Vaqueros, Mexican cattle ranchers, entertained each other and locals by showing off tricks performed on horses. During and after the American Civil War, by which time California had come under American control and received statehood, vaqueros gave way to cowboys, some of whom were American cattle ranchers. They, too, performed rodeos, but they were grounded in speed and strength more than showmanship.

Rodeo is a word of Spanish origin that loosely means "roundup." As it connects to the sport, however, rodeo was not regularly called rodeo until the early 20th century. In the 1800s it had many names, including but not limited to roundups, stampedes, and Wild-West shows. The most popular Wild-West shows, such as Bill Cody's Buffalo Bill's Wild West, traveled the world. They drew huge crowds across all demographics, whether it was the American frontier, the Midwest, the metropolitan Northeast, and even parts of Africa and Europe. Often Wild-West shows included reenactments of famous military battles. Other times they featured events that became staples of rodeos, such as horseback riding and bulldogging, the act of wrestling a steer to the ground by grabbing its horns and twisting

Rodeo, which rose to popularity in the 1800s in Canada and the United States, remains most popular in those two countries. Animal-rights activists have helped to prevent the sport's globalization. (iStockPhoto.com)

its neck. Sometimes, rodeo cowboys performed tricks like the vaqueros did, not feats of speed and strength.

The first modern rodeo took place July 4, 1888, in Prescott, Arizona, at the time an American territory. Historians of the sport consider the Prescott event the first rodeo, because today's rodeos mirror many of the Prescott's traits, including charging for admission and standardizing events and rules. The Prescott rodeo's events included bronco riding and steer roping. Both events are part of modern rodeos. A year later rodeos introduced steer riding, and by the second decade of the 1900s, calf roping had become a regular event. Under the leadership and promotion of William T. Johnson, rodeos thrived during the Great Depression, with many of the athletes earning more than athletes in other sports, and some, according to historians, earning more than workers in other professions, such as dentistry.

As rodeo grew, so did the expectations of its athletes, who began to organize in the late 1920s. They demanded larger shares of prize money, refused to participate in events after tickets had been sold, to pressure promoters into sharing the wealth, and formed organizations such as the Rodeo Association of America and the Cowboys Turtle Association, who named themselves after the reptile because turtles were willing to stick their necks out. The two organizations merged in 1945 and changed their name to the Rodeo Cowboys Association, and eventually to the Professional Rodeo Cowboys Association (PRCA) in the 1970s. The PRCA remains the largest governing body of rodeo in the United States, and therefore the world, since the sport has never caught on as much outside North America as inside.

GLOBALIZATION

As stampedes and Wild-West shows gained popularity in the United States in the late 1800s and early 1900s, they found similar success in parts of western Canada, including Alberta and Manitoba. The longest-running annual rodeo in the world, the Raymond Stampede, began in 1902 in Raymond, Alberta, Canada. The first Raymond Stampede included just two events: steer roping and bronco riding. Rodeo has such a rich history in western Canada that three Canadian Football League teams based their mascots on rodeo terms: the Calgary Stampeders, Saskatchewan Roughriders, and Ottawa Rough Riders.

While rodeo thrived in North America's largest countries—Canada, Mexico, and the United States—to the rest of the world it was a novelty act. North American competitors traveled the world, thrilling fans in parts of Africa and Europe, but their show remained little more than a visiting spectacle. Whatever traction rodeo might have gained outside of North America was minimal. The closest another continent got to establishing a solid foundation of rodeo was Australia.

Australian Wild-West shows enjoyed significant success in the 1880s and 1890s, and they continued well into the 1930s. They toured New Zealand, South America, and India. American cowboys were invited to participate in Australian shows. By the 1960s, the term *roughriders* had been edged out by *cowboys*—the American version of rodeo competitors. Australian rodeo cowboys also began to dress like American cowboys and take part in events known for taking place in American rodeos. By the early 1980s, Australian cowboys and Australian rodeo organizations regularly traveled to North America to compete in North American rodeo competitions, often finishing in the Top 10.

WHERE IT'S PLAYED TODAY

Although amateur rodeos are held throughout the world, including Asia, Europe, and South America, professional rodeo almost exclusively occurs in Australia and North America, with Canada and the United States leading the way. Western Canada remains the most popular region for rodeo in Canada.

In the United States, the West and Southwest hold the most interest, but other parts of the country also enjoy the sport. The PRCA annually holds events in states such as Connecticut, Florida, Idaho, Iowa, Kansas, Minnesota, Montana, Nebraska, Oregon, and Washington, as well as more traditional rodeo states like Arizona, California, Colorado, New Mexico, and Utah.

ECONOMICS AND MEDIA

The amount of prize money awarded to rodeo competitors has risen steadily over the last half century. In 2017 total prize money for the season reached nearly $50 million. To date, more than 100 cowboys have achieved at least $1 million in career earnings, four have reached $3 million, and one $6 million. Over the years the PRCA and other organizations regularly have struck deals with Canadian and

American broadcasters to cover the sport. The value of the contracts is on par with other sports with dedicated but smaller fan bases, such as bowling.

DIMENSIONS OF THE SPORT

The ProRodeo Hall of Fame lists seven events as the core of rodeo:

Bareback Riding. This event is exactly what it sounds like—a rider trying to stay on a bucking horse for eight seconds without the aid of a saddle. There are rules. For example, riders must start with their feet above the horse's shoulders. Also, they can only hold onto the rigging with one hand. If at any time the rider grabs the rigging or any other part of the horse with the other hand, the rider is disqualified.

Barrel Racing. Think of this as an agility course for a rider and horse. This event is about speed and precision. The rider enters the course at full speed and is required to steer the horse around an arrangement of barrels. The pair is allowed to make contact with the barrels, but if a barrel tips over, the result is a five-second penalty.

Bull Riding. Even though this event involves a two-ton bull, it is judged similarly to events such as gymnastics. Not only must riders stay on for eight seconds but they also have to look good doing it. The bull also must perform, as the judge is looking at both the wildness and degree of difficulty posed by the bull and the rider's ability to stay on. Riders who use their free hand are disqualified.

Saddle Bronc Riding. Rodeo's most historic event dates to the 1800s, when cowboys and ranchers competed to see who could most competently ride untamed horses. Riders drive their spurs into the horse at various moments to earn extra points from the judges, and the length of time the rider is able to apply the spurs also improves chances of a high score. Riders are disqualified if they get thrown off in less than eight seconds, improperly use their free hand, or if either foot slips out of the stirrup.

Steer Wrestling. Also known as bulldogging, this event challenges a rider to dismount a galloping horse onto a running steer, which the rider must grab by the horns, twist, and wrestle to the ground. Whichever competitor does it the quickest wins. A rider may be disqualified for starting too early and not giving the steer enough of a head start.

Team Roping. Two cowboys work together to rope a steer, one from the front and the other from the rear. The front cowboy, or header, works first, trying to get her rope around the steer's shoulders or horns. Once that is accomplished, the heeler tries to get in and rope the back feet. A five-second penalty is assessed to teams when the heeler manages to rope just one of the back feet.

Tie-Down Roping: This event blends elements of steer wrestling and team roping. In this event, a rider, while on the horse, ropes a calf, then dismounts, and attempts to tie together three of the calf's legs. Once accomplished, the rider gets back on the horse. The try is completed if the calf does not get up in six seconds from when the rider gets back on the horse.

IMPORTANT FIGURES

Someone who wants to learn about rodeo can start with one name: Bill Pickett. Born in 1870, Pickett was one of the first celebrity rodeo cowboys. He traveled the world with Wild-West shows and early Hollywood stars like Will Rogers. Pickett even starred in two films, including 1921's *The Bull-Dogger*, which was appropriate since Pickett basically invented the technique, known more commonly today as steer wrestling.

POP CULTURE

In the early 1990s Hollywood decided to take a chance on rodeo. Seeking to reach an untapped market, the American film industry produced two major motion pictures that used the sport as their backdrop. First, in 1991, came *My Heroes Have Always Been Cowboys*, starring Scott Glenn as a retired rodeo cowboy who comes out of retirement to win money to buy back the family ranch. The movie did not perform well at the box office, but it received modest reviews and performed well on cable TV and DVD sales.

A few years later, *8 Seconds*, a biopic about former rodeo champion Tuff Hedeman that starred Luke Perry, performed a little better. Although not a box-office smash, it earned nearly three times what it cost to make and, like *My Heroes*, it earned a cult following among rodeo fans.

SCANDALS

Rodeo has long struggled to achieve gender equality. The in-competition death of bronc rider Bonnie McCarroll in 1929 set off a chain of events from which the sport has never fully let itself recover, including banning women from competitive bronc riding even though men have also died from it. Some women have since competed, but in men's divisions. The Women's Professional Rodeo Association had to be formed separate of men's leagues in 1948 to ensure women's rodeo could hold events and receive promotion. To this day, the PRCA receives criticism for insufficiently representing women rodeo athletes alongside men.

POLITICS

Rodeo officials and cowboys find themselves in a constant public relations fight with animal-rights groups such as People for the Ethical Treatment of Animals (PETA) and Showing Animals Respect and Kindness (SHARK). The rights groups call rodeo inherently unethical since the animals have no say in whether they will participate. Rodeo organizations say the animals are treated well. Because rodeo cannot exist without animals, and because rights groups exist to protect animals, the two sides most likely will never resolve their dispute.

PATRIOTISM AND NATIONAL PRIDE

Rodeo in the Olympics? The sides have flirted—twice—but since 2002 the International Olympic Committee (IOC) has given no indication that it would again include rodeo. In 1986, with rodeo lobbyists pressing at every turn, the sport became a "cultural" event at the Olympics Arts Festival, a component of the 1986 Winter Games in Calgary, Alberta, Canada. The festival is one step below "exhibition sport," the designation given to sports the IOC is considering for formal admission into future Olympic games. Its inclusion made sense, given rodeo's legacy in Canada, but after the Calgary Games, rodeo could not make additional headway within the IOC.

It returned, again to Arts Festival status, when Salt Lake City, Utah, United States, hosted the 2002 Winter Olympics. Rodeo officials were again optimistic this could be an important step toward Olympic inclusion, but hopes were dashed when animal-rights groups demonstrated against rodeo, which embarrassed the IOC. Matters worsened when a local Utah politician referred to the rights organizations as "terrorist groups" just one year after actual terrorists caused the September 11, 2001, attacks on the American East Coast. After that, the IOC wanted nothing else to do with rodeo. If cowboys ever get to compete to wear Olympic gold around their necks, it will not be anytime soon.

Timeline

2000 BCE – Cretans create art that depicts people performing athletic feats against bulls.

1851 CE – Following the Mexican-American war, American state California, founded just a year earlier, passes a law that farms with certain animals should host at least one "rodeo" every year, an event designed to ensure cattle owners do not lose any of their animals when mingled with other owners' herds.

1870 – Bill Pickett, who becomes one of the first celebrity American rodeo cowboys, is born in Jenks-Branch, Texas.

1872 – Organized rodeo debuts in Cheyenne, Wyoming.

1883 – Buffalo Bill's Wild West, a show built around Bill Cody's professional life, forms in North Platte, Nebraska, United States.

1888 – A rodeo event held in Prescott, Arizona, becomes the first to charge fans admission.

1897 – Cheyenne Frontier Days, an annual event that includes rodeo events to this day, is held for the first time in Cheyenne, Wyoming.

1900s – The term *rodeo* is used for the first time to describe what becomes the sport of rodeo.

1902 – Canada's oldest rodeo, the Raymond Stampede, is founded.

1912 – Calgary, Canada, businesspeople entice American Guy Weadick to manage "stampede" events, a development that helps lead to the standardization of events held at rodeos.

1913 – Tillie Baldwin becomes the first woman bulldogger to perform at public events.

1922 – The first Madison Square Garden Rodeo is held. It helps to revitalize the sport, which nearly dies during the previous decade because of lack of interest and American resources being redirected during World War I.

1924 – A rodeo event is held at Wembley Stadium in London. The sport does not catch on in the United Kingdom.

1936 – The Cowboys' Turtle Association, a version of organized labor for rodeo competitors, forms to protest a wage dispute at a Boston event.

1948 – The Women's Professional Rodeo Association forms to fight for equal pay.

1959 – The first National Finals Rodeo is held in Dallas, Texas. It is organized by the Cowboys' Turtle Association, which became the Rodeo Cowboys Association in 1945.

1966 – U.S. president Lyndon Johnson signs the Animal Welfare Act of 1966 into law. The sport of rodeo is exempt.

1975 – The Rodeo Cowboys Association rebrands once more as the Professional Rodeo Cowboys Association (PRCA), which it is still known as to this day.

2003 – Giving in to fan interest, the PRCA holds its first Xtreme Bulls Tour, an event that brings together the most dangerous bulls and the best bull riders.

2008 – Maggie Parker makes her bull-riding debut at age 16. She becomes the first female bull rider to win prize money competing against men.

2013 – Trevor Brazile becomes the first rodeo competitor to reach $5 million in lifetime earnings.

See also: Bullfighting; Gymnastics; Horse Racing.

Further Reading
Canutt, Y. (2009). *My Rodeo Years: Memoir of a Bronc Rider's Path to Hollywood Fame.* McFarland & Company: Jefferson, North Carolina.
Harris, L. and Jones, R. A. (2015). *Lecile: This Ain't My First Rodeo.* Clowning Around Enterprises, LLC: Collierville, Tennessee.
Murray, T. (2003). *King of the Cowboys.* Atria Publishing Group: New York.
Peter, J. (2005). *Fried Twinkies, Buckle Bunnies, & Bull Riders: A Year Inside the Professional Bull Riders Tour.* Rodale Books: Emmaus, Pennsylvania.
Phillips, T. (2006). *Blacktop Cowboys: Riders on the Run for Rodeo Gold.* Thomas Dunne Books: New York.
Richards, R. (2010). *Casey Tibbs: Born to Ride.* Moonlight Mesa Associates: Wickenburg, Arizona.
Snyder, A. (2018). *Walk Ride Rodeo: A Story about Amberley Snyder.* Self-published.
Stratton, W. K. (2006). *Chasing the Rodeo: On Wild Rides and Big Dreams, Broken Hearts and Broken Bones, and One Man's Search for the West.* Mariner Books: Boston.
Warren, L. S. (2005). *Buffalo Bill's America: William Cody and the Wild West Show.* Knopf Doubleday: New York.
Wolman, D. and Smith, J. (2020). *Aloha Rodeo: Three Hawaiian Cowboys, the World's Greatest Rodeo, and a Hidden History of the American West.* William Morrow Books: New York.

Rowing/Crew

Casual observers of competitive rowing—or crew, as it is known in the United States—will say it is about speed and strength. Rowers and rowing devotees know there is one thing more important than either of those: precision. It is one thing to go fast, but in rowing all rowers need to work together, moving in sync. It does not matter how big, strong, or fast a crew is if all members' motions do not line up. Synchronization matters so much to rowing that a position was created specifically to help align the rowers. The *coxswain* (pronounced "COX-in") brings no discernable athletic ability to the sport of rowing. Coxswains are more like symphony conductors who call out time, who alert rowers to the moments they must go faster or slower, or turn or go straight ahead. Coxswains are human metronomes, helping rowers keep the beat, making sure everyone works together, that multiple bodies are moving in one motion. Through training rowers get stronger to move quicker, but only when they embrace their role on the crew—only when they devote themselves to precision and synchronicity—do they become champions.

HISTORICAL CONTEXT

Rowing ranks among the ancient sports. Long before humans rowed competitively, they rowed to survive and migrate, to hunt and engage in trade. Poems by the ancient Roman writer Virgil contained references to rowing. Ancient Egyptians relied on rowing and played a crucial role in the development of its technological advancement. A funerary carving, which dated to 1400 BCE and was made for Pharaoh Amenhotep II, depicted evidence of competitive rowing. Dragon boat racing, a specific form of rowing with roots in China, dates back at least 2,000 years. Ancient Polynesians rowed, and according to some historians, Polynesian nations such as Samoa first became inhabited when voyagers rowed and sailed to the islands. There is not an inhabitable region of earth that excludes rowing in its history. Rowing's history parallels humanity's history.

There is a tendency in history written in Romance languages and English to give too much credit to Western Europe for the development of, well, basically everything. Western historians trace the history of competitive rowing to what is now the United Kingdom in the early 1600s. Without a doubt some of the earliest documented competitive rowing races took place in the United Kingdom, but to say competitive rowing began in the United Kingdom is at worst incorrect and at best incomplete. Competitive rowing began in Western Europe, but also in China, among North America's First Nation and Indigenous People's tribes, in Polynesian regions, and up and down the coasts of the African continent. Rowing, like running and swimming, evolved from a functional activity to a form of entertainment.

What is true about Western Europe's claim to the development of competitive rowing is its enthusiasm to document. The British excelled at writing down their activities and preserving their documentation in archives, libraries, and private collections. Because of those, we know that Britain's lust for competitive rowing incubated in its public and private schooling systems. Many schools by the mid-1700s formed what were known as boat clubs. They fulfilled a few functions, including the promotion of physical fitness, camaraderie, and an outlet for competition. By the early 1800s, as the schools produced graduates who did not want to leave their rowing careers behind, public clubs began to form. Some clubs included athletes who did not attend public school, which showed the sport was beginning to extend its reach into the collective British psyche. Clubs formed at the

University of Oxford, the oldest English-speaking university in the world, around 1815, and about a decade later at its chief rival, the University of Cambridge. The two squared off in rowing competition for the first time in 1829 and continue an annual race to this day called "the Boat Race." It remains competitive, with each university winning 5 times during the 10 races of the 2010s.

Around the same time that ancient Greeks organized the Olympic Games, Chinese people who lived along what is now called the Yangtze River began to hold dragon boat races. Dragon boats, simply put, are just a type of boat, with cultures around the world each developing boats with regional character and distinctions. Dragon boats typically hold 20 rowers, a coxswain, and a drummer to help keep a beat for the rowers. Dragon boat races, which continue to this day, emerged as a way to celebrate important agricultural markers, such as the completion of planting season or a successful harvest. Technically, dragon boat athletes do not row, they paddle, a distinction that has to do with which way the rowers/paddlers sit in the boat. Traditionally rowers face backward and move their boats in the opposite direction from which they face, while paddlers move their boats in the direction they face. Most of the physical motion is the same and the concept is the same. Both use paddles or oars.

GLOBALIZATION

Rowing owns a unique distinction. Whereas many sports achieved globalization through imperialism and human migration, globalization itself was achieved largely because of rowing. The Vikings, for example, would not have had such a major influence on human civilization were it not for their long ships, which had up to 50 oars. Competitive rowing never globalized. It was inherently global.

Still, as a sport, rowing eventually became a uniform activity. Two 19th-century human events—the Industrial Revolution and the reinvigoration of the Olympic Games—sparked rowing's modern age, which over the following century saw the world finally agree on common boats, common rules, and training techniques. As North American sports such as baseball, American football, and lacrosse began to find their way in the late 19th century, they aspired to reach the popular heights of competitive rowing, which captured the imagination thanks to rowing competitions between American colleges, most notably the annual Harvard-Yale contest that began in 1852.

The International Olympic Committee (IOC) added rowing before the 1900 Paris Games, the first Olympiad to include team sports. Today the Olympics host seven different rowing events, but in 1900 it was just two: single scull (a lone rower) and coxed eight—a boat with eight rowers plus a coxswain (for more descriptions and terminology, see "Dimensions of the Sport"). In single scull France took gold and silver and a British rower took bronze. It was expected that European rowers would sweep rowing events for two reasons. First, only European and North American countries were invited to compete in the early modern Olympics. Second, the European rowing community did not think much of Canadian and U.S. rowing programs. That changed after 1900, when the United States won gold in the coxed eight. In 1904 U.S. rowers won gold in all five Olympic men's rowing events: single scull, double scull, coxless pair, coxless four, and coxed eight.

As the Olympics became more culturally and internationally inclusive, the medal count began to spread as well. A history of rowing exists in many countries, so it made sense that many countries earned Olympic gold once given the opportunity. At the 2016 Summer Olympics in Rio de Janeiro, Brazil, 20 different countries across five continents earned medals in men's and women's rowing, which was added at the 1976 Montreal Olympics. The only two continents without a rowing medal were South America and Antarctica.

WHERE IT'S PLAYED TODAY

Competitive rowing takes place across the world. Sometimes it is done recreationally at the hyperlocal levels. Other times it is more organized and legislated by governing bodies in countries such as South Africa and England. In the United States, crew remains a presence on university campuses. In 1972 the U.S. Congress passed Title IX, a law that among other things intended for men's and women's sports to receive equal opportunities at institutions that receive federal funds.

That led to the creation of women's crew teams at many American colleges, to help balance scholarships for women with scholarships offered to men, especially American football. Today more than 100 American universities support women's crew teams with scholarships and on-campus resources.

ECONOMICS AND MEDIA

The initial costs of rowing can be substantial. A single shell starts around $5,000 and a double at nearly $10,000. However, once the original cost is absorbed, the cost of rowing itself is fairly reasonable: oars, equipment storage, and if one is part of a club, membership dues to pay for coaching and event entry fees. Rowers say one key to keeping costs down is boat maintenance. A properly maintained shell might last decades.

Other than salaries for coaching, money earned by boat manufacturers, and athletic scholarships for American college students, there is not much money to be made in rowing. For many it is a hobby, an amateur endeavor to keep fit and be part of a team. Members of adult and youth rowing clubs around the world pay money to be part of a club. Television networks rarely, if ever, broadcast rowing. Even the sport's more popular periods, such as during the Olympics, rarely garner much recognition. If rowing receives Olympics television coverage, it often is on replay or during the middle of the night, since it does not generate ratings—and therefore revenue—for the networks.

DIMENSIONS OF THE SPORT

Racing boats are called shells. They vary in sizes depending on the number or rowers: one, two, four, or eight—not counting the coxswain. The coxswain sits in the stern and coordinates the rowers like an orchestra conductor. In smaller or more specialized clubs, the coxswain might also serve as the coach. The coxswain also controls a boat's rudder, if it has one, which means that in addition to overseeing the rowers, the coxswain steers the boat so the rowers can focus on rowing.

Rowing oars are called blades, but rowers usually do not take any offense when casual observers refer to them simply as oars. They range between 2.5 and 3.5 meters long. For millennia shells and oars were made from wood. Today they are made from longer-lasting, easier-to-manufacture composite materials, usually carbon fiber and plastic. A standard race for adults is just 2,000 meters and can be finished in six to eight minutes, depending on the quality of the crew. Because of the distance and short racing time, competitive rowing is considered a sprint event that exhausts its competitors.

IMPORTANT FIGURES

Unlike so many other sports, rowing relies less on individuals and more on the momentum of history. The ancient Chinese, Egyptians, Greeks, Indigenous Americans, Polynesians, and people of other cultures did not record who perfected the shape of an oar 3,000 years ago. They marked key moments. Depiction of rowing in art also helps to preserve the sport's history. Still, that did not prevent the United States' National Rowing Foundation from throwing its support behind a National Rowing Hall of Fame in the 1960s. The NRF recognizes that the Hall might not appeal to everyone but thought its history was worth archiving. Until the 21st century, the Hall was more symbolic than tangible, but in 2008 the NRF was able to move the Hall into a physical location in Mystic, Connecticut, where rowing fans and casual tourists could learn about the history of U.S. rowing.

POP CULTURE

In 1984 young, up-and-coming actor Rob Lowe appeared in the film *Oxford Blues*, about an American college student who believes the only way to win the girl of his dreams is to follow her to England, get into Oxford University, and join its world-famous rowing team. He learns life lessons along the way. Although the film had a small budget, Lowe's charisma—he became an international star during the 1980s—and a fun story propelled the film to modest box-office success.

Oxford Blues was fictional. The 2010 biopic *The Social Network*, a three-time Oscar winner about the early days of Facebook and its founder, Mark Zuckerberg, included a more realistic portrayal of college rowing. In the film, two characters, twins Cameron and Tyler Winklevoss, are members of Harvard's crew team who aspire to the U.S. Olympic team. In real life they succeeded, representing the United States in the 2008 Olympics. They later attended graduate school at Oxford and took part in the Boat Race.

SCANDALS

In 2020 American actor Lori Loughlin, best known for playing Aunt Becky on the long-running television show *Full House*, pleaded guilty to charges brought by federal prosecutors for her involvement in a nationwide college admissions scam. Hers and her husband's alleged role in the scandal involved them trying to get their two daughters into the University of Southern California by having at least one of their daughters falsely pose as a college-level rower. Prosecutors charged Loughlin and her husband with fraud, bribery, and a money-laundering conspiracy.

The scandal, which extended well beyond Loughlin's family, led to charges nationwide against more than 50 people, including another actor, Felicity Huffman, an Academy Award nominee and Emmy and Golden Globe winner. Although Loughlin and Huffman were the faces of the scandal, the overall scheme spread awareness about economic class disparity in the United States, with the wealthy using bribes to get their unqualified children into colleges while more academically able students in lower economic classes were left out. Huffman, who received a 14-day prison term, said, "I especially want to apologize to the students who work hard every day to get into college, and to their parents who make tremendous sacrifices supporting their children."

The scandal involved some of the top U.S. colleges, including Yale University, Georgetown University, and Stanford University.

PATRIOTISM AND NATIONAL PRIDE

The first Boat Race between Cambridge and Oxford took place in 1828. The first occurrence of "the Race" between Yale and Harvard was in 1853. Yet it took nearly another century and a half for all four teams to come together in one completion. In 1996 in Gainesville, Georgia, on the eve of the Olympics that was held down the road, in Atlanta, the four universities took part in their first eight-event regatta. It turned out to be a split decision: Cambridge won the 2,000-meter men's heavyweight race, considered the most prestigious race, but Harvard won the most races overall.

Timeline

c. 1400 BCE – Ancient Egyptians make a funerary carving for Pharaoh Amenhotep II that depicts evidence of competitive rowing.

1315 CE – Boat races are held along the waterways of Venice, Italy.

1683 – An anonymous British artist paints *The Lord Mayor's Water-Procession on the Thames*, a painting—later acquired by Queen Victoria—that captures competitive rowing.

1715 – The world's oldest annual rowing contest, Doggett's Coat and Badge, is held for the first time along the River Thames.

1756 – The first recorded boat race is held in the American colonies, in New York Harbor.

1815 – The Oxford University rowing team, the most famous college rowing team in the world—and the first—is founded.

1828 – The first Oxford-Cambridge University rowing competition, known as "the Boat Race" is held on the River Thames in London.

1852 – The first Harvard-Yale Regatta, the United States' answer to the Oxford-Cambridge rivalry, is held.

1856 – The Boat Race becomes an annual race. The only times it will be canceled are during World War I, World War II, and the 2020 COVID-19 pandemic.

1863 – A boat club is founded in Australia.

1865 – The first boat club is founded in Japan.

1870s – Racing shells—the name for boats used in competitive rowing—are made from a composite material for the first time. They previously had been made exclusively from wood.

1892 – The Fédération Internationale des Sociétés d'Aviron, otherwise known as the International Rowing Federation, forms in Turin, Italy.

1896 – Rowing is included in the first modern Olympic Games, but the event is canceled because of weather conditions.

1962 – The first World Rowing Championships, hosted by the International Rowing Federation, are held. Although intended to be held every four years, they become an annual event in 1974.

1976 – Women's rowing debuts at the Olympics.

1984 – Romania's Elisabeta Lipa wins the first of her five Olympic gold medals in rowing. That same year, Great Britain's Steve Redgrave wins the first of his five golds. Both are records within the sport.

1997 – The World Rowing Cup debuts.

2001 – The World Rowing Cup holds an event outside of Europe for the first time when one leg is held in Princeton, New Jersey, in the United States.

2013 – Australia hosts a leg of the World Rowing Cup for the first time. It hosts again the following year.

2019 – A federal investigation in the United States reveals that colleges and wealthy parents used crew—the American term for rowing—as a tool within a college admissions bribery scandal.

See also: Diving; Sailing and Yachting; Swimming.

Further Reading

Ayer, T. (2016). *The Sphinx of the Charles: A Year at Harvard with Harry Parker*. Lyons Press: Lanham, Maryland.

Bond, H. and Murray, E. (2016). *The Kiwi Pair: The Story behind Our World-Beating Rowers*. Penguin Books: New York.

Boyne, D. J. (2005). *Red Rose Crew: A True Story of Women, Winning, and the Water*. Lyons Press: Lanham, Maryland.

Boyne, D. J. (2019). *The Seven Seat: A True Story of Rowing, Revenge, and Redemption*. Lyons Press: Lanham, Maryland.

Brown, D. J. (2014). *The Boys in the Boat: Nine Americans and Their Epic Quest for Gold at the 1936 Berlin Olympics*. Penguin Books: New York.

Gilder, G. (2016). *Course Correction: A Story of Rowing and Resilience in the Wake of Title IX*. Beacon Press: Boston.

Halberstam, D. (1996). *The Amateurs: The Story of Four Young Men and Their Quest for an Olympic Gold Medal*. Ballantine Books: New York.

Kiesling, S. (2017). *The Shell Game: Reflections on Rowing and the Pursuit of Excellence*. Nordic Knight Press: Ashland, Oregon.

Lewis, B. A. (2011). *Assault on Lake Casitas.* CreateSpace Independent Publishing Platform: Scotts Valley, California.

Livingston, D. and Livingston, J. (2011). *Blood over Water.* Bloomsbury Publishing: London.

Rugby

Over the last 150 years, rugby has become one of the most popular team sports in the world. A handful of international games share the same family tree as rugby, including soccer, American football, and Australian rules football. Of those, rugby most purely retains what the sport was intended to be. In rugby, players work together to move a ball into the other team's territory. Defenses have only their bodies to stop offenses. They do not wear pads. They do not wear helmets. Relying only on their teammates along with their own wits, strength, and speed, rugby players end up forming a unique bond with their fellow players—even their opponents. Rugby games are a mix of skillful artistry combined with a car crash. Rugby tournaments between clubs look like something else altogether. Teams set up tents and drink with one another. On the field they might knock out an opponent's tooth. Off the field they will give that opponent a hug and share a meal. Rugby is its own culture.

HISTORICAL CONTEXT

What do rugby and baseball have in common? Both have dubious origin stories. Baseball's is rooted in the myth of a Civil War officer inventing the game, a story disproven but still perpetuated. Some rugby enthusiasts, meanwhile, enjoy the story of Rugby School in Rugby, England, and a clergyman named William Webb Ellis, who allegedly picked up a ball in the 1820s, thus inventing the rugby style of play. The apocryphal tale makes for a fun story, but the actual history of rugby's origins run deeper—and not quite as exciting—than the story of Ellis.

Rugby, similar to American football, partially grew from traditional football (soccer), a game with roots to at least the 12th century, and likely even deeper when one considers a game called *episkyros*, a team game played by ancient Greeks that called for teams of players to try to work a ball downfield against another team. Episkyros players, like rugby players, were allowed to progress the ball using their hands or feet, and the game was considered violent.

Although Ellis did not pick up the ball and run, players at Rugby School did contribute to the game's evolution. In soccer, only goalies may use their hands, but at Rugby School players evolved the game to create a version in which players may run while holding the ball, one of the key components of rugby and the defining difference between rugby and traditional football. By the 1840s the Rugby School's version of the game proved so popular that the school put down a set of rules in writing.

Two sects of rugby emerged: rugby union and rugby league. League broke off from union in 1895 over the issue of amateurism. Twenty clubs moved

Rugby matches, such as this one pictured between Australia and Italy, do not end when the match is over. Teams routinely celebrate together afterward, making camaraderie a rugby staple. (Antonio Ros/Dreamstime.com)

away from the union because the rogue clubs wanted to provide "broken-time" payments, which were payments to players who needed to miss time from work in order to play. Rugby union considered this a breach of amateurism, while rugby league rightly noted that many players came from working-class backgrounds and could not afford to play rugby if they had to miss work in order to play it. The split lasted a century, until rugby union finally turned professional in 1995.

GLOBALIZATION

The game spread through various avenues of British imperialism. The British invented the game. It was brought to Canada, a British colony, where Canadian college students learned the game. Students from McGill University in Montreal introduced rugby to American college students, mostly at Ivy League universities such as Yale and Columbia. Interestingly, it was also McGill where the game of ice hockey grew in international popularity.

Argentina learned rugby from English and Scottish migrants. Australia and New Zealand, where rugby is hugely popular and successful, are former British colonies. Some contradictory evidence exists as to how rugby arrived at another of the sport's most dominant regions, the Pacific Ocean nations of Fiji, the Independent State of Samoa, and Tonga. Some credit New Zealand missionaries, which would fall in line with rugby's British lineage, while others credit

Marist Brothers, a French-founded group of Christian missionaries. Rugby was introduced to Japan after World War II, when British forces occupied the area.

WHERE IT'S PLAYED TODAY

Consider the 2019 World Cup of Rugby as an example of how rugby has grown into one of the most popular games in the world. The following nations, from across six continents, qualified for the World Cup: from Africa, Namibia and South Africa; from Asia, Japan, Georgia, and Russia (the last two straddle Asia and Europe); from Europe, England, France, Ireland, Italy, Scotland, and Wales; from North America, Canada and the United States; from Oceania, Australia, Fiji, New Zealand, Samoa, and Tonga; and from South America, Argentina and Uruguay.

Players come to rugby at different ages. For example, many American players become introduced to rugby through a club while in college, because while there are some youth rugby leagues in the United States, there are not many. Youth rugby is far more common in Europe and Oceania than in North America.

Rugby sometimes served as an Olympic sport at the early modern Olympic Games (1896–1924). The International Olympic Committee removed it from the slate after the 1924 Games. It returned to Olympic status at the 2016 Games in Rio de Janeiro, Brazil, where Fiji won gold in the men's competition and Australia in the women's event.

ECONOMICS AND MEDIA

The world's best rugby players earn more than a million dollars in annual salary in the currency of the country in which they play. That does not include endorsements and other sources of income. Some regions pay more than others. As of 2018, the professional rugby player with the highest base salary in the world was New Zealand's Israel Folau, who earned about $2 million.

The top players in Europe and Oceania, where the game is hugely popular, earn more than the top players from countries such as Argentina and the United States, where some significant fandom exists but nothing near the levels that are achieved in other parts of the world.

For example, in 2016 a group of American rugby investors and fans started the Professional Rugby Organization (PRO). The average salary hovered around $25,000 per season, while top players with national and international experience could earn up to $70,000 per season. By contrast, the highest annual salary in Major League Baseball the same year was a little less than $4 million.

Rugby broadcasts are carried by different networks across the world. In the United Kingdom, most rugby union matches are carried by one of three networks: ITV Sport, the British Broadcasting Corporation (BBC), and Sky Sports, formerly under the control of Rupert Murdoch's 21st Century Fox and now a subsidiary of Comcast, a U.S.-based media company that runs NBC Sports, the world's dominant broadcast rights holder of the Olympic Games.

DIMENSIONS OF THE SPORT

A typical rugby field is 120 meters long by 70 meters wide. The in-play surface is 100 meters in length, with 10 meters on each end reserved for a team's goal.

Rugby is played with 15 players per side, with each match lasting 85 minutes (40 minutes per half with a 5-minute halftime). Individual players score five points for their team when they touch the ball to the ground inside the opponent's goal. This is called a "try." The team can earn an additional two points—called conversion points—by kicking the ball over the opposing team's crossbar after a try. This is similar to the "extra point" in American football. A team is awarded a penalty kick when the opposing team commits a penalty. If the penalty kick is successful, the kicking team earns three points. A drop goal, also worth three points, occurs when a player lets the ball bounce on the ground and then kicks it over the crossbar.

One of the more iconic images of rugby is the "scrum," a way for the referee to restart play after a stoppage. In a scrum, eight players from each side line up head to head. The referee puts the ball in the middle, and the two sides engage each other until one team has control of the ball. Once a team has possession, it may never advance the ball by throwing it forward. It must be run forward, so a player seeking to pass to a teammate must do so with a backward pass or toss.

IMPORTANT FIGURES

New Zealand's Richie McCaw is the most capped test rugby player of all time and a three-time World Rugby Player of the Year. His first appearance in a test match came in 2001. By the time he retired in 2015, he had earned 148 caps. As New Zealand's captain, he led the All Blacks to World Cup championships in 2011 and 2015. Most impressively, he made his first national team in 2001 after playing just eight minutes of Super 12 rugby—a professional division of the sport—and in his first contest was named the Man of the Match. It was a sign of great things to come.

Emily Scarratt proved essential to her English squad the moment she joined it in 2008. She scored 12 tries in her first 12 matches. By 2014 she was firmly cemented as one of the greatest players in English women's rugby history. During that year's Rugby World Cup, Scarratt led all players with 70 points, including 16 during England's win in the championship match against Canada. She became so invaluable to her team that by the time the 2016 Summer Olympics rolled around, she was named Great Britain's team captain.

Australian Rod Macqueen is one of the top rugby coaches in the history of the sport, and his accolades are too numerous to mention. He was among the recipients of the Australian Sports Medal, an honor bestowed upon the nation's top athletes and other sports figures in 2000—the only year the award was given. He coached Australia to the 1999 Rugby World Cup championship and the 2000 Tri Nations Series championship, and he is a member of the Australia Sports Hall of Fame and the World Rugby Hall of Fame.

POP CULTURE

Invictus, a 2009 film that stars Morgan Freeman and Matt Damon, is based on the true story of South Africa's improbable championship at the 1995 Rugby World Cup. Freeman stars as Nelson Mandela, the political dissident and champion of the anti-apartheid movement who becomes South Africa's president following 27 years in jail. Few expected the Springboks—the nickname of the South African team—to be competitive in the tournament, much less win the championship.

On a less-sunny note, the 1993 movie *Alive,* also based on a true story, depicts the story of the 1972 Uruguayan rugby team. The team plane crashed into the Andes Mountains. Although the movie is about camaraderie and survival, it became most notable for its subplot of cannibalism, in which surviving members of the crash must decide whether to eat the flesh of their dead friends and teammates to stay alive while they wait to be rescued.

SCANDALS

His nickname was "Quiet Man." Marc Cecillon was a former captain of France's national rugby team. He took part in 46 matches as well as the 1991 and 1995 Rugby World Cups. He exemplified French rugby, but he had a dark side.

In 2004, in front of nearly 60 people at a party, Cecillon shot and murdered his wife, Chantal. He pulled the gun from his waistband and shot her multiple times. Cecillon blamed alcohol and his own narcissism. He was convicted of the crime and sentenced to 20 years in prison, but in 2011 he was paroled. In 2018 Cecillion was arrested again for violent behavior after being found drunk.

POLITICS

Perhaps it should be little surprise that Cecillon committed his crimes while drunk. One of the biggest debates surrounding rugby that doesn't involve competition is whether the game is too heavily intertwined with drinking culture. For example, even in the face of players getting into trouble and hurting others and themselves, one British sportswriter wrote that it was just part of the game that society has to learn how to accept.

The connection between rugby and alcohol is so prevalent and so rooted in the game's history that how to separate the two has become a matter of public debate. One rugby-focused website wrote that alcohol consumption seemed like "a normal part of the rugby experience" before flipping it on the readers to show how alcohol damages on-field performance (Rugby Renegade 2015). Other rugby sites note rugby's culture of drinking as the reason for players' regular behavior of getting into fights after matches, in hotels, and on airlines.

Academic studies have been performed on the history of rugby and alcohol consumption, and old encyclopedias—in their entries on rugby—include references to alcohol. Even the website Rugby Football History, in its section on the origins of the game, includes a story about a team that lost entry into a key league in the late 19th century because its representative drank too much and went to the wrong location.

PATRIOTISM AND NATIONAL PRIDE

Sports are about far more than winning and losing. Sports drive emotion, and they deliver feelings of pride in the accomplishments of our fellow people, pride in ourselves, and pride in our heritage.

In Hamilton, New Zealand, in 2017, New Zealand's famed All Blacks prepared for a match against Tonga, one of its regional rivals. Tonga won, 28 to 22, but the game's result was moot compared with a respectful pregame showdown between the squads. The All Blacks performed a haka, a ceremonial dance that traces to the Maori, one of New Zealand's indigenous people. It is common for New Zealand sports teams to perform a haka in international competition.

But this haka sparked an especially deep emotional response from the crowd. They roared as the All Blacks hollered and postured toward the Tongans. When they were done, they stood face to face with their opponents. The Tongans responded with a sipi tau, their own ceremonial dance of posturing and challenge, this one even more coordinated than the All Blacks' haka. And even though Tonga was the visiting team, the crowd roared for them too. Viewers from across the world also loved it, watching on YouTube and other platforms several million times.

When the Tongan team was done, members of the All Blacks smiled and nodded in appreciation at the symbolism and choreography. Although the two dances have histories rooted in pride and conflict, on this day, they were about respect for each other and national pride in themselves.

Timeline

1823 – William Webb Ellis is alleged to have invented rugby while a student at Rugby School. The story is untrue.

1845 – The actual year in which the Rugby School's rules for the sport were first published.

1866 – The drop goal as a method of scoring is created.

1871 – England and Scotland play rugby's first international match.

1886 – The International Rugby Football Board is formed. It is known today as World Rugby and includes more than 100 member countries.

1895 – Rugby league splits from rugby union over whether to compensate athletes who lose wages while playing. Union, in support of amateurism, is against the practice but finally relents 100 years later, in 1995.

1900 – Rugby appears in the second modern Olympic Games.

1920 – Rugby's last inclusion as an Olympic sport until 2016 takes place.

1968 – The first documented women's rugby match takes place (in France).

1968 – Organized rugby officially lets teams replace injured players on the field with substitutes.

1978 – The first Women's U.S. National Championship is held.

1982 – The first sanctioned women's international match is held between Netherlands and France.

1983 – The Women's Rugby Football Union is formed.

1987 – The first Rugby World Cup is held.

1991 – The first Women's Rugby World Cup is held.

2016 – Rugby returns to the Olympics and includes women's and men's competitions. Australia wins the women's gold; Fiji the men's.

See also: Football; Ice Hockey; Soccer.

Further Reading

Bills, P. (2018). *The Jersey: The Secrets Behind the World's Most Successful Team*. MacMillan Publishers: London.

Carlin, J. (2008). *Playing the Enemy: Nelson Mandela and the Game that Made a Nation*. Penguin Books: New York.

Kerr, J. (2013). *Legacy. What the All Blacks Can Teach Us about the Business of Life*. Little, Brown and Company: New York.

McKittrick, J. and Williams, T. (2016). *Rugby Skills, Tactics and Rules*. Firefly Books: Richmond Hill, Ontario, Canada.

Nauright, J. (2013). *Making the Rugby World: Race, Gender, Commerce*. Taylor & Francis: London.

O'Connell, P. (2016). *The Battle*. Penguin Books: New York.

Owens, N. (2012). *Half Time: My Autobiography*. Y Lolfa: Ceredigion, Wales.

Parrado, N. and Rause, V. (2007). *Miracle in the Andes: 72 Days on the Mountain and My Long Trek Home*. Broadway Books: New York.

Richards, H. (2007). *A Game for Hooligans: The History of Rugby Union*. Mainstream Publishing: Edinburgh, United Kingdom.

Rugby Renegade (2015). "The Effects of Alcohol on Rugby Players." Rugby Renegade Strength and Conditioning, Jan. 10, 2015. https://rugbyrenegade.com/effects-alcohol-rugby-players.

S

Sailing and Yachting

The craft and art of sailing are nearly as old as humanity itself. For as long as people have existed, they have yearned to explore, migrate, travel, and colonize. They built boats to navigate waters, to discover what lies beyond, and they learned to understand seas and rivers, lakes and gulfs. Like so many other common activities, such as running, jumping, and climbing, humans became curious not just about who could sail but about who could sail better than whom. One way to determine superiority came through naval wars, but during times of peace, they turned to racing. For nearly 400 years people have raced boats for sport.

There are different types of boats. Yachts represent luxury—the ultrawealthy. Someone who loses another type of boat race—kayaks, for example—will feel the sting of defeat not just in pride but in the wallet. If one loses a yacht race, however, odds are the person will still be among the socioeconomic upper class, because to be able to compete in a yacht race means one has the means to afford a yacht in the first place.

HISTORICAL CONTEXT

In 1661 King Charles II of England helped captain a ship in a round-trip race from Greenwich to Gravesend. He lost, but that race, along with some that were documented in the Netherlands, marked the beginning of competitive yacht racing. From there yacht races occasionally appear in history books, but the sport significantly took off in 1815 with the founding of the Royal Yacht Squadron (RYS), an organization that still exists with the reigning monarch of the United Kingdom, Queen Elizabeth II, serving as its patron. Membership first included men who owned vessels that weighed at least 10 tons and who had an active interest in yachting. RYS is headquartered on the Isle of Wight, United Kingdom, in Cowes Castle.

Cowes Week, a series of yacht races that take have taken place each summer since 1826, celebrates the sport. The only years they did not take place were during the world wars. Participants the first few years were unsure whether the event would survive, but when King George IV attended and awarded a cup to one of the winners in 1834, its chances for long-term survival solidified. Cowes Week has grown to include 1,000 ships competing over the week of racing, with between 7000 and 10,000 crew members plus spectators of varying fame and social status.

America's Cup, an occasional contest between RYS and the New York Yacht Club, began in 1851. The New York Yacht Club won the first race and every race in the America's Cup until it finally lost in 1983 to an Australian team sponsored by the Royal Perth Yacht Club, with the New York club winning it back in 1987 (see "Patriotism and National Pride"). As the RYS was a private club, in 1875 the Yacht Racing Association (YRA) was founded to standardize rules and regulate membership. Among the founders was Gusztáv Batthyány, a Hungarian count known for breeding horses in the United Kingdom. Not all of the YRA's early rules survived, but one that did is the "flying start," which calls for crews to understand wind and other elements to get ahead of the pack as the race begins.

One reason some historians believe yacht racing emerged from the Netherlands is that the word *yacht* comes from the Dutch word *jacht*, which means "hunt" but has also come to denote vessels of war or pleasure. Yachting today bears close resemblance to yachting's early days, with the biggest exception being modern technology.

GLOBALIZATION

Sailing is one of the oldest contests at the Summer Olympics. It was supposed to be included in the first modern games in Athens, Greece, in 1896 but was canceled because of bad weather. It has appeared in every Olympic Games since then except for 1904, when the Games were held in St. Louis, Missouri, and the only nearby body of water was the Mississippi River, which has unpredictable water depths that make it not ideal for sailing.

Across various classes, Great Britain had won 28 gold medals as of the 2016 Games, the most among any nation. The United States stood second with 19 golds, Norway third with 17, and Spain fourth with 13. The most successful non-European countries other than the United States are Australia (11 gold medals), New Zealand (9), and Brazil (7). China has won 2 golds, while the Bahamas, Hong Kong, and Israel each have won one.

WHERE IT'S PLAYED TODAY

Yachting events take place in waters across the world, but less important than where yachting takes place is who participates. The sport of yachting breeds a cross section of skilled sailors and wealthy sponsors, and sometimes skilled, wealthy sailors such as Larry Ellison (see "Economics and Media"). Wild Oats XI, the maxi yacht used to win multiple Sydney to Hobart races, a historic event that starts in Australia and ends in Tasmania, was owned by Bob Oatley, the late businessperson best known for winemaking and owning—yes, owning—Hamilton Island in Queensland, Australia. Australian Mark Richards skippered Wild Oats XI for Oatley when he was not overseeing the building of other ships.

The 2017–2018 Ocean Race, formerly known as the Volvo Ocean Race, which includes ports throughout Europe, was won by a crew sponsored by the Dongfeng Motor Group (DFG). DFG, which showed revenues of about $120 billion in 2017, is made up of a conglomerate of some of the world's largest automakers, including

Honda, Peugeot, and Nissan, with business interests in China. The winning boat was skippered by French sailor Charles Caudrelier, a naval officer.

Yacht racing takes place all over the world. Wherever there is water, money, royalty, celebrity, and yachting enthusiasts, there can be a yacht race. Yet not all yacht racing involves the upper crust. In the United States, regattas take place annually, with local enthusiasts racing one another on the Fourth of July or Memorial Day weekend, on regional lakes and other bodies of water, such as Spirit Lake in northern Iowa, Idaho's Snake River, and for the Camden Classics Cup, the sea just off the coast of Camden, Maine.

Regional and national regattas are held around the world with varying classes of boats and competitors, from Hong Kong to Rio de Janeiro to Monaco to Tunisia. The organization Rowing South Africa hosts numerous events each year, including events for senior citizen and para-athletes, in its headquarters of Roodeplaat Dam northeast of Pretoria, South Africa. Rowing South Africa also supports its country's national team while providing resources for sailors who are looking to compete in international competitions.

ECONOMICS AND MEDIA

Many yacht enthusiasts are so well off that they do not even bother competing for money. They compete for trophies and prestige. For example, during Cowes Week, the Queen's Cup will be awarded to the Class 0 winner. The Cup first was awarded in 1897. It once went missing for years until it turned up in a thrift shop in Cardiff, Wales, in the 1930s, after which it was returned to the Royal Southampton Yacht Club so that it could once again be awarded during Cowes Week.

Boat International estimated that American businessperson Larry Ellison spent $300 million to win the 2013 America's Cup. He paid staff up to $20,000 per month and also sunk money into research, construction, and other resources. In 2019 *Forbes* estimated Ellison's total personal worth at nearly $70 billion. At the America's Cup founding in 1851, the creators of the event challenged any takers at a wager of £10,000. When later that year the yacht *America*, for which the cup is named, soundly defeated 15 other yachts, demand for the ship was so great that the owners sold it for $25,000, or about $800,000 in today's dollars.

Media coverage of yachting events usually falls under one of two categories: niche media or parachute journalism, which are stories that journalists "drop into" to cover one time to show their viewers or readers something they do not often get to see. Niche publications include titles such as *Boat International* and the magazines *Yachting* and *Power & Motoryacht*. Television personality Robin Leach often took his viewers onto yachts as part of his program, *Lifestyles of the Rich and Famous*.

DIMENSIONS OF THE SPORT

Sailing and yachting include many different race formats, classes, ratings, distances, bodies of water, and disciplines, that is, how the race is conducted.

Additionally, the boats themselves hold to different standards and requirements that can vary greatly.

One race format is the short-course race, which usually can be completed in a few hours or less. These races are conducted around triangle-shaped courses marked by buoys—anchored navigational markers. Olympic sailing and the America's Cup are both considered short-course events. Oceanic racing, a different format, requires a team or individual to traverse all or part an ocean. Yet another format, offshore racing, takes place in various bodies of open waters over long distances. One example of this is the Newport Bermuda Race, a 635-nautical mile race from Newport, Rhode Island, USA, to Bermuda that held its first race in 1906.

Each class of boat has to meet certain requirements to be considered part of that class. Box rules determine what size a boat needs to be in order to fall under a certain class, and if a boat meets certain rules, then it is free to be constructed as the designer sees fit. For example, the Transpac 52 yacht class requires a fixed-keel monohull with just one rudder. The hull may not exceed 52 feet, and the boat must weigh a minimum of 6,975 kilograms.

IMPORTANT FIGURES

In yachting, ships are often as recognizable as the captains who skipper them. The yacht *Partridge* remains the world's oldest fully operational racing yacht. Built in England in 1885, *Partridge* was once thought lost until it was located wrecked off an eastern shore of Great Britain in the late 1970s. Once the identity of the ship was confirmed thanks to an entry certificate and original building materials, restoration began. Partridge relaunched in 1998 after final fixes were made in—where else?—Cowes. Restorers used as many original materials as they could find, using modern, updated materials only when they had no other choice. *Partridge* took part in the 2001 America's Cup jubilee regatta. It finished third in its class.

It has been said that a yacht race is not truly a yacht race if Peter Montgomery is not the broadcaster. Nicknamed "the Voice of the America's Cup," New Zealand's Montgomery to date has broadcast 11 America's Cup events, 9 Olympic sailing competitions, and many other major regattas across the world. Montgomery came to enjoy yachting in the 1960s, which helped him learn and understand yacht races in a way that other commentators could not. Producers of the 1992 film *Wind*, a fictional movie about the America's Cup (see "Pop Culture"), recruited Montgomery to star as himself to lend authenticity to the film.

POP CULTURE

The 1992 film *Wind*, starring Matthew Modine and Jennifer Grey, took inspiration from Dennis Conner's America's Cup loss in 1983 to create the story of an American captain who loses the Cup and tries to find sponsors so that he can compete to win it back. The movie bombed at the box office, earning back less than

25 percent of its near $30 million budget, a sign that mainstream moviegoers care about as much for fictional yachting as mainstream sports fans care about competitive yachting. The movie also received criticism for putting the boat in unrealistic situations with members of the crew in wrong places, a move later explained as necessary for being able to get shots to help the audience follow along.

Slightly more successful was the 2013 independent film *All Is Lost*, starring Robert Redford as a sailor all alone at sea trying to salvage his ship after it begins to take on water. The film earned 22 award nominations from various organizations, and Redford won Best Actor from the New York Film Critics Circle.

Few yachts are as famous in pop culture as *The Flying Wasp*, the boat owned by the fictional judge Elihu Smails, played by Ted Knight, in the 1980 comedy *Caddyshack*. In the film, Smails's attempt to christen the boat is spoiled first when his wife breaks the ship's bow with a champagne bottle and then later when another character drops an anchor through it.

SCANDALS

In 1969 Great Britain's Donald Crowhurst began the Golden Globe race, a one-person yacht race around the world. It is believed that not long after the race started, he found damage to his boat, but he kept going. Against race rules, he stopped at least once—allegedly in South America—to make repairs. However, he realized he could not win and began to slip into what can only be described as madness as he hopelessly wandered the seas.

He could not stop and turn back without risking humiliation in the face of his sponsors and supporters. He could not continue on without repairs, which would lead to disqualification. Occasionally Crowhurst radioed his position to officials, but they doubted the authenticity of his whereabouts. He falsified details in his journal to make it seem as if he had passed various global markers, which he had not. Ultimately, Crowhurst died during the race, most likely by suicide. Officials began to piece together what had happened once his boat and journal were recovered.

Crowhurst's story has been told numerous times, most recently in the 2018 film *The Mercy*, starring Academy Award–winning actor Colin Firth as Crowhurst. Crowhurst has also been the subject of multiple documentary films.

PATRIOTISM AND NATIONAL PRIDE

The cover of the February 16, 1987, *Sports Illustrated* magazine featured Dennis Conner after he regained the America's Cup as the challenger. Conner, with beard stubble on his face, wore a nice sport coat and flashed a wide grin as he held half the cup. Holding the other half was then U.S. president Ronald Reagan under the headline, "Aye, Aye, Sir! President Reagan Welcomes Home Dennis Conner and the America's Cup" (Ballard 1987, 10–17).

It had been a long road back to the Cup for Conner, who had lost the Cup in 1983. Having regained it, Conner enjoyed international media accolades in what must be considered the historical peak of modern yachting coverage. *Sports Illustrated* began its story this way: "With his America's Cup triumph, Dennis Conner redeemed himself of his '83 loss and became a hero even to the vanquished Aussies." In all, Conner won three America's Cups—1980, 1987, and 1988—plus a bronze medal in sailing at the 1976 Summer Olympics.

Timeline

c. 58,000 BCE – Human beings first learn to sail.

4000 BCE – Egyptians and others incorporate cloth sails into their boats.

500 BCE – Phoenicians build ships that use two masts.

1100 – Vikings build ships up to 80 feet long to conduct trading and war.

1588 – The Spanish Armada, a fleet of approximately 130 ships sent to wage war on England, fails because of poor planning, British defenses, and bad weather.

1661 – King Charles II of England partially captains a ship in what many consider the first yacht race.

1815 – The Royal Yacht Squadron is founded in England. Eleven years later it hosts the first of what would become Cowes Week, an annual yachting and sailing tradition that continues to this day.

1851 – The first America's Cup is held.

1875 – The Yacht Racing Association is formed, standardizing some rules and classes.

1896 – Sailing is included in the first modern Olympics, although the sailing events do not take place, due to bad weather.

1906 – World Sailing, the governing body for organized competitive sailing and yachting, forms and a year later adopts a formal constitution at a meeting in Paris.

1960 – The Yachting Association of India is formed.

1983 – The United States loses an America's Cup event for the first time, to a team from Australia.

1987 – The United States wins back the America's Cup.

2013 – American businessman Larry Ellison bankrolls a reported $300 million to help the United States win the America's Cup.

See also: Olympics; Rowing/Crew.

Further Reading

Ballard, S. (1987). "Victory at Sea: With His America's Cup Triumph, Dennis Conner Redeemed Himself for His '83 Loss and Became a Hero Even to the Vanquished Aussies." *Sports Illustrated*, Feb. 16, 1987, 10–17.

Conner, D. and Levitt, M. (1998). *The America's Cup: The History of Sailing's Greatest Competition in the Twentieth Century*. St. Martin's Press: New York.

Conner, D. and Rousmaniere, J. (1978). *No Excuse to Lose: Winning Yacht Races with Dennis Conner*. W. W. Norton & Company: New York.

Le Carrer, O. (2015). *Yachting*. Adlard Coles Nautical: London.

Melges, B. and Mason, C. (1987). *Sailing Smart: Winning Techniques, Tactics, and Strategies*. Holt Paperbacks: London.

Melville, H. (1851). *Moby-Dick*. Harper & Brothers: New York.

O'Brian, P. (2004). *The Complete Aubrey/Maturin Novels*. W. W. Norton & Company: New York.

Sheahan, M. and Ascenti, B. (2017). *Nautor's Swan: Through 50 Years of Yachting Evolution*. Skira: Milan, Italy.

U.S. Sailing Association and B. Dellenbaugh. (2017). *2017–2020 Sailor's Guide to the Racing Rules*. U.S. Sailing Association: Bristol, Rhode Island.

Walker, S. and Little, C. (1991). *The Tactics of Small Boat Racing*. W. W. Norton & Company: New York.

Soccer

Soccer is the world's most popular sport. Nothing else comes a close second. From South America to Europe, to Africa, to North America, to Asia, and to Australia, soccer draws hundreds of millions of players and billions of fans. It's a game so simple yet demanding of great skill: one team tries to kick the ball through a goal more than the other team does. Nothing else is quite like it. A soccer game might end 0-0 but be considered a classic, a player might be praised for the ability to convincingly pretend to be hurt, and when the game reaches the international level, a single team's victory will lead an entire nation to dance in the streets, hug strangers, and declare a national holiday. Soccer is more than a sport. It's an international cultural force that drives foreign policy, affects national socioeconomics, and inspires billions of sports fans to sit on the edges of their seats in suspenseful anticipation.

HISTORICAL CONTEXT

Ancient games across multiple continents hold elements of soccer and permeate sport's historical landscape. Tsu Chu, for example, was a 2,000-year-old Chinese activity for military training that involved kicking a ball, and it denied the use of hands. Soccer's remedial skill set necessitates further exploration. All that is required to play are human beings, a cheaply manufactured ball, and some wide-open space to run around in. Like wrestling, boxing, and track and field, much of soccer's popularity grew because it could be played just about anywhere around the world and is affordable, and at the recreational level it requires almost no expensive equipment, unlike sports such as cricket, ice hockey, and American football.

As Great Britain played games in the 8th century that involved the kicking of a ball, Central American and Mexican people played a game on a standardized field in which they tried to get a ball through a small goal. Ancient Greeks developed a team game with spacing similar to soccer. Japan created its own team game on a field. Canadians and eastern Alaskans played games with a ball stuffed with grass. Indigenous people from what is now the United States played a game called *pasuckuakohowog*, which some historians translate to "they gather to play ball with their feet" or "they gather to play ball with a foot."

With hundreds of millions of recreational and professional players worldwide, soccer is far and away the world's most popular sport. The top professional teams pull the best players from across the globe. (fstockfoto/Dreamstime.com)

Soccer as the world knows it today incubated in Western Europe in the early and middle part of the 19th century, when clubs formed and began to formally publish rules for other organizations to follow. It created a uniformity to the game that, coupled with increased globalization sparked by imperialism and the Industrial Revolution, allowed it to transcend both literal and figurative international borders.

In 1815 Eton College in Berkshire, England, published what is believed to be the first set of written rules for soccer. It looked more like rugby, players could use their hands, and it was common for players to suffer severe injuries. Institutions of higher education in the northeastern United States, such as Princeton and Brown Universities, played a version of the game. By 1860 divided factions in the sport appeared between those advocating for different applications of the rules. The divisions were fierce, and in December 1863 a formal split occurred, and two organizations were formed: Rugby Football, which allowed players to advance the ball with their hands, and Association Football, which became soccer. Six years later, Association Football officials tweaked their rules once more to make any use of hands on the field by anyone other than the goalkeeper a rule violation. Soccer finally had its modern framework. By 1920 some women's matches in the United Kingdom were being played in front of at least 40,000 fans.

GLOBALIZATION

Although there are records of China and Japan playing a team-type game against each other in the 7th century, for the most part the basic elements of soccer—teammates working together to advance a ball—grew wherever there was sport. Nevertheless, history sometimes trends toward a Western European version of history, which is why sport historians often credit an 1872 match between England and Scotland as the first "official" international soccer match. This match is notable because it was the first international match of record to take place using what is known as the Cambridge Rules, developed in 1848 at Cambridge University and amended over the years to become the modern game.

In 1885 the United States hosted Canada in Newark, New Jersey, in what some view as the first non-European international match. The game enamored Europeans, who fought to have it included in the second modern Olympic Games in 1900 in Paris. Four years later in 1904, also in Paris, representatives from the nations of Belgium, Denmark, France, the Netherlands, Spain, Sweden, and Switzerland gathered to form the Federation Internationale de Football Association, or FIFA, an organization that went on to become the most dominant, organized sports entity in world history, surpassing even the International Olympic Committee because of its ability to impact national economies and morale.

The South American game also grew around this period. A 1906 goodwill visit to Argentina by a South African squad resulted mostly in blowout wins for the South Africans, but when one Argentinian club won 1-0, fans crowded the field to celebrate their players. From there, the number of professional teams in South American nations rose. In 1910 Chile and Uruguay played the first international match between two national teams on South American soil. Uruguay's infrastructure and local interest was one reason FIFA selected it as the host country for the first World Cup, held in 1930, in which Uruguay defeated Argentina for the championship. In all the first World Cup featured 13 nations: 7 from South America (Argentina, Bolivia, Brazil, Chile, Paraguay, Peru, and Uruguay), 4 from Europe (Belgium, France, Romania, and Yugoslavia), and 2 from North America (Mexico and the United States).

The second World Cup, held in 1934, took place in Italy and expanded to 16 teams, including Egypt, the first nation from the African continent to take part. In 1938 Cuba partook for the first time, but the World Cup was suspended by FIFA in 1942 and 1946 because of World War II and its fallout. Turkey's qualification in 1954 marked the first time a nation with some land in Asia entered the World Cup, while North Korea's entrance in 1966 signaled the World Cup's expansion into East Asia. Finally, in 1974 Australia qualified, which meant that all six of the earth's continents with a sustainable human population had sent a team to the World Cup. FIFA expanded the World Cup field in 1982 to 24 teams, enabling for the first time at least one nation from each continent to qualify a team, with the Soviet Union, which has land in both Europe and Asia, counting as the Asian nation.

WHERE IT'S PLAYED TODAY

With nearly 300 million people registered to play in some form of soccer league and countless more playing recreationally, an easier question to answer would be,

> ### The Team that Changed the World
>
> When the iconic U.S. sporting magazine *Sports Illustrated* went to pick its annual Sportsperson of the Year in 1999, it realized that no one person deserved the honor. The most memorable, satisfying, and inspirational sports figure of 1999 was not a person but a team. For decades American soccer fans liked to declare that soccer was the next big thing in the United States, that it was only a matter of time before it rivaled basketball and baseball. The rallying cry became co-opted by fans of other sports, as well as by cynical, male-dominated sports media, as a bit of a joke. Few believed that day would ever come.
>
> In 1999 it finally happened, when the U.S. women's soccer team won the Women's World Cup. Hosted at sites across the United States, the sport finally, at last, captured America's attention. The 32 matches drew an average of 37,000 spectators, nearly 10,000 more per game than that season's Major League Baseball daily attendance average. Television networks recorded record viewership for soccer matches, even some that did not involve the U.S. squad.
>
> The phenomenon culminated in the World Cup final between the United States and China, which after a scoreless draw the United States won in a 5-4 shootout before 90,185 fans at the Rose Bowl in Los Angeles, California, one of the country's most iconic sports venues. Brandi Chastain's left-footed penalty kick sealed the victory. She spun toward her teammates, arms raised, and then back around toward the goal where she fell to her knees in celebration. Chastain seized the moment for a squad that created a generation of household names, including Mia Hamm, Michelle Akers, Briana Scurry, and Julie Foudy.

Where is soccer *not* played? There are even organized teams that occasionally gather for matches in Antarctica.

One indicator of a country's soccer success, although there are exceptions, is the strength and size of its youth soccer programs. Organized programs appeared in South America pre–World War II, even in poor neighborhoods in countries such as Argentina, Bolivia, and Brazil. The same happened in parts of the African, Asian, European, and North American continents. Generally, youth programs are a sign of some level of affluence, families using disposable income to supplement children's activities, so the fact that organized soccer programs appeared in low-income communities signaled the sport's global appeal.

ECONOMICS AND MEDIA

Media analysts estimate that between three and four billion people—about half of the world's population—watch at least one soccer match per year on television during years when there is no World Cup. During men's and women's World Cup events, that many people could watch a soccer match during a single three-week period.

The total value of the sport is nearly incalculable once professional, recreational, media, corporate, and political forces are all factored in. Some industry analysts place the sport's total global value at well more than $1 trillion.

DIMENSIONS OF THE SPORT

Soccer fields can differ in size based on the age of the players and format of the game (outdoor vs. indoor, etc.). However, standard international fields—called "pitches"—are rectangular in shape, 100 to 130 yards in length, and 75 to 100 yards in width. A match starts in the center circle with 11 players per side: one goalkeeper plus some combination of forwards (offensive players), midfielders, and backfield (defensive) players.

Only goalkeepers may regularly use their hands. They can block the ball from going in their team's goal, catch the ball, and throw or roll it to their teammates. Nongoalkeepers may only use their hands on a "throw-in," a way of putting the ball back in play when a ball goes out of bounds along a sideline. Players score for their team by using their feet or head to put the ball into the opposing team's goal. Matches typically last 90 minutes, which includes two 45-minute halves plus a halftime break.

IMPORTANT FIGURES

To his family he was first known as Edson do Nascimento, but to the rest of the world he became known as Pelé, soccer's first international superstar, a prolific goal scorer from Brazil and ambassador for soccer throughout the mid- to late 20th century. Pelé did not like the nickname—he preferred his childhood nickname of "Dico"—but it stuck and became synonymous with the game itself. To this day he remains the only male soccer player to be part of three World Cup–winning squads, helping Brazil to the 1958, 1962, and 1970 titles. He significantly cut back his match schedule in 1974 but returned in 1975 to play for the New York Cosmos of the North American Soccer League. The lesser quality of play helped Pelé remain competitive, but his real impact was increasing soccer's exposure in the United States, and his games occasionally sold out as he received mainstream exposure in the sporting press.

What started as a fun celebratory pose for American soccer player Megan Rapinoe turned into an iconic symbol of confidence and equity. After scoring a goal for the U.S. Women's National Team during 2019 World Cup qualifying play and then during the World Cup, Rapinoe turned to the crowd, placed her feet together, stood up straight, lifted her chin in the air, and threw her arms out wide as fans roared and teammates jumped on her back. It was the natural extension of her call earlier that year for athletes on the women's team, one of the top soccer programs in the world, to earn equal pay to athletes on the men's team, an international afterthought. The iconic American magazine *Sports Illustrated* captured Rapinoe's pose on its cover during the World Cup and then featured her again months later, when it named her its Sportsperson of the Year.

Jules Rimet of France proved so adept at running the French Football Federation that just two years after ascending to its leadership, he became president of FIFA in 1921. Under Rimet's leadership, FIFA launched the first World Cup in 1930. He tried to grow the sport and found some success, holding the position of president until 1954. The original World Cup trophy was named in his honor and awarded to each champion until it was stolen in the early 1980s.

POP CULTURE

No one expected much when the low-budget film *Bend It Like Beckham* debuted in 2000. The British film, starring Parminder Nagra and Keira Knightley, about teen girl soccer players with big dreams and cultural expectations became a smash hit in the United Kingdom and United States, earning more than 20 times at the box office than what it cost to make. The "Beckham" in the film referred to David Beckham, then one of the United Kingdom's top soccer players.

The opposite of *Beckham* could be the 2015 film *United Passions*, a historical work about the creation of FIFA. Released on multiple continents as well as at France's historic Cannes Film Festival, the film should have been a surefire hit, right? Hardly. Considered by multiple critics to be "the worst film of all time," *United Passions* was laughed off as FIFA propaganda. It lost millions of dollars and—most staggering of all—made less than $700 in the United States despite a cast that included multiple Oscar nominees.

SCANDALS

In 2015 numerous world soccer administrators faced bribery and other chargers for receiving funds related to the awarding of the World Cup to nations and sponsorships. Allegations included money laundering, bribery, and fraud. With monetary figures in the hundreds of millions, the charges, brought by U.S. federal prosecutors and later involving the international justice agency Interpol, led to guilty pleas and much public embarrassment. At least eight international soccer figures pleaded guilty in a case that began when a whistleblower came forward from the nation of Qatar to admit her nation had illegally used funds to secure the 2022 World Cup. The event is still scheduled to take place there.

POLITICS

The country of Brazil spent between $3 and $4 billion on constructing facilities to host the 2014 men's World Cup. Government officials also dislocated its own citizens, razed homes, and attempted to hide many of the city's social problems. This led to numerous embarrassments for Brazil's government, including worldwide coverage of antigovernment demonstrations. In the years after the World Cup, some of the facilities Brazil worked hard to provide fell into ruin, further cementing the 2014 World Cup's legacy of financial failure.

Even before the 2022 men's World Cup in Qatar began, it faced political pressure on a different front. Allegations that the government was using slave labor to build facilities received worldwide coverage. Brazil's and Qatar's problems, coupled with FIFA's bribery charges, have led some nations to conclude that while competing in the World Cup is an honor, hosting one is not worth the effort.

PATRIOTISM AND NATIONAL PRIDE

Beyond the World Cup, international soccer includes many regional tournaments and organizations. Examples include CONCACAF (the Confederation of North, Central American and Caribbean Association Football) and the Asian Football Confederation. Some regional events serve as qualifying events for the World Cup.

Timeline

5000–500 BCE – Games showing some resemblance to modern soccer are played in China, Greece, and Egypt.

1863 CE – The Football Association forms and splits Rugby Football into two organizations, paving the way for separate sports: one that allows the regular use of hands to handle a ball and one that does not.

1872 – Scotland ties England, 0-0, in Glasgow, Scotland, in the first recognized international match.

1885 – In Newark, New Jersey, the United States host the first international competition outside of Europe, losing 1-0 to Canada.

1888 – The penalty kick is introduced.

1900 – In the second edition of the modern Olympic games, men's soccer debuts, with Great Britain defeating France for the gold medal.

1904 – Seven European nations form the Federation Internationale de Football Association (FIFA) at a meeting in Paris.

1930 – FIFA hosts 13 countries in Montevideo, Uruguay, for the first World Cup. The host team beats Argentina, 4-2, for the championship.

1940 – Brazilian footballer Pelé is born. In 1999 numerous soccer organizations name him the Football Player of the 20th Century.

1942 – FIFA suspends the World Cup and then does so again in 1946 because of World War II and its fallout.

1943 – Professional men's soccer comes to Mexico.

1950 – The first organized women's soccer league in the United States debuts in St. Louis.

1991 – The first Women's World Cup is held in China and won by the United States.

1996 – Women's soccer debuts at the Olympics. The United States wins gold.

2007 – Iran's Ali Daei retires as the all-time leading scorer in international soccer competition, with 109 goals.

See also: Cricket; Football; Rugby.

Further Reading

Buford, B. (1993). *Among the Thugs*. Vintage Books: New York.

Foer, F. (2010). *How Soccer Explains the World: An Unlikely Theory of Globalization*. Harper Perennial: New York.

Goldblatt, D. (2008). *The Ball Is Round: A Global History of Soccer*. Riverhead Books: New York.

Holt, N. (2014). *The Mammoth Book of the World Cup*. Running Press: Philadelphia.

Kuper, S. and Szymanski, S. (2014). *Soccernomics: Why England Loses, Why Spain, Germany, and Brazil Win, and Why the U.S., Japan, Australia–and Even Iraq–Are Destined to Become the Kings of the World's Most Popular Sport*. Bold Type Books: Lebanon, Indiana.

Lloyd, C. and Coffey W. (2017). *When Nobody Was Watching: My Hard-Fought Journey to the Top of the Soccer World*. Mariner Books: Boston.

Part, M. (2017). *The Flea: The Amazing Story of Leo Messi*. Sole Books: Beverly Hills, California.

Pelé (2007). *Pelé: The Autobiography*. Simon & Schuster: London.

Robinson, J. and Clegg, J. (2018). *The Club: How the English Premier League Became the Wildest, Richest, Most Disruptive Force in Sports*. Houghton Mifflin Harcourt: Boston.

Wilson, J. (2018). *Inverting the Pyramid: The History of Soccer Tactics*. Bold Type Books: Lebanon, Indiana.

Softball

What does it feel like to try to get a hit off a hard-throwing softball pitcher? Just getting your bat on the ball in an accomplishment in itself. First, it's important to know that softball is not baseball. When Monica Abbott threw a pitch 77 miles per hour in 2012, setting a new fast-pitch softball record, people reacted one of two ways. Those who knew the game couldn't believe it. A softball pitcher throwing that hard was previously unheard of. Those who did not understand softball wondered, What's the big deal? The fastest baseball ever thrown was 105 mph, nearly 30 mph faster. There are key differences. A baseball is thrown overhand and requires different muscle mechanics. The ball is smaller than a softball, making it easier to grip. A softball is thrown underhand, windmill style. It's larger than a baseball, making it more difficult to grip while putting added emphasis on the release point. Lastly, the distance between a baseball pitcher's mound and home plate is 60.5 feet, while the distance between a softball pitcher's mound and home plate is between 43 and 46 feet. Taking into account the lesser distance, trying to hit Abbott's 77-mph softball pitch would be the equivalent of hitting a baseball coming at you at 104 mph.

HISTORICAL CONTEXT

Rugby and baseball created tall tales to describe the origins of their sports. Softball's origin also exists as legend, except this one by most accounts appears to be true.

In Chicago in 1887, a group of people gathered at Farragut Boat Club to learn the outcome of the Harvard-Yale college football game. After Yale won 17-8, one of the men threw a boxing glove at another man, who hit it with a pole he had been holding. George Hancock picked up the glove, tied it until it looked like a ball, drew a baseball diamond on the floor that was smaller than regulation size because of space limitations, and grabbed a broom handle for a bat.

Softball was born.

The game became popular so quickly that Hancock designed a real ball and bat, and the game spread. In the United States, it was especially popular in Chicago, Minneapolis, Philadelphia, and other cities in the American Midwest and parts of the East Coast. The first organized softball league formed in Toronto, Canada, in 1897. Sometime around 1920—conflicting sources offer different years—Hancock's sport officially became known as "softball." Although the site of the original boat club was razed in the early 1950s, a monument to the game's creation still stands near the site.

The National Collegiate Athletic Association (NCAA) recognized softball in 1910. Eventually, softball became one of just two NCAA-sanctioned sports available only to women, joining field hockey. In the sport's early days, it was played nationally by both men and women. The game went national in 1933 at the World's Fair in, fittingly, Chicago, softball's birthplace. Michael Pauley and Leo Fischer brought 55 softball teams to Chicago for 3 tournaments: men's fast-pitch, men's slow-pitch, and women's softball. An estimated 350,000 people visiting the fair from across the country watched the tournaments.

GLOBALIZATION

Softball was invented in the United States, where today it remains one of the most popular recreational and college sports, but the countries most fanatical for professional softball are Australia and New Zealand. The game's journey to Australia followed a path similar to its spreading across North America: softball originated in Chicago and spread to nearby large midwestern cities such as Detroit. From there it spread to Canada, and it was a Canadian, Gordon Young, who then brought the game to Australia in the late 1930s.

Still, the game needed one more push to really take off. That occurred a few years later, during World War II, when U.S. nurses stationed throughout Australia shared softball with Australians. Melbourne, Australia, hosted the first Women's Softball World Championship in 1965 and won the event.

New Zealand's love for softball goes back slightly further, when American sailors played softball while they were in the country in 1935. It took New Zealanders just two years—1937—until they were playing organized contests and one more until they had formed the governing body, Softball New Zealand. New Zealand's women's softball team won the Women's Softball World Championship in 1982 and hosted the event in 1986. In the 16 times the Women's World Championship has been held, New Zealand or Australia has finished in the top three 10 times.

New Zealand has hosted the Men's World Championship 3 times and won 7 championships, finished runner-up another 4 times, and third twice. Australia has won the championship once.

WHERE IT'S PLAYED TODAY

Over the last decade, Japan has emerged as one of the most dominant women's softball powers in the world. Japan won the gold medal at the 2008 Olympics, and Japan was scheduled to host the 2020 Summer Olympics—before the COVID-19 pandemic—when softball returned to the fold after being removed from Olympic competition during 2012 and 2016. Japan has won five consecutive gold medals in softball at the Asian Games, including a performance so dominant in 2018 against Taiwan in the championship game that Japan won via mercy rule, which means it was winning by so many runs that the game ended early to save the other team further embarrassment.

Softball's popularity also has been growing in China. Chinese softball officials, recognizing their country's interest in the game, consulted with softball coaches and other officials across the world to help Chinese people better learn the game. Already the relationships are paying off for China. China won the Asian University Women's Softball Championship titles in 2017 and 2018. The team also tried to train in Alabama in the United States, but problems concerning the coach, an American who used to coach in Alabama before running into legal problems, prevented that from happening.

ECONOMICS AND MEDIA

Recreational and youth softball is big business. From 2007 to 2017, the sporting-goods industry made between $27 and $32 million annually from just the sale of softballs. Sales of softball and baseball bats, which are measured as one piece of equipment, fluctuated between $172 million and $216 million annually. Kids' softball makes up a major part of the United States' $15 billion youth sports industry.

About 10 million people take part in organized softball leagues each year in just the United States, and many more in countries such as Australia and Japan. Youth softball is most often played by girls starting around age 6 and ending around 18, through high school. Community youth leagues charge fees of between $30 and $50 to play, but more competitive travel teams cost upward of hundreds of dollars per year in fees, not counting travel costs such as hotels, gas, and food.

Recreational softball played by adults includes men and women, with the ages of league participants ranging from college-age (late teens) through people in their 80s, such as the Cape Cod Senior Softball League in Massachusetts. Professional leagues exist for men and women in various countries, but in the United States professional softball is almost exclusively for women.

Professional softball revenue in the United States pales next to revenue for more established sports such as basketball, auto racing, and football, but it compares favorably to baseball's growth when professional baseball was still in its infancy. Women's professional softball debuted in the United States in the early 21st century. Abbott, the pitcher who threw a softball a record 77 miles per hour, signed a six-year contract worth $1 million to play professional softball, but most American professional softball players earn less than $20,000 annually.

DIMENSIONS OF THE SPORT

Field dimensions differ by age group, slow-pitch, and fast-pitch softball. Little League softball, a division for girls ages 4 through 18, runs bases that are 60 feet apart. The distance from the pitcher's mound to home plate is 46 feet. The distances are the same for the National Softball League, a slow-pitch organization in the United Kingdom. However, for National Pro Fastpitch, a professional league in the United States, the distance between the pitcher's mound and home plate is just 43 feet.

The average distance from home plate to a home run wall is about 220 feet, although it may fluctuate by 10 to 20 feet, depending on the ballpark. The ball comes in three sizes: 11 inches, 12 inches, and 16 inches. Eleven-inch balls are used for fast-pitch, 12-inch balls are used for slow-pitch, and 16-inch balls are used for leagues in which the game is played without gloves. The 16-inch ball is slightly softer in construction than the 11- and 12-inch balls.

One benefit to pitching in softball versus baseball is that softball's windmill technique is a more natural motion compared with baseball's overhand approach. The pitching motion of a baseball player is so unnatural that it is common to cause damage to the shoulder or elbow beginning at a young age. To prevent injury, coaches and athletic trainers only let starting pitchers throw once every five days. Softball pitchers, meanwhile, can pitch every two days or even one day after pitching, if necessary, because of a less physically taxing throwing motion. Although injuries to pitchers happen in softball, the rate of injuries to softball pitchers as compared to baseball is far less—and, proportionally, they throw the ball just as hard.

Fast-pitch softball players are able to throw five primary different types of pitches. The first is a fastball, of which there are a few variations. The basic fastball is the first pitch a softball pitcher learns. The goal is to throw the ball as fast and accurately as possible. There are two main types of fastballs: a two-seam fastball, for which the pitcher has two fingers on the seam of the ball, and the four-seam fastball, for which they make contact with four parts of the seam. The four-seam is the easier of the two to control, but the two-seam is considered the better pitch because it moves around a little bit more, which confuses the hitter.

The drop pitch is similar to baseball's sinkerball. They both come in fast toward the hitter, except the drop pitch at the last moment sinks, leaving the hitter almost no time to adjust. A release that creates a downward spiral causes the ball to drop. Softball pitchers can also learn a changeup, which throws off the timing of a hitter because it comes in slower than most pitches; and a curveball, which moves left to right or right to left, depending on which arm the pitcher throws with. The last pitch, which is the hardest to learn, is a rise ball, for which baseball has no equivalent. It moves up through the batter's box. The batter sees the ball coming, starts to swing, but often misses contact because by the time the ball arrives, it is too high for the batter to hit.

IMPORTANT FIGURES

Whether Dot Richardson is the greatest American women's softball player is a matter for debate. Whether she is its most diversified is not. Richardson burst onto the national scene in the early 1980s, helping UCLA to the NCAA women's softball championship. She played professionally until 1994, working during the off-season toward her medical degree. During her residency at the University of Southern California, Richardson took time off to play for the United States in the 1996 Summer Olympics—the first time that women's softball had been an Olympic sport. The United States won. Richardson had a gold medal. She played for the United States again in 2000, making her the only two-time, gold-medal-winning softball player/medical doctor.

It would be tough to one-up Richardson's overall accomplishments, but Lisa Fernandez did surpass Richardson in one area. Fernandez helped lead the United States to three Olympic gold medals (1996 and 2000 with Richardson, and again in 2004 after Richardson had retired). Fernandez starred as a pitcher and a hitter. She holds the Olympic record for striking out the most batters in a game: 25. Notably, Fernandez did not play for the 2008 team, the only year the United States failed to win the gold before softball ceased being an Olympic sport.

POP CULTURE

More Hollywood films have been made about boxing and baseball than any other sport. Softball? Not so much. The sport occasionally pops up in TV and film, but not often. One example is *Beer League*, a 1996 film starring Artie Lange and Ralph Macchio about a down-on-his-luck man whose only joy in life is softball. He risks losing his team if they don't learn to be better players. The movie made less than $500,000, a staggeringly small amount by any box-office metric.

Softball's most visible ambassador into the pop-culture sphere might be Ramona Shelburne, but her public notoriety has nothing to do with softball. Shelburne, who played softball at Stanford University in Palo Alto, California, from 1998 to 2001, went on to become a popular journalist and on-air personality for ESPN, the all-sports cable network. She mostly covered the National Basketball Association. Her close professional relationship with mixed martial arts competitor Ronda Rousey, one of the most popular athletes in the United States during the early 21st century, allowed Shelburne to write a series of high-profile stories.

SCANDALS

In 2015 the Little League softball team from Snohomish, Washington, lost on purpose. It was reported that Washington's coaches purposely made their team lose to a team from North Carolina because had Washington won, a team from Iowa would have advanced in the Little League World Series, and Iowa posed a greater threat to Washington's chance at a championship. Against North Carolina, Washington did not let its best players play, North Carolina won, 8-0, and Iowa was eliminated.

World Series officials said it was clear Washington had lost on purpose and ordered them to play another game against Iowa, with the winner moving on in the tournament. Iowa won, 3-2. Washington was eliminated and had to go home, while Iowa got to keep playing.

POLITICS

Sometimes politics finds its way into sports. Other times, politics is sports. In 2009 women from the U.S. Congress formed a softball team to play against women from the Washington, DC, press corps. It was the start of an annual softball game between the two sides to raise money for the Young Survival Coalition, a charity that benefits women under 40 who are diagnosed with breast cancer.

Some of the more notable players past and present from the bipartisan congressional team included Kirsten Gillibrand, a senator from New York; Joni Ernst, a senator from Iowa who previously earned the rank of lieutenant colonel in the National Guard; and Debbie Wasserman Schultz, a congresswoman from Florida whose diagnosis with breast cancer helped inspire the first game. As of 2020, Schultz remains a cancer survivor.

PATRIOTISM AND NATIONAL PRIDE

The softball world was thrilled when after more than a century of existence it finally became an Olympic sport in 1996. The sport was dropped from the Olympics, however, after only four cycles, with the 2008 Games being its last. The absence was short-lived. Recognizing the game's growing presence across the globe, the International Olympic Committee restored Olympic softball in time for what would have been the 2020 Summer Games in Japan, had the pandemic not struck. Coincidentally, the host nation of the 2020/what are projected to become the 2021 Games won the last Olympic gold medal awarded for softball in 2008.

Timeline

1887 – Softball is invented in Chicago by a group of college football fans when one throws a boxing glove at another, who hits it with a pole.

1897 – The first organized softball league forms in Toronto, Canada.

c. 1920 – The sport is officially named "softball."

1933 – Softball, which already has a loyal niche following in large midwestern American cities, explodes on the national scene after more than 350,000 people watch games played at the World's Fair in Chicago.

1935–1939 – Softball is introduced to New Zealand and Australia by Canadians and Americans. The two Oceanic countries will become among the most rabid and successful softball nations in the world.

1951 – The International Softball Federation is formed to oversee women's and men's softball championships for both fast-pitch and slow-pitch competitions.

1965 – Australia hosts the first Women's Softball World Championships.

1982 – The University of California, Los Angeles, wins the first NCAA Women's Softball championship behind Dot Richardson, who goes on to become a two-time Olympic gold medalist.

1996 – Softball becomes an Olympic sport.

2008 – Softball appears in the Olympics for the final time until 2021 (to substitute for the 2020 Games at the time of this writing). Japan wins the gold medal and then goes on to win five consecutive gold medals at the Asian Games.

2012 – Monica Abbott pitches a softball 77 miles per hour, the fastest softball pitch on record.

See also: Baseball; Mixed Martial Arts; Rugby.

Further Reading

Finch, J. and Killion, A. (2011). *Throw like a Girl: How to Dream Big & Believe in Yourself.* Triumph Books: Chicago.

Maddox, J. (2014). *Softball Surprise.* Stone Arch Books: Mankato, Minnesota.

McCree, M. (2018). *Mind of a Superior Hitter: The Art, Science, and Philosophy.* Self-published.

McGinnis, M. (2019). *Heroine.* Katherine Tegen Books: New York.

Reilly-Boccia, C. (2014). *Finished It: A Team's Journey to Winning It All.* Self-published.

Richardson, D. and Yaeger, D. (1997). *Living the Dream.* Kensington Books: New York.

Sammons, B. (1997). *Fastpitch Softball: The Windmill Pitcher.* McGraw-Hill Education: New York.

Smith, M. and Hsieh, L. (2008). *Coach's Guide to Game-Winning Softball Drills: Developing the Essential Skills in Every Player.* Ragged Mountain Press: New York.

Walker, K. (2007). *The Softball Drill Book.* Human Kinetics: Champaign, Illinois.

Westly, E. (2017). *Fastpitch: The Untold Story of Softball and the Women Who Made the Game.* Touchstone: New York.

Speed Skating

Speed skating is the natural cousin of sprinting in track and field, developed largely by cold-climate countries where running would have been impractical because of all the ice and snow on the ground. As in track and field, the goal of speed skating is to see who can go the fastest over different distances. There are indoor and outdoor races, short sprints and distance events. In more recent years,

Speed skating began as a form of transportation in Northern Europe around the 13th century. Early forms of the sport also appeared in Scotland. (Lukas Blazek/Dreamstime.com)

short-track speed skating has increased in popularity and in some regions even surpassed traditional speed skating, because short-track can be done on hockey rinks, whereas traditional speed skating requires a more sport-exclusive sort of track. Short-track speed skaters can go as fast as 30 miles per hour, while long-track skaters reach 35 mph.

HISTORICAL CONTEXT

Speed skating began not as a sport but as a practical form of transportation over icy terrain during the 13th century. Skaters used canals between villages to deliver messages, and speed was of the essence. It took more than 500 years for speed skating to evolve from exclusively a logistical function to a sport. The first official speed-skating event took place in Oslo, Norway, in 1863, although some accounts claim that speed-skating events took place earlier than that, in Scotland. What is for certain is that speed skating began in Northern Europe and found its way west to the United Kingdom. Skating's popularity extended to British royalty.

The Netherlands, the United Kingdom, Russia, and the United States—four regions of the world that include cold climates—showed the earliest interest in speed skating as a competitive sport. Those four nations came together in 1889 in the Netherlands for the first Speed Skating World Championships. Three years later the International Skating Union formed in the Netherlands to ensure the sport's growth was legitimate and that standards remained consistent. Part of this standardization included creating long-track distances of 400, 500, 1,500, 5,000, and 10,000 meters as well as the tradition of skaters going off in pairs rather than all skating at once. That standard remains in place to this day, although in 1932 American organizers of the Olympics decided to hold a mass start, which led many of Europe's best racers to boycott the Games.

One of the sport's first stars was the Netherlands' Jaap Eden, who in 1894 set a 5,000-meter record so dominant that it stood until 1911. At the turn of the century, Eden proved to be one of the world's best athletes. He was the first recognized speed-skating world champion, and in addition to setting the 5,000-meter mark, he held a world record in the 10,000 meters. As if that weren't impressive enough, Eden also held a world record in cycling. Each year the Dutch Sportsperson of the Year receives the Jaap Eden award.

Eden's success helped popularize the sport. It earned inclusion in the inaugural Winter Olympic Games in 1924 as a men's sport. Women's Olympic speed skating began at the 1932 Games as a demonstration sport, meaning that it did not apply to the medal count, and it did not become a medal sport until 1960. As speed skating's popularity grew, so did a realization: outside of regional interest and the Olympics, the sport still did not draw enough fans to grow the sport. Beginning in the late 1960s and early 1970s, numerous groups tried to create professional speed-skating leagues. Nearly all failed for one reason or another, mostly financial.

Also, long tracks, while fun to watch, could serve little function outside of speed skating. Hockey rinks, however, proved more hospitable to the sport's growth. Ice hockey's growth across the world far outpaced speed skating, and since hockey rinks were just sitting there when games or practice were not going on, speed skaters began to develop what is now known as short-track racing. It officially became an Olympic sport at the 1992 Games in Albertville, France, and since then has grown more rapidly than long-track skating for the simple reason that hockey rinks can be found nearly everywhere, while long tracks cannot.

GLOBALIZATION

King James II of England, while in exile in the Netherlands in the mid-17th century, took a personal fancy to ice skating. His return to the United Kingdom brought speed skating along with it, and suddenly the sport had two points of interest: Northern and Western Europe. By the early 19th century, the French had taken to ice skating, but not as much for the speed aspect. According to author Laura Gascoigne, French men used ice skating to publicly show off their combinations of grace and strength to attract sexual partners. Nonetheless, some became enamored with how fast they could go.

As the sport trickled through Europe, it also found its way to the United States, either by Europeans visiting the America and exporting the sport or by American citizens traveling abroad and bring the sport home with them. Americans in cold climates took a quick liking to speed skating and found success. New York's Charles Jewtraw won gold in the 500 meters at the first Winter Olympic Games. To date, Americans have won more medals in speed skating than in any other Winter Olympic sport.

WHERE IT'S PLAYED TODAY

Competitive speed skating began in cold-climate countries and generally remains most popular in those regions today—at least as far as long-track competition is concerned—with some minor exceptions, most notably wealthier countries with the resources to build and maintain indoor facilities. A look at the home countries of recent speed-skating Olympic medalists affirms the popularity, culture, and resources needed to succeed in such a niche sport.

In the 2018 Winter Olympics, for example, the Netherlands won the gold medal in the women's 1,000, 5,000, and 3,000 meters, and in the 3,000 the Netherlands won gold, silver, and bronze. In 2014 the Netherlands swept every medal in the men's 10,000 meters race, while in 2018 it took silver while Ted-Jan Bloemen of Canada won gold. Since 1976, when 1,000 meters was introduced at the Winter Olympics, every gold medal has been won by a skater from Canada, Germany, the Netherlands, Russia/Soviet Union, or the United States.

Although cold-weather and wealthier countries tend to dominate long-track skating, the sport has welcomed competitors from across the world—mostly Europe and East Asia. South Korea has won more short-track Olympic medals than any other country. Austria, Belgium, China, Czech Republic, Finland, Italy, Japan, North Korea, Norway, and Sweden have medaled in long track, as has Kazakhstan's Lyudmila Prokasheva in 1998. Kazakhstan, which has territory in both Asia and Europe, is known for its warmth but also has freezing winters.

Short-track speed skating, because of its easier accessibility, draws competitors from more parts of the world. Since it became an Olympic sport in 1992, nations that have sent athletes to the Olympics include Australia, Belarus, Bulgaria, Hong Kong, Israel (which rarely gets more than snow flurries twice a year), Latvia, Lithuania, Mongolia, New Zealand, Poland, Romania, Taiwan, and Ukraine.

ECONOMICS AND MEDIA

Speed skaters do not make much money from the sport itself, anywhere from $50,000 to $125,000 a year; even then, that is just for a select few from each country. Numerous organizations have tried to start professional speed-skating organizations over the years, but they never last more than a handful of years.

The world's most notable speed skaters earn their money from endorsements. American Apolo Ohno (see "Important Figures") has earned nearly $10 million and nearly all through nonskating means. Eric Heiden (see "Important Figures") became a physician after retiring from the sport.

DIMENSIONS OF THE SPORT

Speed skating runs counterclockwise. A standard long track stretches 400 meters around. Short tracks run 111 meters, with skaters' speeds and their frequent need to bank so great that it has become standard for short-track speed skaters to put their fingers on the ground as they turn, to help maintain balance.

Long-track speed skating includes the following distances for its events: 500, 1,000, 1,500, 5,000, and 10,000 meters. There is also a team event. Short-track speed skating competes at the following distances for its events: 500, 1,000, and 1,500 meters for women and men, 3,000 meters for women, and 5,000 meters for men.

Depending on the height and weight of the athlete, a skater's blade can range between 28 and 45 centimeters. Blades on short-track skates attach in two places—behind the ball of the foot and again at the heel—while long-track blades attach just once. Additional equipment includes helmets, a must since the fastest recorded times have neared 40 miles (just over 60 kilometers) per hour, as well as knee, ankle, and shin protection. Some speed skaters choose to wear rib protection in case they wipe out at a high speed and glide unprotected into a wall or other protective barrier. They also wear spandex to reduce friction and build speed. In recent years competitive skaters have chosen—or sometimes been required—to wear Kevlar suits, which protects them from being cut by the skates of their competitors. Serious injuries in speed skating are no joke. Whereas an athlete in any sport can break a bone or tear ligaments, speed skaters sometimes suffer injuries such as what happened to J. R. Celski of the United States in 2010, who slipped on a turn and cut himself with his own blade so severely that he reported, "I saw my femur" (Almond 2010).

IMPORTANT FIGURES

Speed skating might have originated in the Netherlands, but at the 1980 Winter Olympics, American Eric Heiden single-handedly won more gold medals than all athletes from the Netherlands (and Norway and Finland) combined. Heiden didn't just earn five gold medals but set five Olympic records and one world record, earning him the nickname Heiden the Great. Then Heiden did something that few expected: he retired at the end of the 1980 speed-skating season. Yet that was hardly the end of his athletic run. Heiden went on to climb mountains. He moved into cycling and, like the Netherlands' Jaap Eden nearly a century earlier, found success, winning the United State Professional Cycling Championship in 1985. Heiden eventually returned to speed skating as a broadcaster.

There must be something about speed skaters being attracted to cycling. Canadian Clara Hughes won Olympic medals in both sports. To date she is the most decorated Olympic athlete in Canadian history, earning six medals. Perhaps most impressively, Hughes is the only athlete in Olympic history to have won multiple medals in both the Summer and Winter Games, earning her numerous Canadian civic and governmental honors. Hughes won her gold in long-track speed skating in the 5,000-meter event at the 2006 Games in Turin, Italy.

Shani Davis set nine world records during his speed-skating career. At the 2006 Games, where Hughes made her mark, Davis won gold in the 1,000 meters to become the first Black athlete to win a gold medal at the Winter Olympics. In 2010 in Vancouver, Canada, Davis defended his gold. In all he won four Olympic medals and at least 11 world championships in different speed-skating events.

POP CULTURE

Even those who have never watched speed skating might know the name Apolo Anton Ohno. The American short-track speed skater understood how little interest his sport garnered at home, so he did what he could to keep his name in the spotlight. Ohno grew his hair out and wrapped it in what became a signature bandana. He appeared twice as a contestant on the popular reality show *Dancing with the Stars*, winning the championship in the fourth season. He has guest-starred on other shows as well, written two books, and appeared on the cover of *Sports Illustrated*, a popular American magazine.

And what of his on-ice accomplishments? Let's just say Ohno more than backed up his off-ice bravado: he won two Olympic gold medals and at least nine world championships.

Steven Bradbury's Gold Medal Strategy

By any metric, Australia's Steven Bradbury should have had zero chance of winning a gold medal in short-track speed skating at the 2002 Winter Olympics. For one thing, he was old by speed-skating standards: 29 years old and competing in his fourth Olympics. For another, Australia is a Southern Hemisphere nation. So what? No athlete from a Southern Hemisphere nation had ever won an individual gold medal at the Winter Olympics.

Until Bradbury.

So how did he do it? Simple: He stayed on his feet and followed the rules. In the quarterfinals of the 1000 meters in Salt Lake City, Bradbury, who had been part of Australia's bronze-medal relay team in 1994, qualified to advance only because the skater in front of him was disqualified for a race rules violation.

His pace through the first two races suggested he had no chance to advance past the semifinals, so he and his coaches devised a plan for Bradbury to stay just behind the race leaders and hope for a crash—an occasional occurrence in short-track racing. Remarkably, the strategy worked. All skaters in front of him wiped out, and Bradbury won to advance to the finals where he would face, among others, Apolo Anton Ohno, the race favorite from the host nation United States.

Bradbury quickly fell behind again, this time by an insurmountable distance of 15 meters. Then—again—on the final lap, all four skaters ahead of him crashed while fighting for position. Clear of the wreck, Bradbury glided ahead of his competitors to win the gold medal. Sometimes, experience beats youth. Bradbury, one of the oldest competitors in his event, later said that he "might as well stay out of the way and be in last place and hope that some people get tangled up" (Al-Razouki 2018).

SCANDALS

South Korean authorities sentenced former speed-skating coach Cho Jae-beom to prison time in early 2019 after he was found guilty of assaulting one of his former athletes, who also later accused Cho of sexual abuse. The crimes devastated South Korea's speed-skating community and its fans. South Korea has won the most short-track Olympic gold medals since the sport became recognized by the Games in 1992.

South Korea's program fell under further scrutiny later that year after two skaters publicly shunned a teammate in a team-pursuit event: three skaters working in unison and taking turns in front. Two of Noh Seon-Yeong's teammates left her behind on the track. When the event was over, they skated away without acknowledging Noh, a display of unsportsmanlike conduct and overall show of disrespect. In defense of Noh, more than 400,000 South Koreans wrote to South Korean President Moon Jae-In to ask that official sanctions be brought against Noh's teammates.

PATRIOTISM AND NATIONAL PRIDE

When it comes to long-track speed skating and who does it best, look to the originators. At the 2014 Winter Olympic Games, the Netherlands won 24 medals, all of them in speed skating. By the time the Games had ended, over the history of the Olympics they had won nearly 40 more speed-skating medals than the next-closest nation.

Looking for a good children's book? Go online and you will find several thousand copies of the Mary Mapes Dodge's *Hans Brinker, or the Silver Skates*, the classic Dutch best seller. It was first published in 1865.

Timeline

12th century – The Dutch skate along frozen canals to send messages between villages. The faster they skate, the better.

1642 – The Skating Club of Edinburgh is formed in Scotland.

1763 – The Skating Club of Edinburgh hosts what it considers to be the first official speed-skating competition.

1863 – Oslo, Norway, hosts what the International Olympic Committee now considers to be the first recognized speed-skating competition.

1884 – Norwegian Alex Paulsen wins numerous skating championships while on a tour of the United States and is unofficially named "Amateur Champion Skater of the World."

1889 – Teams from Great Britain, the Netherlands, Russia, and the United States compete in the Netherlands for the first Speed Skating World Championships.

1892 – The International Skating Union (ISU) forms in the Netherlands.

1909 – The Elfstedentoch, an outdoor distance skating race, is held for the first time in the northern part of the Netherlands.

1924 – Speed skating debuts at the 1924 Winter Olympics, the first year the Winter Olympics are held.

1932 – Women's speed skating debuts at the Olympics as a demonstration sport.

1932 – Many European competitors boycott speed skating at the Lake Placid, New York, Olympic Games because the Americans insisted on a mass start—all competitors going off at the same time—instead of the traditional two-at-a-time format. As a result, Americans win four gold medals.

1960 – Women's speed skating officially becomes part of the Olympic program.

1964 – The Soviet Union's Lidia Skoblikova wins four gold medals at one Olympics, adding to the two she won four years earlier.

1974 – The International Speedskating League, a professional organization, folds after three seasons because of financial problems.

1980 – American Eric Heiden becomes the first, and to date (2020) only, speed skater to win five individual gold medals in a single Olympics.

1988 – West Germany's Uwe-Jens Mey wins Olympic gold in the men's 500 meters. Four years later he wins again, this time for a unified Germany.

1992 – Short-track speed skating debuts at the Albertville, France, Olympics. Short track includes mass starts similar to the ones that led to boycotts during the 1932 Games.

1994 – American Bonnie Blair competes in her fourth and final Olympic Games. She finishes her career with five gold medals and a bronze.

2006 – American Shani Davis wins gold in the 1,000 meters, becoming the first Black athlete to win a gold medal at the Winter Olympics.

See also: Ice Hockey; Olympics; Track and Field.

Further Reading

Aaseng, N. (1981). *Eric Heiden: Winner in Gold.* Lerner Publishing Group: Minneapolis, Minnesota.

Almond. E. (2010). "Speed Skater J. R. Celski Overcomes Scary, Bloody Accident to Reach Olympics." *San Jose Mercury News*, Feb. 10, 2010. https://www.mercurynews.com/2010/02/10/speed-skater-j-r-celski-overcomes-scary-bloody-accident-to-reach-olympics.

Al-Razouki, M. M. (2018). "Carpe Diem: Entrepreneurial Lessons from Olympian Steven Bradbury." *Entrepreneur*, Feb. 28, 2018. https://www.entrepreneur.com/article/309667.

Blair, B. (1996). *A Winning Edge.* Taylor Trade Publishing: Lanham, Maryland.

Hughes, C. (2017). *Open Heart, Open Mind.* Touchstone: New York.

Le May Doan, C. (2002). *Going for Gold.* McClelland & Stewart: Toronto, Ontario, Canada.

Munshower, S. (1980). *Eric Heiden: America's Olympic Golden Boy.* Ace Books: New York.

Ohno, A. A. (2002). *A Journey: The Autobiography of Apolo Anton Ohno.* Simon & Schuster: New York.

Ohno, A. (2011). *Zero Regrets: Be Greater Than Yesterday.* Atria Books: New York.

Publow, B. (1998). *Speed on Skates: A Complete Technique, Training and Racing Guide for In-Line and Ice Skaters.* Human Kinetics: Champaign, Illinois.

Squash

Squash might be the most popular sport in the world that does not seem to get the respect it deserves. More than 25 million people identify as regular squash players, from Australia to South Asia to North America and to Western Europe. National governing bodies run the sport well. Squash athletes compete locally and globally, recreationally and competitively. Despite these achievements, squash cannot seem to land a place at the Olympics despite trying year after year for inclusion. It cannot land any sort of regular broadcast deal, instead relying on ways to broadcast itself, mostly livestreaming online. The game itself, played in singles or doubles with rackets inside a room enclosed by walls on all sides, requires speed, endurance, and precision. A truly global game with 150 years of history, one can only assume that it will be just a matter of time until squash gets its reward. Then again, people have been saying that for 100 years.

HISTORICAL CONTEXT

The most fascinating aspect of squash is its social trajectory. The game found life in a prison, but today it owns a special place in the hearts of the wealthy. British imperialists introduced it to many of its subjects, but it was those former subjects who came to dominate the imperialists on the squash court.

Historians trace squash's birth to Fleet Prison in 1782 England. A version of handball already existed inside the prison walls. Prisoners fashioned rackets and used those walls to volley a ball. They called the game "rackets," a game that exists today. It is similar to squash, but it is not squash. It was more like squash's inspiration. Rackets proved so popular that when prisoners were discharged, they found ways to bring the game home with them. Prison workers, who observed the game, also brought it home, and eventually rackets was as popular outside the prison as inside it. By the 1830s rackets made its way to Harrow School in London. Players there modified the ball, putting extra holes in it, which changed how it reacted upon impact with the wall. The ball appeared to squash when it hit the wall before ricocheting. The new game was called "squash."

Both rackets and squash continued to grow during the second half of the 19th century. Courts with ceilings appeared in England in the 1840s. Charles Dickens described games played with rackets in his books. By 1890 lawn tennis captured England's imagination, but squash was not forgotten. In his book *The Badminton Library of Sports and Pastimes*, Great Britain's Duke of Beaufort, whose estate, Badminton, gave its name to another racket sport, mentions squash by name. Lawn and tennis clubs helped devise rules, but around the turn of the 20th century, clubs turned up devoted exclusively to squash. The first was in the United States, in the state of New Hampshire. That was in 1904. Three years later the Tennis, Rackets & Fives Association finalized rules for squash, most of which exist to this day with some minor tweaks.

Squash permanently surpassed rackets in popularity over the first few decades of the 20th century. The games are similar. Scoring is slightly different. The biggest difference is the rackets and the ball. Squash rackets have longer handles with narrower heads, and the ball plays slower than do racket balls, which makes playing the angles more vital to winning. One sports historian argued that squash overtook rackets not because it was vastly better but because the two sports were so similar that it was unnecessary for both to exist. One had to emerge, and it just so happened to be squash, although both are played today and enjoy various levels of popularity.

The first women's world championship was held in 1922, a number of years before the first men's world championship occurred. Around this period courts began to be built at a standard size (see "Dimensions of the Sport"). Courts often were built inside community centers and private clubs, which meant that in order to play squash, players had to be able to afford membership dues. That was the beginning of squash's growth among higher-income people, a trait that remains to this day. In the United States the median household income of squash players is $300,000 with a net worth exceeding $1 million. According to U.S. Squash, the governing body of squash in the United States, 98 percent of U.S. squash players have college degrees, compared with just 34 percent of the overall population.

GLOBALIZATION

The British spread squash throughout the globe as they spread so many other sports: through colonialism and imperialism. They introduced squash to the following regions: South Asia, North America, Oceania (Australia and New Zealand), and parts of the African continent.

Countries reacted differently to the sport. In the United States, for example, players sometimes had to choose between pursuing squash or racquetball because the courts are slightly different. Playing racquetball in a squash court or playing squash in a racquetball court could jeopardize the authenticity of both games. It also required them to buy different rackets and balls. Therefore, the two games could not develop at an equal pace. If a local community center built a squash court, its members would choose to play squash because there was no opportunity to play racquetball.

WHERE IT'S PLAYED TODAY

Squash remains popular around the world. As of 2020, the four top-ranked players in the world (women's, men's, and junior players) were from England, Egypt, France, and Malaysia, while Pakistan remained the country with the most distinguished and decorated squash legacy. World championships have been hosted in Australia, Canada, the Cayman Islands, Egypt, Hong Kong, Germany, Qatar, South Africa, and many other countries.

The United States boasts a healthy relationship between squash and its universities. More than 200 U.S. colleges have squash courts on campus, which both domestic and international students enjoy. More than 70 universities have men's teams and nearly 50 have women's teams. South America also has a growing squash presence, with athletes from Argentina, Brazil, and other nations performing well at regional events, such as the Pan-American Games, where Argentina's Robertino Pezzota won a bronze medal.

ECONOMICS AND MEDIA

In 2018 the Professional Squash Association awarded total prize money of $3.8 million to its men's players and $2.6 million to its women's players. Squash fans applauded the PSA for its 31 increase in pay to women from just one year earlier while acknowledging it was still 32 percent less than the men. The top men's player earned about $275,000. In setting up purses and awards, the PSA chose to spread winnings around rather than make it so top heavy that the best players earned millions while the middle and lesser players could barely afford a living. They tried to look at the big picture: still let the top players earn a comfortable living while providing enough money in the middle and the bottom so that all players on the tour could focus their time on the game, make a career out of it and, hopefully, help grow the sport. Players, especially the most successful ones, supplement their incomes through product endorsements, including rackets and protective gear.

When it comes to the less-visible sports in the world, squash officials are among the hardest promoters and marketers. They work tirelessly to increase the visibility of their game, whether in their attempts to get squash into the Olympics (so far unsuccessful) or to deliver the product to its fans. To help, they have aggressively built ways to view professional squash online through a number of livestreaming options. If television networks will not compete to broadcast squash, then squash will broadcast itself and take the sport directly to fans.

DIMENSIONS OF THE SPORT

Squash courts are 6.4 meters wide by 9.75 meters long by at least 5.7 meters high. The height is to provide for adequate lighting and may be higher than 5.7. Games are played to 11 points, called PAR (point-a-rally). Either the server or the receiver can score a point on a rally.

Another way of playing is games to 9 PARs, but in games to 9, players can only score by winning rallies in which they were the server. On the serve the server must keep at least one foot inside the serving box and hit the ball above the service line on the front wall.

IMPORTANT FIGURES

Maria Toorpakai loved sports, but as a girl in Pakistan, a country under threat from the Taliban, sports were considered an unacceptable activity with dangerous consequences for women. With her parents' blessing she disguised herself as a boy and participated in powerlifting. She turned to squash in 2002 at the age of 12 and came out as a girl since the sport required a birth certificate.

She excelled, turning professional in 2006 at 16. Despite great success and national awards, she went into hiding for three years shortly after turning pro to hide from the Taliban, which disapproved of a woman competing in sports. Finally, in 2011 she made her way to Canada to live and train in squash. She now competes internationally.

POP CULTURE

When director James Cameron's film *Titanic* debuted in 1997, critics expected a box-office disaster beset by production drama and massive budget overruns. Instead it became the most financially successful film in history and won 11 Academy Awards. The docudrama included British actor Bernard Fox playing an elderly, slightly drunk, and situationally clueless passenger named Archibald Gracie, who was concerned about getting back to a party as the legendary ship began to sink. In reality Gracie, who did indulge himself on the ship, was not elderly, British, or clueless. Colonel Archibald Gracie of the New York National Guard was a historian and real-estate investor. He also played squash.

He was scheduled to play squash on the Titanic the day it sank. Available only to first-class passengers, the Titanic's squash court cost 50 cents to reserve for one hour. Gracie, who cared deeply about fitness, wrote that he intended to use squash aboard the Titanic to reengage his fitness after a couple of days of partying. Of course, he never got to play aboard the ship. He did, however, manage to survive its sinking despite being one of its many passengers who went into the water rather than onto a lifeboat, and once in the water he helped at least one other passenger onto a piece of debris in order to await rescue—hardly the bumbling partier as he was portrayed to be in Cameron's film.

Alas, Gracie did not survive long after his rescue. He wrote about his experience in one of the more popular books published by survivors, but he was diabetic, and in 1912 medical care was not what it is today. In December 1912 in New York, about eight months after Titanic sank, Gracie died at age 54 from health-related complications tied to diabetes and injuries sustained the night Titanic went down. He was the first adult survivor of Titanic to die. According to the *New York Times*'s 1912 obituary of Gracie, some of his last words, spoken in delirium, were, "We must get them into the boats. We must get them all into the boats" (*New York Times* 1912, 1).

SCANDALS

The squash community erupted in anger in May 2019 when a club hosting a women's tournament in Spain awarded the top performers with women's hygiene products and sex toys along with trophies. No one individual stepped forward to claim responsibility for these prizes as the winner, runner-up, and third- and fourth-place finishers grew furious upon discovering them. Calling the prizes sexist, among other things, the athletes made sure everyone knew what had happened.

Local media supported the athletes, calling the prizes degrading. The event organizer, Club Squash Oviedo (CSO), half-heartedly apologized and said it did not mean to offend anyone. However, after the Royal Spanish Squad Federation took the matter to the Asturian Institute of Women, an agency that represents the European Union in matters of gender equity, CSO canceled all their organized squash events for the remainder of the year, and three people resigned.

POLITICS

Squash athletes are sick and tired of feeling disrespected, and they do not want to take it any longer. They petitioned the International Olympic Committee (IOC) for inclusion at the 2012 Games in London and were denied. Then they applied for the 2016 Rio de Janeiro Games and were denied again. And then they were denied a third time for inclusion at the 2020 Games that were scheduled for Japan before the COVID-19 pandemic forced the event's postponement. Meanwhile, the IOC either approved or was strongly considering approval of the following events for inclusion or exhibition status: break dancing, climbing, karate, kite surfing, rugby, skateboarding, and surfboarding.

Some squash athletes and administrators have grown so frustrated that they are starting to talk about legal action. Although a lawsuit would almost certainly go nowhere—the IOC is under no legal obligation to include any sport—squash's frustration is understandable. The game is played by millions and has taken steps to achieve the regional oversight that the IOC requires of all of it sports. Asked British squash player Nick Matthew, "Can the sport take the IOC to court over past bids? . . . It's very frustrating, and I don't see anything that will change if we carry on doing the same things" (Morgan and Gilmour 2019).

PATRIOTISM AND NATIONAL PRIDE

Nicol David has given her fellow Malaysians reason to take pride in their place in the sport of squash. For decades squash has thrived in Malaysia. The country consistently produces some of the world's best players. It has hosted the world championships six times.

David took their pride to a new level when in August 2006 she became the top-ranked women's squash player in the world. She held the top ranking for a staggering 108 consecutive months, until September 2015. It was the longest any squash player in any gender or age class has consecutively held the world's top ranking. She also has won gold at the Squash World Championships eight times, a squash record.

Timeline

1148 – The French begin to play *la paume*, which loosely translates to "the palm," a game in which a ball is hit against a wall with one's hand.

1782 – In England's Fleet Prison, a game played by prisoners to pass time, "rackets," like handball but with a racket, is so appealing that the British begin to play it outside of the prison.

1822 – Some records indicate Fleet inmate Robert Mackey as the first rackets "champion."

1830 – Rackets makes its way to Harrow School in London, where students alter the ball in a way that causes it to "squash" upon impact with the wall, which dramatically alters the game's strategy.

1836 – Charles Dickens publishes *The Pickwick Papers*, which includes a scene in which prisoners play rackets.

1840s – The first racket courts built with ceilings begin to appear in England.

1884 – The first squash court in North America, in Concord, New Hampshire, USA, opens.

1890 – Great Britain's Duke of Beaufort, whose estate, Badminton, gave its name to another racket sport, mentions squash in his book, *The Badminton Library of Sports and Pastimes*.

1904 – The U.S. Squash Rackets Association, today known as USA Squash, is founded as the world's first national organization dedicated exclusively to squash.

1907 – In a crucial moment for squash, the Tennis, Rackets & Fives Association finalizes rules for squash that combine all three sports.

1912 – A squash court permanently sets up home at the bottom of the Atlantic Ocean when it goes down with the RMS *Titanic*. The court was available to first-class passengers.

1922 – The Women's British Open, then considered the de facto world championship, is played for the first time.

1923 – The first squash amateur championship is held in England, prompting one writer to predict—correctly, to some degree—that its popularity would overtake that of rackets.

1924 – Squash officials begin discussions about standardizing court sizes.

1930s – British imperialists introduce squash to India, including the region that becomes the independent nation of Pakistan in 1947.

1934 – The Squash Rackets Association of Australia forms about 20 years after the sport has entered the region.

1948 – Stanley W. Pearson Jr., wins the U.S. Squash Championship, an event won six times by his father between 1915 and 1923.

1960 – A non-Briton wins the Women's British Open for the first time.

1966 – Australia, Canada, Great Britain, India, New Zealand, Pakistan, South Africa, United Arab Republic, and the United States agree to form the International Squash Rackets Association.

1975 – The Professional Squash Association forms in Leeds, England. Today it governs women's and men's professional tours and oversees world rankings.

1987 – Pakistan's Jansher Khan wins the first of his record eight men's World Squash Championships.

1995 – Squash debuts at the Pan-American Games.

2000 – The new double-yellow-dot ball, which slows the game and bounces less than other balls, becomes the new standard for competitive squash play.

2006 – Malaysia's Nicol David earns the world's number-one women's ranking, a spot she holds until 2015, a record 108 consecutive months.

2012 – Squash officials try, and fail, to earn inclusion at the Olympics, the first of three consecutive Olympics in which the IOC says no to squash.

2018 – Squash debuts as a demonstration sport at the Summer Youth Olympics.

See also: Badminton; Surfing; Tennis.

Further Reading

Assaiante, P. and Zug, J. (2012). *Run to the Roar: Coaching to Overcome Fear.* Portfolio: New York.

Correa, J. (2015). *Creating the Ultimate Squash Player: Discover the Secrets Used by the Best Professional Squash Players and Coaches to Improve Your Conditioning, Nutrition, and Mental Toughness.* CreateSpace Independent Publishing Platform: Scotts Valley, California.

Gilmour, R. (2017). *Jahangir Khan 555: The Untold Story Behind Squash's Invincible Champion and Sports Greatest Unbeaten Run.* Pitch Publishing: Sussex, United Kingdom.

Millman, R. and Morque, G. (2006). *Raising Big Smiling Squash Kids: The Complete Roadmap for Junior Squash.* Mansion Grove House: Austin, Texas.

Morgan, T. and Gilmour, R. (2019). "Squash 'Could Launch Legal Battle' over Olympic Snub in Favour of Breakdancing." *The Telegraph*, Feb. 21, 2019. https://www.telegraph.co.uk/squash/2019/02/21/squash-could-launch-legal-battle-olympic-snub-favour-breakdancing.

Nayar, J. (2020). *Lucky-Anil Nayar's Story: A Portrait of a Legendary Squash Champion.* Five Rivers Press: Brossard, Quebec, Canada.

New York Times (1912). "Col. Gracie Dies, Haunted by Titanic: 'We Must Get Them All in the Boats,' Last Words of the Man Who Helped Save Many." *New York Times*, Dec. 5, 1912, 1.

Toorpakai, M. and Holstein, K. (2016). *A Different Kind of Daughter: The Girl Who Hid from the Taliban in Plain Sight.* Twelve: New York.

Willstrop, J. and Gilmour, R. (2012). *Shot and a Ghost: A Year in the Brutal World of Professional Squash.* CPI Group: Croydon, England.

Zug, J. (2003). *Squash: A History of the Game.* Scribner: New York.

Sumo

Sumo wrestling is one of the most recognizable sports in the world. Its competitors, massive in size and weight, stand across from each other wearing almost nothing. They wrestle, each trying to force the other out of the ring. Nothing else, not even comparable sports such as wrestling or mixed martial arts, looks quite like it. A survey taken in the 1980s found that American sports fans, when shown a photo of different athletes in their sport-appropriate uniforms, more successfully identified sumo than any other sport, including those popular in their own country, like baseball and American football. This matters for sumo because sumo

In recent years the Japanese sport of sumo has been beset by scandal, but the sport's 1500-year history assures its place in Japanese culture. (J. Henning Buchholz/ Dreamstime.com)

takes place almost exclusively in Japan, one of the most industrialized nations on earth but one with just 1.7 percent of the earth's population. Everyone, it seems, knows what a sumo wrestler looks like and has a general idea of how the sport works. Sumo wrestling has a historic place in Japanese culture, a place that has been sullied in recent years as the outside world learns more about the sport's inner workings, from training to the treatment of young competitors. Still, the sport perseveres. Whether it chooses to adapt to modern times—and whether it should adapt or even wants to adapt—remains a matter that is yet to be decided.

HISTORICAL CONTEXT

Japan established sumo as its national sport in 1909, but the sport itself dates back at least 1,500 years. A popular form of leisure and entertainment among its consumers, sumo, similar to lacrosse, once was used in rituals to stimulate agriculture, spirituality, and personal growth. However, sumo differs from lacrosse because of how early it became an organized sport with governing bodies. Various sumo organizations and historians have stated that sumo was the world's first organized sport. Sumo became professionalized during the 17th century, during Japan's Edo period, when Sumo tournaments were held as fundraising events for government or charitable causes.

As with many sports that date back centuries, sumo's popularity grew under the watchful eye of a monarchy. Emperor Tenmu helped Japan become an empire in the 7th century. From there, tales emerged of sumo matches taking place to commemorate ceremonial moments. The Japanese word *sumo* translates in English to "also," but spelled with Chinese characters, sumo means "mutual bruising." This suggests that sumo's origins come from a mix of Japanese, Mongolian, Chinese, and Korean wrestling, and that the sport had a gradual migration before finding a cultural and historical home in Japan. To this day Mongolia remains one of the most dominant countries for producing world-class wrestlers.

The Japan Sumo Association, housed in Tokyo, formed in 1925 when organizations from Tokyo and Osaka merged. The oldest international amateur sumo championships date to 1915. Competitors in amateur sumo came from across the world, but the most common countries were those nearest Japan or with strong wrestling histories, including Russia, Mongolia, and Greece. Today, the International Sumo Federation is recognized by the International Olympic Committee and says it has members from 87 countries.

Athletes who want to compete in sumo professionally become part of a *heya* (or "stable")—groups of competitors who live and train together. Higher-ranked wrestlers earn certain social privileges, such as having less experienced and less successful wrestlers cook for them. They eat large amounts of food to gain weight and sleep right after eating—considered by dieticians as a cause of digestive problems—to maximize weight gain. Estimates vary, but the average sumo wrestler weighs 148 kilograms (326 pounds) and stands about 6 feet tall (182 centimeters).

GLOBALIZATION

The most notable global expansion of sumo is among women sumo wrestlers. Women are banned from competing in professional Japanese sumo. Not only that, they are banned from even setting foot in some *dohyo* (see "Dimensions of the Sport"). In 2018 a local mayor was giving a speech when he collapsed after suffering a brain hemorrhage. When female medical professionals rushed to his aid, a referee ordered them out of the ring. The Japan Sumo Association apologized for the referee's behavior but made no effort to change the sport's rules.

The expansion of women's sumo has taken place mostly at the amateur level, and while competitors come from all over the world, many events are still held in Japan. Championships are held in Japan as well as other countries, including Russia and the United States. The fourth International Women's Sumo Invitational Championship, held in Osaka, Japan, in 2018, included women from Japan, Hong Kong, Thailand, Taiwan, and Mongolia. Events were held in five classes. All women were required to compete as amateurs because of Japan's professional gender restrictions.

WHERE IT'S PLAYED TODAY

Nearly all sumo happens in Japan, although the International Sumo Federation says its membership includes wrestlers from 87 countries. Events are held throughout the world, but the prestigious events, as well as events with the most talented pools of competitors, take place in Japan.

Outside of Japan one of sumo's more popular destinations is Hawaii, the Polynesian island that became the 50th state of the United States in 1959. Two Hawaiians earned the rank of *yokozuna*—sumo's highest rank—in the 1990s. As recently as 2018 sumo was a youth sport in Hawaii for children ages 5 to 15.

ECONOMICS AND MEDIA

At the peak of his career, Hakuhō made $400,000 annual from sumo. That amount did not include additional income he earned through endorsements. Sumo wrestlers also earn money from *kenshokin*—prize money offered by companies to win specific bouts or matches. This practice is similar to that of professional golf, in which companies sponsor specific tournaments or events and reward victors with cash prizes beyond their typical earnings.

Broadcasting network Nippon Hōsō Kyōkai (NHK, also known as the Japan Broadcasting Corporation in English-speaking countries) has carried sumo tournaments since 1953. In the United States, the ABC network's defunct sports-television show *Wide World of Sports* introduced many viewers to sumo when it began running highlights of the sport.

The sport itself has struggled in recent years to attract new participants. At one point, administrators of the sport hoped it might someday join the Olympics, but now they can barely find enough young people to compete and sustain sumo's long-term health. In 2011 just 60 people applied to train as wrestlers. That number fell to 55 in 2012. In 2018 the Japan Sumo Association said no one had applied to join professional sumo ahead of a major tournament.

DIMENSIONS OF THE SPORT

Professional sumo wrestlers, called *rikishi*, are ranked, or seeded, by the number of matches they win. There are five designations: the lowest, *maegashira*, are considered not ranked; *komusubi*, the lowest ranked sumos, struggle to maintain their status because once they achieve *komusubi* they compete against higher-ranked sumos; the rank of *sekiwake* is reserved for sumos who have won at least 30 matches; 33 wins earns a sumo the rank of *ozeki*, but the rank usually is only temporarily because a loss or two can send them back down to *sekiwake*. The highest rank, *yokozuna*, has been earned less than 100 times since it was first achieved in the early 17th century. Wrestlers Taihō and Hakuhō both earned the rank of *yokozuna*.

Sumo matches take place in a *dohyo*, a circle 4.55 meters in diameter that is surrounded by bales of straw. The circle is within a 6.7- by 6.7-meter square that is built atop a clay platform. A 25-centimeter strip of dirt, known as "snake eyes" sand, surrounds the ring to help judges determine whether a sumo has been pushed out or has stepped out of the ring.

A sumo match generally is won in either of two ways: by forcing an opponent out of the ring, or by forcing the opponent to touch the ring with a part of the body other than the feet. Matches have no time limits, and while they sometimes can last a few minutes, they often last just a few seconds because of the disparity between the skill and size of the athletes. A tournament lasts up to 15 days.

IMPORTANT FIGURES

Poor Chiyonfuji Mitsugu. He was a *yokozuna* and one of the greatest sumos of his era. Unfortunately, he had the misfortune of timing his career around the same time as Taihō's. Chiyonfuji won 31 tournament championships; Taihō won 32. Chiyonfuji did have one thing going for him, however: longevity. His career lasted until his late 30s—well past the usual retirement age for most *yokozuna*. Even Taihō bowed out at the age of 30.

From his youngest moment, American Emanuel Yarbrough stood out. A native of New Jersey, Yarbrough stood 6 feet 8 and weighed between 600 and 800 pounds. He was also athletic, a standout wrestler. It was as if he was made to be a sumo. Turns out, he was pretty good at it. Although he did not have a long career, Yarbrough, who held the title of world's heaviest living athlete according to Guinness World Records, won the World Amateur Sumo Championship in 1995 at age 31.

Yet few could compare to Taihō Kōki. The crowd applauded when, in March 2013, Hakuhō Shō had won yet another sumo championship. Then Hakuhō did something unexpected. He asked the crowd for a moment of silence. Less than two months earlier, one of Hakuhō's mentors, Taihō Kōki, died at the age of 72. Taihō was more than a retired sumo wrestler. Japan has plenty of those. Many, including Hakuhō, considered Taihō the greatest sumo ever. From 1960 to 1971 Taihō won 32 championships—and between 1968 and 1969 he won 45 consecutive matches. Hakukō would go on to win 33 championships, breaking Taihō's record, and Hakukō also set the record for most match wins, but Taihō was still the greatest.

Children loved Taihō. Taihō loved sumo. He remained in the sport long after he retired. He opened his own training stable, assisted in the curation of sumo history, and contributed to the sport's administration. In 2009 he became the first sumo to receive the Person of Cultural Merit, an honor bestowed by Japan upon those who have made significant cultural contributions.

POP CULTURE

In Japan, sumo ranks among the most historic of sports rituals. It carries rich meanings and instills cultural pride. Although an appreciation for sumo extends beyond Japan, recent art in Western Europe and the United States—particularly the motion-picture and entertainment industries—has disrespectfully appropriated sumo for its own uses, including moments of humor, nationalism, and commentary on body image.

From 1992 and 1996, the World Wrestling Federation (now World Wrestling Entertainment) employed Rodney Anoa'i, an American of Samoan heritage, to portray the character Yokozuna. Yokozuna, named after the highest ranking a sumo wrestler can achieve, was billed as a Japanese sumo wrestler who weighed more than 500 pounds and was guided to the ring by Mr. Fuji, another American portraying an "evil" Japanese intruder.

The 2002 movie *Austin Powers in Goldmember* included a character named Fat Bastard, portrayed by the actor Mike Myers, who served as a henchman for the movie's antagonist while moonlighting as a sumo wrestler. Fat Bastard, who suffered from extreme flatulence and expressed interest in eating babies, often revealed an emotional side, including the revelation that he ate to hide emotional trauma.

A late-2016 television commercial produced by the insurance company GEICO featured a sumo wrestler who had become a figure skater. The wrestler gingerly skated around the ice rink performing moves such as the "baby bird." A couple of months after its debut, the trade publication *Ad Week* found GEICO's sumo ad among the most digitally engaging on the internet, meaning social-media users were sharing the ad on their social-media feeds.

SCANDALS

Japanese sumo stables have long been known to engage in mentally and physically abusive practices against younger, less experienced, and less successful competitors. During practices, senior wrestlers beat other wrestlers across the back with bamboo sticks called *shinai* to correct poor form or technique. In 2007 this practice led to the death of 17-year-old Takashi Saito. The stable master moved beyond using just shinai. Saito was found to have been beaten with a metal baseball bat and beer bottle and to have received cigarette burns.

Another scandal arrived in 2011, when multiple wrestlers were found to have rigged matches—won or lost on purpose to increase gambling profits. As a result, the Japan Sumo Association canceled a tournament, and the local channel that broadcast the tournament had to find something else to fill 15 days of programming.

Matters got even worse in 2018, when every Japanese sumo wrestler submitted to questioning from the sport's officials about harassment and violence within sumo. The inquiry was sparked by a grand champion's forced retirement following his attack on a junior wrestler.

POLITICS

Sumo cannot seem to get away from politics and controversy. As detailed earlier, sumo has been used for agricultural and spiritual fulfillment, as a form of entertainment for royalty and other political figures, to boost Japanese national pride, as an arena to contest gender roles, and most recently as an example of changing cultural norms—namely, new attitudes toward confronting hazing and other legalized forms of assault.

PATRIOTISM AND NATIONAL PRIDE

Japanese Americans, prior to World War II, took as much pride in sumo wrestling as the Japanese did. However, following the war and the American internment along the West Coast of Japanese Americans, many began to distance themselves from the sport. Looking to prove themselves as Americans, some abandoned sumo as a form of entertainment in favor of what they saw as more "American" activities, such as baseball, another American sport that is popular in Japan.

Around 1870 American professor Horace Wilson, working in Tokyo, had introduced some Japanese people to baseball. Slowly but passionately some Japanese citizens took a liking to baseball. Games were organized in local neighborhoods, and clubs began to form. By 1920 Japan fielded its first professional team and, by 1936, its first professional league. Today it is one of the few countries in the world, along with the United States, to field collegiate baseball teams, and Japanese professional baseball is considered the second most competitive league in the world after the United States' Major League Baseball.

Nevertheless, baseball does not have a comparable historical underpinning to sumo. Baseball is fun; sumo reflects history and culture. For example, in the mid-19th through the early 20th centuries, the Japanese used sumo, as well as other symbols such as cherry blossoms and Mount Fuji, as examples of Japanese exceptionalism. As the culture has grown and sumo has suffered through scandal, some have soured on the sport but still understand and appreciate its place in Japanese history.

Timeline

8th century – Japan's Imperial Court hosts a sumo tournament to ensure good harvests.

17th century – Sumo becomes one of the first professionalized sports in the world.

1853 – The Japanese hold a sumo exhibition for American commodore Matthew Perry, who is taken aback by the size of the athletes.

1909 – Japan's government names sumo its national sport.

1915 – The first Japan amateur solo championship is held.

1925 – The Japan Sumo Association forms in Tokyo.

1960 – Taihō Kōki begins an 11-year stretch in which he wins 32 championships, a record at that time.

1993 – American Rodney Anoa'i, performing under the stage name "Yokozuna" and portraying a sumo wrestler, wins the World Wrestling Federation's heavyweight championship. His act is criticized for being racist and stereotypical of Japanese people.

1995 – American Emanuel Yarbrough, who weighed about 700 pounds, wins sumo's world amateur championship.

2009 – Taihō becomes the first sumo to receive the Japanese Person of Cultural Merit award.

2015 – Hakuhō Shō wins his 33rd championship, breaking Taihō's record.

2018 – Every professional sumo wrestler in Japan is questioned by officials about the sport's long history of hazing and other forms of harassment.

See also: Golf; Lacrosse; Wrestling.

Further Reading

Benjamin, D. (2010). *Sumo: A Thinking Fan's Guide to Japan's National Sport.* Tuttle Publishing: Clarendon, Vermont.

Buckingham, D. (1994). *The Essential Guide to Sumo.* Bess Press: Honolulu, Hawaii.

Deninger, D. (2012). *Sports on Television: The How and Why behind What You See.* Routledge: Abingdon, England.

Hall, M. (1997). *The Big Book of Sumo: History, Practice, Ritual, Fight.* Stone Bridge Press: Berkeley, California.

Newton, Clyde (1995). *Dynamic Sumo.* Kodansha International: Tokyo, Japan.

Panek, M. (2011). *Big Happiness: The Life and Death of a Modern Hawaiian Warrior.* University of Hawaii Press: Honolulu.

Sargeant, J. A. (2012). *Sumo: The Sport and Tradition.* Tuttle Publishing: Clarendon, Vermont.

Sharnoff, L. and Matsuoka, L. (1993). *Grand Sumo: The Living Sport and Tradition.* Weatherhill: Boston.

Wenjen, M. (2019). *Sumo Joe.* Lee & Low Books Incorporated: New York.

Zabel, T. (2014). *Sumo Skills: Instructional Guide for Competitive Sumo.* Ozumo Academy Publishing: Mico, Texas.

Surfing

Surfing is one of the world's oldest physical activities but also one of its newest sports. It wasn't until just a half century ago that it transformed from a functional recreation to a financial competition.

So what is surfing? Simple. It's the process of standing on a board in the ocean while the waves move you around—and hopefully not falling off. If you do, grab your board and try again. Everything about surfing is designed to connect humans to nature, from the board, which originally came from trees, to the water, which comes from the earth, to the mind, which simultaneously requires calm and focus in order to be successful.

Today, surfing happens in many of the world's coastal regions. It began in ancient Polynesia and spread largely because the people who did it taught others. Surfing is something to be shared, like a life lesson. If that sounds emotionally deep, it should, because at its core, that is what surfing is supposed to be. The author William Finnegan said of surfers, "What are they doing this for? It's just pure. You're alone. That wave is so much bigger and stronger than you. You're always outnumbered. They always can crush you. And yet you're going to accept that and turn it into a little, brief, meaningless art form" (Finnegan 2016, 443).

HISTORICAL CONTEXT

While research suggests that the practice of surfing goes back at least 3,000 years, the claim to the first documentation of surfing is conflicted. One claim puts it in Tahiti around 1767. Another puts it in Hawaii around 1778 by the crew of British explorer James Cook. Wherever the more truthful account lies, what is almost certain is that surfing's rich, historical roots rest heavily with the Pacific Ocean.

Surfing was both cultural and functional throughout Polynesia. Boards could be used for fishing, but the creation of a board could also be a spiritual experience. The boards, likely carved from trees, were big and heavy, too, ranging from 10 to 25 feet long and weighing up to 200 pounds.

Interest in surfing spread in the late 19th century. One key reason was the ambassadorship of Hawaii's Duke Kahanamoku, a medal-winning Olympic swimmer who toured the world and taught people how to surf. He introduced surfing to both Australia and the United States, with U.S. representatives in turn teaching the sport to people in Southeast Asia.

Surfing wasn't professionalized until rather late, as modern sports go. Although surfers competed against one another for centuries, often for fun or bragging rights or local rewards, it became a professional global sport in the mid-1960s with the founding of the International Surfing Federation. Other leagues popped up over the years. Some stuck around for a while, while others did not. The Association of Surfing Professionals formed in 1983, rebranded in 2014 as the World Surf League, and today is the most recognized organization for the administration of professional surfers.

GLOBALIZATION

There are 195 countries in the world. Of them, 48 are land-locked nations, which means the remaining 147 give their citizens an opportunity to regularly surf. If one is going to measure surfing by how many people have turned professional, the result will be exceedingly small. Despite its visibility—its natural beauty makes it spectator-friendly—surfing remains a niche sport. The number of professional surfers rests somewhere in the thousands.

However, if one counts by the number of people who surf, including those who do it for recreational or pragmatic purposes, the total rises to between 23 and 35 million around the globe, depending on which estimates one trusts. It's a hard number to pin down. That is far less than some sports, such as cricket, basketball, and soccer, but more than others, like American football or yachting.

The spread of surfing from Polynesia and the western coast of South America to the rest of the world can be contained in one 60-plus-year period: from 1870 to the 1930s. The activity itself is at least 3,000 years old, and explorers first witnessed surfing at the dawn of the 18th century, but surfing became something that people wanted to try during that half-century boom period. Starting around 1870, Polynesians who loved surfing and wanted to share it with the world brought it to

Australia—Sydney first—and North America, particularly Southern California. From there it spread north up the coast of California. Then enthusiast James Jordan helped it migrate to the East Coast, demonstrating it off the coast of Virginia in 1912. From there, Americans who had gone to Hawaii to better learn to surf took it to the Indonesian province of Bali. All it took was a few acts of enthusiasm and goodwill to spark surfing's growth.

In modern times, the World Surf League annually hosts events in the following locations: Australia, Indonesia, Brazil, South Africa, Tahiti, California, France (mostly off its western and northern borders), Portugal, and Hawaii.

Surfing finally became an Olympic sport in 2020, but between its late start as a sport and the Olympics' recent changes to how a sport comes to be included, admission proved difficult. The Olympics, trying to add sports that are popular in many places all over the world, want at least 100 countries to belong to some sort of an oversight body before it will be considered for admission. In mid-2015, surfing's chances looked slim because only 85 countries had partnered with the International Surfing Association. Nevertheless, in August 2016 the International Olympic Committee (IOC) voted to admit surfing for the 2020 Games in Tokyo (postponed due to COVID-19). Competition will be limited to shortboard events only, with 20 women and 20 men selected to compete.

WHERE IT'S PLAYED TODAY

Coastal regions across the world—mostly those in warm-climate areas—welcome surfers. It remains popular in Polynesia, the western coast of South America and North America, and parts of Southeast Asia. South Africa and France also have become destination spots for surfers.

One unique spot is off the coast of Rhode Island, the smallest of the 50 United States. Long one of the nation's most historic states for sailing and boating, Rhode Island, along the country's eastern seaboard, in recent decades has also become a destination for surfing. Its most distinct trait is its range of water temperature, which fluctuates between 30 and 75 degrees depending on the time of year.

ECONOMICS AND MEDIA

A handful of the world's most successful professional surfers, such as Kelly Slater and Laird Hamilton, earn about $1 million a year exclusively from surfing, plus additional revenue from endorsements and other business endeavors. A second tier of 30 to 50 surfers might earn $250,000 to $500,000 annually, while most professional surfers do not earn anywhere near that much. Sponsorships are key in surfing because of the travel involved. Events are held all over the world, and sponsors help cover travel costs, among other expenses.

Surfboards, compared to overhead costs in other sports, cost surprisingly little, ranging from $150 up to about $1,000. Compare that to cycling, where a top-end bike might cost $15,000, or golf, where a set of professional-level clubs might run several thousand dollars.

> ### Hamilton Gets Back on the Board
>
> The morning of October 31, 2003, was like many others for Bethany Hamilton, then a 13-year-old surfer who lived in Hawaii. She went for a surf and thought that when she was done, she would likely check in on her father, who was scheduled to have a medical procedure that day on his knee. Those plans were waylaid when a 14-foot tiger shark attacked Hamilton, biting off her left arm below the shoulder. She went into shock as friends and family rushed her to the hospital. The injury, obviously, was bad, and survival was not guaranteed.
>
> Thanks to the doctors and nurses, Hamilton survived and recovered more quickly than anyone could have imagined. According to her book, *Soul Surfer: A True Story of Faith, Family, and Fighting to Get Back on the Board*, Hamilton first attempted to surf again just four weeks after the injury, using a specially constructed surfboard that would allow her to relearn balance. She now had just her right arm for balance. In January 2004, a little more than two months after the attack, Hamilton got back into competitive surfing.
>
> Her story caught the attention of the sporting world. She appeared on television shows across the world, such as the *Oprah Winfrey Show* and the *Ellen DeGeneres Show*, and in magazines ranging from *Time* to *People*. Capitalizing on the moment, she released her autobiography in 2004. It made numerous best-seller lists. In 2011 her story became a movie, also called *Soul Surfer*, and starred Academy Award–winner Helen Hunt and Dennis Quaid. That too proved successful, earning 2½ times at the box office what it cost to make. Hamilton also hit it big as a professional surfer, winning numerous competitions. As recently as 2016, 13 years after the shark attack, Hamilton finished third at the Fiji Women's Pro Event in the World Surf League.

DIMENSIONS OF THE SPORT

There are four primary categories of surfing: longboarding, shortboarding, bodyboarding, and stand-up paddleboarding (SUP).

Longboards work best for beginner surfers because they catch waves more easily than shorter boards do. Waves that typically would not propel a shortboard forward can be caught by longer boards. Surfers, according to their age and size, can select longboards that range from 9 to 14 feet. Longboards also create more stability for inexperienced surfers than do shortboards.

Shortboards work better inside barrels, which is the hollow part of a wave when it is breaking. For experienced surfers, shortboards are also easier to maneuver and may work better in certain bodies of water, depending on how the waves break. Most competitive surfers ride shortboards, which can run between 6 and 7 feet long.

Bodyboarding, sometimes called boogie boarding, calls for the rider to surf toward the shore on either the belly or knees. This was one of the forms of surfing witnessed by Cook's crew during the 18th century. Within bodyboarding are three forms of riding: dropknee, stand-up, and prone. Surfers who are bodyboarding in the prone position are riding on their stomach while strategically holding onto the board to assist with turning and managing the waves. SUP, meanwhile, is, relatively speaking, a newer professional approach that has surfers holding paddles while standing on their boards. They use the paddles to hurl themselves through the water.

IMPORTANT FIGURES

It can be said without hyperbole that Hawaiian Duke Kahanamoku is the most influential surfer the world has ever seen. A multiple-time winner of gold medals in swimming across multiple Olympic Games in the early 20th century, Kahanamoku's true passion was surfing. Serving as an advocate for the sport, he traveled to California and Australia to share his love. Through his advocacy, surfing spread across two continents. Those who learned from him in the United States in turn brought their skills to Southeast Asia, which means that because of Kahanamoku, surfing became a truly global sport. He died in 1968, but his legacy has lived on as he has been honored by the U.S. Postal Service and Google, among others, as well as through his nickname, "Father of Modern Surfing."

Margo Oberg had become the top-seeded women's surfer in all of California by the age of 15. So it only made sense several years later when, at the age of 22 in 1975, Oberg became the first professional women's surfer. As an amateur she began winning age-division championships before she had even become a teenager. She won the first three professional women's championships (1975–1977); then she won again in 1980, 1981, and 1983; and she was among the first to receive sponsorships. In 2000 *Sports Illustrated* named her one of the top 100 women's athletes of the 20th century.

Kelly Slater is the youngest man to ever earn the World Surf League championship. He's also the oldest. In all, he's won 11 championships, making him the most decorated men's professional surfer in the short history of the sport. Still an active competitor, there remains a chance that Slater will add to his decorated trophy case. In the meantime, he also has become a successful businessman within surfing. He is an author, an advocate for environmental issues, and a musician.

POP CULTURE

The 1966 documentary *Endless Summer*, meant to tell the story of two surfers in search of the perfect wave, ended up starting a movement. It began with a simple idea: if someone wanted to surf year-round and had the time and money, where would the person go? The movie's iconic soundtrack, supported by the song "The Theme to Endless Summer," coupled with its innovative, beautiful cinematography, led it to become a worldwide hit that was honored in 2002 with preservation by the U.S. National Film Registry.

Annette and Frankie. Frankie and Annette. In the 1960s no Hollywood duo came to symbolize surf and beach culture quite like American actors Annette Funicello and Frankie Avalon. Their movies were fun, whimsical—and loved by millions. Their films included *Beach Blanket Bingo*, *Bikini Beach*, and *Muscle Beach Party*, among others. Their message last well beyond their Hollywood prime. In 1987 the duo reunited for *Back to the Beach*, a comedy that blended fact and fiction without losing their playful legacy.

SCANDALS

Overcrowded beaches are not so much a scandal as they are a problem. Between 2004 and 2016, the number of Americans who identified as surfers increased by 40 percent, from 1.8 million to 2.5 million. The concern is that while the number of surfers has grown significantly, the earth can't grow more beaches and more waves. What may have been a quiet place to surf at dawn can now be overrun with "kooks," the term used for people who either are not good at surfing or do not follow surfing etiquette.

A longtime surfer told *Newsweek* magazine in 2016 that a beach that used to feel private 40 years ago now has between 30 and 60 people surfing it on any given morning. Any number of those people might be kooks, which means not only has it become more challenging to find a wave but one also has to be on the lookout for inexperienced surfers who could put others or themselves in danger.

PATRIOTISM AND NATIONAL PRIDE

The American state of Hawaii takes great pride in its surfing history and its role in developing the sport. Surfing developed in ancient Polynesia. Millennia later, Hawaii became its unofficial ambassador to the world. Hawaiians have such great love for the sport that when the IOC selected surfing for admission into the 2020 games, it led one journalist to ask whether Hawaii should be allowed to enter as its own country, rather than as part of the United States, because of its rich surfing heritage.

Timeline

1700 – European explorers witness surfing.

1767 – European explorers document surfing near Tahiti.

1778 – Surfing is documented by the crew of British explorer James Cook.

1821 – Scottish and German missionaries arrive in Hawaii and other Polynesian areas. They try to ban surfing and other cultural practices.

1885 – Young Hawaiian men, in California for school, surf in Santa Cruz and are believed by some to have introduced surfing to California.

1890 – Instructed by two Hawaiian students, John Wrightson becomes the first British surfer.

1907 – George Freeth, considered a pioneer in modern surfing, is hired to come to California and surf as part of a publicity stunt by a railroad company.

1912 – James Jordan introduces surfing to the eastern United States, mounting a board on the beach of Virginia Beach, Virginia.

1915 – Hawaiian Duke Kahanamoku introduces surfing to Australia during a visit.

1919 – Freeth dies during the flu pandemic that, from 1918 to 1920, wiped out between 3 and 5 percent of the world's population.

1930s – American surfers who learned the sport in Hawaii visit Bali, a province of Indonesia, starting the sport's growth along Asian coasts.

1959 – Columbia Pictures releases *Gidget,* a lighthearted film about a young woman's introduction to surfing in California. The movie is a hit and reignites Americans' interest in the sport.

1964 – Professional surfboarding begins. Both men and women compete, but only men earn the prize money required to be labeled a professional.

1975 – American Margo Oberg becomes the first female professional surfer after earning a $1,000 prize.

1980 – Australian Simon Anderson creates the thruster, a form of surfboard that provides surfers with more control, and revolutionizes professional surfing.

1992 – Kelly Slater wins the first of his 11 world surfing championships, a record.

2015 – William Finnegan releases his memoir *Barbarian Days: A Surfing Life* to rave reviews, with the *New York Times* writing, "There isn't a line the most mischievous critic could single out for ridicule."

See also: Olympics; Sailing and Yachting; Swimming.

Further Reading
Burkard, C. (2015). *High Tide: A Surf Odyssey.* Lannoo Publishers: Tielt, Belgium.
Finnegan, W. (2016). *Barbarian Days: A Surfing Life.* Penguin Books: New York.
Hamilton, B., Bundschuh, R., and Berk, S. (2006). *Soul Surfer: A True Story of Faith, Family, and Fighting to Get Back on the Board.* MTV Books: New York.
Hamilton, L. (2010). *Force of Nature: Mind, Body, Soul, and, of Course, Surfing.* Rodale Press: Emmaus, Pennsylvania.
Heimann, J. (2019). *Surfing: 1778–Today.* Taschen: Cologne, Germany.
Kenvin, R. (2014). *Surf Craft: Design and the Culture of Board Riding.* MIT Press: Cambridge, Massachusetts.
Slater, K. (2004). *Pipe Dreams: A Surfer's Journey.* It Books: New York.
Smith, C. (2014). *Welcome to Paradise, Now Go to Hell: A True Story of Violence, Corruption, and the Soul of Surfing.* It Books: New York.
Soderquist, E. and Burkard, C. (2009). *The California Surf Project.* Chronicle Books: San Francisco.
Warshaw, M. (2010). *The History of Surfing.* Chronicle Books: San Francisco.

Swimming

Millennia before the British built the first indoor pool, constructed explicitly for swimming, people swam. They swam in oceans and lakes, rivers and ponds, seas and gulfs. As with other remedial movements with human kinesiology—running and walking—the skill of swimming was first used to achieve practical goals. Then, because human nature is human nature, we became curious about not just who could swim, but who could swim fastest. Today swimming remains one of

American Katie Ledecky stunned the world when she won a gold medal at the 2012 London Olympics when she was just 15 years old. She went on to win more golds in her career and set numerous world records. (Zhukovsky/Dreamstime.com)

the most popular recreational and competitive athletic activities in the world. Five-year-olds learn to swim for safety and fun. Older athletes, their joints worn down by effort and time, swim to remain active, the water far more welcoming of their aching bodies than asphalt and pavement are. Some of the world's best athletes swim to test their limits and abilities, spending hours each day in a pool just to someday be able to say they were 1/100th of a second faster than anyone else in the world.

HISTORICAL CONTEXT

The key to discussing the history of swimming is to distinguish swimming from competitive swimming. Swimming—just the basic act of propelling oneself through the water—began out of necessity. No anthropologist or historian can pinpoint exactly when, but it was millennia ago. Learning how to move through water without drowning helped in the gathering of food and the process of migration. Even now, in the 21st century, adults enroll children in beginning swim classes not in the hopes of Olympic glory but so the children can learn to exist in and around water without drowning.

Competitive swimming began in earnest around the 1830s in Great Britain. The British, as they were wont to do during this era, laid out rules and built facilities. They took the whim out of competitive swimming—*OK, let's see who can swim quickest to that small island*—and made it proper: *We shall now swim exactly 100 meters.* Not coincidentally, the formalization of competitive swimming aligned almost to the moment with the 1837 coronation of Queen Victoria, whose 60-plus-year reign marked Great Britain with, among other things, etiquette and a required social behavior. Every activity came with steadfast rules, classist hierarchy, and devoted equipment and facilities. So it was only natural that in 1862 Great Britain constructed the first swimming pool built specifically for competition. Although crude by today's standards, conceptually it modestly resembled today's pools, which are 50 meters long by 25 meters wide. More than 250 swim clubs existed in England by the time the Amateur Swimming Association formed in 1880.

By 1898 similar swim federations appeared in France and Germany, and the American Athletic Union (AAU) oversaw swimming in the United States. At first nearly all swimmers competed using the breaststroke, a stroke that dates back thousands of years. The Cave of Swimmers, located near the Libyan-Egyptian border, includes cave paintings of swimmers who appear to be doing the breaststroke. A 16th-century German professor's book on swimming includes breaststroke instruction. The butterfly stroke, developed in 1933 by a University of Iowa swim coach, is an adaptation of the breaststroke. By then, however, another stroke, introduced just 30 years earlier by Australian Richmond Cavill, was quickly becoming the world's choice of swim stroke. Freestyle swimming—also known as the front crawl—while not as sustainable over long distances as the breaststroke, allowed for greater speed over short distances. It was a sprinter's stroke, and as competitions called for races as brief as 100 meters, a freestyle swimmer could dominate a breaststroke swimmer. It forced the sport to consider segregating events not just by distance but by stroke. Although breaststroke was rooted in earliest human history, competitive swimming history rests mostly with the front crawl.

The final of the four primary swim strokes, backstroke, also owns historical roots. It was most likely developed as a rest stroke. Swimmers who needed to travel a long distance, exhausted from constant motion, could roll onto their backs and continue swimming, therefore simultaneously resting and progressing toward their destinations. Backstroke was the second stroke adopted for Olympic competition, following the front crawl.

GLOBALIZATION

Recreational and social swimming never globalized. It was global from inception. Any culture constructed near a body of water had to learn how to swim to survive. Unlike so many other sports, the act of swimming did not spread through the world via Mongolian, European, or American imperialism.

Competitive swimming is an entirely different matter. Or rather, organized competitive swimming is a different matter, as many cultures hosted competitive swimming before British influence standardized the sport. The sport's rise timed impeccably with the first modern Olympic Games in Athens, Greece, in 1896. The first games included nine sports, including four events in swimming. One of those events was the 100-meter freestyle, which still exists today. Hungary's Alfréd Hajós won the first 100-meter gold. Greece's Ioannis Malokinis won gold in the "100 meters for sailors," an actual Olympic event that appeared only in the 1896 Games before being removed by the International Olympic Committee (IOC).

The IOC finally allowed women to compete in 1912, but countries such as Scotland, which had a history of introducing gender equity into sport well before the IOC got around to it, had created swimming federations for female competitors some 20 years earlier. Like male swimmers, female swimmers had a millennia-rich history of recreational swimming. The IOC granted women just 2 events in which to compete in 1912, compared to 7 for men. The genders finally received an equal number of events in 1976, when each competed in 13 Olympic events.

It is common in Olympic history for certain countries to dominate sports they invented until the rest of the world can catch up, such as Norway and speed skating or the United States and basketball. No such balance of power ever happened in swimming, since the activity of swimming had existed across the globe for thousands of years. By 1960 more than two dozen countries on four continents had won Olympic swimming medals. For example, in the 400-meter freestyle between the 1928 and 1932 Olympics, the six awarded medals (two golds, silvers, and bronze) went to six different swimmers from six different countries from four different continents: Argentina from South America, Australia, Japan from Asia, France and Sweden from Europe, and the United States from North America.

WHERE IT'S PLAYED TODAY

According to the sport's governing bodies, acting officials, and historians, recreational swimming takes place or has taken place on every country on earth that exists or once existed. Organized competitive swimming has taken place on every continent except Antarctica.

Swimming has been among the most popular sports at the African Games since the event was first held in 1965. The African Games have been held 13 times and have been hosted by nine different countries: Algeria, Egypt, Kenya, Morocco, Mozambique, Nigeria, Republic of the Congo, South Africa, and Zimbabwe. South Africa has dominated most of the swimming events. Out of 42 total events, South African women and men swimmers hold 27 African Games records. Egyptian swimmers hold seven records, Zimbabwean swimmers hold six, and Algerian swimmers hold two.

ECONOMICS AND MEDIA

Professional and Olympic swimmers make little money from the sport itself, instead earning the bulk of their income through product endorsements and other deals. The best American swimmers earn about $36,000 per year from USA Swimming, the sport's governing body in the United States. Some of America's top swimmers come from the country's university system; college swimmers receive just $21,000 per year, plus expenses, toward their international training. There are incentives. A gold medal comes with a $75,000 bonus. The world's best swimmers might earn more than $1 million per year thanks to endorsements. American Michael Phelps, the most successful swimmer in history (see "Important Figures"), possesses a net worth totaling $60 million. American Katie Ledecky has turned her success in the pool into career earnings topping $5 million.

International and local news media rarely cover swimming beyond the Olympics, World Championships, and each country's national championships, which sometimes count toward Olympic qualifying. One study showed that more articles are written each year in American newspapers about high school swimmers than Olympic-level swimmers, since the Olympics happen just once every four years, while every community in every town in the United States has at least one high school swim program.

DIMENSIONS OF THE SPORT

Competitive swimming pools are required to have 10 lanes, with each lane about 8 feet (2.5 meters) wide. The pools are 160 feet (50 meters) long and must have a minimum depth of at least two meters. Different types of strokes and events include backstroke, breaststroke, butterfly, freestyle, medleys (a combination of styles), and relays (team events in which the team members take turns). Distances

---

Wait—She's How Old?

Casual sports fans cheered during the 2012 London Summer Olympics as Katie Ledecky swam to a gold medal in the 800-meter freestyle. Not many people had heard of her, but that was not unusual in a sport like swimming, which only enters the mainstream consciousness once every four years, when the Olympics come around. She had the look and style of other swimmers who emerged from obscurity to reach Olympic glory, like American Janet Evans in 1988 or Australia's Dawn Fraser in 1956. Ledecky stood nearly six feet tall and, like all competitive swimmers, boasted a strong upper body and top physical conditioning.

Then broadcast announcers gave a few more details about Ledecky, and the world's collective jaw dropped in disbelief. Ledecky had set an American record, and this was her first first-place finish at any international event.

Most notably, she was only 15 years old.

Out of 174 American athletes in London, Ledecky was the youngest. Her career was just getting started. The following year at the World Championships she won four gold medals while setting two world records. In 2015 she won five more World Championship gold medals, and in her second Olympics. In 2016 in Rio de Janeiro, Brazil, Ledecky won another four golds while setting two world records. She was scheduled to compete at the 2020 Olympics in Japan before the COVID-19 pandemic forced their postponement. It was scheduled to be her third Olympic Games and yet she was still just 23 years old, an age at which some athletes are just beginning to hit their prime. As of this writing of this book, Ledecky has won a total of 20 Olympic and World Championship gold medals and set 14 world records in 4 different swimming events.

vary by stroke and event but may include 50 meters, 100 meters, 200 meters, 400 meters, 800 meters, and 1,500 meters. Relay events can be 4 by 50 meters, 4 by 100 meters, and 4 by 200 meters.

IMPORTANT FIGURES

Four decades separated the careers of Americans Mark Spitz and Michael Phelps, but their accomplishments in the pool assured that their names would forever be intertwined in the competitive swimming community. In 1972 Spitz pulled off what remains the greatest feat in Olympic Games history: seven events, seven gold medals, and seven world records. Phelps won eight gold medals in 2008, but unlike Spitz, he did not set world records in every event.

Still, Phelps etched his name in history alongside Spitz's, and by the time Phelps retired after the 2016 Olympics, his career achievements dwarfed every competitive swimmer in history: 23 gold medals among 28 medals total. Spitz retains his title as the most successfully Olympian ever to compete in one Olympic Games, while Phelps's total success remains unparalleled.

Dara Torres also achieved Olympic success, but then she won another victory that inspired the world. She finished her Olympic career in 2008 with 12 total medals, including 4 golds, plus 3 world records. What made Torres so remarkable was that she competed at the Olympics in 1984, 1988, and 1992, retired, returned to compete in the 2000 Games, stepped away to focus on family, and returned again in 2008 at the age of 41. She won 3 silver medals in 2008, when she was the oldest member on the U.S. swim team. She also volunteered for rigorous forms of performance-enhancing drug testing to preemptively dispel potential rumors that she cheated to get her aging body in shape. In 2012, at age 45, she tried again to qualify for the Olympics but fell just short, at which point she announced her retirement from the sport.

POP CULTURE

After boxers, the pool of most popular international athletes during the early 20th century came from swimming. The most successful male swimmers were tall and strong, which made them ideal to star as leading men in Hollywood movies. First came Johnny Weissmuller, the Austria-Hungary–born star who immigrated to the United States with his family at a young age. Weissmuller won three Olympic swimming medals at the 1924 Paris Games and two more in 1928 in Amsterdam.

Weissmuller needed something to do when his swimming career ended. Hollywood called, and Weissmuller went on to become one of the biggest celebrities in the world over the next 15 years. His big break came as the title character in the film *Tarzan the Ape Man*, based on the famous, heavily racist, imperialist books by British author Edgar Rice Burroughs. Weissmuller starred in 12 Tarzan movies between 1932 and 1948, earning $2 million—about $20 million by today's standards.

The same year Weissmuller debuted as Tarzan, Buster Crabbe won 400-meter freestyle gold at the 1932 Los Angeles Olympics. Weissmuller's flame burned hotter, but Crabbe's burned longer. After swimming Crabbe also turned to acting, and he proved a far better student of the craft than his swimming predecessor. He appeared in 113 films and television shows from the 1930s until 1982, the year before he died. His most famous roles came as the science fiction heroes Flash Gordon and Buck Rogers and in his portrayal of legendary American West outlaw Billy the Kid.

SCANDALS

Hungarian swimmer Katinka Hosszu and her husband, Shane Tusup, insisted their relationship was healthy. They met in 2008 while at college in the United States. By the 2016 Summer Olympics she had won three gold medals and nine first-place finishes at the world championships. The bigger story, however, was her relationship with Tusup, whom she asked to be her coach several years earlier during a career slump.

From the sidelines he screamed like a maniac, flexed his muscles, and bounced around like he was at a mixed martial arts event, not a swimming meet. His behavior and their vocally volatile public interactions overshadowed her success in the pool. International media fixated on their relationship. She won championships, but Tusup received as much attention as Hosszu. Media critics blasted sports journalists for not giving Hosszu enough credit, but their interactions truly had become a distracting spectacle. It did not last. In 2018 the two divorced, and in 2019 Hosszu won yet another world championship, this time in the 400-meter medley. "I wasn't scared at all," she told reporters. "As a woman, it is sometimes a bit different than [it is] for male athletes. Sometimes the coaches get more credit than the athletes" (Forde 2019).

PATRIOTISM AND NATIONAL PRIDE

Sun Yang filled his fellow Chinese citizens with pride in 2012 when he became the first from his country to win an Olympic gold medal in swimming. He won two, actually, in the 400- and 1,500-meter freestyles, and another in the 200 freestyle in 2016. So it came as no surprise in 2020 that his fans reacted with anger and disbelief when Sun received an eight-year suspension for a drug-testing violation. He will be 36 years old when the suspension ends and will have missed the 2021 and 2024 Olympics, plus much of the qualifying period for 2028, which means, mathematically, he will not be able to compete in another Olympics until 2032, at age 40.

Dara Torres's return at age 41 proved so exceptional that it was historic. Unless Sun can perform a similar feat—or have his suspension by the Court of Arbitration for Sport lifted early—his Olympic career is likely over. The announcement led his fans to social media to support him, search for holes in the Court's case, and defend him against accusers from around the world. Sun caused their patriotism to soar. A doping ban threatened to bring it crashing down.

Timeline

c. 800 BCE – The ancient Greek epic poems *The Iliad* and *The Odyssey* both contain references to swimming.

1837 – England becomes the first nation to classify swimming as a sport, and the National Swimming Society is formed.

1844 – Indigenous Americans, on a tour of England, bring the front crawl to Europe.

1862 – England builds the first swimming pool to be used primarily for competitive racing.

1875 – Great Britain's Matthew Webb becomes the first person to swim the 21-mile English Channel between the United Kingdom and France.

1892 – Scotland hosts the first women's swimming championship.

1896 – Men's swimming is included in the first modern Olympics.

1902 – Australian Richmond Cavill popularizes freestyle swimming.

1908 – The Fédération Internationale de Natation is formed.

1912 – Women's swimming becomes an Olympic sport.

1914 – Swimwear company Speedo is founded in Australia and becomes the most popular maker of swim gear in the world.

1924 – Weissmuller wins three Olympic gold swimming medals. He will win two more in 1928.

1932 – The success of the film *Tarzan the Ape Man* turns the actor who plays the title character, Weissmuller, into an international superstar.

1934 – University of Iowa swim coach David Armbruster modifies the breaststroke to create the butterfly stroke, which goes on to become an Olympic event.

1972 – Mark Spitz wins seven gold medals and sets seven world records at the Olympic Games in Munich, Germany.

2000 – Inge de Bruijn becomes the first woman from the Netherlands to be named *Swimming World* Women's Swimmer of the Year. She wins again in 2001.

2008 – Using a new type of swimsuit that reduces friction in water, swimmers from across the world set 70 world records in one year. The suits are banned in 2010.

2012 – American Katie Ledecky wins gold in the 800-meter freestyle as a 15-year-old.

2016 – Michael Phelps competes in his fourth and final Olympics and retires as the most decorated Olympian in history, with 28 medals, including 23 gold medals.

See also: Diving; Marathon; Track and Field.

Further Reading

Evans, J. (2007). *Janet Evans' Total Swimming*. Human Kinetics: Champaign, Illinois.

Forde, P. (2019). "Hungary's Katinka Hosszu Roared Back in 2019—and She's Not Done Yet." *Sports Illustrated*, Dec. 11, 2019. https://www.si.com/olympics/2019/12/11/katinka-hosszu-2019-season-husband-coach-shane-tusp-divorce.

Foster, R. (2008). *Mark Spitz: The Extraordinary Life of an Olympic Champion*. Santa Monica Press: Solana Beach, California.

Franklin, M. and Franklin, D. (2016). *Relentless Spirit: The Unconventional Raising of a Champion*. Dutton Books: New York.

Fury, D. and Brown, H. (2000). *Johnny Weissmuller: Twice the Hero*. The Artists' Press: White River, South Africa.

Knox, A. (2017). *Eat Right, Swim Faster*. FriesenPress: Victoria, British Columbia, Canada.

Phelps, M. (2012). *Beneath the Surface: My Story*. Skyhorse Publishing: New York.

Ransom, M. (2018). *Keep Calm and Swim to France: Tales of an English Channel Swimmer*. Self-published.

Walker, A. (2017). *Man vs. Ocean: One Man's Journey to Swim the World's Toughest Oceans*. John Blake Publishing: London.

Walker, S. (2016). *Where the Crazy People Swim: Outrageous Goals, Failure, and Success*. CreateSpace Independent Publishing Platform: Scotts Valley, California.

T

Tennis

Tennis is a social game that is played between two or four people at a time. Everyone holds a racket and uses it to strike a ball back and forth over a net. The opposing players face each other the whole time. Players track their opponents' movements: side to side, front to back. It is a game of anticipation, of trying to figure out where one's opponent cannot go. It is also a game of speed, power, endurance, and geometry. Culturally, it is a game that once represented class and opportunity. And it is a game of power. The one who controls the ball, who can fire it more than 100 miles per hour at a waiting opponent, is expected to win, while the person on the receiving end is expected to lose. Then the players swap roles and the person who was serving now has to receive. The game swings in favor of one of the players when the person without the power seizes control, or "breaks serve." Tennis, therefore, more than anything, is a metaphor for control over one's own outcomes.

HISTORICAL CONTEXT

This needs to be said up front: tennis belonged to the wealthy. Rich people created it, played it, and spread it. Other than France's King Francois I, European monarchies prevented commoners from playing it. Tennis originated in the 12th century in France. The French called out *tenez* (translation: "here you go" or "here it is") before service. Noted sportsperson King Henry VIII of England, who also had a hand in promoting bowling during his 16th-century reign, took to tennis and built a court at Hampton Palace in London. The court exists today as the oldest used court in the world.

The tennis we see today differs from the original game, which still exists in a handful of countries as "real tennis." Real tennis uses a corked ball, players use wood rackets, and if a ball bounces twice it does not necessarily result in a point for the opposing player. Real tennis so permeated royal life that Shakespeare included it in his play *Henry V*, when the character of Exeter says to Henry, "Tennis-balls, my liege."

Technically, the tennis we play and watch today is called "lawn tennis." Two friends, English lawyer and soldier Thomas Henry Gem and Spanish merchant Augurio Perera, created modern tennis over a period of years during the mid-19th century. They played it on a croquet lawn, and it became an instant sensation because it allowed "real tennis" players to enjoy the game outside. From the

Tennis can be played on one of three surfaces: hardcourt, grass, or clay, like the one shown here from Madrid, Spain. Pictured is Serena Williams, considered by many the greatest women's player ever. (Alberto Mihai/Dreamstime.com)

beginning it was played on a rectangular court, just as it is today, but the ball changed from wood and cork to one made of vulcanized rubber—a product of the Industrial Revolution that also impacted bowling and lacrosse.

A tennis fan who traveled to the present from the early 20th century would instantly recognize the game. Little about the rules, equipment, and court have changed, although improvements to equipment and athletic training significantly sped up the game. Tennis's biggest difference today from a century ago is the diversity of the players. Whereas tennis courts used to exist behind the gates of palace walls or exclusive clubs—a bastion of the wealthy—in many countries today they exist out in communities, where they were built to give recreational opportunities to nearby residents. For example, American Jimmy Connors grew up in the blue-collar town of East St. Louis, Illinois, in the 1950s and early 1960s. The Williams sisters—Serena, by any metric one of the greatest tennis players to ever live, and her older sister, Venus—were born in working-class Compton, California.

GLOBALIZATION

Tennis's origins have French, Spanish, and English (and therefore by default Australian and South African) influence, so it has always had global flavor. It came to the United States in the late 19th century. The world's four major professional tennis events take place on three separate continents: Europe boasts the

French Open (Paris) and Wimbledon (England); the Australian Open plays in Melbourne; and the U.S. Open takes place in New York.

Additionally, tennis has found growth in South America and parts of Asia. Beijing hosts the China Open, Tokyo hosts the Japan Open, and Seoul hosts the Hansol Korea Open, to name just a few. The Brasil Open takes place in São Paulo, the Chile Open takes place in Vina del Mar, and Copa Claro is held in Buenos Aires, Argentina. Tournaments are also held in Malaysia, Morocco, Qatar, Singapore, Thailand, United Arab Emirates, and other countries throughout the world.

WHERE IT'S PLAYED TODAY

Tennis takes place just about everywhere regardless of region or climate. In fact, a large portion of today's tennis courts are indoors, whereas lawn tennis used to be primarily an outside game. Tennis is played by people of varying socioeconomic backgrounds and all ages. Still, the professional circuit is dominated by players who grew up in affluent or middle-class homes. To excel, players need to pay for lessons, entries into tournaments, and equipment.

The four major women's and men's professional events are held in Australia (Australian Open), France (French Open), the United Kingdom (Wimbledon), and the United States (U.S. Open). For nearly a half century, World TeamTennis, a professional coed league, has existed in the United States, but it receives little media coverage and exists, at best, on the far fringes of professional team sports.

ECONOMICS AND MEDIA

Although the sport of tennis has opened up to different groups of people, it remains for many an expensive endeavor. Private tennis clubs in Western Europe, Australia, South Africa, and the United States charge thousands of dollars annually in membership fees.

Outdoor community courts usually are open to anyone and are free to use, but their condition varies from court to court. Some have cracks in the foundation, while others may have missing or damaged nets. Not all tennis clubs require upper-class incomes. Some charge by the hour for a chance to play on well-maintained courts.

The best professional tennis players are among the world's top-paid athletes. Switzerland's Roger Federer has earned more than $100 million in prize money during his career plus millions more through endorsements. Through 2018 Serena Williams had a net worth of $180 million.

Between 10,000 and 15,000 people list their careers annually as "professional tennis player." About half will make nothing or very little money throughout their careers because they will be unable to advance past the minor-league circuits. Players who reach and stay at the highest levels of women's and men's professional tennis easily can make more than $250,000 per year at bare minimum simply because of the amount of prize money offered, but not many players reach that level. Most who do reach that level will earn well over $1 million during their careers.

Because of the quantity of events, tennis tournaments are broadcast across various networks throughout the world. Most famously, the premium cable channel Home Box Office (HBO) carried coverage of England's Wimbledon (known also as "The Championships") from 1975 to 1999. Cable subscriptions in the 1980s were a luxury item and not as widespread as they are today, which allowed HBO to connect those with disposable incomes with tennis, a sport traditionally consumed by those with money to spend.

DIMENSIONS OF THE SPORT

For singles players, a tennis court is 27 feet wide by 78 feet long (39 feet on each side of the net). The playing area for doubles tennis is 36 feet wide—nine feet longer than the singles width. The back line is called the "baseline," and for singles player the sideline is called the "alleyline" (it's just "sideline" for doubles players). A service line is drawn 21 feet from both sides of the net.

Scoring goes as follows: point, game, set, match.

Point: A player earns a point upon winning a rally. The ball is put into play when one player serves into the opposing player's service court. The server gets two chances to serve into the service court; if the server fails both times, it is called a double fault and the receiving player receives a point. Once the ball is in play, the two players volley the ball back and forth over the net. A player wins a point by skillfully hitting so that the opponent cannot reach it before it bounces a second time, or if the opponent hits the ball out of bounds or into the net.

Game: A game is earned by winning four points, but they are not counted 1 through 4. Instead, they are counted 15, 30, 40, game. Some evidence points to this method of scoring being tied to the face of a clock, but there is no definitive proof. A game must be won by two points, so if a game is tied 40-40, the players keep playing until someone wins consecutive points.

Set: The first player to wins six games wins a set. A set must be won by two games, so if a set is tied five games apiece, the players keep playing until someone wins consecutive games.

Match: The first player to win two or three sets (depending on whether the players are playing two out of three or three out of five) wins the match.

To recap: If you win one rally, you win a point. You win a game by winning four points. You win a set by winning six games. You win a match by winning two or three sets, as applicable.

IMPORTANT FIGURES

Technically, the U.S. Tennis Association (USTA) did not tolerate racism. There was nothing in its rules that prohibited Althea Gibson, an African American woman born in South Carolina and raised in New York, from competing in the

U.S. Open. All she had to do to qualify for the Open was take part in tournaments at sanctioned events at tennis clubs across the region. Once she accumulated enough points, she could play in the Open.

Most of the clubs had white-only policies. Although she was allowed to play in the U.S. Open, she was not allowed to qualify for it. In 1950 a retired player wrote a letter admonishing the USTA and had it published in a popular tennis magazine. Under pressure, the USTA invited Gibson to play in the U.S. Open, where she won her first match and lost her second. Six years later she won the French Open. A year later—1957—she won Wimbledon and the U.S. Open, and in 1958, she won them again.

Martina Navratilova didn't just win more major titles than any tennis player in history. She helped change how women look at themselves as athletes. Her longtime friend and greatest rival, Chris Evert, exemplified the perception of how women were supposed to play tennis in the 1970s and look while doing it. Evert glided across the court, gently smiled for television cameras, and married the hunky star athlete.

Navratilova exemplified none of that—nor cared to. She relentlessly worked on her body, eventually publishing books on fitness. She ignored ridicule from fans and journalists who mocked her as not feminine enough, and in the 1980s she was one of the first openly gay elite athletes in the world. By the end of her 30-year professional tennis career, she had spent 332 weeks as the number-one women's player in the world and 237 weeks as the top-ranked doubles player. Between singles, doubles, and mixed doubles, Navratilova won 59 majors.

POP CULTURE

In 2016 one of the most popular music stars on the planet, Beyoncé, released her signature album *Lemonade*. The album was accompanied by a one-hour performance video on HBO and included the song "Sorry," about Beyoncé's husband cheating on her. The video included a cameo by the number-one women's tennis player in the world at the time, Serena Williams.

Williams, winner of 23 major singles championships and the only tennis player with lifetime accomplishment comparable to Navratilova's, moved beyond tennis and into pop culture thanks to her success and successful marketing. She graced the cover of *Sports Illustrated* in 2015 when the magazine named her its Sportsperson of the Year. A sports columnist claimed she had denigrated women's sports because she wore lace and high heels on the cover, but when it was revealed she picked out her own outfit, fans from across the world praised her for her self-confidence and condemned the columnist for his outdated worldview.

Williams has made nearly $200 million in her career, more than half through endorsement contracts with high-profile companies such as IBM, Pepsi, Chase Bank, Delta Airlines, and Nike. She also owns a share of the Miami Dolphins NFL franchise and owns and operates a clothing line for the Home Shopping Network—all this, plus nearly two dozen acting credits.

Chang Beats the Heat

Not even Michael Chang's father thought he had a chance.

Chang was just a teenager in 1989 when he advanced to the Round of 16 of the French Open, one of professional tennis's four major events. His opponent, Ivan Lendl, held the world's top men's ranking. So Chang's dad, an engineer, boarded a plane home for California because he had to get back to work, confident that there was no point to watch his son try to get by Lendl.

At first, Dad appeared correct. Lendl won the first two sets and needed to win just one more to win the match. Chang won the third, but then horrible cramps overtook both of his legs. No matter how many bananas he ate or how much water he drank, Chang could not recover his legs. He could have quit. Instead, he worked around his body by doing things that fans and his fellow players had never seen. He served underhanded, much to the delight of the crowd, who laughed and cheered in wonderment. He hit ridiculous lob shots that slowed the match down and let him use his legs less intensely.

Lendl, who later credited—and never begrudged—Chang for his tactics, fell apart mentally. It was clear he was unprepared for this type of match. Chang won the 4-hour, 37-minute match, which lasted an hour longer than the average 5-set men's tennis match. The crowd roared in celebration of Chang's 5-set victory after Lendl double-faulted on match point. Chang never won another major, but he did climb as high as number 2 in the world during his career. In all, Chang won 34 singles titles. None, however, was as memorable as that day in Paris against Lendl.

SCANDALS

Tennis would not be the professional sport it is today without the contributions of Billie Jean King, who played from 1968 to 1983. She was the first women's tennis player to earn $100,000 in prize money, but when she won the 1972 U.S. Open and realized her paycheck was $15,000 less than what the men's champion earned, she threatened to boycott the 1973 event. The U.S. Open gave in and became the first tennis event to offer equal prize money.

King helped organize women's tennis players into a union, the Women's Tennis Association, in a hotel room during the summer of 1973. The union drove raises to the prize money offered to women's tennis players. King also defeated Bobby Riggs, an openly chauvinistic, retired men's tennis player, in a highly publicized tennis match on national television, and when transgender athlete Renée Richards sued to be allowed to compete as a woman in the U.S. Open, King was one of the first to support her.

The real scandal was the inequitable treatment of women. Without King, it's difficult to imagine justice would have occurred as swiftly.

PATRIOTISM AND NATIONAL PRIDE

First, Andy Murray cheered when he won Wimbledon in 2013, then he showed respect to his opponent, then he lay on the ground and cried. He had become the first male Briton to win Wimbledon, Great Britain's signature tennis event, since 1936. If the Scot wasn't his nation's tennis hero after winning a gold medal at the 2012 Olympics in London, he certainly was now. In 2016 Murray won Wimbledon again.

Murray expanded his fan base around the same time period by becoming an advocate for gender equity in tennis, a sport notorious for its history of treating women unfairly. Murray, whose mother is a professional tennis coach, is notable because of how attuned he is to institutional misogyny and not just the public blunders that become media spectacles. For example, in 2017 at Wimbledon a reporter asked Murray how it felt to be playing Sam Querrey, "the first U.S. player to reach a major semifinal since 2009" (Hurrey 2017). Murray cut off the reporter to correct him. American Serena Williams had reached multiple semifinals. The reporter had only considered male players.

In 2016, while participating at the Summer Olympics in Rio de Janeiro, a reporter asked Murray about being the first athlete to win two tennis gold medals. Here, Murray replied that the Williams sisters—Venus and Serena—had won four each. That response drew the attention of another famous Briton, author J. K. Rowling, who wrote, "As if we needed more reasons to worship Andy Murray: he just reminded [journalist] John Inverdale that women are people, too" (Guarino 2016).

Timeline

1860s – Thomas Henry Gem and Augurio Perera develop lawn tennis in its modern form in Great Britain.

1881 – The U.S. Tennis Association is established.

1887 – Wimbledon, the world's best-known tennis tournament, is played for the first time in London.

1891 – The first French Open is played.

1900 – The first international tennis competition, later to be known as the Davis Cup, is played in Massachusetts.

1940–1945 – Wimbledon and the French Open cease operation during World War II.

1951 – Althea Gibson debuts at Wimbledon.

1953 – Margaret Connolly becomes the first woman to win the "Grand Slam"—all four major tennis events in a single year.

1967 – In what will mark the start of the end of the wood-racket era, the first metal racket is used. Graphite and fiberglass rackets are introduced in 1976.

2002 – Venus Williams earns the world's number-one ranking, while her sister Serena simultaneously earns number two.

2017 – Roger Federer wins his record eighth Wimbledon title, breaking the previous mark of seven held by Pete Sampras and William Renshaw.

See also: Bowling; Olympics; Squash.

Further Reading

Agassi, A. (2010). *Open: An Autobiography.* Vintage: New York.

Ashe, A. and Rampersad, A. (1994). *Days of Grace: A Memoir.* Ballantine Books: New York.

Fisher, M. J. (2009). *A Terrible Splendor: Three Extraordinary Men, a World Poised for War, and the Greatest Tennis Match Ever Played.* Crown Archetype: New York.

Gallwey, W. T. and Kleiman, Z. (1997). *The Inner Game of Tennis: The Classic Guide to the Mental Side of Peak Performance.* Random House: New York.

Guarino, K. (2016). "Andy Murray Corrects Reporter Who Forgot Women's Tennis." NBC Boston, Aug. 15, 2016. https://www.nbcboston.com/news/sports/andy-murray-corrects-a-reporter-reminds-him-womens-tennis-is-still-tennis/81927.

Hurrey, A. (2017). "Andy Murray Gives Journalist Short Shrift by Issuing Stern 'First Male Player' Correction." *The Telegraph*, July 13, 2017. https://www.telegraph.co.uk/tennis/2017/07/13/andy-murray-gives-journalist-short-shrift-issuing-stern-first.

McPhee, J. (2011). *Levels of the Game*. Farrar, Straus and Giroux: New York.

Navratilova, M. (1985). *Being Myself*. Grafton: London.

Wallace, D. F. (2016). *String Theory: David Foster Wallace on Tennis*. Library of America: New York.

Williams, S. (2010). *My Life: Queen of the Court*. Simon & Schuster: New York.

Track and Field

Track and field falls into the same category of ancient sporting events that includes sports such as weightlifting, swimming, and rowing. Such sports were discovered not for leisure or competitive purposes but out of a basic yearning to understand the human body. Who can run faster? Who can run farther? Who can throw something the farthest? Track and field brings together numerous skills, most notably running, throwing, and jumping. The "track" in track and field refers to the area where running events are contested, while the "field" refers to other areas, just off-track, where nonrunning events take place. Field events include throwing skills (javelin, shot put, and discus and hammer throwing); jumping skills (high jump, long jump, and triple jump); and an event called pole vault, in which athletes use a long pole to catapult themselves over a bar high in the air. Track and field is a sport appreciated throughout the world.

HISTORICAL CONTEXT

Organized track and field events first appeared during the ancient Olympic Games in Greece, in the 8th century BCE. The games continued into the 4th century CE until Roman emperor Theodosius I banned them. Track and field would not undergo a resurgence until the 1860s.

The formations of the Amateur Athletic Club (later Amateur Athletic Association) in the United Kingdom in 1866 and the Amateur Athletic Union in North America in 1887 reignited interests in competitive track and field and helped set the stage for the first modern Olympics in 1896 in Athens. From there, interest grew quickly, and in 1912 the International Amateur Athletic Federation (IAAF) formed to ensure that athletes maintained amateur status, to standardize rules, and to govern world records. The original 17 nations in the IAAF were Australia, Austria, Belgium, Canada, Chile, Denmark, Egypt, Finland, France, Germany, Great Britain, Greece, Hungary, Norway, Russia, Sweden, and the United States.

Track and field's amateurism helped keep commercialism and potential corruption out of the sport, but it also prevented many impoverished and lower-income people from competing. College teams and university clubs provided a breeding

In 1988 Florence Griffith Joyner set the 100 and 200 meter world records, both of which still stood as of 2020. She died in 1998 at the age of 38. (Jerry Coli/Dreamstime.com)

ground for track and field athletes to work on their crafts and compete against one another. In the early 20th century, college was a luxury reserved for the wealthy or the unusually gifted, while those without the means to go to college often went to work at a young age, unable to train or to even know whether they had athletic talent.

The International Olympic Committee (IOC) admitted women into the Olympics during the second games, 1900 in Paris, but only for tennis and golf. Women's track and field's first Olympic appearance happened in 1928 in the Netherlands. Without evidence, the IOC ruled after the 1928 Games that the 800 meters was too grueling for women, and it would not let them compete in any race longer than 200 meters until 1960. Frustrated but undeterred, more women joined the Fédération Sportive Féminine Internationale, a French-based organization founded in 1921 to create more athletic opportunities for women. In all, the FSFI staged four Women's Olympics, with the final one taking place in 1934 in London.

Title IX, an act of the U.S. Congress passed in 1972 that called, among other things, for equal funding for athletic opportunities for men and women when federal funding was involved, had a big impact on women's track and field. From 1972 to 1988, the first 16 years of Title IX, the men's world record in the 100 meters improved from 9.95 seconds to 9.92 seconds, an improvement of 0.004 percent. During the same period, with women finally receiving some semblance of athletic opportunity, the women's 100 record improved from 11.07 seconds to 10.49, a 5.3 percent improvement and just 0.57 seconds behind the men's record.

GLOBALIZATION

In the history of one of the world's oldest sports, it would be a challenge to find anyone who ascended an international stage as rapidly and broadly as Jamaican sprinter Usain Bolt. In 2008, at the age of just 21, Bolt broke the 100m men's record and took the title of "World's Fastest Human." Two months later, at the 2008 Beijing Olympics, he broke his own record. A year later to the day in 2009, in Berlin, he broke it yet again.

Sports fans mobbed Bolt wherever he went: Jamaica, China, the United States, Europe. Children mimicked Bolt's signature pose: one arm bent, the other extended, both hands pointing to the horizon as he leans to the right. His fame continued to climb as he won three gold medals at the 2008 Olympics, three at the 2012 Olympics, and three more at the 2016 Games. He took part in nine Olympic events over three Olympics and won nine golds (a 2016 relay gold was taken away after one of his teammates tested positive for performance-enhancing drugs).

On ESPN's 2017 list of the world's 100 most famous athletes, Bolt ranked seventh. No other track athlete made the list. In contrast, the list included 38 soccer players.

WHERE IT'S PLAYED TODAY

Competitive track and field takes place across the world. The relative low cost of many of the events opens lanes of access across different economic planes. Furthermore, a country's gross domestic product (GDP) has limited impact on its ability to compete in different sports. For example, Jamaica ranks 141st in GDP yet dominated track and field for nearly two decades. Kenya's GDP ranks 75th, but its runners lead the world in distance running.

A country's wealth plays a role in some areas. Countries with greater wealth have more opportunities to train in events that require the purchase and maintenance of expensive equipment, such as hurdling events and pole vault. Six of the top eight finishers in the men's 110m hurdles at the 2016 Olympics came from countries with a GDP in the world's top 18 (but not the winner, who came from Jamaica). Seven of the top eight women in the 100m hurdles came from a top 18 GDP country, and the one who did not was from the Bahamas but attended a United States university, where she trained. Eleven of the top 12 finishers in women's pole vault and all top 12 finishers in men's pole vault came from what would be considered a "wealthy" country.

ECONOMICS AND MEDIA

Like most Olympic sports, the world's best athletes make a comfortable living, while the less competitive do not. Sprinter Usain Bolt earned more than $20 million in a year through race winnings and endorsements, but steeplechaser Andrew Poore, who finished fourth in the 2013 U.S. Nationals event, earned just $5,000 that year from track and field. The best way for a track and field athlete to earn a living is to sign a contract with an apparel company, such as Nike and New Balance. New Balance, for example, signed middle-distance runner Boris Berian to a three-year contract worth $125,000 annually, plus performance bonuses for accomplishments like winning Olympic medals.

The IOC prefers to work with national-level organizations, such as USA Track and Field, British Athletics, Athletics South Africa, and the Japan Association of Athletics Federations. Events are held throughout the world, often hosted by these associations. In 2014 Nike signed a $500 million deal with USATF, which will contribute to training, facilities, and prize money awarded at hosted track and field events. Olympic qualifying events are also hosted by these organizations, but unlike some meets, which are open internationally, they are restricted to the host country to ensure there is balanced representation at the Olympic Games.

DIMENSIONS OF THE SPORT

International track and field meets traditionally include 14 running events, 4 jumping events, 4 throwing events, 2 walking events, and 2 multievent competitions.

The running events include 3 sprints (100m, 200m, and 400m); 2 middle distances (800m and 1500m); 4 long-distance races (3000m, 5000m, 10,000m, and steeplechase); a marathon; 2 hurdling events (100m or 110m and 400m); and 2 relays (4x100m and 4x400m).

The jumping events are long jump, high jump, triple jump, and pole vault. The throwing events are javelin, discus, hammer throw, and shot put. The two race-walking events are the 20km and 50km.

One multievent competition is the heptathlon, which includes 100m hurdles, high jump, shot put, 200m, long jump, javelin, and 800m. The other multievent competition is the decathlon, which includes 100m, long jump, shot put, high jump, 400m, 110m hurdles, discus throw, pole vault, javelin, and 1500m. Both multievent competitions are held over the course of two days.

IMPORTANT FIGURES

American sprinter Florence Griffith Joyner burst onto the world track and field scene. Then, too soon, she was gone. Flo-Jo, as she was known, qualified for three Olympics: 1980, when she was just 20 years old, 1984; and 1988, although she did not compete in the 1980 Games because of the U.S. boycott (see **Olympics**). She won three gold medals at the 1988 Games: 100m, 200m, and 100m relay. It was in Seoul, South Korea, that Flo-Jo, with her dominant speed, styled fingernails, unique running outfits, and flowing hair became an international superstar. Her world records in the 100m and 200m, both set in 1988, have stood for 30 years, prompting allegations of doping, even though she never failed a drug test. She retired in 1989 at the age of 29. In 1998, at age 38, she died in her sleep after suffering an epileptic seizure. Her death renewed allegations of doping by her former competitors, but an autopsy again revealed no foul play.

Caitlyn Jenner set the world record in the men's decathlon during the 1976 Olympics. Jenner, then competing as Bruce Jenner—she came out as a transwoman and underwent sex-reassignment surgery between 2015 and 2017—finished first in only one of the 10 events, but as was her habit in decathlete competition,

> ### Where No Human Had Gone Before
>
> There was a time when what Roger Bannister accomplished in 1954 was considered impossible. No human could ever run a mile in less than four minutes. Bannister, a medical student from Britain, was one of three runners pushing each other to see who could break the mark first. The others were John Landy, an Australian, and American Wes Santee, who was the first to publicly declare he wanted to accomplish the feat.
>
> Wind swept through the campus of Oxford University, where Bannister studied, the morning of the race. Because of the wind Bannister considered not running, but the wind lessened and Bannister decided to race in front of an approximate crowd of 3,000 people. He had a strategy. Teammate Chris Brasher ran in front of Bannister as the first pacemaker, with Bannister behind him and another teammate, Chris Chataway, in the rear. Chataway took the lead when Brasher tired. Two hundred yards from the finish, Bannister separated from his teammates and sprinted for the finish line, which he crossed before collapsing in exhaustion into the arms of friends and well-wishers.
>
> Pandemonium erupted when news of Bannister's time swept through the crowd: 3 minutes, 59.4 seconds. The impossible mark was impossible no more. Bannister did not have much time to enjoy his position as the world's fastest miler. Landy broke his old rival Bannister's record just 46 days later, finishing in 3 minutes, 58 seconds. Santee never broke 4 minutes; the closest he ever came was 4 minutes, one-half second.
>
> Records exist to be broken, and two years after Landy set the mark, Briton Derek Ibbotson bested Landy's record by nearly a full second. By 1999 the record had been broken 16 more times, with the current record as of the publishing of this book held by Morocco's Hicham El Guerrouj, who ran the mile in 3 minutes, 43.13 seconds.

she was so competitive in all events that she won gold. Jenner appeared on the front of Wheaties cereal boxes, starred in television shows, and became a sports broadcaster.

POP CULTURE

The 1981 film *Chariots of Fire* told the story of two British friends who won gold at the 1924 Olympics: Eric Liddell, who won the men's 400 meters, and Harold Abrahams, who won gold in the 100 in the face of anti-Semitism. The film won the Academy Award for Best Picture, but its most enduring legacy is its score, an electronic and piano tune by the Greek composer Vangelis that became an anthem for great feats of athleticism.

In 2014 actor and filmmaker Angelina Jolie produced and directed *Unbroken*, a biopic based on the challenges faced by Louis Zamperini, an Olympic distance runner whose plane crashed in the ocean during World War II. Zamperini survived at sea for nearly seven weeks, only to hit land on the Japanese-occupied Marshall Islands, where he was tortured as a prisoner of war. Zamperini survived and lived to the age of 97. He died in July 2014. The film came out four months later, in November. The film was a big hit, earning $163 million worldwide on a budget of just $65 million.

SCANDALS

At the 1988 Olympic Games in Seoul, South Korea, Canadian Ben Johnson didn't just set a new world record in the 100 meters; he obliterated the old record, and he did so while dispatching his rival, American Carl Lewis. Johnson ran the 100 meters in 9.79 seconds. His fellow Canadians basked in his accomplishment for a little more than two days, which is when his drug test came back positive for steroids, a banned substance used to enhance athletic performance.

The IOC stripped Johnson of his gold medal. His time was erased from the record books. He claimed he did not know he took the steroid, but it was a moot point because it was clear he had benefited from it. His 9.79 time was so fast that no sprinter running naturally or unaided by wind was able to beat it until Jamaican Asafa Powell ran 9.768 in 2005, 17 years later.

Lewis had tested positive during the Olympic trials. He also claimed that he did not realize what he had ingested, but after his supplements were tested, he was cleared and allowed to compete. Of the top five finishers in the race, only Calvin Smith never failed a drug test. Smith ended up with the bronze medal, while sports fans learned just how corrupt sprinting had become. It took years for the sport to clean up its reputation.

POLITICS

In 1968 American sprinters Tommie Smith and John Carlos delivered the most visually political statement the Olympic Games had ever seen. Standing on the podium for the 200m—Smith had won gold and Carlos bronze—the two African American men raised black-gloved fists above their heads, the Black Power sign, to protest the lack of human rights around the world and in the United States, and they were shoeless to represent Black poverty. Photographs of the gesture were reprinted around the world. Australian silver-medalist Peter Norman joined Smith and Carlos in protest by wearing a human-rights badge on his jacket but did not raise his fist. The two American athletes served as pallbearers at Norman's 2006 funeral.

PATRIOTISM AND NATIONAL PRIDE

African American Jesse Owens stuck his thumb in the eye of Adolf Hitler's alleged "Aryan supremacy" when he won four gold medals at the 1936 Olympics in Berlin. He won the 100m, 200m, 4x100m, and long jump. Hitler did not shake Owens's hand, choosing instead to shake just the hand of German athletes, and when IOC officials told him to shake the hand of all the winners or none at all, Hitler stopped shaking hands altogether. It was not better at home for Owens, who because he was African American was not invited to shake hands with President Franklin Roosevelt either.

Timeline

1866 – The Amateur Athletic Club opens in Great Britain, reigniting interest in organized track and field that had been dormant in Europe for nearly 1,400 years.

1912 – Sixteen countries come together to form the International Amateur Athletic Federation, which standardizes track rules and world records.

1921 – Alice Milliat, a French athlete and activist who was frustrated by the lack of track opportunities for women, organizes the Fédération Sportive Féminine Internationale. Four Women's Olympics are held between 1922 and 1934.

1936 – Sprinter Jesse Owens wins four Olympic gold medals at Adolf Hitler's Olympic Games in Berlin.

1954 – Roger Bannister becomes the first human to run the mile in less than 4 minutes.

1968 – Tommie Smith and John Carlos accept their 200m medals shoeless and with their black-gloved fists in the air to protest human rights injustices.

1968 – Al Oerter wins gold in the discus throw to become the first athlete to win a gold medal in the same event at four different Olympics (1956, 1960, 1964, and 1968).

1972 – The U.S. Congress passes Title IX, which delivers new athletic opportunities for women and begins a new era of women's athletic performance.

1982 – *Chariots of Fire*, a film set around track and field at the 1924 Olympics, wins the Academy Award for Best Picture.

1984 – Women's marathon is held at the Olympics for the first time.

1988 – Florence Griffith Joyner wins three Olympic gold medals and sets the 100m women's world-record mark.

2006 – Smith and Carlos serve as pallbearers for Peter Norman, the Australian sprinter who supported their 1968 protest by wearing a human rights badge on the medal stand.

2008 – Usain Bolt wins three Olympic gold medals and twice sets the 100m men's world-record mark.

See also: Marathon; Olympics; Soccer.

Further Reading
Bascomb, N. (2005). *The Perfect Mile: Three Athletes, One Goal, and Less Than Four Minutes to Achieve It*. Mariner Books: Boston.

Carlos, J. and Zirin, D. (2011). *The John Carlos Story: The Sports Moment that Changed the World*. Haymarket Books: Chicago.

Fagan, K. (2017). *What Made Maddy Run: The Secret Struggles and Tragic Death of an All-American Teen*. Little, Brown and Company: Boston.

Jordan T. (1997). *Pre: The Story of America's Greatest Running Legend, Steve Prefontaine*. Rodale Books: Emmaus, Pennsylvania.

Joyner-Kersee, J. and Steptoe, S. (1997). *A Kind of Grace: The Autobiography of the World's Greatest Female Athlete*. Grand Central Publishing: New York.

Krull, K. and Diaz, D. (2000). *Wilma Unlimited: How Wilma Rudolph Became the World's Fastest Woman*. Voyager Books Harcourt, Inc.: Orlando, Florida.

Lomong, L. and Tabb, M. A. (2012). *Running for My Life: One Lost Boy's Journey from the Killing Fields of Sudan to the Olympic Games*. Thomas Nelson: Nashville, Tennessee.

Moore, K. (2007). *Bowerman and the Men of Oregon: The Story of Oregon's Legendary Coach and Nike Cofounder.* Rodale Books: Emmaus, Pennsylvania.

Moore, R. (2012). *The Dirtiest Race in History: Ben Johnson, Carl Lewis and the 1988 Olympic 100m Final.* Wisden: London.

Reynolds, J. (2016). *Ghost.* Atheneum Books: New York.

Volleyball

Volleyball emerged from the United States' recreational sport scene in the late 19th and early 20th centuries. Its history lagged behind sports such as soccer and wrestling by a few thousand years, but that did not keep it from achieving great popularity. The reason? Anyone can do it, regardless of age and physical ability. Although world-class athletes compete in volleyball at the international level, it is possible to walk into a primary school or a local recreational facility to find five-year-olds or nonagenarians playing some form of the sport. The rules are simple. In three hits or less, one team needs to volley a ball over a net to the other side without catching it or letting it hit the ground. If that sounds easy enough, it is, which is why volleyball continues to experience growth among all skill levels and ages.

HISTORICAL CONTEXT

In 1892 James Naismith, the inventor of basketball, taught a student at Springfield College named William G. Morgan, who also wanted to teach physical education. Morgan went to work as an instructor at a Young Men's Christian Association (YMCA). He appreciated basketball, but it proved too strenuous for older players, while businessmen, looking to stay active, found basketball too strenuous—or rather, too sweaty. Morgan tasked himself with creating a new game to get older people and businessmen exercise without having to overtax themselves on the court.

Morgan came up with a game called mintonette, a compound word combining badminton and net. In 1895 he raised a tennis net 6 feet, 6 inches off a court and had players from each team volley a ball back and forth over the net from side to side. Another student at the school, Alfred Thompson, wondered why Morgan did not just name the sport volley ball (two words), to which Morgan agreed. In 1896 the first recorded volleyball game took place at a YMCA conference at Springfield College. Springfield College, a school that in 2020 enrolls barely 2,000 students, is the home of two of the world's most popular sports: volleyball and basketball.

At first, players used the bladder of a basketball, but in 1900 the first true volleyball was made and eventually adopted throughout the sport. Rules were all over the place, or nonexistent, during the sport's first few decades, so in 1928 the U.S. Volleyball Association formed to bring order to volleyball, including three hits per side—which some officials in the game had adopted several years earlier—and rules about front-row and back-row play.

Brazilian volleyball players (pictured) have achieved worldwide success. The sport began as a recreational activity in the United States. (Pavel Losevsky/Dreamstime.com)

Beach volleyball, which eventually would be governed as a separate sport by separate organizations, is believed by historians to have emerged in Hawaii around 1915. Two-on-two beach volleyball, which today is the most common form of beach volleyball, grew up a couple of years later in Southern California—most likely Santa Monica.

GLOBALIZATION

Women's and men's volleyball spread through the United States on the strength of its ties to the YMCA, an interconnected network of community that stressed fitness and recreation. Religious missionaries brought volleyball to Central America a few years later. From there the YMCA network as well as Playground for America, which later became the National Recreational Association, sent volleyball abroad. In 1910 volleyball advocates spread their gospel to the Philippines, putting the sport on a second continent. It reached Japan in 1913, Poland in 1915 (a third continent), Uruguay in 1916 (a fourth continent), and Syria, an Asian country with geographical ties to a fifth continent, Africa, in 1922.

The first recognized, non-American volleyball competition took place at the inaugural Far Eastern Games, held 1913 in Manila in the Philippines and sponsored by the United States. Although it included international sports such as swimming and tennis, the Far Eastern Games served mostly to export U.S. games abroad. In addition to volleyball, the eight-day event included baseball, basketball, and football. Six countries took part: China, Federated Malay States,

Hong Kong, Japan, the Philippines (under U.S. jurisdiction at the time), and Siam.

Volleyball expanded in Europe after World War I, especially Eastern Europe since volleyball arrived to Europe via Poland. Around the same time the YMCA opened an office in Brazil. Volleyball grew in South America as a result. In the Philippines volleyball found not only popularity but new approaches. Filipino players invented the spike—or kill—a common tactic in the modern game in which one player sets the ball high in the air near the net so that a teammate can jump and drive the ball down toward the ground with an overhead swing with tremendous force. That necessitated development of the setter position to help set good balls to spike, and it forced opposing teams to develop detailed blocking and defensive schemes. Volleyball may have been born in the United States, but it took its modern form in Asia.

Volleyball debuted as a demonstration sport at the 1924 Olympics in Paris but did not get official status for women and men until 1964 because the International Olympic Committee worried about administration of regional contests, those that help determine which teams qualify for the Olympics.

WHERE IT'S PLAYED TODAY

Volleyball is played around the world at inside and outside venues. Hard-court volleyball, played six on six at recreational, academic, and international levels, takes place indoors and is the most common form of volleyball played in the world because of its history and instructional value.

Beach volleyball gained momentum in the 1960s and 1970s and has become a staple of spectator sports played during warm months in traditionally warm climates, such as the beaches of Brazil, South Africa, and the United States. Top American college hard-court volleyball players who seek to play professional volleyball often turn to beach volleyball because of greater financial opportunities. No substantive professional six-on-six volleyball league has taken hold in the United States—there has been more success in other countries—but two-on-two beach volleyball has been broadcast nationally on American television, most notably on the American networks NBC and ESPN, the most financially successful cable network in the world.

ECONOMICS AND MEDIA

The average beach volleyball player earns about $65,000 annually. Top players might earn $200,000 to $400,000 per year. Over the course of a career, the world's best players will earn $2 million to $5 million, while the majority earn far less from playing on tour. Players supplement their incomes through product endorsements such as apparel and volleyball equipment.

Far fewer opportunities exist for hard-court volleyball players to earn a substantial living. Some earn stipends through their regional Olympic committees and others through endorsements. Most hoping to build careers in volleyball, however, do so by becoming college volleyball coaches in the United States or by transitioning their playing careers into the beach game.

DIMENSIONS OF THE SPORT

Volleyball courts are 9 meters wide by 18 meters long, divided into two equal 9-meter by 9-meter sides. The top of the net for women should be set at 2.24 meters and 2.43 meters for men and should be measured from the center of the court. Net height may differ based on skill and age levels.

IMPORTANT FIGURES

Kerri Walsh Jennings finished her career as the most decorated volleyball player in American history. She won, on the hard court and on the beach, college championships, league championships, and Olympic gold medals. As a student at Stanford University, one of the top academic institutions along the American West Coast, Walsh Jennings earned first-team All-American honors after all four of her college seasons. Stanford won four conference championships and two national titles. She played professional beach volleyball after graduation where, along with partner Misty May-Treanor, she at one point won 8 consecutive tournaments, 90 consecutive matches, and a world championship. Walsh Jennings and May-Treanor cemented their legacy as the most successful beach volleyball team in the sport's history by winning gold medals at the 2004, 2008, and 2012 Olympics. Walsh Jennings went on to win bronze at the 2016 Olympics at age 38 with a new partner after May-Treanor retired.

Few American male players capitalized on the success and fame of the 1984 and 1988 gold medals as much as Karch Kiraly (pronounced "KEER-eye"), who seamlessly transitioned from hard-court volleyball to beach volleyball to broadcaster. As a professional beach player, Kiraly played 28 seasons, winning at least one tournament championship in 24. He won his last title in 2005, just a few months shy of his 45th birthday. Three years later, he became a broadcaster for Olympic beach volleyball. Kiraly has been inducted into numerous volleyball halls of fame and, like Walsh Jennings, earned four consecutive All-American honors while in college.

Sometimes fledgling sports need an infusion of outside fame to gain notoriety. Beach volleyball, which boasted some of the best volleyball players in the world regardless of surface, found that boost from former National Basketball Association player Wilt Chamberlain, a 7-foot-1 player whom basketball historians consider one of the five best players in NBA history. After retiring from basketball in 1974, Chamberlain, a longtime recreational beach volleyball player, became involved professionally as a player, team owner, and league administrator. He played in the International Volleyball Association and became president of the IVA. The league folded in 1979, but one of its all-star games was broadcast nationally because Chamberlain agreed to play in it. He was named the game's MVP. In 2008 the California Beach Volleyball Association inducted Chamberlain, who died in 1999, into its Hall of Fame.

POP CULTURE

In 2011 Caroline Found, a high school senior in Iowa City, Iowa, died in a moped accident. The tragedy rocked her loved ones and the entire community. Two books detailed Found's life and her profound effect on others, and in 2018 Academy Award winners Helen Hunt and William Hurt starred in the film *The Miracle Season* about Found, her death, and the volleyball team she left behind as they fought to win a state championship.

One cannot talk about the 1986 movie *Top Gun*, the film that launched actor Tom Cruise into superstardom, without discussing a volleyball scene in which Navy fighter pilots play beach volleyball in blue jeans. The scene inspired curiosity—as in, Why are they wearing jeans on the beach in California?—and also led a then up-and-coming actor and writer, Quentin Tarantino, to declare in the independent movie *Sleep with Me* that *Top Gun*'s volleyball scene should be considered not as a sports scene but as a text for understanding the film's true narrative: unexplored homosexuality.

SCANDALS

The University of Pennsylvania has a reputation as one of the top universities in the country. Founded in the mid-18th century by Benjamin Franklin, Penn is part of the Ivy League, the nation's most prestigious consortium of colleges that also includes Harvard, Yale, and Princeton.

Yet in recent years, problems with its women's volleyball program have shown that even the top academic schools are not immune to the trials of college athletics. In 2018 Penn hired Iain Braddak, its third head coach in three years. By the end of his first season, local news organizations reported that some of his players had alleged verbal mistreatment, filing eight grievances through the college. The players then expressed frustration that the college was not taking their concerns seriously.

The university canceled the end of their 2019 season because "offensive" posters appeared inside the team's locker room—posters that the university said had nothing to do with the coach. Then in 2020 Braddak resigned from Princeton without offering any public reason. As scandals go, Penn volleyball fails to rise to the level of some of sport's more notorious moments, but it does prove that even the institution that Ben Franklin built is not above reproach.

POLITICS

The Cold War between the Soviet Union and the United States extended beyond politics. For the latter half of the 20th century, the Olympics served as a bitter—but peaceful—outlet for the nations to compete with one another.

By the late 1970s it had become clear that the Soviets and Americans fielded the two most competitive men's hard-court volleyball programs in the world. They appeared headed for a showdown at the 1980 Olympics in Moscow, but led by U.S.

President Jimmy Carter, the U.S. Olympic Committee boycotted the Moscow Olympics to protest the Soviets' military confrontation in Afghanistan. The Soviets won the gold medal, but the two international powers would have to wait until 1984 to square off.

Los Angeles, California, USA, hosted the 1984 Summer Olympics. As payback for the United States boycotting the 1980 Olympics, the Soviets and some of their Eastern European allies boycotted the 1984 Games. The Americans won gold in men's volleyball, but the two international powers would have to wait until 1988 to square off.

At last, at the 1988 Summer Olympics in Seoul, South Korea, both the Americans and Soviets competed. The anticipation paid off as the two countries rolled through the early rounds. The Soviets ran through Pool A, 4-1, losing only to Brazil while winning 14 of 18 sets. The United States swept through Pool B, going 5-0 while winning 15 of 18 sets.

Neither team lost a set in the semifinals, with the United States beating Brazil, 3-0, and the Soviet Union beating Argentina by the same score. It was finally time to see which nation could boast the world's best men's volleyball program. The United States won, 3-1. The Soviets won the first set, but the United States won the last three to earn the gold medal in one of the most watched events of that year's Olympics. Several of the players on the 1984 and 1988 U.S. men's teams capitalized on their fame to launch long, successful careers in volleyball or other sports, including Kiraly.

Timeline

1895 – William G. Morgan, a physical education instructor at a YMCA in Holyoke, Massachusetts, raises a tennis net more than six feet off the floor to create the game of "mintonette," renamed "volley ball" less than a year later at the urging of a colleague.

1896 – The first recorded game of volleyball is played at Springfield College in Massachusetts, the same college where basketball's first game took place.

1900 – The ball specific to volleyball is created.

1916 – Setting and spiking become part of the sport, introduced in the Philippines.

1920 – Sport officials decide that each team gets just three hits per side to return the ball to the opposing team.

1928 – The U.S. Volleyball Association, which later becomes USA Volleyball, forms and standardizes rules across the sport.

1934 – American volleyball finally adopts referees as a permanent part of the sport.

1947 – The Fédération Internationale de Volleyball (FIVB) is formed in Paris.

1948 – The first two-on-two beach volleyball tournament takes place.

1949 – The first Volleyball World Championships are held in Prague, Czechoslovakia.

1964 – The Summer Olympics in Tokyo become the first to include volleyball.

1974 – The World Championships, held in Mexico, are broadcast in Japan, signaling the sport's worldwide growth.

1975 – The U.S. Women's national team begins training year-round. Two years later, the men's team creates its year-round regimen.

1978 – The International Volleyball Hall of Fame opens in Holyoke, Massachusetts.

1983 – In Newport Beach, California, the Association of Volleyball Professionals is founded for beach volleyball.

1984 – The United States wins gold in men's volleyball and silver in women's, at the Summer Olympics in Los Angeles.

1996 – Two-on-two beach volleyball debuts at the Olympics.

See also: Basketball; Olympics; Tennis.

Further Reading

Bresnahan, K. (2018). *The Miracle Season.* KCI Sports Publishing: Stevens Point, Wisconsin.

Cook, J. and Vogel, B. (2017). *Dream Like a Champion: Wins, Losses, and Leadership the Nebraska Volleyball Way.* University of Nebraska Press: Lincoln.

Dearing, J. (2018). *Volleyball Fundamentals: Master the Basics and Compete with Confidence.* Human Kinetics: Champaign, Illinois.

Hebert, M. (2013). *Thinking Volleyball: Inside the Game with a Coaching Legend.* Human Kinetics: Champaign, Illinois.

Hoeft, B. (2018). *Live like Line, Love like Ellyn.* Ice Cube Press: North Liberty, Iowa.

Kiraly, K. and Shewman, B. (1999). *The Sandman: An Autobiography.* Renaissance Books: Folkestone, England.

Mayer, J. and Allen, B. (2019). *Coach Your Brains Out: Lesson on the Art and Science of Coaching Volleyball.* Self-published.

May-Treanor, M. (2011). *Misty: My Journey through Volleyball and Life.* Scribner: New York.

Mewhirter, T. (2018). *We Were Kings: A Deep Dive inside the Lives of Professional Beach Volleyball Players.* Paper Courts: Costa Mesa, California.

Uribe, D. (2019). *The Volleyball Psychology Workbook: How to Use Advanced Sports Psychology to Succeed on the Volleyball Court.* CreateSpace Independent Publishing Platform: Scotts Valley, California.

Water Polo

In the beginning, water polo's rules allowed players to nearly drown opponents in order to get the ball. The days of attempted murder passed, but water polo's brutality did not. Many water sports are associated with less violent tendencies. Swimmers showcase speed. Synchronized swimmers show grace. Divers combine daring and precision. Water polo? Players kick, grab, tug, and punch each other. What goes on beneath the surface would shock casual observers of the sport. Above the water, players look for the right angle to pass the teammate the ball, to shoot the ball past the goalkeeper. What happens above versus below the water looks like two entirely different sports, but the sides work together to create a unique game, one of physical toughness, endurance, skill, and resilience. Players no longer attempt to drown each other, but water polo remains serious business.

HISTORICAL CONTEXT

Before water polo was called water polo, some called it water rugby. Others did not have a name for it, referring to it simply as football in the water. The sport emerged during the mid-1800s in the United Kingdom, as so many of today's most popular sports did, primarily in Scotland and England. Locals played their own versions of it in regional bodies of water: lakes, ponds, and rivers. It offered something unique, something previously unseen in the United Kingdom and possibly across the world. Never had there been a team sport played in water. Early forms of soccer, rugby, rounders, and cricket were played on land. In the water, individuals squared off to see who was the fastest.

In 1870 the London Swimming Association wrote the first official set of water polo rules. Writing rules was common practice in the mid- to late 1800s, very much in line with the properness of Victorian-era England. There were right and wrong ways of doing things, courtesies that extended to sports. Putting rules on paper was a way of staking claim to a game's ownership. As water polo took on elements of football and rugby, it was only natural that one of those elements was violence. Water polo was a game of offense and defense, and it was in the defensive strategy that brutality ruled. The goal was to get the ball away from the opponent—by any means necessary. Underwater tackling, or dunking, was allowed. This meant that, yes, defensive players were allowed to hold their opponents underwater, which could, of course, lead to death. Evidence shows that death rarely, if ever, occurred, but the threat was real. If you were an offensive player with the ball who found himself in the clutches of a stronger opponent, you had two choices: give up the ball or drown.

As human civilization became more humane, so did water polo in most parts of the world. The game's fan base grew. The game grew, too, and as it did, local clubs rethought the dunking rule. The Scottish Amateur Swimming Association held its first water polo tournament in 1886, an event that continues to this day. Its members were among the first to reconsider a more modern set of rules. Punching, throwing elbows, and kicking opponents beneath the surface continued (and sometimes still take place today), but at least players no longer had to worry about being forced underwater. Fans seemed OK with these rules adjustments. It was common for thousands of people to show up to watch a match between competitive clubs or to descend upon a town hosting a tournament. The International Olympic Committee (IOC) took notice and made water polo the first team sport to take place at the Olympic Games when it debuted in Paris in 1900, the second modern Olympiad.

The Swimming Association of Great Britain welcomed water polo in 1885, but it became clear that water polo had become so popular it could be self-sustaining. In 1889 the London Water Polo League was founded. A year later the first international water polo match took place in London between England and Scotland, two countries within the United Kingdom. As it had with soccer, rugby, cricket, tennis, and other sports, Great Britain had taken a regional sport and made its rules uniform, which allowed for the game's expansion. Water polo was well on its way to popularity beyond the United Kingdom's borders.

GLOBALIZATION

Water polo rolled across Europe. Hungary, which would become a world water polo power, and Belgium found the game in 1890, Germany in 1894, and France in 1895. By then the Canadians had been playing water polo for nearly 20 years thanks to the country's Scottish immigrants. By 1876 the Montreal Swim Club formed Canada's first recorded water polo team, although teams informally existed well before that, mostly regionally and each adhering to slightly differing rules.

European and Canadian clubs played mostly by British rules, which meant water polo remained a rough game but far less violent than it had been a half century earlier. It was far more a game of skill than one of brute force. One country that chose to play by the old-school rules was the United States, which played a version of water polo so rough that clubs in America could mostly only play against other clubs in America. European teams refused to take part in water polo tournaments that adopted the uncivilized American rules, which included far more underwater action. A Briton, John Robinson, brought water polo to the United States, but even though he introduced Americans to the game, he could not get them to accept the more skillful version of it.

As the Olympics continued to grow in prestige, and with water polo holding its place of honor as the Olympics' first team sport and international matches becoming more common, it was only a matter of time before one of the sides had to give.

Either the Europeans would have to accept the violent U.S. version of water polo or the Americans would have to abandon the violence. The European game won out. By the time World War I ended in 1918 and the world began to resume international sports competitions, the original American version of the game was no more. In 1930 the International Amateur Swimming Federation helped write and implement a set of international water polo rules that, to some great degree, still exist to this day.

One interesting note about water polo is Europe's continued dominance. If one traces the lineage of other world sports, it is common over time to see the dissemination of success. Japan found success in soccer, a sport developed in Western Europe. Argentina won championships in basketball, a game born in the United States. But not water polo. As of the 2016 Olympic Games, no men's team outside of Europe has ever won the gold medal. Ten different nations—all European—have won men's water polo gold through 26 Summer Olympic Games.

Women's water polo suffered greatly from administrative misogyny. Women's clubs formed throughout the world, but for decades individual nations refused to throw their resources behind it, and when nations do not support a sport's growth, the IOC refuses to admit it into the Games. It took a full 100 years from the time men's water polo became an Olympic sport for women's water polo to earn admission into the Olympics. After a public-relations campaign shamed the IOC and the 2000 host nation, Australia, women's water became an Olympic sport. Appropriately, Australia won the first women's water polo gold. Italy, the Netherlands, and the United States have won since, meaning that through the first five Olympics in which women's water polo has been included, champions have come from three different continents, a level of international diversity that men's water polo has not been able to achieve in more than a century.

WHERE IT'S PLAYED TODAY

Water polo is popular across Europe, whether Western, Eastern, Northern, or Southern. World and Olympic champions have included Hungary, Italy, Spain, the United Kingdom, Serbia, and Russia, among others. The game has its supporters across the world, from Canada and the United States to Brazil, Australia, and parts of North Africa, but Europe remains the center of the water polo universe.

Since 2003 the Junior Water Polo Championships have taken place for boys across Europe every two years, and for girls every two years since 2011. The events have been held in Spain, Turkey, Serbia, Azerbaijan, Georgia, and other nations.

ECONOMICS AND MEDIA

The top players in some countries, such as Egypt and India, make little to no money playing water polo, because they play only for their national teams. Benefits might include health insurance, a small stipend to make ends meet, and a government job with hours that allow them time to train in water polo. The most successful players from Europe and the United States might make between $75,000 and $150,000 per year plus additional money in endorsements. The exact number of players able to earn a living playing water polo is unknown, but the number is small. Most of the world's best players compete for their countries. Any professional success is a bonus that most players will not achieve.

DIMENSIONS OF THE SPORT

Under international rules, water polo games are broken into four 8-minute quarters. Similar to basketball, the clock stops when the ball goes out of play or there is another stoppage of play, so in real time a quarter might last 12 to 15 minutes and, including halftime, a full game between 60 and 90 minutes. Water polo players are among the best physically conditioned athletes in the world. Not only do they have to pass, shoot, and defend the ball but they have to do so while constantly swimming or treading water. They are not allowed to touch the floor of the pool while the game is going on.

Two teams compete against each other, and each team fields seven players at a time. One player on each team plays goalkeeper, while the other six play offense and defense. Each team defends a goal while trying to score on the other goal, like many other sports, including soccer and field hockey. The game begins with players from each team starting along the wall by their goal. The ball is in the middle of the pool. The first team to reach the ball gets to go on offense first.

Players advance the ball by swimming with it or throwing it to teammates. Other than the goalkeeper, who may use two hands, players may only touch the ball with one hand at a time. There are fouls that often revolve around regulating physicality. Beyond that, scoring is done in a traditional way for sport, with one player throwing the ball toward the goal while the goalkeeper tries to defend it.

IMPORTANT FIGURE

It is nearly impossible to find a more successful, decorated water polo player than Spain's Manuel Estiarte, who competed at the highest levels of the sport from 1977 to 2000. Estiarte led Spain to a gold medal at the 1996 Games in Atlanta, Georgia, USA. Where he really stands out are in the individual accolades. In 1986 he was voted the top water polo player in the world. He won the award again in 1987, 1988, 1989, 1990, 1991, and 1992. For seven straight years Estiarte dominated international water polo. His career ended in style. At the 2000 Olympics in Sydney, Australia, Estiarte served as Spain's flag bearer. He retired right after the Games, ending a career that spanned four decades.

POP CULTURE

Not a lot of movies or other forms of pop culture feature water polo in a prominent role. One of the most famous water polo movie cameos came in the form of a joke in the legendary 1959 film *Some Like It Hot*, starring Marilyn Monroe, Jack Lemmon, and Tony Curtis. In one scene Monroe's character, Sugar, asks Curtis's character, Joe, "Isn't water polo terribly dangerous?" to which Joe replies, "I'll say. I had two ponies drowned under me."

SCANDALS

In 2019 Fiona Viotti, a former model who became a teacher and water polo coach in South Africa, resigned when officials learned she had slept with at least five of her students, all of whom were at least 10 years younger than she and some who were still teenagers. Viotti was 32 at the time. Her uncle was Nick Mallet, a well-known South African rugby player who played for the national team and later served as head coach for the Italian national rugby team.

POLITICS

In October 1956 Hungarian students began to rebel against their government and communist rule. Post–World War II treaties put Hungary under communist rule, so troops from the Soviet Union intervened to squash the rebellion. The clash lasted only 23 days, but it was bloody. More than 2,000 Hungarians and 700 Soviet troops were killed, and 200,000 Hungarian tried to flee the country as refugees. The uprising drew so much international attention that it became known as the Hungarian Revolution of 1956.

Less than two weeks after the revolution, the 1956 Summer Olympics began in Melbourne, Australia. Australia is in the Southern Hemisphere, where November and December are warmer months. Two of the best water polo squads in the world at that time were Hungary and the Soviet Union. On December 6, the teams met in one of the most violent water polo matches of the modern era. Players from both sides barely tried to disguise their kicks and punches from the referees.

One Hungarian player got hit in the nose and bled into the pool, which gave the match the nickname, the "Blood in the Water Match." Hungary won 4-0 and went on to win the gold medal; the Soviets won bronze. Before the Hungarian players could be rounded up for their flight back to Hungary, about half the team defected—the practice common during times of communist rule of seeking asylum in another country to gain citizenship. It was the ultimate act of defiance against Soviet oppression.

PATRIOTISM AND NATIONAL PRIDE

In 1904 St. Louis, Missouri, hosted North America's first Olympic Games. The United States won gold in men's water polo. Remarkably, as of 2020 it remains the only time a non-European nation has won gold in the event. Nevertheless, it was not exactly an American patriotic moment for the ages. The U.S. squad did not defeat a single European team during the Olympic tournament.

No European teams even traveled to the United States to compete. European water polo teams were upset about a rules disparity and chose to skip the 1904 Olympics.

Timeline

1850s – Water polo, also originally known as "water rugby" because of its resemblance to the land game, is first played in England and Scotland in local lakes, ponds, and rivers.

1857 – A Kent, England, newspaper references a water polo match, although the term "football" is used instead of "polo."

1870 – The London Swimming Association writes a set of rules for water polo, which is still not called water polo but the more colloquial "football in the water."

1876 – The Montreal Swimming Club forms Canada's first water polo team.

1885 – New rules prevent players from dragging and dunking opposing players underwater.

1886 – The Scottish Amateur Swimming Association holds its first water polo club tournament, an event that still takes place.

1888 – Water polo debuts in the United States thanks to an introduction from a British visitor.

1900 – Men's water polo debuts as one of the first Olympic team sports, alongside tug-of-war, soccer, and a few other events.

1904 – The United States wins Olympic gold in men's water polo, marking the only time to date that a non-European team has taken the top Olympic men's spot.

1914 – Two years after disavowing itself of any association with U.S. water polo because of its rough nature, the American Athletic Union (AAU) reassociates itself with the sport after the Americans adopt less violent international rules.

1928 – The "dry pass," in which one player throws the ball to a teammate with the ball never touching the water, is developed by Hungarian water polo coach Béla Komjádi.

1929 – Water polo organizations from across the world finally agree on a single set of rules, which helps avoid situations like 1904, when European teams skipped the Olympics.

1936 – Jimmy Smith, a water polo coach and teacher in the United States, invents what becomes the modern water polo ball.

1956 – Hungary's men's team defeats the Soviet Union 4-0 in what becomes known as the "Blood in the Water Match," which took place right after the Soviet military crushed a Hungarian uprising.

1973 – The first World Water Polo Championship takes place.

2000 – Women's water polo debuts at the Olympics exactly one century after the men are allowed to play. Australia wins gold.

2016 – European nations sweep the gold, silver, and bronze medals in men's water polo at the Summer Olympics, marking the 20th time in 26 Olympics that European teams have completed the sweep.

See also: Diving; Rugby; Swimming.

Further Reading

Balline, G. (2012). *Water Polo Basics: All about Water Polo.* CreateSpace Independent Publishing Platform: Scotts Valley, California.

Cutino, P. J. (2001). *101 Offensive Water Polo Drills.* Coaches Choice: Monterey, California.

Greenwald, J. (2014). *A Parent's Guide to Water Polo.* Self-published.

Hines, C. (2008). *Water Polo the Y's Way.* AuthorHouse: Bloomington, Indiana.

Ivovic, I. (2011). *Secrets of a Serbian Water Polo Coach.* Self-published.

Kacic, Z. (2017). *Water Polo Goalkeeper.* CreateSpace Independent Publishing Platform: Scotts Valley, California.

Lyle, D. A. (2016). *Swimming through Life: Terry Schroeder and the USA Olympic Men's Water Polo Team.* CreateSpace Independent Publishing Platform: Scotts Valley, California.

Rockwell, T. (2018). *How to Play Water Polo: The Complete Guide to Mastering the Game.* Pegasus Books: New York.

Solum, J. (2010). *Science of Shooting: Water Polo Fundamentals.* Self-published.

Stein, A. (2019). *Water Polo Explained.* Self-published.

Weightlifting and Powerlifting

No premise in sport is more basic than the premise of powerlifting or weightlifting. Determine the strongest person. Find the limits of human strength, and then break them. Casual sports fans sometimes confuse powerlifting and bodybuilding, but the two could not be more different. Bodybuilding is about how you look to others; powerlifting is about how you feel about yourself. Bodybuilding is about looking like the strongest person on earth; powerlifting is about being the strongest person earth. In 2011 Iceland's Benedikt Magnússon set a world record by deadlifting 1,015 pounds. That is more than the heaviest Harley-Davidson motorcycle, more than some adult horses, and nearly as much as the entire starting lineup of the 1955 Boston Celtics. Weightlifting is not pretty. Athletes scream, grunt, and turn red, but their accomplishments inspire awe. No human should be able to accomplish what they do, which is one of the main reasons they do it.

HISTORICAL CONTEXT

Between 3,000 and 4,000 years ago the ancient Chinese, Greek, and Persian cultures engaged in sporting battles of strength. Within their own cultures, each used stones and other natural objects to see who was the strongest. The competition might have called on individuals to move a stone from one spot to another or merely to lift it or to progressively determine who could achieve a successful list of the most weight. Feats of strength were included in the ancient Olympics.

As hundreds of sports came and went over the next few thousand years, powerlifting—or weightlifting as the sport sometimes is known, even though the two differ in terms of some required Olympic events—remained. How could it not? Few sports hold such a basic concept as to see who is the strongest (or fastest, or most nimble). However, just because weightlifting was omnipresent does not mean it was well administered. As some sports in countries such as India, the United Kingdom, Brazil, China, and the United States became more institutionalized, which led to their globalization, powerlifting stumbled along. Each country, it seemed, prioritized different events, which made it hard to get together for international events. Record keeping was spotty. Powerlifting record books from the early 20th century are littered with asterisks to indicate unofficial records or to suggest that a documented record might not be accurate. Powerlifting organizations, whether for-profit or national programs, have at times expressed skepticism about the validity of other organizations.

Even the Olympics could not decide what to do about weightlifting. First, the International Olympic Committee (IOC) included it (1896), then it did not (1900), then it did again (1904), then it did not (1908), and then finally in 1920 it did again, but with a new weight-class system that exists to some degree to this day. Despite the IOC finally coming around to powerlifting, the rest of the world was slow to follow. It took until the 1950s for international standards to start to take hold. The Soviet Union, United Kingdom, and United States played key roles in its development, as did some influential figures such as Bob Hoffman (see "Important Figures"). Powerlifters can compete in any number of lifts, including bench press (laying horizontally on a bench and pushing weight off the chest), deadlift (standing over a bar that is on the ground and lifting it), and squat (bending the knees and hips with a bar resting on the upper back).

Technically, powerlifting is the deadlift, squat, and bench press, while Olympic weightlifting is two other lifts: the clean and jerk, and the snatch. It is this sort of semantic and logistical differentiation that has led to confusion in the sports' developments. Are they the same sport, or are they not? Powerlifting emerged in the 1950s because its competitors did not like the moves performed in weightlifting, even though some of the motions are the same. Different governing bodies tried to oversee it but found record keeping and attempts to host events frustrating. In the United States the American Athletic Union oversaw powerlifting starting in the 1950s, planned the first national championship, and had to cancel it. They later tried to hold international events but could not decide whether to measure in kilograms or pounds. Other private organizations also tried to oversee it, including the International Powerlifting Federation and the World Powerlifting Congress.

In the 1980s some competitors broke away and formed their own organization, the American Powerlifting Federation, which promised to not drug-test their athletes. This led to professional opportunities and potentially huge lifts, but they could not have any direct affiliation with the IOC, which strictly drug-tests its competitors in nearly all sports. Today weightlifting and powerlifting are better regulated, as the IOC requires strong local and regional oversight of sports in order for them to be included in the Olympic Games. The AAU lost control over the sports in the late 1970s. The International Powerlifting Federation now serves as the sport's more influential governing body.

GLOBALIZATION

For decades globalization was powerlifting and weightlifting's problem, not its goal. Turkey, Mongolia, the United States, Ecuador, the Soviet Union, Nigeria—the sports were everywhere, which is what most sports want. The problems came because they acted independently, and when one federation tried to unify the world's strongest athletes, it ran into a host of other problems such as which events to include, how to merge or compare record books, the standardization of equipment, the standardization of grips (e.g., how one holds a weight bar), which units of measurement to use, and how—or if—to test for performance-enhancing drugs.

Like track and field, swimming, rowing, and other sports with origins in the ancient world, the globalization of weightlifting occurred organically. Humans like to compete, and figuring out the strongest person was an easy, natural avenue for competition for the world's cultures. Getting everyone to recognize universal rules and regulations has proved far more difficult. Were it not for the Olympics, weightlifting would not be as organized as it is today. It is not challenging to imagine what weightlifting might look like without the Olympics; it would look like powerlifting, a sport with divisions and fractures.

WHERE IT'S PLAYED TODAY

Weightlifting and powerlifting competitions take place all over the world, just as they have for millennia. Recreational athletes and regular, everyday people use lifts as general fitness activities. Some doctors recommend that elderly patients engage in exercises such as low-impact squats to retain bone density and flexibility.

Nearly every gym with weights has barbells, which means patrons can do powerlifting and weightlifting exercises. Weightlifting must be done with free weights, not machine weights. Free weights, which slide over a 45-pound barbell, typically come in the following sizes: 2.5, 5, 10, 25, 35, and 45 pounds. Powerlifters also will train with dumbbells, smaller—but equally heavy—weights that are designed to be lifted with one hand. Barbells require two hands.

ECONOMICS AND MEDIA

Journalists who cover powerlifting and weightlifting stress that there is not much money to be made in the sports outside of a few top competitors. Prize money is nominal, and Olympic stipends do not cover much outside of cost-of-living expenses—and few lifters even reach that level to begin with. Most lifters hold jobs outside of the sport and treat the sport as either a hobby or as a way of promoting their careers, sometimes as gym owners, professional trainers, and as salespeople or endorsers of fitness products and supplements. Various organizations around the world hold what are called "strongman competitions," in which powerlifters and weightlifters compete in a series of events, yet even the most valuable of these competitions tops out at a winning purse of $75,000 for the champion. That is a valuable sum of money, significantly above the cost-of-living line in nearly all parts of the world, but it is paltry compared to what the top athletes in many other sports earn.

DIMENSIONS OF THE SPORT

Olympic weightlifting consists of two lifts. One, clean and jerk, contains two motions. In the first motion the lifter bends at the knees and hips to hoist the barbell with weights off the ground. From there the lifter is able to rest the barbell across the deltoids, toward the top of the arm. It is imperative to not let it rest on the shoulders, to avoid injury. The second motion is lifting the weight from the deltoids to straight up in the air with both arms extended. The other lift, snatch, resembles clean and jerk in that the lift must move the barbell from the ground to directly above the head, but it differs because it must be done in a single motion instead of in two. This creates a higher degree of difficulty and, therefore, results in the lifting of less weight than can be achieved in clean and jerk.

Olympic weightlifting includes seven weight classes each for women and men. Both genders include featherweight, lightweight, middleweight, heavyweight, and super heavyweight. Men have bantamweight and middle heavyweight, and women have flyweight and light heavyweight.

IMPORTANT FIGURES

In the early 1930s, Bob Hoffman, a decorated World War I veteran who lived in Pittsburgh, Pennsylvania, got involved with the AAU. An avid rower and fitness nut, Hoffman turned his attention from the work of running his company, which made parts for the oil-burning business, to physical wellness. He founded *Strength & Health* magazine, which published from 1932 to 1986, and bought a bankrupt barbell company that he used to start his own business. Like Joe Weider, the entrepreneur who came to influence bodybuilding, Hoffman became a leader of weightlifting and powerlifting. He coached the U.S. Olympic Weightlifting Team for 32 years, ending his tenure in 1968. In 1966 he founded a second magazine, *Muscular Development*, which prints to this day.

Naim Süleymanoglu stood just 4 feet, 11 inches, but pity the poor person who messed with the man nicknamed "Pocket Hercules." Süleymanoglu, from Turkey, from 1985 through 2000 became one of the most successful weightlifters of all time. He won a gold medal in three consecutive Olympics (1988, 1992, and 1996) in addition to seven world championships, five while competing for Turkey and two early in his career for Bulgaria, from which he defected in the 1980s. Perhaps then it was fitting that his last major medal was a bronze at the European Championships in Sofia, Bulgaria.

Women's weightlifting in the United States might never have been were it not for Judy Glenney. Glenney, who competed against men before there were women's competitions in the United States, won the first women's competition when it was held in 1981 in Waterloo, Iowa. She went on to become an International Weightlifting Federation coach, referee, and administrator and oversaw women's weightlifting during a pivotal period of growth.

POP CULTURE

In 1988 the late-night American comedy show, *Saturday Night Live*, included a segment called the All-Drug Olympics, in which a sportscaster, played by Kevin Nealon, broadcasts a weightlifting competition in which all athletes are encouraged to take whatever legal and illegal drugs they want. After anchor Dennis Miller declares 115 world records have been shattered, the scene switches to a powerlifter, played by Phil Hartman, attempting to clean and jerk more than 1,500 pounds, which at the time was nearly 1,000 pounds more than the actual world record. As Hartman attempts the lift he tears both arms off at the shoulders. Blood spouts everywhere as Nealon declares, "That's got to be disappointing for the big Russian!"

Powerlifter Mark Henry won gold, silver, and bronze medals at the 1995 Pan-American Games. A two-time Olympic competitor (1992 and 1996), Henry went on to become a wildly successful professional wrestler for World Wrestling Entertainment between 1996 and 2017. Henry started off strong, entering the ring with the gimmick of the "World's Strongest Man," but the WWE's creative team often struggled to find storylines for Henry, who bounced from one forgettable plot to another. Finally in 2011, 15 years after Henry's debut, he was scripted to win the world championship after WWE writers decided to simply embrace who Henry was: a 400-pound powerhouse. The fans got behind Henry like never before, and he spent the last five years of his career as a beloved character before retiring.

SCANDALS

Doping, doping, doping. Like a sport closely related to weightlifting and powerlifting—bodybuilding—the greatest concern always has been and will always be to try to figure out which athletes reach their achievements naturally and which use performance-enhancing drugs. The following list of drugs, all of which have earned lifters suspensions from the sport, makes the sport sound like a pharmacy: buprenorphine; drostanolone; metandienone; methandriol; methylhexaneamine; methyltestoserone; methyltrienolone; nandrolone; stanozolol; steroids; testosterone; turinabol.

Most of the drugs help muscle growth and recovery. Performance-enhancing drugs are so vital to the sport that in the early 1980s some lifters formed their own federation, the American Powerlifting Federation, on the promise they would never subject their athletes to drug tests. That might sound like an idea doomed to fail, but the APF exists to this day. Lifters no longer interested in the Olympics and other amateur events, which regularly test for performance-enhancing drugs, might try to compete in the APF, which is popular mostly with lifters interested in professional competition.

The IOC began testing for performance-enhancing drugs before the 1968 Olympics. Since then, 2 weightlifters tested positive before or during the 1972 Games; 8 in 1976; 5 in 1984; 5 in 1988; 5 in 2000; 13 in 2004; 26 in 2008; and 31 in 2012.

POLITICS

Equality has never come quick or easy for women in athletics. Women in many sports have had to either form their own organizations or wait for the misogynistic power structure of sports run by men to become more inclusive. That was especially true in women's weightlifting and powerlifting. Women were not allowed to compete in Olympic weightlifting until the turn of the 21st century, at the 2000 Games in Sydney, Australia. That was more than two decades after the first internationally sanctioned women's strength events took place and more than a century after men were permitted to compete internationally in the sport.

PATRIOTISM AND NATIONAL PRIDE

Turkey has become one of the world's most successful nations in weightlifting and powerlifting. Its national federation, the Türkiye Halter Federasyonu (THF), formed in 1956, a crucial moment in world weightlifting as powers such as the Soviet Union also raced toward athletic success. Turkey's international success is indisputable. Few Olympians have won three Olympic weightlifting gold medals, but two of them are Turkish: the 4-foot-11 Süleymanoglu and Halil Mutlu, who won in 1996, 2000, and 2004. In 2004 Nurcan Taylan became the first Turk to win Olympic gold in women's weightlifting. She also tied or set three world records.

Timeline

Earliest human civilization – Humans realize the value of strength to survival and prosperity

2000–1000 BCE – Ancient civilizations including China, Greece, and Persia hold strength competitions that today would be considered powerlifting or weightlifting. They used natural objects, such as stones, as their weights.

1896 – Weightlifting is included in the first modern Olympics, in Athens. Although there was no real organization to the sport, it was included because it was considered a core athletic skill, such as running and swimming.

1899 – Estonia's George Hackenschmidt performs the first bench press, although it is first called the "floor press."

1900 – Weightlifting is removed from the second modern Olympic Games, in Paris.

Early 1900s – The sport struggles to find uniformity throughout the world as different countries and organizations host various events with different rules and spotty record keeping.

1904 – After reconsidering their decision to exclude weightlifting, the IOC reverses course again and reinserts it into the rotation of events at the St. Louis Games.

1908 – Weightlifting is again removed from the Olympics.

1920 – Weightlifting again returns to the Olympics, this time with weight divisions, and never again leaves the Olympic rotation.

1959 – The first U.S. national championships are scheduled and then canceled, adding to the sport's reputation for disorganization.

1964 – Weightlifting is added to the Paralympics.

1965 – The United States finally holds its first powerlifting championships.

1971 – Bob Hoffman founds the International Powerlifting Federation (IPF), which today includes more than 100 countries and governs much of the sport.

1980 – The first women's powerlifting competition is held in the United States. Similar competitions are held in other parts of the world, but records about exact dates and countries are murky.

1981 – American Dave Waddington becomes the first person to successfully squat more than 1,000 pounds.

1982 – Upset because the IPF insisted on testing for steroids and other performance-enhancing drugs, the American Powerlifting Federation is founded on the promise it will not test its athletes. It still exists and, not surprisingly, has no official relationship with the drug-wary IOC.

1996 – Turkey's Naim Süleymanoglu wins gold in the men's featherweight division for the third consecutive Olympics. Nicknamed "Pocket Hercules," Süleymanoglu stood just 4 feet, 11 inches.

2000 – Women finally get the OK to compete in Olympic weightlifting.

2008 – China's Chen Yanqing wins Olympic gold in the lightweight division, becoming the first women's weightlifter to win gold in consecutive Olympics.

See also: Bodybuilding; Rowing/Crew; Swimming.

Further Reading

Austin, D. and Mann, B. (2012). *Powerlifting: The Complete Guide to Technique, Training, and Competition*. Human Kinetics: Champaign, Illinois.

Carroll, B. (2017). *10/20/Life: The Professional's Guide to Building Strength Has Gotten Even Bigger and Better*. CreateSpace Independent Publishing Platform: Scotts Valley, California.

Henriques, T. (2014). *All about Powerlifting: Everything You Need to Know to Become Stronger Than Ever*. Mythos Publishing: Winnipeg, Manitoba.

Kroczaleski, M. (2014). *Insane Training: Garage Training, Powerlifting, Bodybuilding, and All-Out Bad-Ass Workouts*. Griffin Publishing: Spokane, Washington.

Lilly, B. (2012). *The Cube Method.* BookBaby Publishing: Pennsauken, New Jersey.
Mathias, R. J. (2018). *How to Deadlift 600 Lbs. Raw: 12 Week Deadlift Program and Technique Guide.* Self-published.
Matthews, M. (2019). *Bigger Leaner Stronger.* Oculus Publishers: Clearwater, Florida.
Rippetoe, M. (2014). *Practical Programming for Strength Training.* Aasgaard Company: Wichita Falls, Texas.
Schuller, R. (2016). *Powerlifting over 50: Mastering the Skills for an Empowered Body and Life.* CreateSpace Independent Publishing Platform: Scotts Valley, California.
Wendler, J. (2011). *5/3/1: The Simplest and Most Effective Training System for Raw Strength.* Self-published.

Wrestling

The ancient sport of wrestling is not as romanticized as some of the other ancient sports, such as track and field. Wrestling fans are devoted to their craft, but the sport has its challenges. The International Olympic Committee (IOC) considered dropping wrestling in the early 2000s until a public relations campaign, led by legendary amateur wrestler and coach Dan Gable, saved it at the last minute. Some view wrestling as they view boxing, a one-on-one competition of skill and will with the goal of either pinning your opponent on their back shoulders or dominating them to the point a referee can determine a clear winner. Both women and men compete. For some nations, such as Mongolia, wrestling represents a country's heritage. For other nations, such as the United States, wrestling lives within the universities, to be consumed alongside other ancient classics. Wrestlers say, more than anything, that wrestling is a battle of the mind, a struggle against the self to find the limits of discipline and training. When they lose, it is because they were not strong enough or smart enough or did not work hard enough. The opponent across the mat is just another obstacle on the way to perfection.

HISTORICAL CONTEXT

Wrestling, considered a combat sport, is one of the world's oldest sports and the first to be documented by humans. Drawings depicting wrestling that appear on caves in France date to 17,000 years ago. Wrestling was used as a form of entertainment, to settle disputes, and as a means of military training. Unlike most sports, which formed in a region of the world before spreading elsewhere, wrestling developed everywhere. Culturally specific tendencies may have migrated between regions, but forms of wrestling grew independently of one another across the globe.

Throughout the world, wrestling's roots reach down thousands of years. Ancient Indians and South Asians practiced Malla-yuddha, a form of combat that dates back more than 4,000 years that incorporates wrestling, grappling, and martial arts. Since 1362, wrestlers in Turkey have engaged annually in oil wrestling to

Former University of Iowa wrestling coach Dan Gable, honored here with a statue in Iowa City, Iowa, won three NCAA championships as a wrestler, and later he won more championships as a coach than anyone in U.S. history. He also won an Olympic gold medal. (Ken Wolter/Dreamstime.com)

determine the baspehlivan, or chief wrestler. Early European settlers of North America brought their versions of wrestling with them in the 17th century and then found that Native Americans already had organized forms of the sport.

Most famously, the Greeks included wrestling in the ancient Olympic Games. Wrestling debuted at the Games in 708 BCE. Eventually, ancient Olympic wrestlers trained at the Palaestra of Olympia, a historic practice facility built in the 3rd century BCE that still exists today as a tourist attraction. The IOC included wrestling in the first modern games in Athens, Greece, in 1896. It did not appear in the 1900 games but returned in 1904 and has been part of the Olympics ever since.

WHERE IT'S PLAYED TODAY

Wrestling is a global sport, but residential survey data revealed six countries that named wrestling as its most popular sport: Bahrain, Democratic Republic of the Congo, Ecuador, Lebanon, Oman, and Trinidad and Tobago. In all, 123 different countries have sent wrestlers to the Olympics and several wrestlers have competed as independents because their home countries did not have Olympic programs.

Many countries have hosted the World Wrestling Championships. Recent hosts include Norway, Kazakhstan, Hungary, France, the United States, Canada, Russia, Turkey, China, Japan, Azerbaijan, Greece, and Bulgaria.

ECONOMICS AND MEDIA

IOC officials claimed it was a simple matter of economics and modernity in 2013 when it announced that wrestling would no longer be a part of the Games starting in 2020. The sport was too slow, and it had not produced any recognizable stars like other sports such as gymnastics, swimming, and track and field had. The world's oldest sport suddenly found itself on the outside looking in.

The IOC took immediate flak for its decision, but it wasn't wrong about wrestling's lack of impact on the Olympics' bottom line. Fans and television viewers flocked to catch a glimpse of Usain Bolt, the Jamaican track and field sprinter, swimmers Katinka Hosszu of Hungary and Michael Phelps of the United States, and any number of athletes from women's gymnastics, one of the IOC's most lucrative draws. Wrestling had no one comparable since Aleksandr Karelin had stopped competing decades earlier (see "Important Figures"). Plus, in an increasingly fast-paced world, wrestling was slow and hard for the average fan to follow; much of it looked like two people lying on top of each other for minutes at a time.

The IOC's decision was purely economic. In recent years public interest in the Games had slipped as scandals mounted and the public learned of the economic rubble left behind after the Olympics came to town. Digital media—particularly social-media companies—detracted from television viewership because results were posted and spread through avenues such as Twitter and Facebook hours before they appeared that night on television. Because the Olympics were a global event and social media were globally used, there were always countries somewhere—or television markets, as the IOC saw them—losing the incentive to watch because they already knew the results. That translated into fewer viewers for advertisers to reach, which could potentially lead to losses of advertising revenue.

Despite these factors, backlash against the IOC for its decision on wrestling was swift. Supporters of the sport lobbied the IOC to reinstate it. Instead, the IOC required wrestling's governing body to reapply for admission along with other excommunicated sports, such as softball and squash. So that is what wrestling did, and when the IOC voted in September 2013—seven months after its initial decision—wrestling received enough votes to return to the Olympic rotation. The IOC also got what it wanted: wrestling's proposal for readmission included revising its rules and improving its gender-equity initiatives.

DIMENSIONS OF THE SPORT

The two main forms of wrestling in international competition are Greco-Roman and freestyle. The main difference between the two is that in Greco-Roman wrestling, no scoring is allowed below the waist, while that is an active form of scoring in freestyle. A third form of wrestling, folkstyle, occurs mostly in American college wrestling but rarely on the international stage.

Wrestlers win matches in one of three ways: if they outscore their opponent on points, if they pin their opponent to the mat, or if their opponent is disqualified. Points are scored when a wrestler takes down an opponent, escapes or reverses the opponent's hold, turns over the opponent on the mat, gets a near fall (pin), or gets a pushout.

A pin occurs when a wrestler pins any part of the opponent's shoulder or shoulders to the mat for three seconds. If no pin occurs after three periods, the wrestler with the most points wins.

IMPORTANT FIGURES

The Soviet Union's Aleksandr Karelin, one of the most dominant international Greco-Roman wrestlers ever, a man who went undefeated for 13 years, did not like wrestling when he first learned it. He wanted to quit until he met coach Victor Kusnetzov. The two clicked, and together they made history. Karelin won gold in the super heavyweight division at the 1988 Olympics in Seoul, South Korea. In 1992 he won gold at the Barcelona, Spain, games. In 1996 he won another gold, in Atlanta, Georgia, United States, without giving up a point. He finally lost in the Olympics in the gold-medal match of the 2000 games in Sydney, Australia, but by then he had already solidified his reputation as one of the greatest ever.

Saori Yoshida had a decision to make. Already one the greatest women's freestyle wrestlers, she needed to decide whether to pursue another Olympic appearance, this time in her home country of Japan, which was hosting, or retire. In 2019 at age 36, she retired. She won gold at the 2004 Olympics in Athens, gold at the 2008 Olympics in Beijing, and gold at the 2012 Olympics in London before falling to silver at the 2016 games in Rio de Janeiro. She also won 13 World Championships. With nothing left to prove, it was no wonder she chose to retire.

Cael Sanderson did what many thought impossible: he equaled, then surpassed, Dan Gable's collegiate accomplishments. Wrestling for Iowa State University, Sanderson finished his college career 159-0 and became the first college wrestler to ever finish a four-year career undefeated. His postcollege career was also a success. Sanderson won a gold medal wrestling freestyle at the 2004 Olympics in Athens. As a coach, through 2018 he had led Penn State University to 7 Division I college championships, 10 shy of Dan Gable's NCAA-record 17 championships.

It is Gable who ties each of these personages together. His life reads like the sad origin of a superhero story, except when tragedy happens in real life, the story doesn't end with the hero standing atop a skyscraper, surveying his domain. The pain just kind of lingers, forever.

Gable, a wrestler and wrestling coach from Waterloo, Iowa, was just 15 years old in 1964 when he heard someone from his neighborhood, John Thomas Kyle, say inappropriate things about his sister, Diane. Gable was out of town with his parents when they got the call: Diane had been murdered. He relayed the conversation he had had with Kyle to his parents, who called the police. They arrested Kyle, who confessed to the murder.

Gable already was a hard worker before Diane's murder. Afterward, her memory and the trauma or her death drove him to another level. He became obsessed with training and competition. He worked toward perfection—and nearly achieved it. He went 64-0 as a prep. In college at Iowa State University, Gable won his first 118 matches. His last college match, the NCAA championship match his senior year, handed him his only loss. Gable was distraught. He said he felt like he had let his sister down by losing. Incensed and obsessed with the lone loss, Gable trained even harder. He qualified for the 1972 Olympics in Munich, Germany, where he won the gold medal in freestyle lightweight by going 6-0 without giving up a single point.

Still, his career in wrestling was far from over. He coached three U.S. Olympic teams and spent 22 seasons as the head wrestling coach at the University of Iowa, where the Hawkeyes finished with an overall record of 355-21-5 with 21 conference championships, 17 NCAA championships, and 12 individual Olympians. There may have been one or two American wrestlers who were better than Gable; there may have been one or two better coaches. But no one in the history of American wrestling has had a career as complete as his.

POP CULTURE

Not a lot of movies have been made about amateur wrestling, although professional wrestling, which is scripted and performed by athletic actors, has been the subject of many. One film about amateur wrestling is *Foxcatcher*, which details the downfall of wrestling benefactor John du Pont (see "Scandals").

Another—and perhaps the most successful—is *Vision Quest*, a 1985 film about a high school wrestler who tries to navigate distractions in his personal life while he prepares to face an undefeated opponent. Although the movie made just $13 million while in theaters, it found new life on cable television and has endured for the authentic quality of its wrestling scenes.

SCANDALS

American John du Pont, heir to a family fortune built first on gunpowder and later the chemical industry, was an avid wrestling fan, taking such an interest that he became a financial benefactor to ambitious amateur wrestlers and even considered himself a de facto coach. One wrestler he supported was Dave Schultz, a former Olympic gold medalist.

Schultz coached du Pont's wrestling club at Foxcatcher Farm in Pennsylvania. Schultz himself was also training for another Olympic bid when du Pont shot and killed Schultz in 1996. Why? No one knows. At du Pont's trial, neither the prosecution nor defense offered a motive. Du Pont was found guilty and mentally ill but not insane and in 1997 was sentenced to 13 to 30 years in prison. He died in prison in 2010.

Years later stories emerged of du Pont's mental illness. He fired his gun into trees because he thought people were following him. He drove his car into ponds on his property. Many at Foxcatcher Farm thought he was eccentric but not dangerous. In addition, du Pont donated millions of dollars to USA Wrestling. The story of Schultz's murder was told in the 2014 film *Foxcatcher*, starring Steve Carell as du Pont, Mark Ruffalo as Schultz, and Channing Tatum as Mark Schultz, Dave's younger brother. The role earned Carell an Oscar nomination.

POLITICS

Wrestling, along with the sports of gymnastics and horse racing, have faced social pressure for their emphasis on "making weight" and their roles in athletes developing eating disorders. Wrestling divides its athletes into weight classes. In Greco-Roman style, for example, there are classes for 59kg, 66kg, 71kg, 75kg, 80kg, 85kg, 98kg, and 130kg. A wrestler who intends to wrestle in the 71kg weight class, for example, and weighs even a gram more than that ahead of the match will be disqualified from wrestling in the event.

This leads some wrestlers to resort to weight cutting, in which they use drastic measures to quickly rid themselves of water weight, which can lead to eating disorders and other health problems, including headaches, hair loss, and menstruation problems. In turn, this has led medical professionals and parenting groups to push the sport to more carefully monitor wrestlers' weights—especially young wrestlers, who in addition to wins and losses have to worry about the long-term development of their bodies.

PATRIOTISM AND NATIONAL PRIDE

Since Mongolia went to its first Olympics in 1964, it has won medals in just four sports: wrestling, judo, shooting, and boxing. That isn't to say Mongolia's Olympic experience has been unsuccessful. To the contrary, Mongolia has been one of the most successful Olympic countries in the world over the last half century, ranking 10th in medals earned per capita. It just so happens that all of Mongolia's success has come through four sports.

Wrestling is a particular point of national pride in Mongolia. It is one of Mongolia's "three manly skills," a historic metric of status that also includes archery and horseback riding. Each year towns across Mongolia host Naadam festivals to showcase the three skills. Mongolian's wrestling style is known as Bökh. Like sumo in Japan, it involves grappling with the intent of throwing your opponent to the ground. Mongolia's wrestling prowess has translated to Olympic success. Although no Mongolian has won gold, the country has earned four silvers and five bronze.

Timeline

15,000 BCE – People living in what is now France make drawings of wrestling on the walls of caves.

3000 BCE – Wrestling events in what is now India are held for entertainment, military, and political purposes.

2697 BCE – The Chinese army practices wrestling as a form of military strategy and training.

708 BCE – Wrestling debuts in the ancient Olympic games.

1240 – The book *The Secret History of the Mongols* includes a passage that details a wrestling match.

1888 – The first organized wrestling meet in the United States is held in New York.

1904 – Freestyle wrestling debuts in the Olympics at the third modern games, in St. Louis, Missouri.

1908 – Greco-Roman and freestyle wrestling are featured in the same Olympiad for the first time.

1912 – The International Federation of Associated Wrestling Styles (FILA; now United World Wrestling) is founded in Belgium.

1948 – Iran wins its first medal in Olympic wrestling. By 2012 it will have won 35 Olympic medals.

1987 – The first women's wrestling championships are held in Lorenskog, Norway.

1988 – The Soviet Union's Aleksandr Karelin wins his first Olympic gold medal. He will win again in 1992 and 1996.

2004 – Women's wrestling debuts in the Olympics.

2013 – The IOC votes to remove wrestling from the games but reinstates wrestling to the Games seven months later.

See also: Gymnastics; Olympics; Sumo.

Further Reading

Angle, K. and Harper, J. (2002). *It's True! It's True!* HarperCollins: New York.

Bernstein, R. (2004). *Grappling Glory: Celebrating a Century of Minnesota Wrestling & Rassling.* Nodin Press: Cambridge, Minnesota.

Gable, D. and Schulte, S. (2015). *A Wrestling Life: The Inspiring Stories of Dan Gable.* University of Iowa Press: Iowa City.

Hammond, J. K. (2014). *The History of Collegiate Wrestling: A Century of Excellence.* National Wrestling Hall of Fame and Museum: Stillwater, Oklahoma.

Jarman, T. and Hanley, R. (1983). *Wrestling for Beginners.* McGraw-Hill Education: New York.

Martell, W. (1993). *Greco-Roman Wrestling.* Human Kinetics: Champaign, Illinois.

Moffatt, J. and Sesker, C. (2016). *Wrestle like a Girl.* Exit Zero: Cape May, New Jersey.

Savage, J. (1996). *Wrestling Basics.* Capstone Press: North Mankato, Minnesota.

Thompson, W. (2019). *The Cost of These Dreams: Sports Stories and Other Serious Business.* Penguin Books: London.

Zavoral, N. (2001). *A Season on the Mat: Dan Gable and the Pursuit of Perfection.* Simon & Schuster: New York.

Bibliography

Agassi, A. (2010). *Open: An Autobiography.* Vintage: New York.
Albergotti, R. and O'Connell, V. (2014). *Wheelmen: Lance Armstrong, the Tour de France, and the Greatest Sports Conspiracy Ever.* Avery Publishing: New York.
Anders, E. R. and Myers, S. (2008). *Field Hockey: Steps to Success.* Human Kinetics: Champaign, Illinois.
Ashe, A. and Rampersad, A. (1994). *Days of Grace: A Memoir.* Ballantine Books: New York.
Askwith, R. (2019). *Unbreakable: The Woman Who Defied the Nazis in the World's Most Dangerous Horse Race.* Pegasus Books: New York.
Baime, A. J. (2010). *Go Like Hell: Ford, Ferrari, and Their Battle for Speed and Glory at Le Mans.* Mariner Books: Boston.
Baines, D. (2014). *Charles Atlas: The Man, the Myth, and the Muscles.* Birch Tree Publishing: New York.
Bascomb, N. (2005). *The Perfect Mile: Three Athletes, One Goal, and Less Than Four Minutes to Achieve It.* Mariner Books: Boston.
Benjamin, D. (2010). *Sumo: A Thinking Fan's Guide to Japan's National Sport.* Tuttle Publishing: Clarendon, Vermont.
Bissinger, H. G. (1990). *Friday Night Lights: A Town, a Team, and a Dream.* Addison-Wesley: Boston.
Blair, B. (1996). *A Winning Edge.* Taylor Trade Publishing: Lanham, Maryland.
Boyne, D. J. (2005). *Red Rose Crew: A True Story of Women, Winning, and the Water.* Lyons Press: Lanham, Maryland.
Brown, D. J. (2014). *The Boys in the Boat: Nine Americans and Their Epic Quest for Gold at the 1936 Berlin Olympics.* Penguin Books: New York.
Carlin, J. (2008). *Playing the Enemy: Nelson Mandela and the Game That Made a Nation.* Penguin Books: New York.
Carlos, J. and Zirin, D. (2011). *The John Carlos Story: The Sports Moment that Changed the World.* Haymarket Books: Chicago.
Chambers, V. (2007). *Kickboxing Geishas: How Modern Japanese Women Are Changing Their Nature.* Free Press: New York.
Chong, W. L. (2012). *Dare to Be a Champion.* Bukuganda Digital & Publication: Butterworth, Malaysia.
Cline, E. (2011). *Ready Player One.* Crown Publishing Group: New York.

Cohan, W. D. (2014). *The Price of Silence: The Duke Lacrosse Scandal, the Power of the Elite,* and *the Corruption of Our Great Universities.* Scribner: New York.

Connelly, M. (2014). *26.2 Miles to Boston: A Journey into the Heart of the Boston Marathon.* Lyons Press: Guilford, Connecticut.

Conner, D. and Levitt, M. (1998). *The America's Cup: The History of Sailing's Greatest Competition in the Twentieth Century.* St. Martin's Press: New York.

Delp, C. (2012). *Muay Thai Basics: Introductory Thai Boxing Techniques.* North Atlantic Books: Berkeley, California.

Demas, L. (2017). *Game of Privilege: An African-American History of Golf.* University of North Carolina Press: Chapel Hill.

Dicks, K. (2017). *Handball: The Story of Wales' First National Sport.* Y Lolfa: Ceredigion, Wales.

Diggins, J. (2020). *Brave Enough.* University of Minnesota Press: Minneapolis.

Dregni, E. (2013). *Let's Go Bowling.* Crestline Books: Sarasota, Florida.

Dryden, K. (2009). *The Game.* Wiley: Hoboken, New Jersey.

Finch, J. and Killion, A. (2011). *Throw Like a Girl: How to Dream Big & Believe in Yourself.* Triumph Books: Chicago.

Finnegan, W. (2016). *Barbarian Days: A Surfing Life.* Penguin Books: New York.

Frank, William D. (2013). *Everyone to Skis! Skiing in Russia and the Rise of Soviet Biathlon.* Northern Illinois University Press: DeKalb.

Fury, D. and Brown, H. (2000). *Johnny Weissmuller: Twice the Hero.* The Artists' Press: White River, South Africa.

Gable, D. and Schulte, S. (2015). *A Wrestling Life: The Inspiring Stories of Dan Gable.* University of Iowa Press: Iowa City.

Gave, K. (2018). *The Russian Five: A Story of Espionage, Defection, Bribery and Courage.* Gold Star Publishing: Ann Arbor, Michigan.

Gilles, R. (2018). *Women on the Move: The Forgotten Era of Women's Bicycle Racing.* University of Nebraska Press: Lincoln.

Gilmour, G. and MacDougall, T. (2018). *Seoul Glow: The Story Behind Britain's First Olympic Hockey Gold.* Pitch Publishing: Sussex, England.

Gilmour, R. (2017). *Jahangir Khan 555: The Untold Story Behind Squash's Invincible Champion and Sports Greatest Unbeaten Run.* Pitch Publishing: Sussex, United Kingdom.

Goldblatt, D. (2008). *The Ball Is Round: A Global History of Soccer.* Riverhead Books: New York.

Goldblatt, D. (2018). *The Games: A Global History of the Olympics.* W. W. Norton & Company: New York.

Grundy, P. and Shackelford, S. (2007). *Shattering the Glass: The Remarkable History of Women's Basketball.* University of North Carolina Press: Chapel Hill.

Haines, R. (2019). *Abused: Surviving Sexual Assault and a Toxic Gymnastics Culture.* Rowman & Littlefield: Lanham, Maryland.

Hamill, D. (2007). *A Skating Life: My Story.* Hyperion: Glendale, California.

Hawk, T. (2010). *How Did I Get Here? The Ascent of an Unlikely CEO.* Wiley: Hoboken, New Jersey.

Helyar, J. (1995). *Lords of the Realm: The Real History of Baseball.* Ballantine Books: New York.

Hemingway, E. (1932). *Death in the Afternoon.* Scribner: New York.

Henriques, T. (2014). *All about Powerlifting: Everything You Need to Know to Become Stronger Than Ever.* Mythos Publishing: Winnipeg, Manitoba, Canada.

Hill, K. (2020). *Abandoned Northwest Florida.* Arcadia Publishing: Mount Pleasant, South Carolina.

Hoeft, B. (2018). *Live Like Line, Love Like Ellyn.* Ice Cube Press: North Liberty, Iowa.

Hogan, B. and Wind, H. W. (1985). *Ben Hogan's Five Lessons: The Modern Fundamentals of Golf.* Touchstone: New York.

Huber, J. J. (2015). *Springboard and Platform Diving.* Human Kinetics Inc.: Champaign, Illinois.

Hughes, C. (2017). *Open Heart, Open Mind.* Touchstone: New York.

Jemni, M. (2011). *The Science of Gymnastics.* Routledge: Abingdon, United Kingdom.

Johnson, S. E. (1994). *When Women Played Hardball.* Seal Press: Seattle, Washington.

Jones, C. (2015). *Throwing Rocks at Houses: My Life In and Out of Curling.* Viking Books: New York.

Kranish, M. (2019). *The World's Fastest Man: The Extraordinary Life of Cyclist Major Taylor, America's First Black Sports Hero.* Scribner: New York.

Leaf, M. (1936). *The Story of Ferdinand.* Viking Books for Young Readers: New York.

Lee, K. and Benner, T. (2019). *Total Archery—Inside the Archer.* Astra Archery: Chula Vista, California.

Lopez, N. and Schwed, P. (1979). *The Education of a Woman Golfer.* Simon & Schuster: New York.

Louganis, G. (1995). *Breaking the Surface.* Random House: New York.

Louison, C. (2011). *Impossible: Rodney Mullen, Ryan Sheckler, and the Fantastic History of Skateboarding.* Lyons Press: Lanham, Maryland.

Loverro, T. (2000). *Cammi Granato: Hockey Pioneer.* Lerner Publishing Group: Minneapolis, Minnesota.

Lyle, D. A. (2016). *Swimming through Life: Terry Schroeder and the USA Olympic Men's Water Polo Team.* CreateSpace Independent Publishing Platform: Scotts Valley, California.

MacCambridge, M. (2004). *America's Game: The Epic Story of How Pro Football Captured a Nation.* Random House: New York.

Macy, S. and Patrick D. (2017). *Motor Girls: How Women Took the Wheel and Drove Boldly into the 20th Century.* National Geographic: Washington, DC.

Marqusee, M. (1999). *Redemption Song: Muhammad Ali and the Spirit of the Sixties.* Verso Books: Brooklyn, New York.

Matthews, L. (2014). *Accept the Challenge: The Autobiography.* Penguin Random House Australia: Melbourne, Australia.

May-Treanor, M. (2011). *Misty: My Journey through Volleyball and Life*. Scribner: New York.

Moffatt, J. and Sesker, C. (2016). *Wrestle Like a Girl*. Exit Zero: Cape May, New Jersey.

Moore, R. (2012). *The Dirtiest Race in History: Ben Johnson, Carl Lewis and the 1988 Olympic 100m Final*. Wisden: London.

Morton, P. E. (2019). *Jai Alai: A Cultural History of the Fastest Game in the World*. University of New Mexico Press: Albuquerque.

Murray, P. (2019). *World Cup Cricket: A Complete History*. G2 Entertainment: East Sussex, United Kingdom.

Nack, W. (2010). *Secretariat*. Hyperion: Glendale, California.

Nauright, J. (2013). *Making the Rugby World: Race, Gender, Commerce*. Taylor & Francis: Abingdon, England.

Navratilova, M. (1985). *Being Myself*. Grafton: London.

Ninan, T. N. (2017). *Turn of the Tortoise: The Challenge and Promise of India's Future*. Oxford University Press: Oxford, United Kingdom.

Panek, M. (2011). *Big Happiness: The Life and Death of a Modern Hawaiian Warrior*. University of Hawaii Press: Honolulu.

Paup, D. (2017). *Skills, Drills & Strategies for Badminton*. Routledge: Abingdon, United Kingdom.

Pelé (2007). *Pelé: The Autobiography*. Simon & Schuster: London.

Pessah, J. (2015). *The Game: Inside the Secret World of Major League Baseball's Power Brokers*. Little, Brown and Company: Boston.

Phelps, M. (2012). *Beneath the Surface: My Story*. Skyhorse Publishing: New York.

Pluto, T. (1990). *Loose Balls: The Short, Wild Life of the American Basketball Association*. Simon & Schuster: New York.

Prescott, S. (2020). *Shredders: Girls Who Skate*. Ten Speed Press: Berkeley, California.

Putnam, R. (2000). *Bowling Alone: The Collapse and Revival of American Community*. Simon & Schuster: New York.

Radu, F. L. and Abalasei, B. A. (2015). *Team Handball 101*. Bloomsbury Publishing: London.

Reddy, N. G. (2012). *Read & Play Kabaddi: With Latest Rules and Regulations*. Nava Ratna Book House: Vijaywada, India.

Remnick, D. (1999). *King of the World: Muhammad Ali and the Rise of an American Hero*. Random House: Crawfordsville, Indiana.

Richards, H. (2007). *A Game for Hooligans: The History of Rugby Union*. Mainstream Publishing: Edinburgh, United Kingdom.

Rider, T. C. (2016). *Cold War Games: Propaganda, the Olympics, and U.S. Foreign Policy*. University of Illinois Press: Champaign.

Rippetoe, M. (2014). *Practical Programming for Strength Training*. Aasgaard Company: Wichita Falls, Texas.

Robinson, J. and Clegg, J. (2018). *The Club: How the English Premier League Became the Wildest, Richest, Most Disruptive Force in Sports*. Mariner Books: Boston.

Rockwell, T. (2018). *How to Play Water Polo: The Complete Guide to Mastering the Game*. Pegasus Books: New York.

Rogers, R., ed. (2019). *Understanding Esports: An Introduction to the Global Phenomenon*. Lexington Books, Rowman & Littlefield Publishers: Lanham, Maryland.

Rosen, C. (2017). *The Chosen Game: A Jewish Basketball History*. University of Nebraska Press: Lincoln.

Rousey, R. and Ortiz, M. B. (2015). *My Fight/Your Fight*. Regan Arts: New York.

Ryan, J. (2018). *Little Girls in Pretty Boxes: The Making and Breaking of Elite Gymnasts and Figure Skaters*. Grand Central Publishing: New York.

Samiudden, O. (2014). *The Unquiet Ones: A History of Pakistan Cricket*. Harper Collins India: Noida, India.

Schaap, J. (2007). *Triumph: The Untold Story of Jesse Owens and Hitler's Olympics*. Houghton Mifflin: Boston.

Schwarzenegger, A. (1993). *Arnold: The Education of a Bodybuilder*. Simon & Schuster: New York.

Seemiller, D. and Holowchak, M. (1996). *Winning Table Tennis: Skills, Drills, and Strategies*. Human Kinetics: Champaign, Illinois.

Sheahan, M. and Ascenti, B. (2017). *Nautor's Swan: Through 50 Years of Yachting Evolution*. Skira: Milan, Italy.

Slater, K. (2004). *Pipe Dreams: A Surfer's Journey*. It Books: New York.

Sorrells, B. (2004). *Beginner's Guide to Traditional Archery*. Stackpole Books: Mechanicsburg, Pennsylvania.

Stewart, J. (2007). *Jackie Stewart: Winning Is Not Enough*. Headline Publishing Group: London.

Switzer, K. (2017). *Marathon Woman: Running the Race to Revolutionize Women's Sports*. Hachette Books Group: New York.

Toorpakai, M. and Holstein, K. (2016). *A Different Kind of Daughter: The Girl Who Hid from the Taliban in Plain Sight*. Twelve: New York.

Turriff, S. (2016). *Curling: Steps to Success*. Human Kinetics: Champaign, Illinois.

Vennum, T. (1994). *American Indian Lacrosse: Little Brother of War*. Johns Hopkins University Press: Baltimore, Maryland.

Vogan, T. (2014). *Keepers of the Flame: NFL Films and the Rise of Sports Media*. University of Illinois Press: Champaign.

Ward, G. C. (2006). *Unforgivable Blackness: The Rise and Fall of Jack Johnson*. Vintage Books: New York.

Warren, L. S. (2005). *Buffalo Bill's America: William Cody and the Wild West Show*. Knopf Doubleday: New York.

Warshaw, M. (2010). *The History of Surfing*. Chronicle Books: San Francisco.

Wertheim, L. J. (2010). *Blood in the Cage: Mixed Martial Arts, Pat Miletich, and the Furious Rise of the UFC*. Houghton Mifflin: Boston.

Westly, E. (2017). *Fastpitch: The Untold Story of Softball and the Women Who Made the Game*. Touchstone: New York.

Wilson, T. (2020). *1989: The Great Grand Final*. Hardie Grant Books: Richmond, Victoria, Australia.

Winkler, H. and Oliver, L. (2005). *My Secret Life as a Ping-Pong Wizard.* Grosset & Dunlap: New York.

Wolman, D. and Smith, J. (2020). *Aloha Rodeo: Three Hawaiian Cowboys, the World's Greatest Rodeo, and a Hidden History of the American West.* William Morrow Books: New York.

Zavoral, N. (2001). *A Season on the Mat: Dan Gable and the Pursuit of Perfection.* Simon & Schuster: New York.

Bibliography by Sport

ACTION SPORTS

Hawk, T. (2010). *How Did I Get Here? The Ascent of an Unlikely CEO.* Wiley: Hoboken, New Jersey.

Louison, C. (2011). *Impossible: Rodney Mullen, Ryan Sheckler, and the Fantastic History of Skateboarding.* Lyons Press: Lanham, Maryland.

Prescott, S. (2020). *Shredders: Girls Who Skate.* Ten Speed Press: Berkeley, California.

ARCHERY

Lee, K. and Benner, T. (2019). *Total Archery—Inside the Archer.* Astra Archery: Chula Vista, California.

Sorrells, B. (2004). *Beginner's Guide to Traditional Archery.* Stackpole Books: Mechanicsburg, Pennsylvania.

AUSTRALIAN RULES FOOTBALL

Matthews, L. (2014). *Accept the Challenge: The Autobiography.* Penguin Random House Australia: Melbourne, Australia.

Wilson, T. (2020). 1989: *The Great Grand Final.* Hardie Grant Books: Richmond, Victoria, Australia.

AUTO RACING

Baime, A. J. (2010). *Go Like Hell: Ford, Ferrari, and Their Battle for Speed and Glory at Le Mans.* Mariner Books: Boston.

Macy, S. and Patrick, D. (2017). *Motor Girls: How Women Took the Wheel and Drove Boldly into the 20th Century.* National Geographic: Washington, DC.

Stewart, J. (2007). *Jackie Stewart: Winning Is Not Enough.* Headline Publishing Group: London.

BADMINTON

Chong, W. L. (2012). *Dare to Be a Champion*. Bukuganda Digital & Publication: Butterworth, Malaysia.

Paup, D. (2017). *Skills, Drills & Strategies for Badminton*. Routledge: Abingdon, United Kingdom.

BASEBALL

Helyar, J. (1995). *Lords of the Realm: The Real History of Baseball*. Ballantine Books: New York.

Johnson, S. E. (1994). *When Women Played Hardball*. Seal Press: Seattle, Washington.

Pessah, J. (2015). *The Game: Inside the Secret World of Major League Baseball's Power Brokers*. Little, Brown and Company: Boston.

BASKETBALL

Grundy, P. and Shackelford, S. (2007). *Shattering the Glass: The Remarkable History of Women's Basketball*. University of North Carolina Press: Chapel Hill.

Pluto, T. (1990). *Loose Balls: The Short, Wild Life of the American Basketball Association*. Simon & Schuster: New York.

Rosen, C. (2017). *The Chosen Game: A Jewish Basketball History*. University of Nebraska Press: Lincoln.

BODYBUILDING

Baines, D. (2014). *Charles Atlas: The Man, the Myth, and the Muscles*. Birch Tree Publishing: New York.

Schwarzenegger, A. (1993). *Arnold: The Education of a Bodybuilder*. Simon & Schuster: New York.

BOWLING

Dregni, E. (2013). *Let's Go Bowling*. Crestline Books: Sarasota, Florida.

Putnam, R. (2000). *Bowling Alone: The Collapse and Revival of American Community*. Simon & Schuster: New York.

BOXING

Marqusee, M. (1999). *Redemption Song: Muhammad Ali and the Spirit of the Sixties*. Verso Books: Brooklyn, New York.

Remnick, D. (1999). *King of the World: Muhammad Ali and the Rise of an American Hero*. Random House: Crawfordsville, Indiana.

Ward, G. C. (2006). *Unforgivable Blackness: The Rise and Fall of Jack Johnson.* Vintage Books: New York.

BULLFIGHTING

Hemingway, E. (1932). *Death in the Afternoon.* Scribner: New York.
Leaf, M. (1936). *The Story of Ferdinand.* Viking Books for Young Readers: New York.

CRICKET

Murray, P. (2019). *World Cup Cricket: A Complete History.* G2 Entertainment: East Sussex, United Kingdom.
Samiudden, O. (2014). *The Unquiet Ones: A History of Pakistan Cricket.* Harper Collins India: Noida, India.

CROSS-COUNTRY SKIING

Diggins, J. (2020). *Brave Enough.* University of Minnesota Press: Minneapolis.
Frank, William D. (2013). *Everyone to Skis! Skiing in Russia and the Rise of Soviet Biathlon.* Northern Illinois University Press: DeKalb.

CURLING

Jones, C. (2015). *Throwing Rocks at Houses: My Life In and Out of Curling.* Viking Books: New York.
Turriff, S. (2016). *Curling: Steps to Success.* Human Kinetics: Champaign, Illinois.

CYCLING

Albergotti, R. and O'Connell, V. (2014). *Wheelmen: Lance Armstrong, the Tour de France, and the Greatest Sports Conspiracy Ever.* Avery Publishing: New York.
Gilles, R. (2018). *Women on the Move: The Forgotten Era of Women's Bicycle Racing.* University of Nebraska Press: Lincoln.
Kranish, M. (2019). *The World's Fastest Man: The Extraordinary Life of Cyclist Major Taylor, America's First Black Sports Hero.* Scribner: New York.

DIVING

Huber, J. J. (2015). *Springboard and Platform Diving.* Human Kinetics: Champaign, Illinois.
Louganis, G. (1995). *Breaking the Surface.* Random House: New York.

E-SPORTS

Cline, E. (2011). *Ready Player One*. Crown Publishing Group: New York.

Rogers, R., ed. (2019). *Understanding E-Sports: An Introduction to the Global Phenomenon*. Lexington Books, Rowman & Littlefield Publishers: Lanham, Maryland.

FIELD HOCKEY

Anders, E. R. and Myers, S. (2008). *Field Hockey: Steps to Success*. Human Kinetics: Champaign, Illinois.

Gilmour, G. and MacDougall, T. (2018). *Seoul Glow: The Story behind Britain's First Olympic Hockey Gold*. Pitch Publishing: Sussex, United Kingdom.

FIGURE SKATING

Hamill, D. (2007). *A Skating Life: My Story*. Hyperion: Glendale, California.

Ryan, J. (2018). *Little Girls in Pretty Boxes: The Making and Breaking of Elite Gymnasts and Figure Skaters*. Grand Central Publishing: New York.

FOOTBALL

Bissinger, H. G. (1990). *Friday Night Lights: A Town, a Team, and a Dream*. Addison-Wesley: Boston.

MacCambridge, M. (2004). *America's Game: The Epic Story of How Pro Football Captured a Nation*. Random House: New York.

Vogan, T. (2014). *Keepers of the Flame: NFL Films and the Rise of Sports Media*. University of Illinois Press: Champaign.

GOLF

Demas, L. (2017). *Game of Privilege: An African-American History of Golf*. University of North Carolina Press: Chapel Hill.

Hogan, B. and Wind, H. W. (1985). *Ben Hogan's Five Lessons: The Modern Fundamentals of* Golf. Touchstone: New York.

Lopez, N. and Schwed, P. (1979). *The Education of a Woman Golfer*. Simon & Schuster: New York.

GYMNASTICS

Haines, R. (2019). *Abused: Surviving Sexual Assault and a Toxic Gymnastics Culture.* Rowman & Littlefield: Lanham, Maryland.

Jemni, M. (2011). *The Science of Gymnastics*. Routledge: Abingdon, United Kingdom.

HANDBALL

Dicks, K. (2017). *Handball: The Story of Wales' First National Sport*. Y Lolfa: Ceredigion, Wales.

Radu, F. L. and Abalasei, B. A. (2015). *Team Handball 101*. Bloomsbury Publishing: London.

HORSE RACING

Askwith, R. (2019). *Unbreakable: The Woman Who Defied the Nazis in the World's Most Dangerous Horse Race*. Pegasus Books: New York.

Nack, W. (2010). *Secretariat*. Hyperion: Glendale, California.

ICE HOCKEY

Dryden, K. (2009). *The Game*. Wiley: Hoboken, New Jersey.

Gave, K. (2018). *The Russian Five: A Story of Espionage, Defection, Bribery and Courage*. Gold Star Publishing: Ann Arbor, Michigan.

Loverro, T. (2000). *Cammi Granato: Hockey Pioneer*. Lerner Publishing Group: Minneapolis, Minnesota.

JAI ALAI

Hill, K. (2020). *Abandoned Northwest Florida*. Arcadia Publishing: Mount Pleasant, South Carolina.

Morton, P. E. (2019). *Jai Alai: A Cultural History of the Fastest Game in the World*. University of New Mexico Press: Albuquerque.

KABADDI

Ninan, T. N. (2017). *Turn of the Tortoise: The Challenge and Promise of India's Future*. Oxford University Press: Oxford, United Kingdom.

Reddy, N. G. (2012). *Read & Play Kabaddi: With Latest Rules and Regulations*. Nava Ratna Book House: Vijaywada, India.

KICKBOXING

Chambers, V. (2007). *Kickboxing Geishas: How Modern Japanese Women Are Changing Their Nature*. Free Press: New York.

Delp, C. (2012). *Muay Thai Basics: Introductory Thai Boxing Techniques*. North Atlantic Books: Berkeley, California.

LACROSSE

Cohan, W. D. (2014). *The Price of Silence: The Duke Lacrosse Scandal, the Power of the Elite,* and *the Corruption of our Great Universities*. Scribner: New York.

Vennum, T. (1994). *American Indian Lacrosse: Little Brother of War.* Johns Hopkins University Press: Baltimore, Maryland.

MARATHON

Connelly, M. (2014). *26.2 Miles to Boston: A Journey into the Heart of the Boston Marathon.* Lyons Press: Guilford, Connecticut.

Switzer, K. (2017). *Marathon Woman: Running the Race to Revolutionize Women's Sports.* Hachette Books Group: New York.

MIXED MARTIAL ARTS

Rousey, R. and Ortiz, M. B. (2015). *My Fight/Your Fight.* Regan Arts: New York.

Wertheim, L. J. (2010). *Blood in the Cage: Mixed Martial Arts, Pat Miletich, and the Furious Rise of the UFC.* Houghton Mifflin: Boston.

OLYMPICS

Goldblatt, D. (2018). *The Games: A Global History of the Olympics.* W. W. Norton & Company: New York.

Rider, T. C. (2016). *Cold War Games: Propaganda, the Olympics, and U.S. Foreign Policy.* University of Illinois Press: Champaign.

Schaap, J. (2007). *Triumph: The Untold Story of Jesse Owens and Hitler's Olympics.* Houghton Mifflin: Boston.

PING-PONG

Seemiller, D. and Holowchak, M. (1996). *Winning Table Tennis: Skills, Drills, and Strategies.* Human Kinetics: Champaign, Illinois.

Winkler, H. and Oliver, L. (2005). *My Secret Life as a Ping-Pong Wizard.* Grosset & Dunlap: New York.

RODEO

Warren, L. S. (2005). *Buffalo Bill's America: William Cody and the Wild West Show.* Knopf Doubleday: New York.

Wolman, D. and Smith, J. (2020). *Aloha Rodeo: Three Hawaiian Cowboys, the World's Greatest Rodeo, and a Hidden History of the American West.* William Morrow Books: New York.

ROWING/CREW

Boyne, D. J. (2005). *Red Rose Crew: A True Story of Women, Winning, and the Water.* Lyons Press: Lanham, Maryland.

Brown, D. J. (2014). *The Boys in the Boat: Nine Americans and Their Epic Quest for Gold at the 1936 Berlin Olympics.* Penguin Books: New York.

RUGBY

Carlin, J. (2008). *Playing the Enemy: Nelson Mandela and the Game That Made a Nation.* Penguin Books: New York.

Nauright, J. (2013). *Making the Rugby World: Race, Gender, Commerce.* Taylor & Francis: Abindgon, England.

Richards, H. (2007). *A Game for Hooligans: The History of Rugby Union.* Mainstream Publishing: Edinburgh, United Kingdom.

SAILING AND YACHTING

Conner, D. and Levitt, M. (1998). *The America's Cup: The History of Sailing's Greatest Competition in the Twentieth Century.* St. Martin's Press: New York.

Sheahan, M. and Ascenti, B. (2017). *Nautor's Swan: Through 50 Years of Yachting Evolution.* Skira: Milan, Italy.

SOCCER

Goldblatt, D. (2008). *The Ball Is Round: A Global History of Soccer.* Riverhead Books: New York.

Pelé (2007). *Pelé: The Autobiography.* Simon & Schuster: London.

Robinson, J. and Clegg, J. (2018). *The Club: How the English Premier League Became the Wildest, Richest, Most Disruptive Force in Sports.* Mariner Books: Boston.

SOFTBALL

Finch, J. and Killion, A. (2011). *Throw Like a Girl: How to Dream Big & Believe in Yourself.* Triumph Books: Chicago.

Westly, E. (2017). *Fastpitch: The Untold Story of Softball and the Women Who Made the Game.* Touchstone: New York.

SPEED SKATING

Blair, B. (1996). *A Winning Edge.* Taylor Trade Publishing: Lanham, Maryland.

Hughes, C. (2017). *Open Heart, Open Mind.* Touchstone: New York.

SQUASH

Gilmour, R. (2017). *Jahangir Khan 555: The Untold Story behind Squash's Invincible Champion and Sports Greatest Unbeaten Run.* Pitch Publishing: Sussex, United Kingdom.

Toorpakai, M. and Holstein, K. (2016). *A Different Kind of Daughter: The Girl Who Hid from the Taliban in Plain Sight.* Twelve: New York.

SUMO

Benjamin, D. (2010). *Sumo: A Thinking Fan's Guide to Japan's National Sport*. Tuttle Publishing: Clarendon, Vermont.
Panek, M. (2011). *Big Happiness: The Life and Death of a Modern Hawaiian Warrior*. University of Hawaii Press: Honolulu.

SURFING

Finnegan, W. (2016). *Barbarian Days: A Surfing Life*. Penguin Books: New York.
Slater, K. (2004). *Pipe Dreams: A Surfer's Journey*. It Books: New York.
Warshaw, M. (2010). *The History of Surfing*. Chronicle Books: San Francisco.

SWIMMING

Fury, D. and Brown, H. (2000). *Johnny Weissmuller: Twice the Hero*. The Artists' Press: White River, South Africa.
Phelps, M. (2012). *Beneath the Surface: My Story*. Skyhorse Publishing: New York.

TENNIS

Agassi, A. (2010). *Open: An Autobiography*. Vintage: New York.
Ashe, A. and Rampersad, A. (1994). *Days of Grace: A Memoir*. Ballantine Books: New York.
Navratilova, M. (1985). *Being Myself*. Grafton: London.

TRACK AND FIELD

Bascomb, N. (2005). *The Perfect Mile: Three Athletes, One Goal, and Less Than Four Minutes to Achieve It*. Mariner Books: Boston.
Carlos, J. and Zirin, D. (2011). *The John Carlos Story: The Sports Moment that Changed the World*. Haymarket Books: Chicago.
Moore, R. (2012). *The Dirtiest Race in History: Ben Johnson, Carl Lewis and the 1988 Olympic 100m Final*. Wisden: London.

VOLLEYBALL

Hoeft, B. (2018). *Live Like Line, Love Like Ellyn*. Ice Cube Press: North Liberty, Iowa.
May-Treanor, M. (2011). *Misty: My Journey through Volleyball and Life*. Scribner: New York.

WATER POLO

Lyle, D. A. (2016). *Swimming through Life: Terry Schroeder and the USA Olympic Men's Water Polo Team*. CreateSpace Independent Publishing Platform: Scotts Valley, California.

Rockwell, T. (2018). *How to Play Water Polo: The Complete Guide to Mastering the Game*. Pegasus Books: New York.

WEIGHTLIFTING AND POWERLIFTING

Henriques, T. (2014). *All about Powerlifting: Everything You Need to Know to Become Stronger than Ever*. Mythos Publishing: Winnipeg, Manitoba, Canada.

Rippetoe, M. (2014). *Practical Programming for Strength Training*. Aasgaard Company: Wichita Falls, Texas.

WRESTLING

Gable, D. and Schulte, S. (2015). *A Wrestling Life: The Inspiring Stories of Dan Gable*. University of Iowa Press: Iowa City.

Moffatt, J. and Sesker, C. (2016). *Wrestle Like a Girl*. Exit Zero: Cape May, New Jersey.

Zavoral, N. (2001). *A Season on the Mat: Dan Gable and the Pursuit of Perfection*. Simon & Schuster: New York.

Index

Page numbers in **bold** indicate the location of main entries.

Action sports, **1–8**
   Back to the Future, 5
   Brown, Sky, 5
   Cooper, Anderson, 6
   dimensions of the sport, 4
   economics and media, 4
   Gleaming the Cube, 6
   globalization, 2–3
   Hart, Carey, 5
   Hawk, Tony, 2, 3, 6
   historical context, 1–2
   Humphrey, John F., 4–5
   important figures, 4–5
   Moore, Alecia, 5
   Motocross des Nations, 2
   On Any Sunday, 1
   patriotism and national pride, 6
   pop culture, 5–6
   scandals, 6
   where played today, 3
   White, Shaun, 6
   X Games, 2
   XXX, 6
Archery, **8–14**
   The Adventures of Robin Hood, 11
   Avengers: Endgame, 11
   Avengers: Infinity War, 11
   dimensions of the sport, 10
   economics and media, 10
   Fairhall, Neroli, 11
   globalization, 9
   Green Arrow, 11
   historical context, 8–9
   The Hunger Games, 12
   important figures, 10–11
   Olympics, 9
   patriotism and national pride, 12–13
   pop culture, 11–12
   Robin Hood, 11
   scandals, 12
   The Secret History of the Mongols, 12–13
   where played today, 9
   World Archery Foundation, 9
Australian rules football, **14–21**
   Australian Football League, 16
   Barassi, Ron, Jr., 18
   Chitty, Peter, 19
   The Club, 19
   dimensions of the sport, 17–18
   economics and media, 17
   Essendon Football Club, 19
   globalization, 16–17
   historical context, 14–16
   important figures, 18–19
   Matthews, Leigh, 18
   Melbourne Grammar School, 14–15
   patriotism and national pride, 19–20
   pop culture, 19
   scandals, 19
   where played today, 17
Auto racing, **21–28**
   Andretti, Mario, 25
   dimensions of the sport, 25
   economics and media, 24–25
   Formula One, 23, 23–24
   globalization, 23
   Gordon Bennett Cup, 23
   historical context, 21–23
   important figures, 25
   Muldowney, Shirley, 24
   Newman, Paul, 25
   patriotism and national pride, 26
   pop culture, 26

Auto racing (Cont.)
   scandals, 26
   Toyota, 26
   where played today, 23–24

Badminton, **29–35**
   Badminton World Federation, 30, 33
   Dan, Lin, 32
   dimensions of the sport, 32
   economics and media, 31–32
   globalization, 30–31
   historical context, 29–30
   important figures, 32
   Nehwai, Saina, 34
   Olympics, 30–31, 33
   patriotism and national pride, 34
   politics, 33–34
   Poona, 29
   pop culture, 32–33
   Premier Badminton League, 31–32
   scandals, 33
   The Theory of the Leisure Class, 30
   Tom and Jerry, 32–33
   where played today, 31
Baseball, **35–43**
   All–American Girls Professional Baseball League, 40
   Anson, Cap, 37
   Clemente, Roberto, 36, 40
   Costner, Kevin, 40
   dimensions of the sport, 38–39
   earthquake, 39
   economics and media, 38
   Federal Baseball Club v. National League, 41
   Flood, Curt, 38
   globalization, 37
   historical context, 36–37
   important figures, 39–40
   Juiced, 41
   Knickerbocker Base Ball Club, 37
   A League of Their Own, 40
   National Association of Base Ball Players, 37
   1919 Chicago White Sox, 40–41
   Oh, Sadaharu, 40
   patriotism and national pride, 41–42
   politics, 41
   pop culture, 40
   Robinson, Jackie, 37
   Ruth, George Herman (Babe), 39
   scandals, 40–41
   Walker, Moses Fleetwood, 37
   where played today, 38
Basketball, **43–51**
   Allen, Phog, 47
   Chamberlain, Wilt, 47
   City College of New York, 45, 49
   dimensions of the sport, 47
   economics and media, 46–47
   Fédération International de Basketball, 46, 47
   globalization, 45–46
   Hammon, Becky, 48
   historical context, 44–45
   important figures, 47–48
   Jordan, Michael, 48
   Leslie, Lisa, 48
   Lieberman, Nancy, 48
   Miller, Cheryl, 48
   Naismith, James, 44, 47
   National Basketball Association, 45
   Olympic Dream Team, 49
   patriotism and national pride, 50
   politics, 49–50
   pop culture, 48
   Rupp, Adolph, 47
   Russell, Bill, 47
   Sabonis, Arvydas, 48
   scandals, 48–49
   Schmidt, Oscar, 48
   Smith, Dean, 47
   Space Jam, 48
   Texas Western University, 49
   where played today, 46
Bodybuilding, **51–58**
   Atlas, Charles, 55
   dimensions of the sport, 54
   economics and media, 53–54
   Ferrigno, Lou, 55
   globalization, 53
   historical context, 52–53
   important figures, 54–55
   Mr. Olympia, 52, 53–54
   Ms. Olympia, 53–54
   patriotism and national pride, 56–57
   politics, 56
   pop culture, 55
   Sandow, Eugen, 52
   scandals, 56
   Schwarzenegger, Arnold, 54–57
   Weider, Joe, 52, 54–55
   where played today, 53

Bowling, **58–64**
   The Big Lebowski, 62–63
   Bowling Alone, 63
   Brunswick, John Moses, 62
   dimensions of the sport, 61–62
   economics and media, 60–61
   globalization, 59–60
   historical context, 59
   important figures, 62
   Kingpin, 62
   politics, 63
   pop culture, 62–63
   Pro Bowlers Association, 60,
   Rip Van Winkle, 59
   scandals, 63
   Tenpin Bowling Federation, 60
   U.S. Bowling Congress, 61
   Weber, Dick, 62
   Weber, Pete, 62
   where played today, 60
Boxing, **64–71**
   ABC's Wild World of Sports, 67
   Ali, Muhammad, 65, 68
   dimensions of the sport, 67–68
   Duran, Roberto, 65
   economics and media, 66–67
   The Fighter, 69
   Girlfight, 69
   globalization, 66
   historical context, 65–66
   important figure, 68
   Johnson, Jack, 65, 69–70
   The Marquess of Queensberry, 66
   Million Dollar Baby, 69
   politics, 69–70
   pop culture, 69
   Rocky movie franchise, 69
   scandals, 69
Bullfighting, **71–78**
   Bully for Bugs, 76
   dimensions of the sport, 74–75
   Dominguín, Luis Miguel, 75
   economics and media, 74
   The Epic of Gilgamesh, 71–72
   globalization, 73
   Hemingway, Ernest, 75
   historical context, 71–73
   important figures, 75
   Manolete, 72, 75
   olé!, 75
   patriotism and national pride, 77
   politics, 77

   pop culture, 75–76
   scandals, 76
   Solis, Merced, 76
   The Story of Ferdinand, 75–76
   where played today, 73–74

Cricket, **79–85**
   Bend It Like Beckham, 83
   Board of Cricket Control, 82
   Cricket World Cup, 79, 81
   dimensions of the sport, 82
   economics and media, 82
   globalization, 81
   Grace, W. G., 83
   Guvaskar, Sunil, 83
   historical context, 79–81
   important figures, 83
   Life, the Universe, and Everything, 83
   Marylebone Cricket Club, 80
   Million Dollar Arm, 83
   politics, 84
   pop culture, 83
   scandals, 83–84
   South African apartheid, 84
   where played today, 81–82
Cross-country skiing, **85–92**
   Boit, Philip, 89–90
   Cologna, Dario, 88
   dimensions of the sport, 88
   economics and media, 87–88
   globalization, 87
   historical context, 86–87
   Holmenkollen Ski Festival, 86
   important figures, 88–89
   Nordic World Ski Championships, 89
   Olympics, 86–87
   patriotism and national pride, 90
   politics, 89–90
   pop culture, 89
   Rantzau, Carl Schack, 88
   scandals, 89
   where played today, 87
Curling, **92–98**
   Canadian Gay Curling Championships, 97
   dimensions of the sport, 95
   Doping, 96–97
   economics and media, 94–95
   globalization, 93–94
   Help!, 96
   historical context, 92–93
   important figures, 95–96

Curling (Cont.)
  Jones, Jennifer, 95
  Men with Brooms, 96
  Olympics, 93–94
  patriotism and national pride, 97
  politics, 97
  pop culture, 96
  Royal Caledonian Curling Club, 93
  Royal Montreal Curling Club, 93
  scandals, 96–97
  Ulsrud, Thomas, 95
  where played today, 94
Cycling, **98–105**
  Armstrong, Lance, 101, 103, 104
  Breaking Away, 102
  dimensions of the sport, 101–102
  economics and media, 101
  globalization, 100
  historical context, 100
  important figures, 102
  Kopchovsky, Annie, 102
  LeMond, Greg, 103
  Mueller-Koronek, Denise, 102
  patriotism and national pride, 104
  pop culture, 102–103
  Premium Rush, 103
  Quicksilver, 103
  scandals, 103
  Taylor, Major, 102
  Tour de France, 100, 101, 103–104
  where played today, 101

Diving, **106–112**
  Back to School, 110
  dimensions of the sport, 108–109
  economics and media, 108
  globalization, 107–108
  historical context, 106–107
  important figures, 109
  Louganis, Greg, 108, 109
  Minxia, Wu, 109
  Olympics, 107
  patriotism and national pride, 110
  pop culture, 109–110
  scandals, 110
  Southeast Asian Games, 110
  where played today, 108

E-sports, **113–119**
  Atari, 113
  Blevins, Richard, 116
  consoles, 115
  dimensions of the sport, 116
  economics and media, 115
  "Gamergate," 117–118
  globalization, 114–115
  historical context, 113–114
  important figures, 116
  Jae-yoon, Ma, 117
  Nintendo, 113–114
  Olympics, 115
  patriotism and national pride, 118
  politics, 117–118
  pop culture, 116–117
  Ready Player One, 116–117
  scandals, 117
  Starcade, 117
  where played today, 115

Field hockey, **120–126**
  Applebee, Constance M. K., 123
  Chak de! India, 124
  dimensions of the sport, 122–123
  economics and media, 122
  Fédération Internationale de Hockey, 121
  Federation of Women's Hockey Associations, 121
  globalization, 121
  Grant, Christine, 123–124
  historical context, 120–121
  important figures, 123–124
  Irish Ladies Hockey Union, 121
  1984, 124
  patriotism and national pride, 125
  pop culture, 124
  scandals, 124–125
  University of Iowa, 122
  where played today, 121–122
Figure skating, **126–133**
  Blades of Glory, 131
  dimensions of the sport, 129–130
  economics and media, 129
  globalization, 128
  Hamill, Dorothy, 130
  Harding, Tonya, 131
  Henie, Sonja, 130
  historical context, 127–128
  important figures, 130
  International Skating Union, 127
  Kerrigan, Nancy, 131
  Lipinski, Tara, 128
  Olympics, 126–127, 129

patriotism and national pride, 132
politics, 131–132
pop culture, 131
scandals, 131
Schindler's List, 131–132
A Treatise for Skating, 127
Weir, Johnny, 128
where played today, 129
World Figure Skating Championships, 127–128

Football, **133–141**
Camp, Walter, 134–135
Canadian Football League, 135
dimensions of the sport, 137
economics and media, 136
globalization, 135
historical context, 134–135
important figures, 137–138
injuries, 138
Kaepernick, Colin, 138–139
Madden NFL, 138
National Football League, 133, 135
patriotism and national pride, 139
politics, 138–139
pop culture, 138
Rice, Jerry, 137–138
Roosevelt, Theodore, 133
scandals, 138
Super Bowl, 135
Super Bowl Shuffle, 138
Thorpe, Jim, 137
University of Miami, 136
where played today, 136

Golf, **142–149**
Caddyshack, 146–147
dimensions of the sport, 145
economics and media, 144–145
globalization, 143–144
historical context, 142–143
Hogan, Ben, 146
important figures, 145–146
Ladies Professional Golf Association, 144
Nicklaus, Jack, 143–144
Palmer, Arnold, 143
patriotism and national pride, 147–148
Player, Gary, 145–146
politics, 147
pop culture, 146–147
Professional Golf Association, 144
Royal & Ancient, 142
Ryder Cup, 147–148
scandals, 147
St. Andrews, 142
Tin Cup, 147
where played today, 144
Wie, Michelle, 146
Woods, Tiger, 144–145, 146, 147

Gymnastics, **149–156**
American Anthem, 153
Biles, Simone, 150, 153
Comaneci, Nadia, 152
dimensions of the sport, 152
economics and media, 151–152
Federation of International Gymnastics, 150
globalization, 150–151
Gymkata, 153
historical context, 149–150
important figures, 152–153
Jahn, Friedrich Ludwig, 150
Nassar, Larry, 154
Ning, Li, 152–153
Old School, 153
Olympics, 151
patriotism and national pride, 155
politics, 155
pop culture, 153
Saturday Night Live, 153
scandals, 154–155
Soviet Union, 151
Stick It, 153
Strug, Keri, 154
where played today, 151

Handball, **157–163**
chwarae pél, 161
dimensions of the sport, 159–160
economics and media, 159
European Handball Federation, 159
globalization, 158
Hansen, Mikkel, 160
historical context, 157–158
important figures, 160
Knockaround Guys, 160
Neagu, Cristina, 160
Olympics, 158, 161
patriotism and national pride, 161
pop culture, 160
scandals, 160–161
where played today, 158–159
Women's World Championship, 158

Horse racing, **163–170**
    dimensions of the sport, 165–166
    Diomed, 166
    economics and media, 165
    globalization, 164–165
    historical context, 163–164
    important figures, 166
    Kentucky Derby, 165
    King Charles, II, 163
    Let It Ride, 166–167
    The Mongol Derby, 166
    patriotism and national pride, 168
    politics, 168
    pop culture, 166–167
    Saudi Cup, 165
    scandals, 167–168
    Seabiscuit, 167
    Secretariat, 167
    Shrimpton, Jean, 168
    where played today, 165

Ice hockey, **171–178**
    dimensions of the sport, 174
    economics and media, 173
    Emrick, Mike "Doc," 174
    fighting, 176
    FoxTrax, 176
    globalization, 172–173
    Gretzky, Wayne, 174
    historical context, 171–172
    Howe, Gordie, 174
    important figures, 174
    International Ice Hockey Federation, 172
    Kontinental Hockey League, 173
    Lord Stanley of Preston, 171
    Miracle, 175
    National Hockey League, 171, 173
    patriotism and national pride, 176–177
    politics, 176
    pop culture, 175
    scandals, 176
    Slap Shot, 175
    Soviet Olympic team, 175
    where played today, 173
    World Championships, 171

Jai alai, **179–185**
    Aldazabal, Ibon, 179
    Callahan, John B., 182–183
    dimensions of the sport, 181–182
    economics and media, 181
    globalization, 180
    historical context, 179–180
    important figures, 182–183
    Orbea, Fernando, 182
    patriotism and national pride, 183
    politics, 183
    pop culture, 183
    scandals, 183
    St. Louis World's Fair, 179
    Tron, 183
    Wheeler, Roger, 182–183
    where played today, 180–181

Kabaddi, **186–192**
    Asian Games, 187
    Cheralathan, Dharmaraj, 189
    dimensions of the sport, 188–189
    economics and media, 188
    globalization, 187
    historical context, 186–187
    important figures, 189
    Jang-kun, Lee, 189
    Ka Bodyscapes, 190
    Kabaddi, 190
    Kabaddi Federation of India, 186
    Kumar, Anup, 189
    Mahabharata, 186
    patriotism and national pride, 191
    politics, 190–191
    pop culture, 189–190
    Pro Kabaddi League, 188
    scandals, 190
    where played today, 188
    World Cup, 190–191

Kickboxing, **192–199**
    dimensions of the sport, 195–196
    economics and media, 195
    Fujiwara, Toshio, 196–197
    globalization, 194
    Goldstein, Leah, 196
    health and fitness, 193, 195
    historical context, 193–194
    important figures, 196–197
    Kickboxer, 197
    muay Thai, 193
    Noguchi, Osamu, 196
    Olympics, 198
    politics, 198
    pop culture, 197
    scandals, 197–198
    where played today, 194–195
    youth participation, 197–198

Index

Lacrosse, **200–206**
   American Pie, 204
   Brown, Jim, 202–203
   Crooked Arrows, 203
   dimensions of the sport, 202
   Duke University, 204
   economics and media, 202
   Federation of International Lacrosse, 201
   First Nations, 200, 204
   First Nations Lacrosse Association, 204
   globalization, 201
   historical context, 200–201
   important figures, 202–203
   Mean Girls, 203–204
   Miller, Cyrus C., 203
   patriotism and national pride, 204
   politics, 204
   pop culture, 203–204
   scandals, 204
   Styres, Curt, 203
   Vennum, Thomas, 203
   where played today, 201–202

Marathon, **207–214**
   Boston Marathon, 208, 209, 211–212
   dimensions of the sport, 209–210
   economics and media, 209
   Farah, Mo, 212
   globalization, 208
   historical context, 207–208
   important figures, 210
   Kipchoge, Eliud, 210
   Marathon Man, 210–211
   Olympics, 207–208
   Pheidippides, 207
   politics, 212
   pop culture, 210–211
   Samuelson, Joan Benoit, 210
   scandals, 211–212
   Switzer, Kathrine, 211
   Waitz, Grete, 210
   where played today, 208–209

Mixed martial arts, **214–221**
   dimensions of the sport, 217
   economics and media, 216–217
   globalization, 215–216
   historical context, 214–215
   Holm, Holly, 219
   important figures, 217
   Jedrzejczyk, Joanna, 217
   Jones, Jon, 218
   McCain, John, 215, 218–219
   McGregor, Conor, 216, 219
   octagon, 217
   patriotism and national pride, 219
   politics, 218–219
   pop culture, 217–218
   Rousey, Ronda, 219
   scandals, 218
   Silva, Anderson, 217
   Ultimate Fighting Championship, 214–215
   where played today, 216
   White, Dana, 215, 217

Olympics, **222–230**
   Ali, Muhammad, 224
   Cool Runnings, 227
   de Frédy, Charles, 226
   dimensions of the sport, 226
   economics and media, 225–226
   Edwards, Michael, 227
   globalization, 225
   historical context, 222–225
   important figures, 226–227
   International Olympic Committee, 222–223, 226, 227
   McKay, Jim, 226–227
   Owens, Jesse, 224
   patriotism and national pride, 228
   politics, 227–228
   pop culture, 227
   scandals, 227
   where played today, 225
   Zappas, Evangelos, 222

Ping-Pong, **231–236**
   Balls of Fury, 234
   dimensions of the sport, 233
   Forrest Gump, 233–234
   globalization, 232
   historical context, 231–232
   important figures, 233
   International Table Tennis Association, 231
   International Table Tennis Federation, 232
   The Office, 234
   Olympics, 232
   patriotism and national pride, 235
   People's Republic of China, 234–235
   politics, 234–235
   pop culture, 233–234

Ping-Pong (*Cont.*)
   scandals, 234
   Table Tennis Association, 231
   Waldner, Jan-Ove, 233
   where played today, 232–233
   World Table Tennis Championships, 235
   Yining, Zhang, 233

Rodeo, **237–243**
   American Wild West, 237
   Cody, Bill, 237
   dimensions of the sport, 240
   economics and media, 239–240
   8 Seconds, 241
   globalization, 239
   historical context, 237–238
   important figures, 241
   My Heroes Have Always Been Cowboys, 241
   Olympics, 241–242
   patriotism and national pride, 241–242
   Pickett, Bill, 241
   politics, 241
   pop culture, 241
   Professional Rodeo Cowboys Association, 238, 239
   scandals, 241
   where played today, 239

Rowing/crew, **243–250**
   the Boat Race, 245
   college admissions scandal, 247–248
   dimensions of the sport, 246–247
   economics and media, 246
   globalization, 245–246
   historical context, 244–245
   important figures, 247
   Olympics, 245
   Oxford Blues, 247
   patriotism and national pride, 248
   pop culture, 247
   scandals, 247–248
   The Social Network, 247
   Title IX, 246
   where played today, 246

Rugby, **250–256**
   Alive, 254
   Cecillon, Marc, 254
   dimensions of the sport, 253
   economics and media, 252
   globalization, 251–252
   haka, 255
   historical context, 250–251
   important figures, 253
   Invictus, 254
   links to alcohol, 254–255
   Macqueen, Rod, 253
   McCaw, Richie, 253
   Olympics, 252
   patriotism and national pride, 255
   politics, 254–255
   pop culture, 254
   Rugby School, 250
   scandals, 254
   Scarratt, Emily, 253
   sipi tau, 255
   where played today, 252
   World Cup, 252

Sailing and yachting, **257–263**
   All Is Lost, 261
   America's Cup, 257–258, 261–262
   Caddyshack, 261
   Conner, Dennis, 261–262
   Cowes Week, 257
   Crowhurst, Donald, 261
   dimensions of the sport, 259–260
   economics and media, 259
   globalization, 258
   historical context, 257–258
   important figures, 260
   Montgomery, Peter, 260
   Olympics, 258
   Partridge, 260
   patriotism and national pride, 261–262
   pop culture, 260–261
   Royal Yacht Squadron, 257
   scandals, 261
   where played today, 258–259
   Wind, 260–261

Soccer, **263–270**
   Bend It Like Beckham, 268
   dimensions of the sport, 267
   economics and media, 266
   Federation Internationale de Football Association, 265
   globalization, 264–265
   historical context, 263–264
   important figures, 267–268
   patriotism and national pride, 269
   Pelé, 267
   politics, 268–269
   pop culture, 268
   Rapinoe, Megan, 267
   Rimet, Jules, 267–268

scandals, 268
United Passions, 268
United States Women's National Team, 266
where played today, 265–266
World Cup, 265, 266, 268
Softball, **270–276**
   Beer League, 274
   dimensions of the sport, 273–274
   economics and media, 272–273
   Farragut Boat Club, 271
   Fernandez, Lisa, 274
   globalization, 271–272
   historical context, 270–271
   important figures, 274
   Little League World Series, 275
   National Collegiate Athletic Association, 271
   Olympics, 275
   patriotism and national pride, 275
   politics, 275
   pop culture, 274
   recreational play, 272
   Richardson, Dot, 274
   scandals, 275
   Shelburne, Ramona, 274
   where played today, 272
Speed skating, **276–283**
   Bradbury, Steven, 281
   Davis, Shani, 281
   dimensions of the sport, 280
   economics and media, 279
   globalization, 278–279
   Hans Brinker, or the Silver Skates, 282
   Heiden, Eric, 280
   historical context, 277–278
   Hughes, Clara, 280
   important figures, 280–281
   International Skating Union, 277
   Ohno, Apolo Anton, 281
   Olympics, 278
   patriotism and national pride, 282
   pop culture, 281
   scandals, 282
   Speed Skating World Championships, 277
   where played today, 279
Squash, **284–290**
   David, Nicol, 288
   dimensions of the sport, 286
   economics and media, 286
   Fleet Prison, 284
   globalization, 285
   Gracie, Archibald, 287
   Harrow School, 284
   historical context, 284–285
   important figures, 286–287
   Olympics, 288
   patriotism and national pride, 288
   politics, 288
   pop culture, 287
   Professional Squash Association, 286
   scandals, 287–288
   Tennis, Rackets & Fives Association, 284, 289
   Toorpakai, Maria, 286–287
   where played today, 285–286
Sumo, **290–297**
   Anoa'i, Rodney, 294–295
   Austin Powers in Goldmember, 295
   dimensions of the sport, 293–294
   economics and media, 293
   globalization, 292
   historical context, 291–292
   important figures, 294
   International Sumo Federation, 292
   International Women's Sumo Invitational Championship, 292
   Japan Sumo Association, 292
   Kōki, Taihō, 294
   Mitsugu, Chiyonfuji, 294
   patriotism and national pride, 296
   politics, 295
   pop culture, 294–295
   scandals, 295
   where played today, 292–293
   Yarbrough, Emanuel, 294
Surfing, **297–303**
   Avalon, Frankie, 301–302
   dimensions of the sport, 300–301
   economics and media, 299
   Endless Summer, 301
   Funicello, Annette, 301–302
   globalization, 298–299
   Hamilton, Bethany, 300
   historical context, 298
   important figures, 301
   International Surfing Federation, 298
   Kahanamoku, Duke, 301
   Oberg, Margo, 301
   Olympics, 299
   patriotism and national pride, 302
   pop culture, 301–302
   scandals, 302
   Slater, Kelly, 301
   where played today, 299
   World Surf League, 298

Swimming, **303–311**
   African Games, 306
   Amateur Swimming Association, 305
   Crabbe, Buster, 309
   dimensions of the sport, 307–308
   economics and media, 306–307
   globalization, 305–306
   historical context, 304–305
   Hosszu, Katinka, 309
   important figures, 308
   Ledecky, Katie, 304, 307
   Olympics, 305–306
   patriotism and national pride, 309–310
   Phelps, Michael, 308
   pop culture, 308–309
   scandals, 309
   Spitz, Mark, 308
   Torres, Dara, 308
   Weissmuller, Johnny, 308
   where played today, 306
   Yang, Sun, 309

Tennis, **312–319**
   Chang, Michael, 317
   dimensions of the sport, 315
   economics and media, 314–315
   Gibson, Althea, 315–316
   globalization, 313–314
   historical context, 312–313
   important figures, 315–316
   King, Billie Jean, 317
   Murray, Andy, 317–318
   Navratilova, Martina, 316
   patriotism and national pride, 317–318
   pop culture, 316
   scandals, 317
   where played today, 314
   Williams, Serena, 313, 316
   Wimbledon, 314, 315
   Women's Tennis Association, 317

Track and field, **319–326**
   Bannister, Roger, 323
   Black Power, 324
   Bolt, Usain, 321
   Chariots of Fire, 323
   dimensions of the sport, 322
   economics and media, 321–322
   globalization, 320–321
   historical context, 319–320
   important figures, 322–323
   International Amateur Athletic Federation, 319
   Jenner, Caitlyn, 322–323
   Johnson, Ben, 324
   Joyner, Florence Griffith, 320, 322
   Lewis, Carl, 324
   Olympics, 319
   Owens, Jesse, 324
   patriotism and national pride, 324
   politics, 324
   pop culture, 323
   scandals, 324
   Unbroken, 323
   where played today, 321

Volleyball, **327–333**
   beach volleyball, 328, 329
   Chamberlain, Wilt, 330
   Cold War, 331–332
   dimensions of the sport, 330
   economics and media, 329–330
   Found, Caroline, 331
   globalization, 328–329
   historical context, 327–328
   important figures, 330
   Kiraly, Karch, 330
   Morgan, William G., 327
   Olympics, 329
   politics, 331–332
   pop culture, 331
   scandals, 331
   Top Gun, 331
   Walsh Jennings, 330
   where played today, 329
   Young Men's Christian Association, 327–328

Water polo, **334–340**
   "Blood in the Water Match," 338
   dimensions of the sport, 337
   economics and media, 336–337
   Estiarte, Manuel, 337
   globalization, 335–336
   historical context, 334–335
   important figures, 337
   London Swimming Association, 334
   Olympics, 335, 338–339
   patriotism and national pride, 338–339
   politics, 338
   pop culture, 337–338
   scandals, 338
   Scottish Amateur Swimming Association, 335

Some Like It Hot, 337–338
  where played today, 336
Weightlifting and powerlifting, **340–347**
  dimensions of the sport, 343
  doping, 344–345
  economics and media, 342–343
  Glenney, Judy, 344
  globalization, 342
  Henry, Mark, 344
  historical context, 340–342
  Hoffman, Bob, 343
  important figures, 343–344
  Olympics, 341
  patriotism and national pride, 345
  politics, 345
  pop culture, 344
  Saturday Night Live, 344
  scandals, 344–345
  Süleymanoglu, Naim, 343
  where played today, 342
Wrestling, **347–353**
  dimensions of the sport, 349–350
  du Pont, John, 351
  economics and media, 349
  Foxcatcher, 351
  Gable, Dan, 348, 350–351
  historical context, 347–348
  important figures, 350–351
  Karelin, Aleksandr, 350
  making weight, 352
  Olympics, 348–349
  patriotism and national pride, 352
  politics, 352
  pop culture, 351
  Sanderson, Cael, 350
  scandals, 351
  Vision Quest, 351
  where played today, 348
  Yoshida, Saori, 350

About the Author

David Asa Schwartz is assistant professor for multimedia journalism and mass communication at Augustana College in Rock Island, Illinois. He spent 15 years as a journalist covering sports, politics, and business.

www.ingramcontent.com/pod-product-compliance
Lightning Source LLC
Chambersburg PA
CBHW082025300426
44117CB00015B/2357